TERRITORIAL HUES

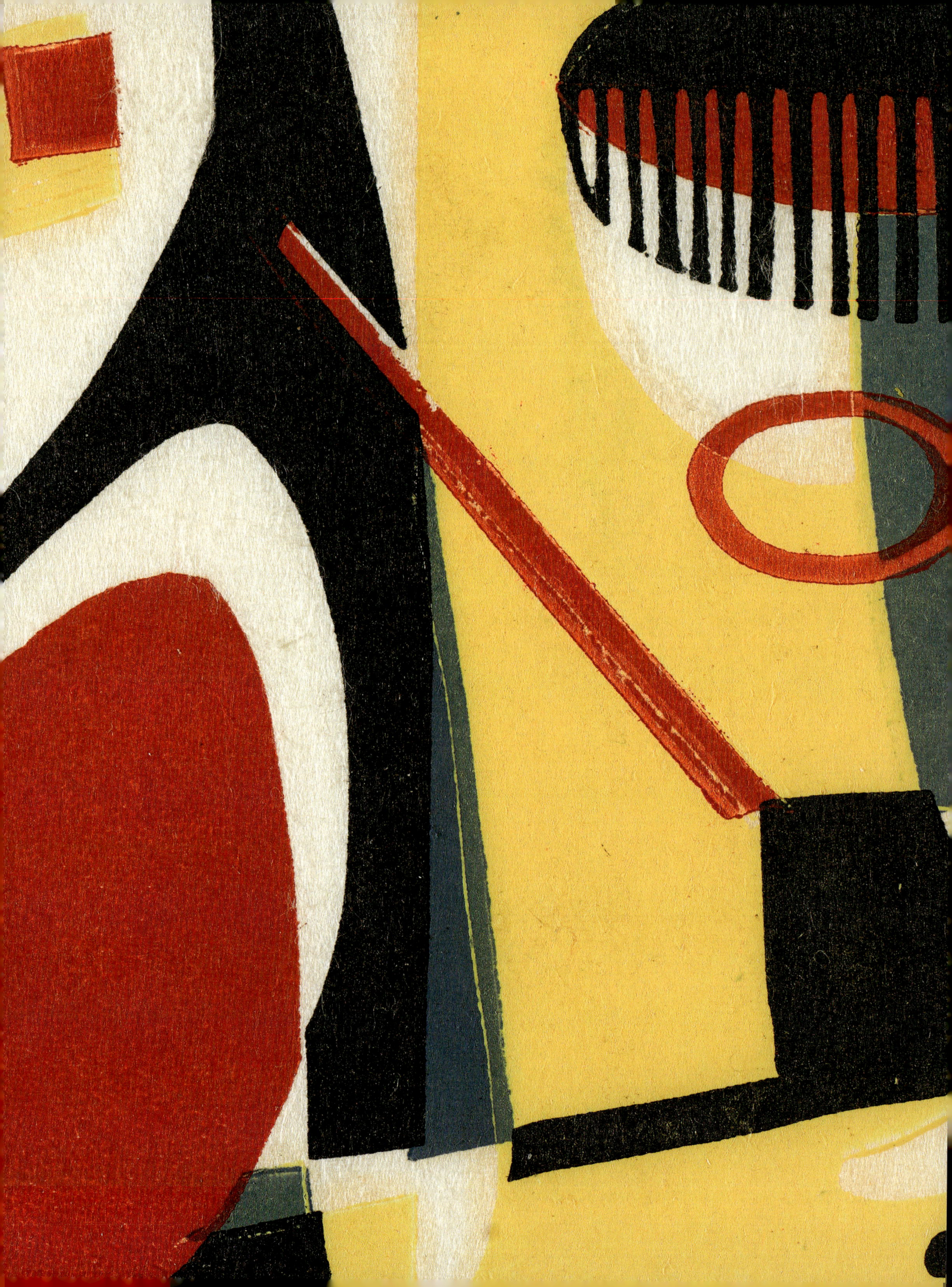

TERRITORIAL HUES

The Color Print and Washington State 1920–1960

DAVID F. MARTIN

Cascadia Art Museum

DISTRIBUTED BY UNIVERSITY OF WASHINGTON PRESS
SEATTLE AND LONDON

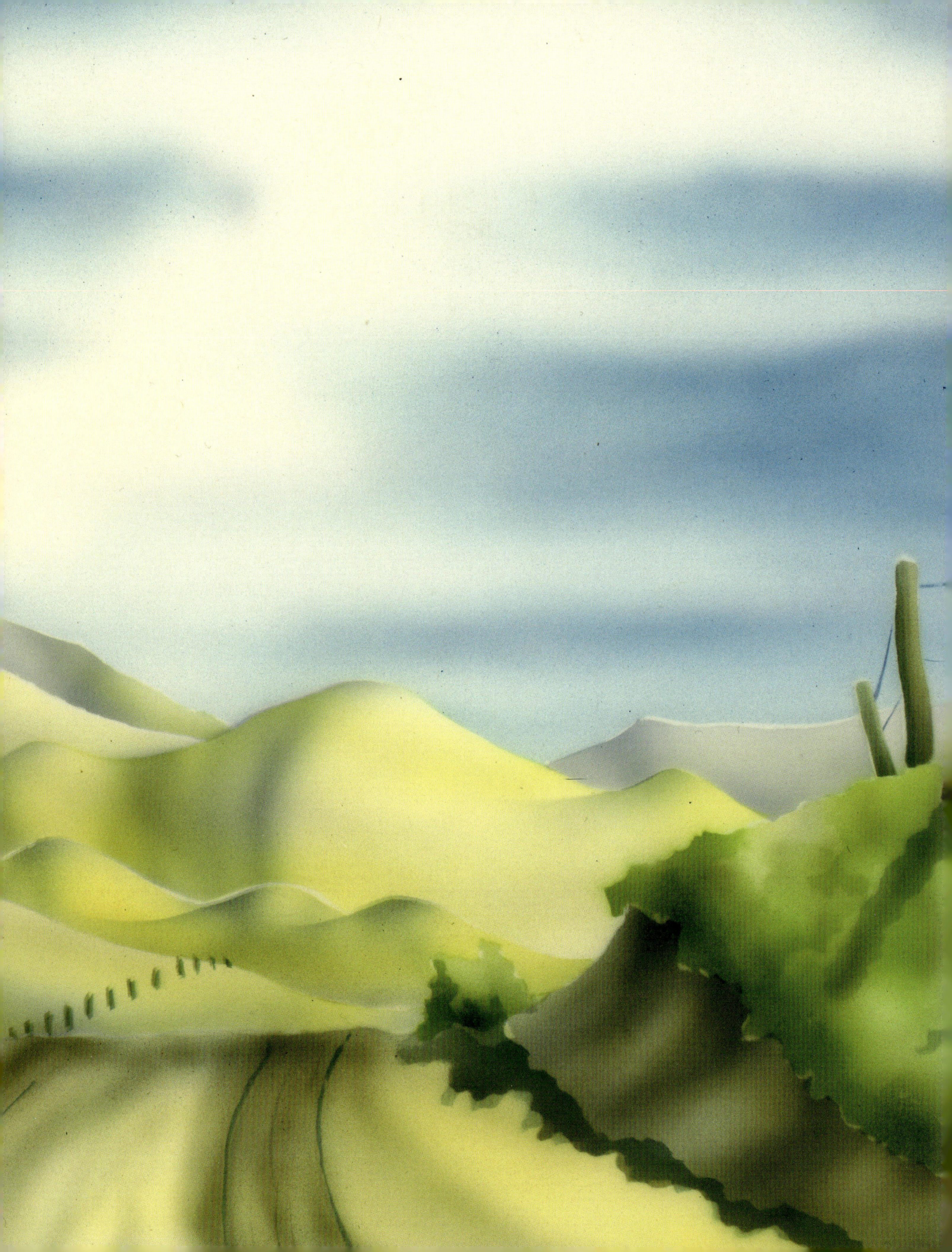

CONTENTS

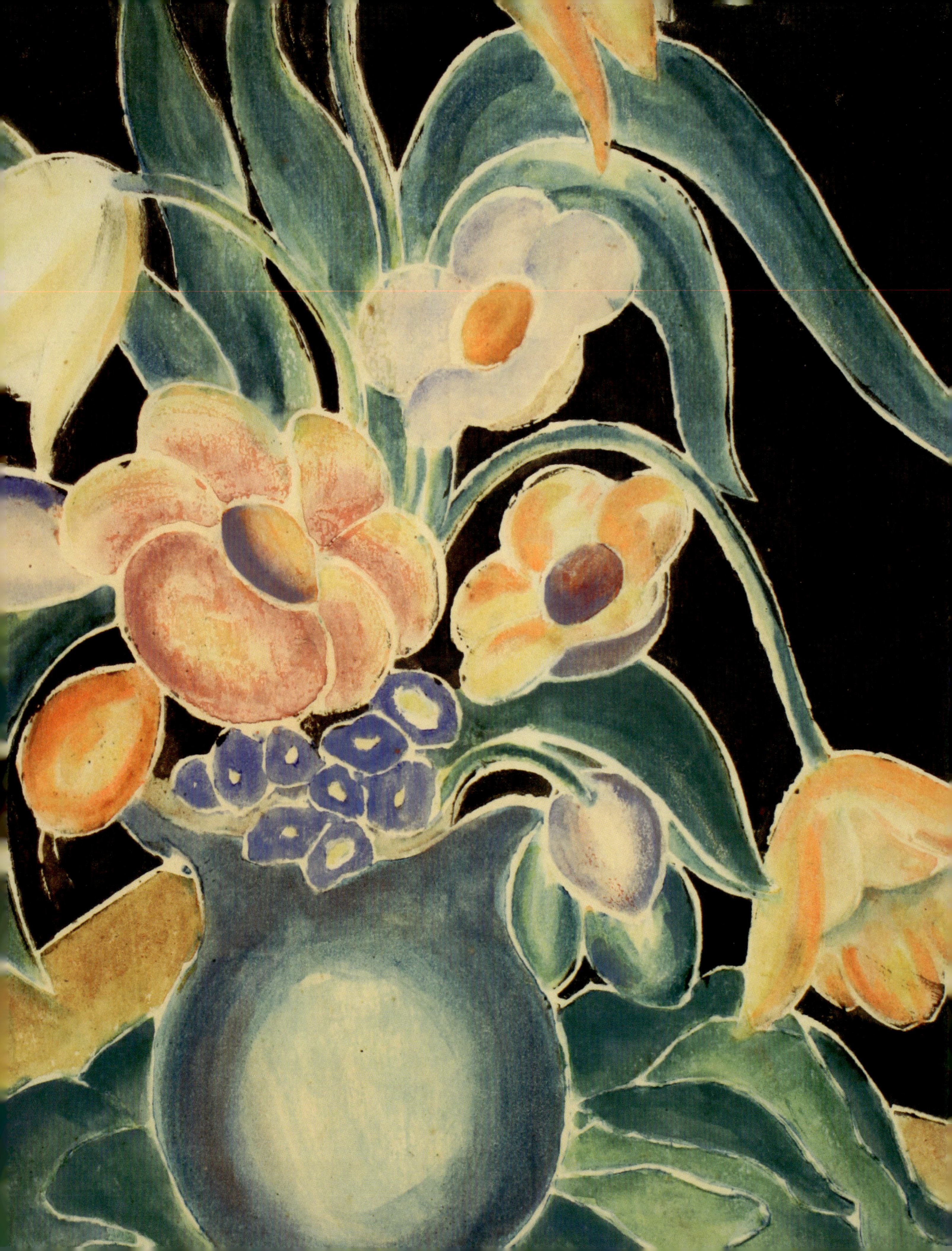

PREFACE

Cascadia Art Museum is proud to publish *Territorial Hues: The Color Print and Washington State, 1920–1960*, written by our consulting curator David F. Martin. Cascadia, the newest art museum in the Seattle metropolitan area, is dedicated to a publishing program that will document our exhibitions and increase the body of knowledge centered on Northwest art. We hope to publish one book each year with an accompanying exhibition.

Just two years old, Cascadia was founded by a small group who wanted to focus strictly on the early art of the Northwest. Other areas of the United States seemed to have a keener appreciation for their regional art, and the past forty years have seen a rediscovery of important activities such as The Old Lyme Art Colony in Connecticut, the Pennsylvania Impressionists, the Taos School of Artists, the Hoosier Group in Indiana, and the California Impressionists. The Northwest created a fascinating range of art during the period from 1860 to 1960, yet curiously we have lagged behind the rest of the country in finding aesthetic value in our historic past. In this, our founding group saw a need and identified a niche that needed to be filled—and Cascadia is the result.

Over the past thirty years that I have known David F. Martin, I have seen him emerge as the premier authority on Northwest art. It hasn't always been an easy path for him, as local "experts" often had little knowledge of or regard for the artists that he championed. Among these were many marginalized minority and women artists; their neglect reflected both the benighted attitudes of the time, and insecurity about the position of the Northwest in the nation's cultural history. Fortunately, attitudes have changed, in part due to David's indefatigable work in (re)introducing artists of the past.

I often hear first-time visitors to Cascadia say "Where have all these great artists been all my life? Why have I never heard of them?" These questions will be repeated dozens of times by visitors to the *Territorial Hues* exhibition as they discover printmakers hitherto unknown to them and realize the great breadth and depth of Northwest art. David has clearly outlined the national and international impact that our printmakers have had in this era. Forgotten printmakers such as Glen Alps, Danny Pierce, and Frances Blakemore all had national or international reputations that equaled or exceeded their local standing.

The deeply grounded and important artistic heritage brought together in this exhibition is one that all Northwesterners should be proud of—and all Americans, too.

LINDSEY ECHELBARGER
Board President

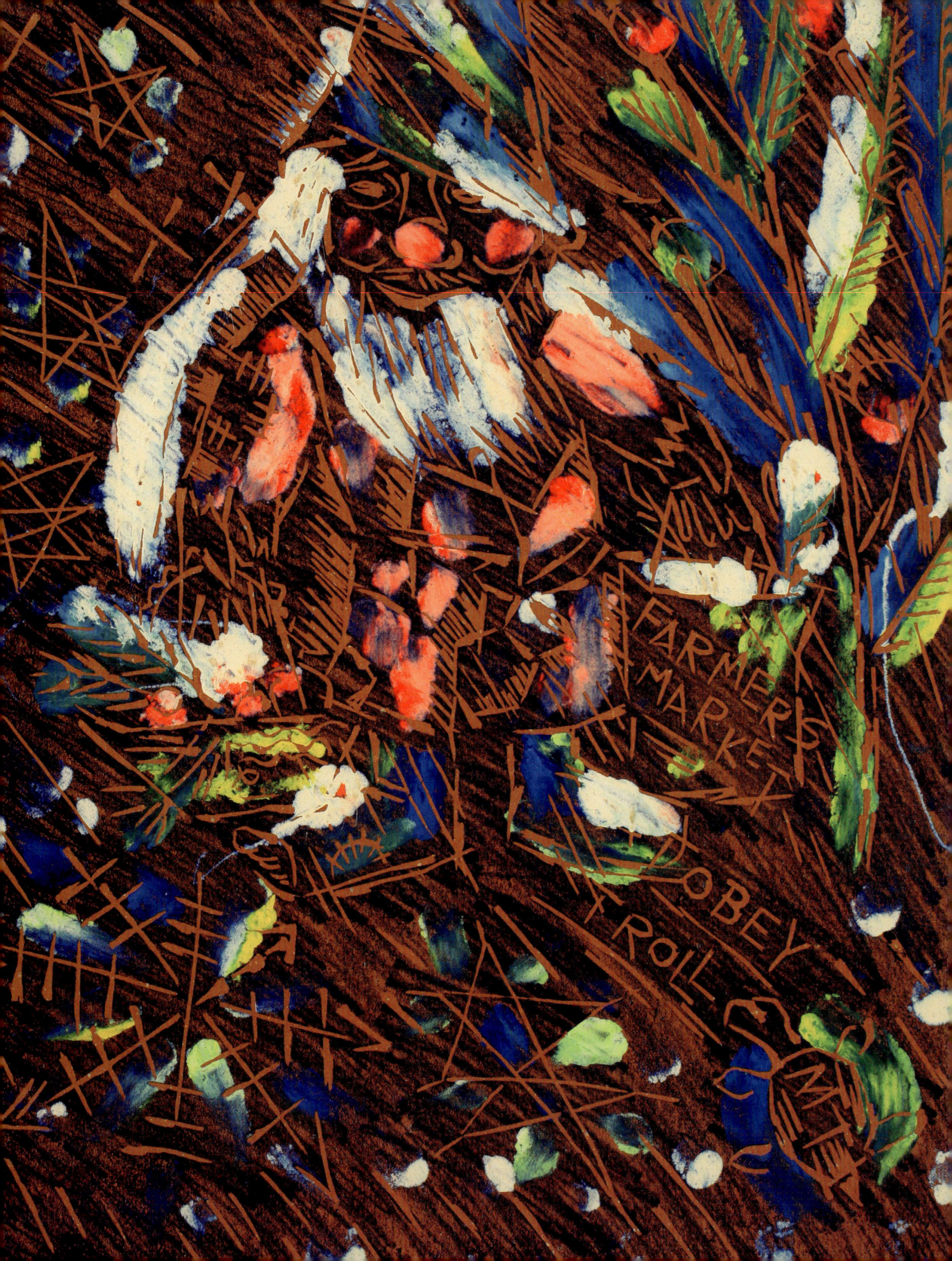
FARMERS
MARKET
OBEY
ROLL

DIRECTOR'S FOREWORD

Cascadia Art Museum opened its doors two short years ago with the goal of introducing the public to artists of the Northwest who have played a significant role in our region's cultural legacy yet remain unfamiliar names today. Although still a very young institution, we have firmly embraced our mission and are working to provide new scholarship on historic Northwest artists where there has been little in the past. Toward that goal, we are committed to publishing a series of books focused on artists who worked in the Northwest between the mid-nineteenth and the mid-twentieth centuries. We are very excited to present the first of this series, *Territorial Hues: The Color Print and Washington State, 1920–1960*.

Territorial Hues is the first study of color printmaking in Washington State during a very fertile period for local art. Curator David F. Martin has spent years researching this region's forgotten artists, and in this book and exhibition brings many of them together to tell the story of how they participated in the rise of printmaking as an innovative art form. *Territorial Hues* assembles an array of prints—including those in color woodcut, intaglio, screenprinting, and lithography—that display the variety of cultural and stylistic influences Washington State artists utilized in producing works that were technically innovative and also unique in their depiction of the distinctive color, light, and atmosphere of this region.

The styles and subject matter of the works range from those inspired by the Arts & Crafts Movement to modernism and abstraction. The influences of Japanese prints and later international movements are explored throughout the varied styles and subjects, including the local appropriation of white-line, or Provincetown, prints.

After looking at the region's artists as a group, David delves more deeply into the aesthetic evolution and work of the brothers Waldo and Corwin Chase. The color prints of the Chase brothers have generated much national interest but very little has been written about their lives and work process until now.

This book has been a labor of love for many people. A very special thank you to David Martin for his passion and all of his tireless work to bring this exhibition and book to life. We would also like to thank Phil Kovacevich for all of his guidance and a book design that is worthy of the amazing works found within its pages, and Sigrid Asmus for all her thoughtful edits that tie the book together. We would also like to offer our heartfelt thanks to all of our supporters for their participation in making this, our first book in an ongoing series, a reality.

BRANDI P. CLARK
Executive Director

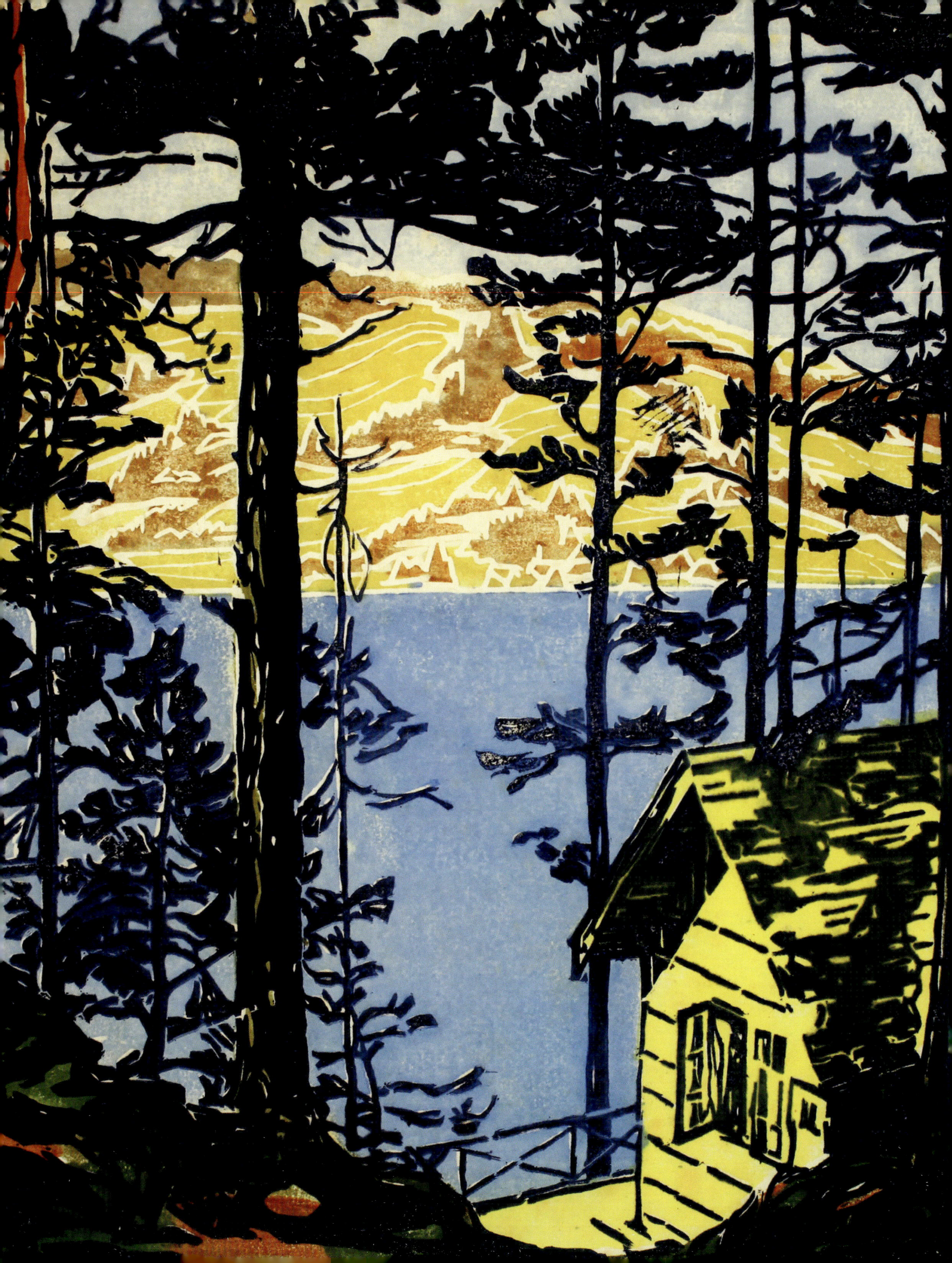

INTRODUCTION AND ACKNOWLEDGMENTS

I selected the title for this publication, *Territorial Hues: The Color Print and Washington State*, because I wanted to document the work of historic color printmakers in the state as well as to illustrate how their work had a national and international impact. For example, the prints of Frances Blakemore and Glen Alps had a significant influence in Japan, while Danny Pierce virtually established the medium in Alaska. Elizabeth Colborne and the Chase brothers are now beginning to be recognized as among the best color printmakers associated with the Arts & Crafts Movement in the United States. Their choice to live in such close proximity to the rugged natural beauty of the Northwest produced works that are distinctly regional through close observation of nature. The fact that they were also experienced mountain climbers gave them unique and direct insights into color, values, and hue when translating these atmospheric territorial nuances to paper.

This catalogue and the accompanying exhibition represent the more than twenty-five years of research that I have conducted on the subject. I was fortunate to know several of these printmakers personally, including Frances Blakemore, Ruth Penington, and James W. Washington, Jr. Another three of them were particularly close friends of mine: Glen Alps, Yvonne Twining Humber, and Danny Pierce. Many of their descendants became friends and allowed me access to important family materials.

Printmaking in Washington State has a substantial and impressive history although it is a subject that remains for the most part understudied. To my knowledge there has never been a curator of prints at any of the major museums in western Washington, and because of the dearth of exhibitions and publications the print medium is not as fully understood or appreciated locally as it should be. I hope this will be the first step in resurrecting the history of our regional printmakers.

This exhibition and publication would not have been possible had it not been for the establishment of the Cascadia Art Museum in Edmonds, Washington. The museum exists because of the foresight of Lindsey and Carolyn Echelbarger, who founded it and have been the primary supporters. The Echelbargers recognized the need for a venue and institution that could document and exhibit the region's art and cultural history, and brought it to life. Without their support and the dedication of the museum's board and staff much of this history would be lost or remain unknown to the public.

I am deeply grateful to the Cascadia Art Museum, where I serve as consulting curator, for taking a chance on my projects even though the art and artists are not yet well known. For the past thirty years, I have made in-depth studies of the region's artists, with a special emphasis on work by women and minorities, who undeservedly became forgotten over the years. It is extremely gratifying to find that their work is being so well received when it is viewed through the museum's groundbreaking exhibitions.

From the Cascadia Art Museum I would like to thank Lindsey Echelbarger, President of the Board; Brandi P. Clark, Executive Director; Nate Hegerberg, Operations Manager; Cameron Overturf, Registrar and Office Manager; Beth Brooks, Development and Membership Manager; and all of the wonderful volunteers whose interest and care allow the museum to flourish.

The following individuals and colleagues were instrumental in assisting me with this publication.

I am indebted to Florence Gilleland Schieve for her assistance with Chase family materials, recollections, and information over the years.

I would like to remember my friend, the late Anthony R. White, independent print scholar and author of the catalogue raisonné of the work of Roi Partridge, for sharing an incredible amount of his personal research on the Northwest Printmakers Society as well as national printmakers and print exhibition archives. Tony was a true scholar and poet who never sought any special recognition although he certainly deserved it.

Thank you to Benjamin Levy, independent print scholar and curator, for assisting me with deciphering Helmi Juvonen's unusual printmaking technique and for photographing works from the Henry Art Gallery's collection.

Thank you to Michiyo Morioka, PhD, art historian and leading authority on Frances Blakemore. Your assistance with Japanese translations over the past two decades is greatly appreciated. どうもありがとう

Phil Kovacevich, who designed this publication, is always a pleasure to work with. Thank you for being so kind and patient and for sharing your talent once again. Thanks are also due to Sigrid Asmus for her expert and sensitive editing.

Thank you to Tod Gangler for repairing the scan of the Virna Haffer negative depicting her nude study of Corwin Chase. Your generosity is much appreciated.

Special thanks to Cornish College of the Arts in Seattle for conferring on me an Honorary Doctorate of Fine Arts, honoris causa, in May of 2017. It is a great honor to receive this recognition from such an important institution and I am deeply grateful.

The following individuals have all been very helpful and I thank them for their assistance: Marilyn Braarud, Janine Blocher, Anita Carmin and Lloyd Carmin, Jim and Rachel Clifton, Neil Collins, John and Lynn Cooper and the Cooper Trust, Leslie Correll, Maureen Duryee, Pat and Mike Green, Lisa Hart Guthrie, Timothy Hagen, Hotie and Larry Hard, Lucy Hart, Mathew Healea, John Impert, Kathy Ince, Kji and Rebecca Kelly, Lawrence Kreisman and Wayne Dodge, Joe Morosco, Richard Nicol, Edward and Susan Nudelman, Ann Matsudaira Otani and the Family of John Matsudaira, Julie Pierce, Waneen Cormier Post-Marks, Rivkah Sweedler, Roger and Jeanna van Oosten, Thomas H. Wake, Virginia Wyman, and Vera Zimmerman.

Thank you to the following colleagues and historians: Steven Thomas, of Steven Thomas, Inc.; Johannes Faber, Galerie Johannes Faber, Vienna, Austria; Ulrich Fritzsche, scholar and expert on Helmi Juvonen; Susan Futterman, print scholar and expert on Frances Gearhart; Marcia Approo, Assistant Registrar, Records, Pratt Institute, Brooklyn, New York; and Chiaki Ajioka, Art Historian, Sydney, Australia.

From the Whatcom Museum, Bellingham, Washington, my thanks go to Rebecca L. Hutchins, Curator of Collections/Registrar; Barbara Matilsky, Curator of Art; and Patricia Leach, Executive Director.

From the Jordan Schnitzer Museum of Art, University of Oregon, Eugene, Oregon, I thank Jonathan Smith, Photographer/Database Coordinator/Rights and Reproductions; Christopher White, Collection Manager; and Danielle Knapp, McCosh Associate Curator.

From The Seattle Public Library, I thank Jade D'Addario, Librarian, Special Collections, The Seattle Public Library; and Jodee Fenton, Managing Librarian, The Seattle Public Library.

From the University of Washington, I thank Conor M. Casey, Labor Archivist, University of Washington Libraries, Special Collections; Nicolette Bromberg, Visual Materials Curator, University of Washington Libraries, Special Collections; and Christine Fish, Office of the Registrar, University of Washington.

From the Frye Art Museum, Seattle, Washington, I thank Cory Gooch, Head of Collections; and Nives Mestrovic, Assistant Registrar.

From the Washington State Historical Society, I thank

Lynette Miller, Head of Collections; Eileen Price, Reference Archivist; and Maria Pascualy, Registrar and Associate Editor of *Columbia, The Magazine of Northwest History*.

For other important assistance I thank Zachariah Selley, Associate Head of Special Collections and College Archives, Lewis & Clark College, Portland, Oregon; Joanna Kiss, Collections Information and Imaging Administrator, Springfield Museums, Springfield, Massachusetts; and Judy Sourakli, Curator of Collections, Henry Art Gallery, University of Washington. Seattle.

From the Tacoma Art Museum, I thank Margaret Bullock, Curator of Collections and Special Exhibitions; Jessica Wilks, Registrar; and Ellen Ito, Exhibition and Collection Assistant.

Further thanks go to Eugene Lee, The Blakemore Foundation; Gail Goodrick, of the Kitsap Regional Library, Bremerton, Washington; and, at the Seattle Art Museum, Patti Junker, Ann M. Barwick Curator of American Art; Ashley Mead, Assistant Registrar, Rights and Reproductions; and Jeffrey Carlson, Collections Coordinator.

I also wish to thank Sam Davidson and Shayla M. Alarie, MA, Davidson Galleries, Seattle, Washington; Emily Laverty, Interim Registrar for Rights and Reproductions, Newark Museum, Newark, New Jersey; Esther Ervin, Program Manager, and the Reverend Laverne Hall, President, of the Dr. James W. Washington, Jr. & Janie Rogella Washington Foundation, Seattle, Washington; as well as Jason Krueger, Permanent Art Collection Curator, Indiana State University, Terre Haute, Indiana; Marge Huang, Library and Archives, Philadelphia Museum of Art, Philadelphia, Pennsylvania; and the Women Painters of Washington.

Finally I want to thank my life partner, Dominic Zambito, for all of his assistance and support.

DAVID F. MARTIN
July 2017

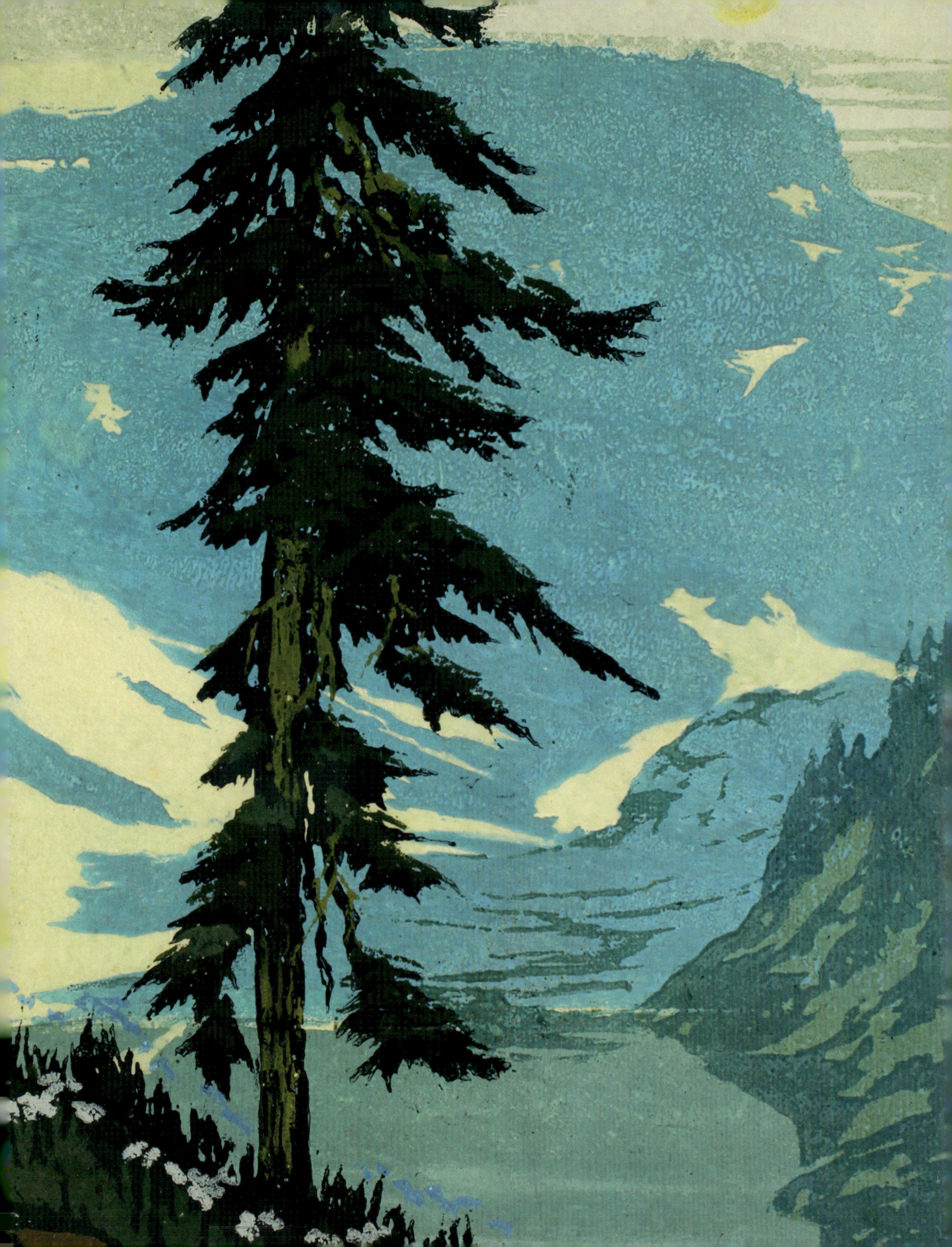

TERRITORIAL HUES

The Color Print and Washington State 1920–1960

DAVID F. MARTIN

The Seattle Art Association was organized in 1883 at the Territorial University, now the University of Washington. Six years later, on November 11, 1889, Washington became the forty-second state in the United States. In Washington State, establishing a cultural identity predated statehood.

As the nascent regional art scene was in its infancy, local citizens looked to other states and countries for collecting art. At the turn of the century, many of Seattle's fashionable homes contained Japanese *ukiyo-e* prints. These prints, woodcuts made with multiple blocks for different colors, could then be purchased in a wide range of prices; whether for decorative purposes in a working-class family, or as rare impressions by masters such as Kitagawa Utamaro (1753–1806), Katsushika Hokusai (1760–1849), and Andō Hiroshige (1797–1858), for wealthier collectors.

In 1904, the *Seattle Daily Times* reported on the collection of Dr. Alfred B. Kibbe, a prominent Seattle physician; his recent demise had left a large group of Japanese prints. The article reflected the growing interest in such prints, especially on the East Coast.

> The collections of these prints [have] assumed the proportions of a mild mania in the eastern cities, and their valuation has undergone a marked change in the last two or three years, for connoisseurs in numbers have developed of the art products of Japan and many valuable collections of vases, pictures and ornaments have come from the Orient gathered together here by those who have made a study of design, the methods of Japanese work, Eastern color schemes and the grouping and arrangements which produce the most striking effects.[1]

Dr. Kibbe, like most prominent early collectors in Seattle, had originally come from the East Coast—or Buffalo, New York, in Dr. Kibbe's case. The initial group of collectors in Seattle and other areas of Washington State and Oregon focused heavily on collecting Japanese prints.

One of the important art dealers on the West Coast at the turn of the century was Frederic C. Torrey (1864–1935) of the San Francisco gallery Vickery, Atkins & Torrey. He

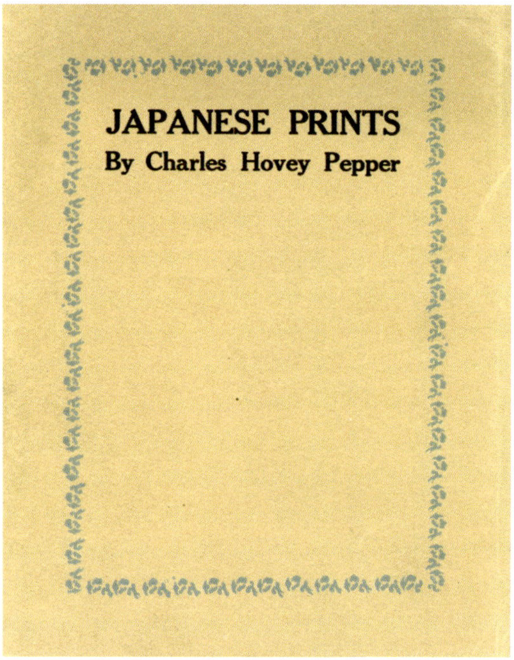

Japanese Prints, by Charles Hovey Pepper et al., Walter Kimball & Co., Boston, Massachusetts, 1905. The Martin-Zambito Archive

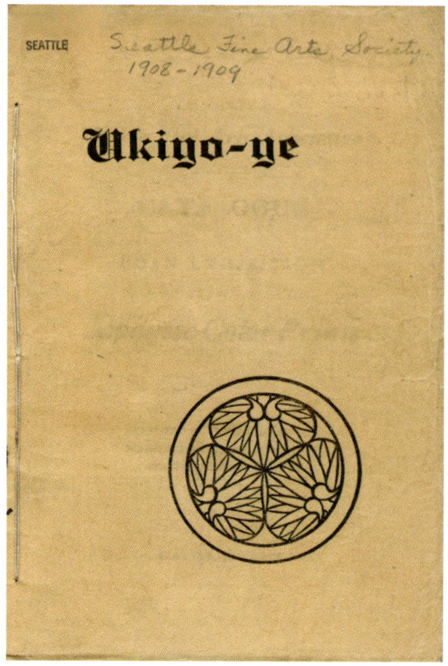

Ukiyo-ye, booklet for the Seattle Fine Arts Association, catalogue of a loan exhibition of Japanese color prints, Seattle, Washington, June 1908. Courtesy of The Seattle Public Library

was a specialist in Japanese prints and Chinese porcelains, and made frequent visits to Seattle at the turn of the century to offer fine works of art to the budding collectors group.

Another frequent visitor to Seattle was Katherine Ball (1859–1952), one of the founders of the Japan Society of America. She was an avid collector of Japanese prints and lectured extensively. In 1906 she gave a lecture in Seattle titled "Color Prints of Old Japan" under the auspices of the Rainier Chapter of the Daughters of the American Revolution. The lecture was illustrated with color stereopticon views, an early version of color slides, and Ball made several visits to local homes, promoting the collecting and study of Japanese prints.[2]

One of the earlier books on the subject was Charles Hovey Pepper's 1905 publication, *Japanese Prints*. Pepper (1864–1950), was an American artist whose own work was highly influenced by Japanese prints. Pepper was raised on the East Coast and traveled to Japan in 1903 initially to study printmaking. He created a collection that eventually became one of the finest in the United States. While in Japan, he produced several watercolors that were used to create woodblock prints by the publisher Kobayashi Bunshichi (1861–1923), who arranged the carving and printing of the blocks based on Pepper's watercolor designs.

Pepper was a frequent visitor to Seattle because his sister was married to University of Washington Professor Frederick Morgan Padelford (1875–1942). Thanks to promotion by his sister, Pepper became well known in the region and later received a solo exhibition at the University of Washington's Henry Gallery in 1928.

In February 1908, Mrs. Padelford gave a lecture on the influence of Japanese prints on contemporary art for the Women's Century Club in Seattle. In March 1908, the Seattle Fine Arts Association was formed, with Dr. Padelford serving as its first President. Mrs. Padelford was already preparing the women's group for a forthcoming June exhibition at the Seattle Fine Arts Association, who were sponsoring a loan exhibition of Japanese color prints at the

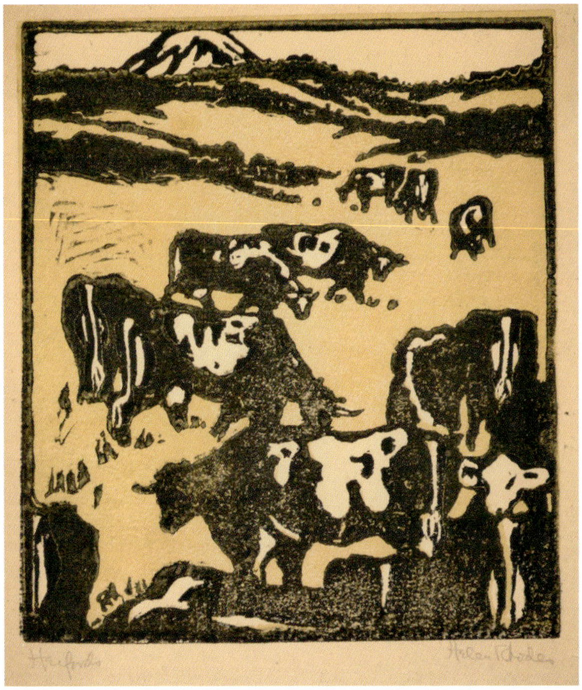

HELEN N. RHODES (1875–1938), *Herefords*, 1910, color woodblock print, 9 1/16 x 7 3/16 in. Henry Art Gallery, University of Washington, Seattle, Gift of Bertha Wiese, 51.11

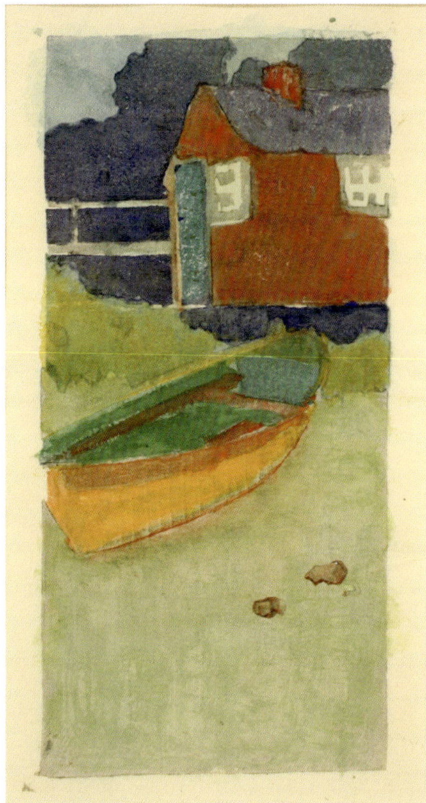

ARTHUR WESLEY DOW (1857–1922), *The Dory*, ca. 1895, color woodblock print, 4 7/8 x 2 1/4 in. Tacoma Art Museum, Museum purchase, 2000.1.1 to 4

Seattle Public Library's rooms at the Washington State Art Society. The exhibit included such rarities as the complete *Fifty-Three Stations of the Tôkaidô* by Hiroshige, and twelve prints by Utamaro.

Seattle was preparing for the 1909 Alaska-Yukon-Pacific Exposition (AYPE), the city's first world's fair that would emphasize the Northwest's industrial and cultural development. The fair naturally displayed the crowd-pleasing prints, but also included the work of regional and national artists in a variety of media. One artist whose work was very popular locally was California's Helen Hyde (1868–1919), who won a gold medal. Hyde, like Pepper, was an American printmaker whose charming work was based on Japanese prints. Another woman exhibiting her work at the AYPE was Helen N. Rhodes (1875–1938). Albeit unknown at the time, she would eventually become a key figure in the region's printmaking activities.

Rhodes was experimenting with three-color printmaking aroung this time, inspired by the chiaroscuro prints of sixteenth-century artists like Ugo da Carpi (1480–1523), who created interesting tonal values that resembled ink washes. Her earliest known print of 1910 utilizes this technique, but she soon adopted the teachings of Arthur Wesley Dow (1857–1922), with whom she studied.

Dow was a revolutionary force in American art and American art education. When he was a student he came under the influence of Ernest Fenollosa (1853–1908), then curator of Japanese Art at the Museum of Fine Arts in Boston. Dow was strongly influenced by Hokusai, whose work was radically different than anything he had experienced in his western training. Around 1890, Dow began creating his own color-woodblock prints; though influenced by the *ukiyo-e* movement, he elected to carve and print his own blocks. Dow traveled to Yokohama in 1903 and received further instruction after meeting Charles Hovey Pepper upon his arrival. Some of Dow's prints display simple shapes, a cropped vertical format, almost no modeling of the forms, and simple variegated colors.

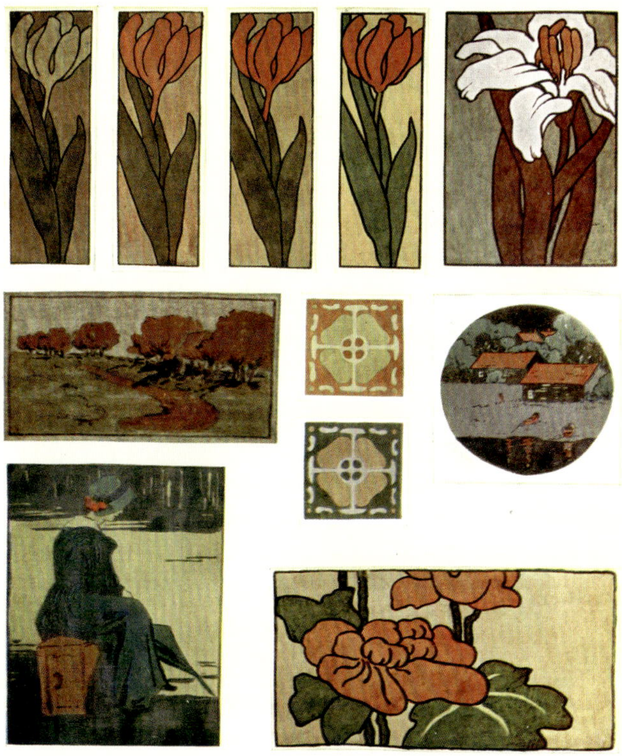

Plate No. 66 from *Composition*, by Arthur Wesley Dow, 7th edition, Doubleday, Page & Company, Garden City, New York, 1913. The Martin-Zambito Archive

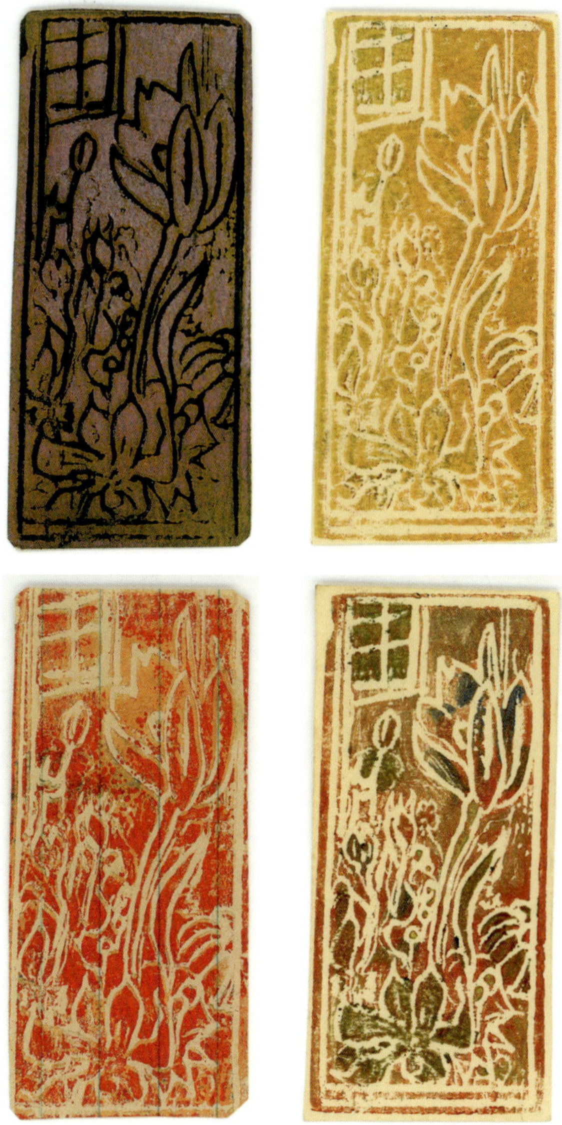

PETER M. CAMFFERMAN (1890–1957) and MARGARET GOVE CAMFFERMAN (1881–1964), four progressive proofs illustrating the multiple overlaying technique in creating a color woodblock print, ca. 1918, color woodblock prints, each 3 ½ x 1 ½ in. Collection of Maureen Duryee

Dow's landmark 1899 publication *Composition* became a standard art instruction book for the following decades.

Several Seattle artists used *Composition* for self-instruction if they were not able to study with Dow in person. His book was profusely illustrated with exercises for art students. Regional artists who experimented with these exercises include Peter Camfferman (1890–1957) and his wife, Margaret Gove Camfferman (1881–1964) who had studied with Robert Henri (1865–1929) in New York. Their four progressive proofs of a flower are obviously inspired by plate number 66 from *Composition*. Lance Wood Hart (1891–1941) produced several studies from Dow's exercises, as his landscape composition of 1916 attests. Another Seattle artist, Elizabeth Cooper (1877–1936), was also influenced by Dow, as seen in her exercises using the same design with variations in color and values. Cooper not only used these exercises in her paintings and prints but also for the production of ceramic tiles and hooked rugs. Regional teachers such as Alfrida Storm (1896–1967), Ruth K. Fisken (1896–?), Maude Irvine Kerns (1876–1965), and Helen

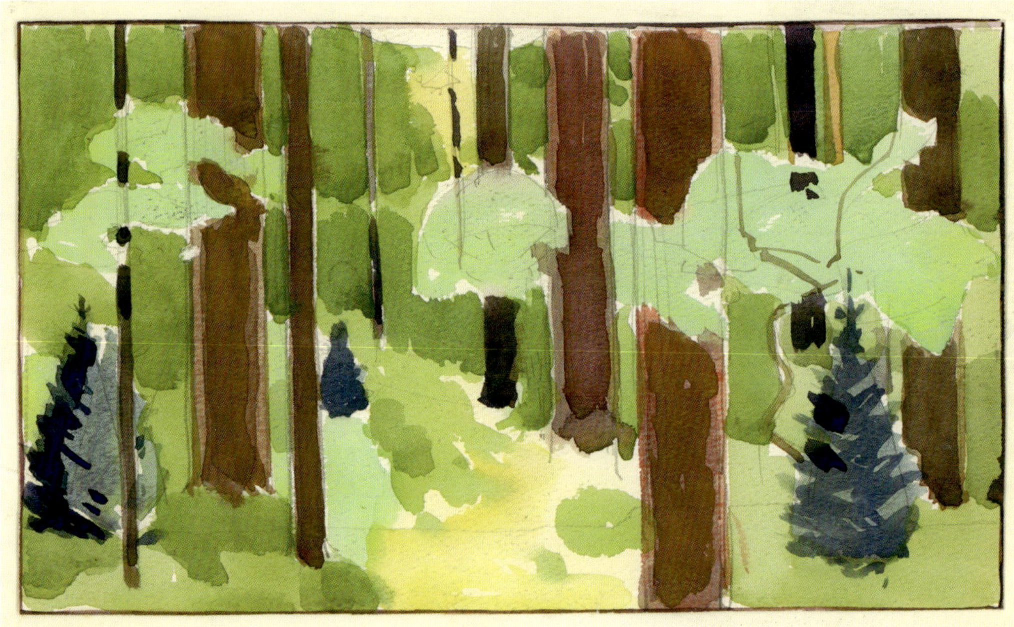

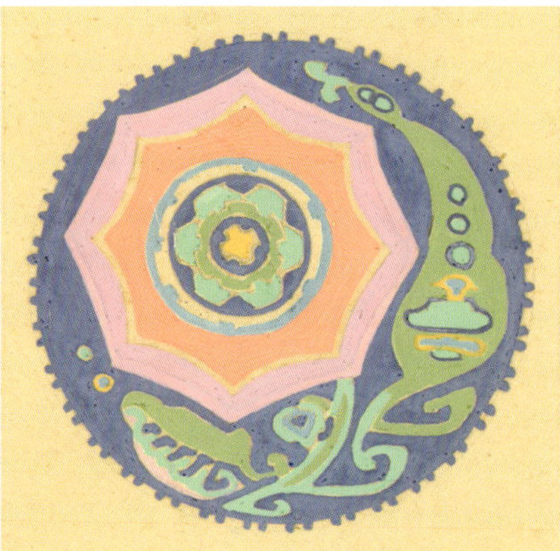

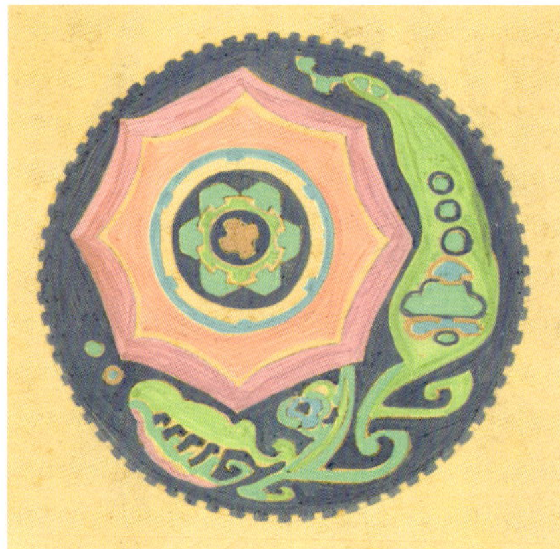

(top) LANCE WOOD HART (1891–1941), compositional study in the manner of Arthur Wesley Dow, 1916, watercolor, 5 x 8 ¼ in. Private collection

(bottom) ELIZABETH A. COOPER (1877–1936), three exercise studies using color, design, intensity, and value variations, ca. 1919, oil on paper, each 5 ½ in. diameter. Collection of the John Marshall Cooper QTIP Trust

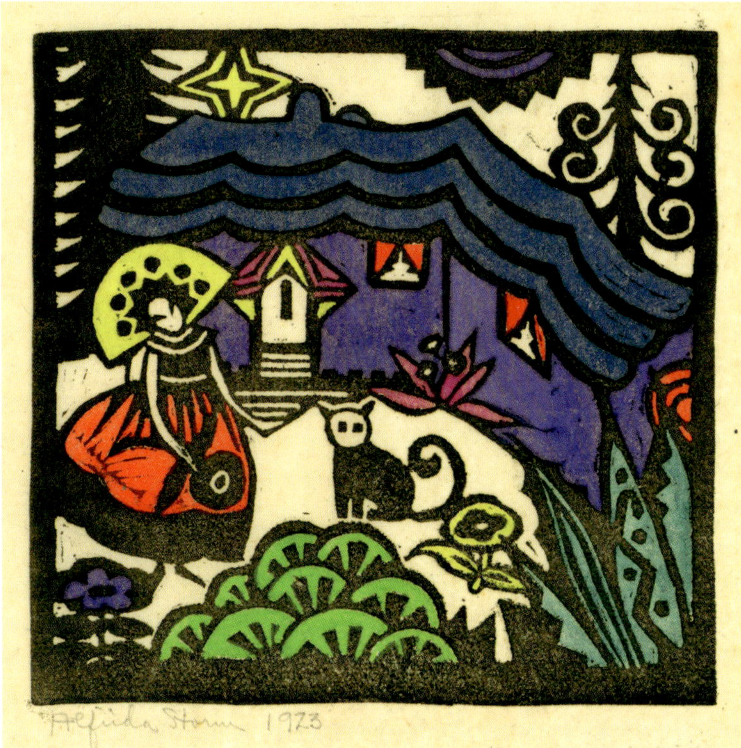

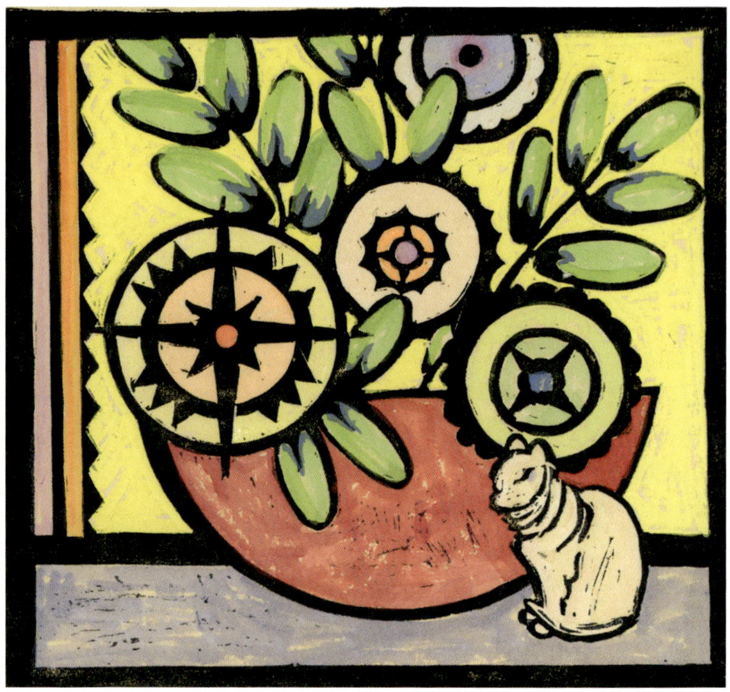

(top) ANNA ALFRIDA STORM (1896–1967), *Untitled*, 1923, color linocut print with additional hand coloring, 5 ½ x 5 ½ in. Private collection

(bottom) RUTH K. FISKEN (1896–?), *Untitled*, ca. 1923, color linocut print with additional hand coloring, 7 ½ x 8 in. Private collection

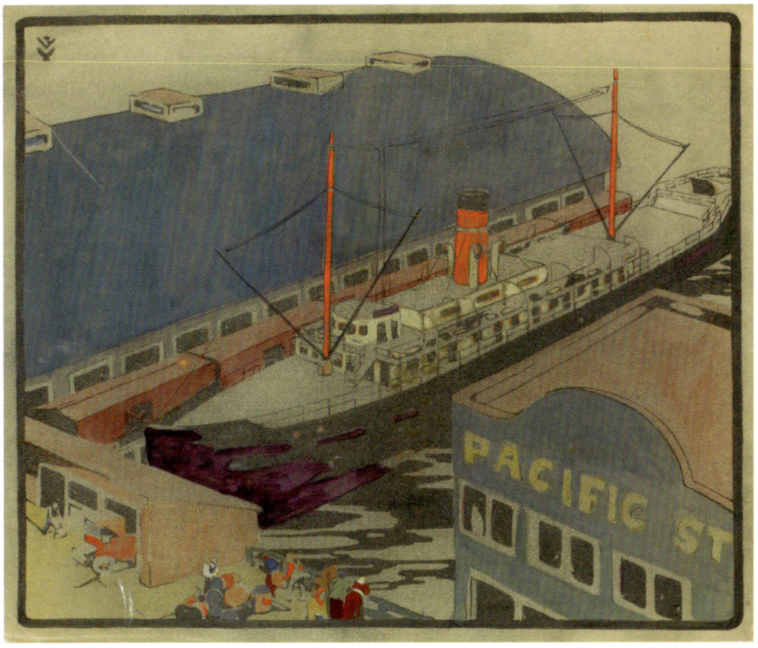

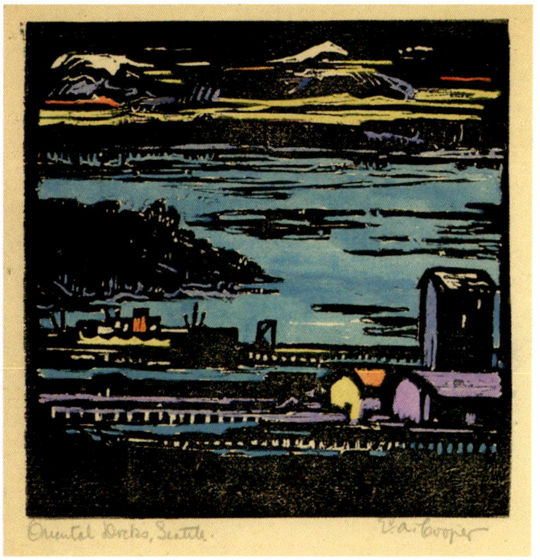

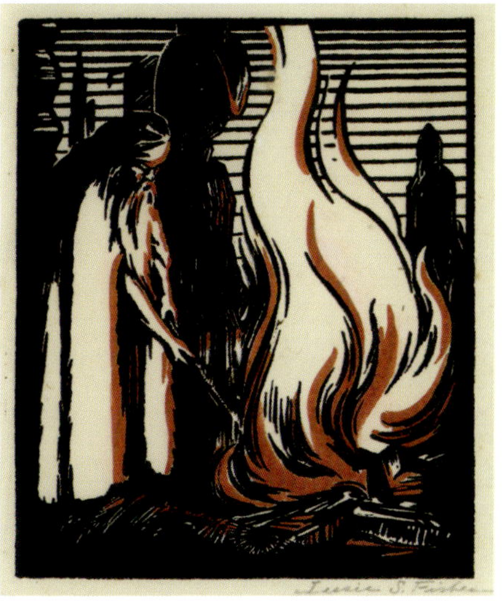

(left) MABEL LISLE DUCASSE (1895–1976), *Untitled*, ca. 1918, linocut print with hand coloring, 11 5/8 x 13 3/8 in. Private collection

(top right) ELIZABETH A. COOPER (1877–1936), *Oriental Docks*, ca. 1920, color linocut print with additional hand coloring, 7 x 6 7/8 in. Collection of the John Marshall Cooper QTIP Trust

(bottom right) JESSIE FISKEN (1860–1935), Untitled, ca. 1920, color linocut print, 5 1/2 x 4 1/2 in. Collection of John Impert

Rhodes were all students of Dow in New York and relayed his concepts to their students.

Younger artists from the University of Washington's art department who had studied with Rhodes and others at the University also tried their hand at printmaking. They would include the first person to receive a MA from the University, Mabel Lisle Ducasse (1895–1976), who hand-colored her prints rather than using separate blocks, and Elizabeth Cooper, whose earlier prints were made in the same manner. Cooper had entered the University of Washington in 1917 and returned over the next two decades when her maternal responsibilities allowed. Her circa 1920 print *Oriental Docks, Seattle* shows a debt to Hiroshige, while Jessie Fisken's (1860–1935) untitled color-relief print is one of the earliest Northwest color prints to depict Native American subject matter.

In 1915, Dow's successor at Pratt, Ralph Johonnot (1880–1940), came to Seattle to teach design classes at Broadway High School and the University of Washington. His instruction further reinforced Dow's methods.[3]

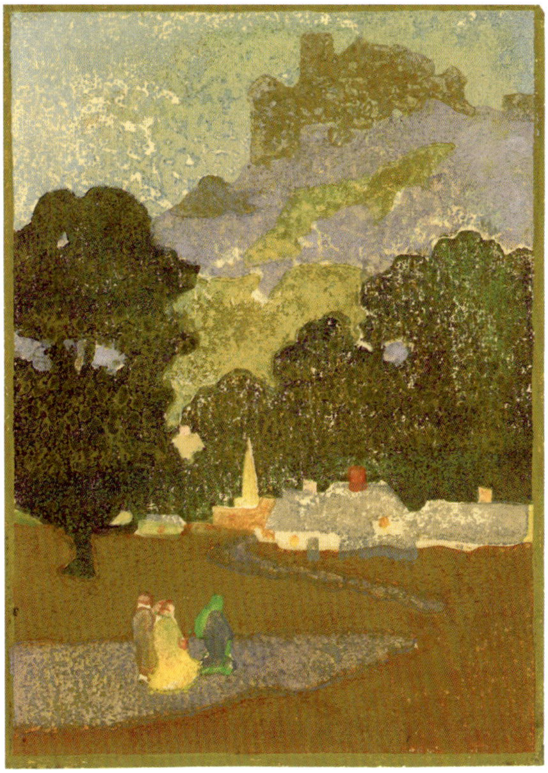

WILLIAM T. MCDERMITT (1884–1961), *Vespers*, 1920, color woodblock print, 6 ½ x 4 ½ in. Collection of John Impert

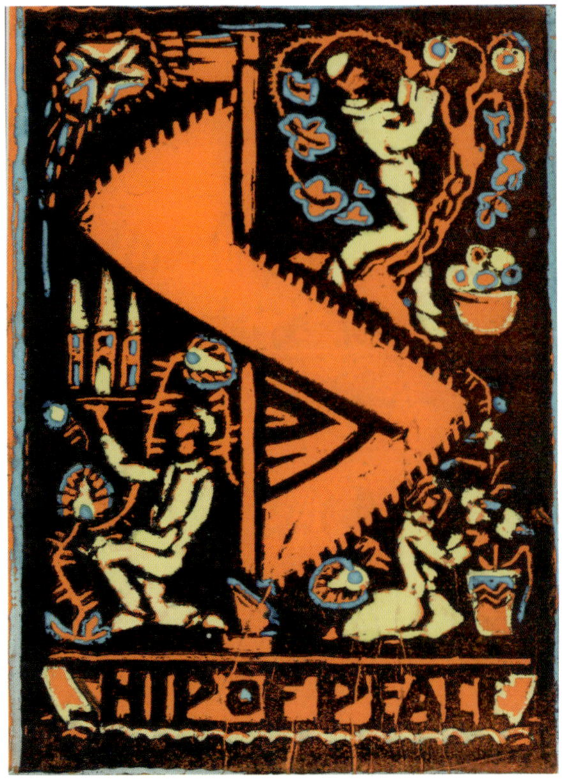

HELEN N. RHODES (1875–1938), *Ship of Peace*, 1924, color linocut print. 6 x 4 ¼ in. Private collection

In November of 1916, Seattle etcher Roi Partridge (1888–1984) arranged the first known exhibition of color prints in the region. Sponsored by the Seattle Fine Arts Society, the exhibition included works by Helen Hyde and Bertha Lum (1869–1954), Charles Hovey Pepper, B. J. O. Nordfeldt (1878–1955), Maud Squire (1873–1955), Elizabeth Colwell (1881–1954), and Gustav Baumann (1881–1971). This was also the first time that Washington State audiences were able to see white-line or "Provincetown" prints:

> It would not be a complete exhibition in the year 1916 if the work of Ada Gilmore, Bror Nordfeldt and Ethel Mars had been omitted, and they furnish the riot of primitive coloring and wood blocky figures that will prove interesting to some – as an indication that modernity has placed its mark on even this expression of art – and of mirth to others, and possibly of annoyance to a few.[4]

Another local review also mentioned the Provincetown printmakers:

> The most extremely modern prints exhibited are the above mentioned group by Ethel Mars, Ada Gilmore, and Mary Jones. The color is so vivid, almost gaudy, and the subjects and their poses so unusual that it takes some little time to become attracted to these prints, but there is something rather live and bright about them that is after all, quite pleasing.[5]

Within a few years, some regional artists began exhibiting their own attempts at color printmaking. William T. McDermitt (1884–1961) produced several color woodblock prints in 1920 while on the faculty at Washington State College in Pullman, Washington. McDermitt's prints did not always reflect regional subjects, but rather he often based them on European and particularly German prints

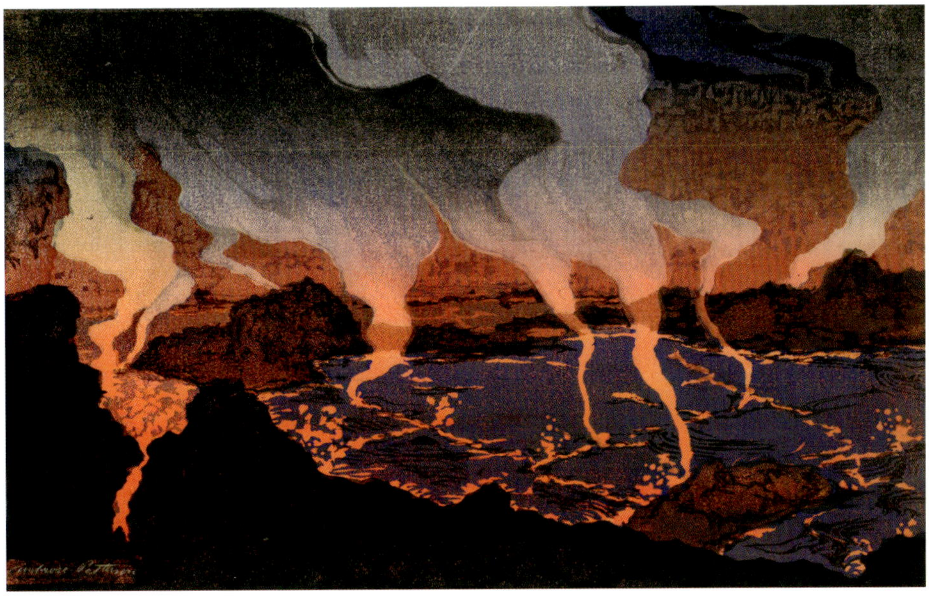

AMBROSE PATTERSON (1877–1966), *Volcano, Kilauea, Hawaii*, 1917, color woodblock print, 9 3/8 x 14 1/2 in. Tacoma Art Museum. Gift of Joan McCrary Wahlman, 1991.32

of the era. Ambrose Patterson (1877–1966) was new to the faculty at the University of Washington by 1918. Having previously lived in Hawaii and briefly in California, the Australian-born artist had developed a significant European exhibition history and was adept at making color woodblock prints and monotypes by the time he began teaching at the university. Soon after his arrival, he was given a solo exhibition at the Seattle Fine Arts Society that included several of his prints, including his masterpiece, *Volcano, Kilauea, Hawaii* of 1917. The only color woodblock print that he made in Seattle during that time was an image of Mount Rainier in 1921, and it is highly influenced by Japanese *ukiyo-e* prints.

Patterson's wife Viola Hansen Patterson (1898–1984) had a special interest in color printmaking and produced several prints in the early 1920s and '30s. Viola gave a class in block printing at the Seattle Fine Arts Society in 1928, teaching the methods for making bookplates, letterheads, and original textiles.

In 1919, Helen Hyde was once again featured in Seattle, this time at the Seattle Fine Arts Society, where sixty of her color prints dating from 1907 to 1918[6] were shown. Owing to this popularity, the SFAS held an exhibition of the work of the Scottish artist Elizabeth Keith (1887–1956) in 1922. Keith too concentrated on Japanese-style color prints.

In 1924, artist Hiroshi Yoshida (1876–1950), one of the greatest Japanese printmakers of that period, visited Seattle as part of an American tour. He was given a solo exhibition of his paintings and prints at the Seattle Fine Arts Society sponsored by the local Japanese Club.[7] During this trip he made several sketches of Mount Rainier to be used for making color woodblock prints upon his return to Japan.

Local artists were now beginning to create their own multi-block color prints. James Allan (1892–1966), a Scottish immigrant who worked in the commercial arts field in Seattle, created a large multiple-block print of Mount Rainier between 1921 and 1924. The effort was so strenuous that he made no other prints after this initial endeavor.

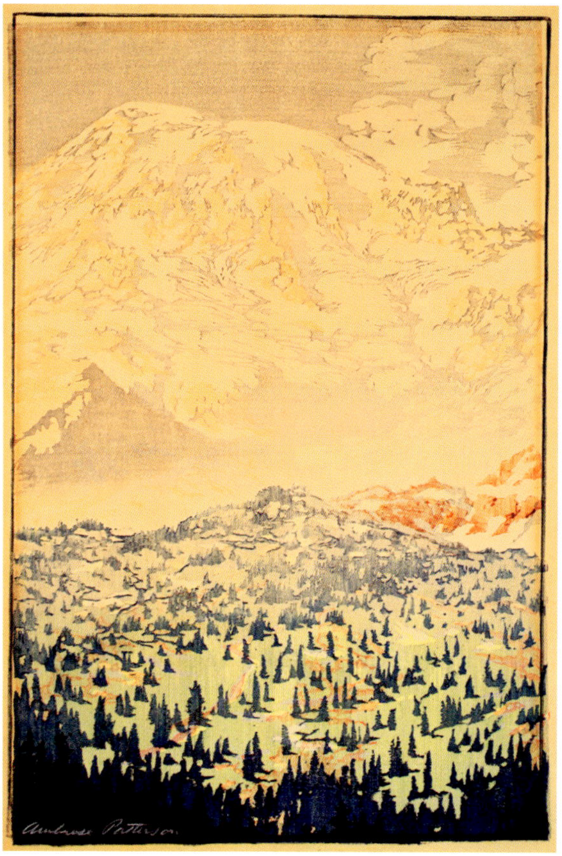

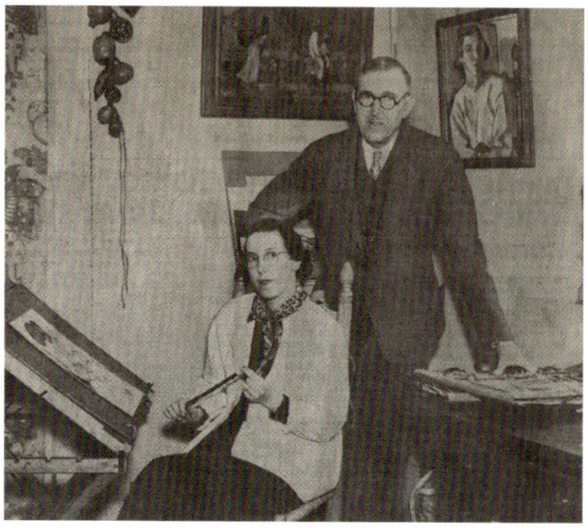

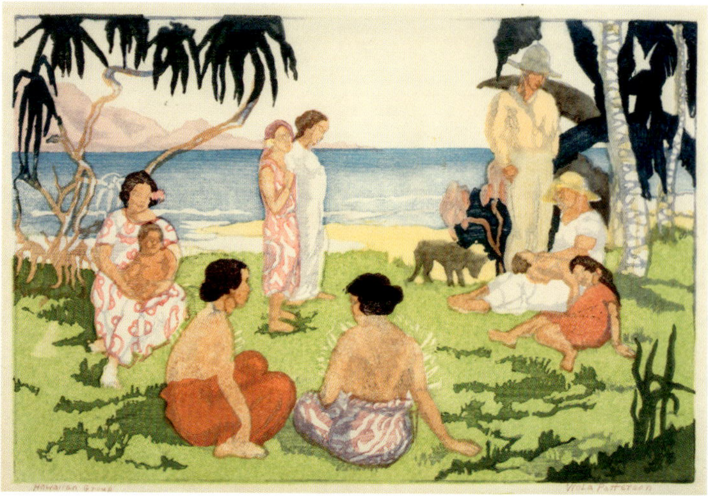

(left) AMBROSE PATTERSON (1877–1966), *Mount Rainier*, 1921, color woodblock print, 14 ½ x 9 ¼ in. Collection of Lawrence Kreisman and Wayne Dodge

(top right) VIOLA PATTERSON and AMBROSE PATTERSON, ca. 1935, newspaper clipping from the artists' scrapbook. Courtesy of The Seattle Public Library

(bottom right) VIOLA HANSEN PATTERSON (1898–1984), *Hawaiian Group*, ca. 1929, color woodblock print, 9 ¼ x 13 ⅜ in. Included in the first exhibition of the Northwest Printmakers Society in 1929. Michele and Donald D'Amour Museum of Fine Arts, Springfield, Massachusetts. Eugene Aston Collection, 2008.D40. Photograph by John Polak

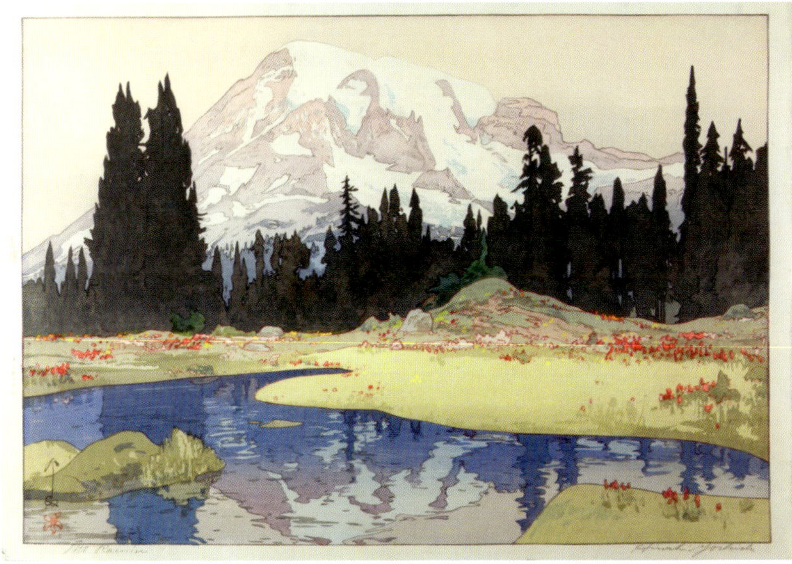

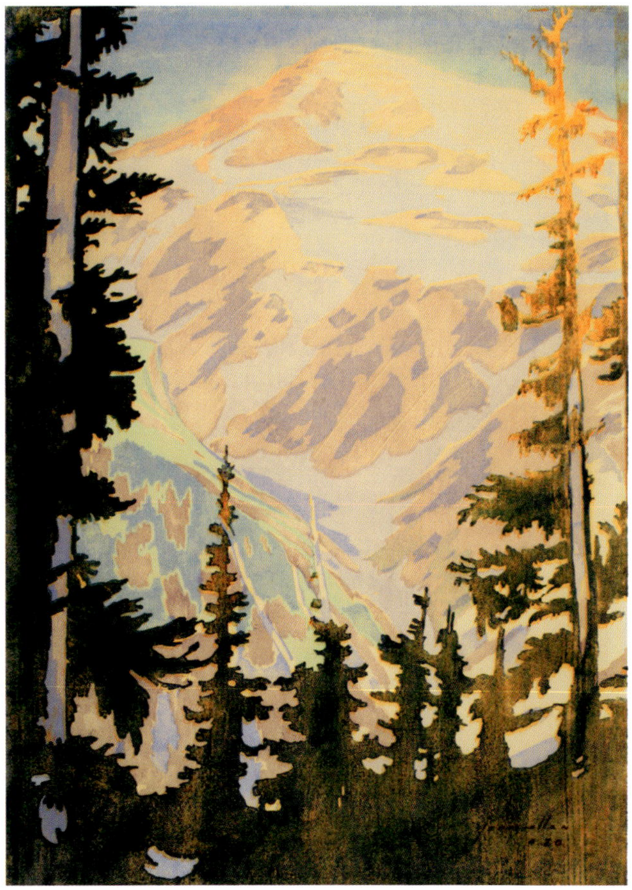

(top) HIROSHI YOSHIDA (1876–1950), *Mount Rainier*, 1925, color woodblock print, 15 7/8 x 21 1/4 in. (double oban). Photograph courtesy Davidson Galleries

(bottom) JAMES ALLAN (1892–1966), *Mount Rainier from Van Trump Park*, ca. 1921–24, color woodblock print, 20 x 14 in. Private collection

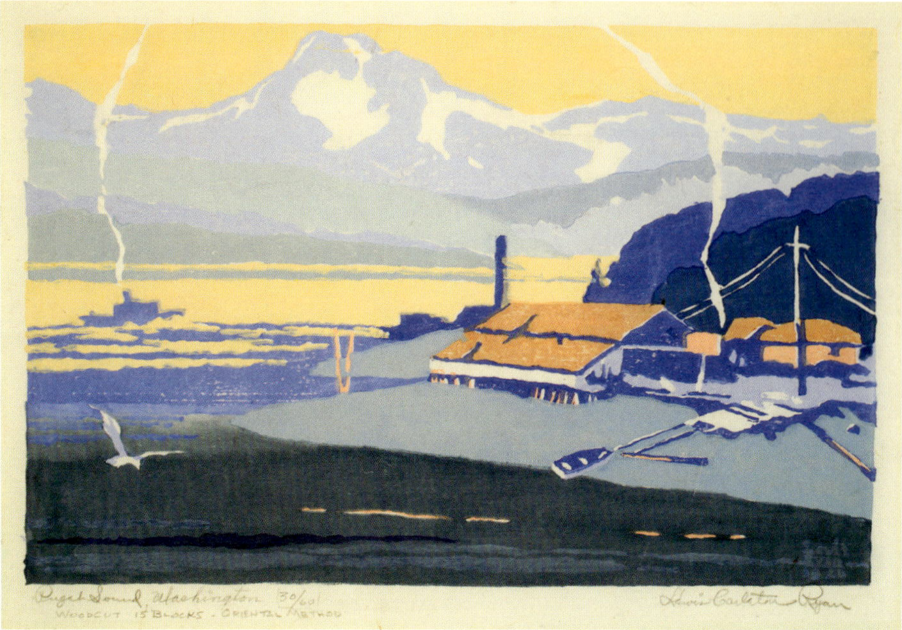

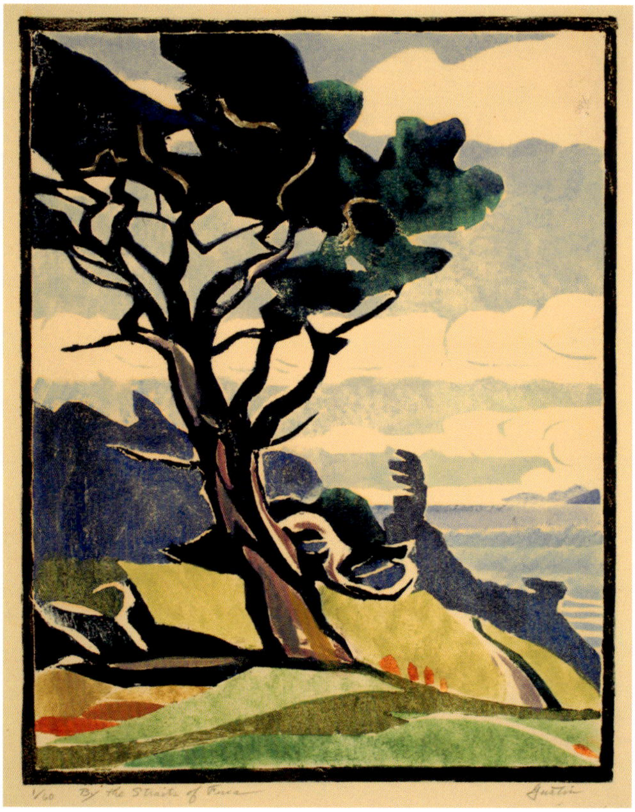

(top) LEWIS CARLTON RYAN (1894–1982), *Puget Sound, Washington*, 1924, color woodblock print, 8 x 12 in. Collection of Thomas H. Wake

(bottom) PAUL MORGAN GUSTIN (1886–1974), *By the Strait of Fuca*, ca. 1925, color relief print, 11 ¼ x 8 ½ in. Private collection

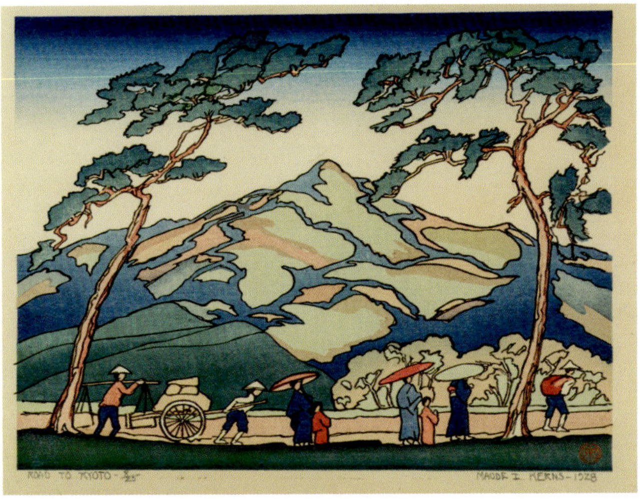

MAUDE I. KERNS (1876–1965), *Road to Kyoto*, 1928, color woodblock print, 7 5/8 x 9 5/8 in. Jordan Schnitzer Museum of Art, University of Oregon, Eugene, Oregon, Murray Warner Collection of Oriental Art, MWA51:K1a

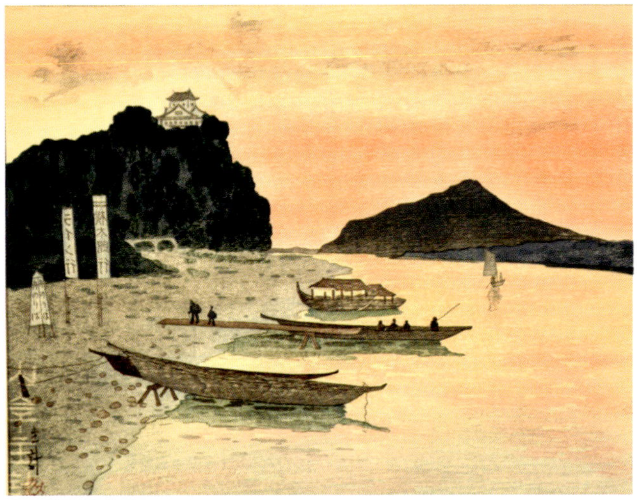

YAMAGISHI KAZUE (1883–1966), *Boat Launch on a River Bank*, ca. 1928, color woodblock print, 11 1/4 x 14 3/16 in. Henry Art Gallery, University of Washington, Seattle, Frances and Thomas Blakemore Collection, FA 96.72

Lewis Carlton Ryan (1894–1982), a California artist who lived for a while in Seattle, produced his print, *Puget Sound, Washington* in 1924, using fifteen blocks

Paul Morgan Gustin (1886–1974), one of the region's most significant artists, produced a number of color relief prints. The majority of his output in that medium was used for creating Christmas cards but he made a few larger prints as well. Rather than carving a block, Gustin used a method that is closer to what we today would call a collagraph. The matrix he used was built up with heavy cardboard shapes that were heavily varnished and printed and didn't require any carving.

Maude I. Kerns (1876–1965) was born in Oregon and attended the University of Oregon in Eugene. In 1904, she attended Columbia University, studying under Arthur Wesley Dow. From 1906 to 1920, she was teaching art at Lincoln High School in Seattle and exhibited in all of the regional venues, winning awards for her paintings. By 1921, she returned to the University of Oregon as Assistant Professor. In 1928, she traveled to Japan to paint and study color printmaking. Her *Road to Kyoto* (1928) was likely made from her original watercolor, with the blocks carved and printed by a Japanese artisan in the modern *Shin-hanga* movement's collaborative manner of the time. Kerns later went on to produce abstractions in the manner of Wassily Kandinsky (1866–1944) and was an early exhibitor at the Museum of Non-Objective Painting in New York, later renamed the Guggenheim.

Kerns had the financial means to travel to Japan but most other local artists did not. However, in 1928, Japanese artist Yamagishi Kazue (1883–1966) arrived in Seattle to teach. He had developed a reputation for carving blocks for some of the finest print artists of the period, including Hiroshi Yoshida, Kōshirō Onchi (1891–1955), and the Parisian *Japoniste*, Paul Jacoulet (1896–1960). Local students included Waldo S. Chase (1895–1988), his brother W. Corwin Chase (1897–1988) and R. Bruce Inverarity (1909–1999).

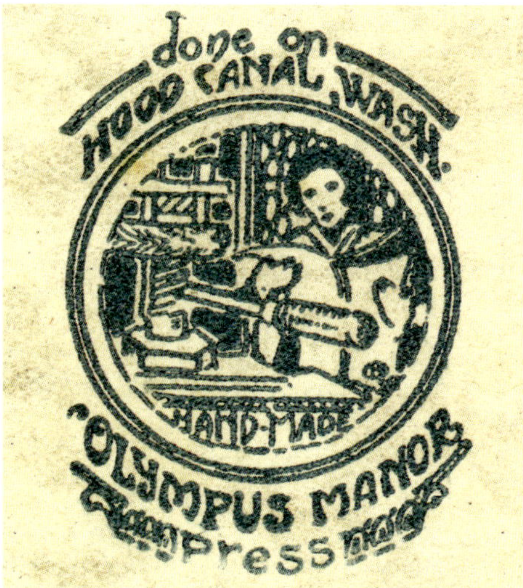

ORRE NELSON NOBLES (1894–1967), *Olympus Manor Press*, ca. 1924, woodblock print, 1 ⅛ x 4 ¾ in. The Martin-Zambito Archive

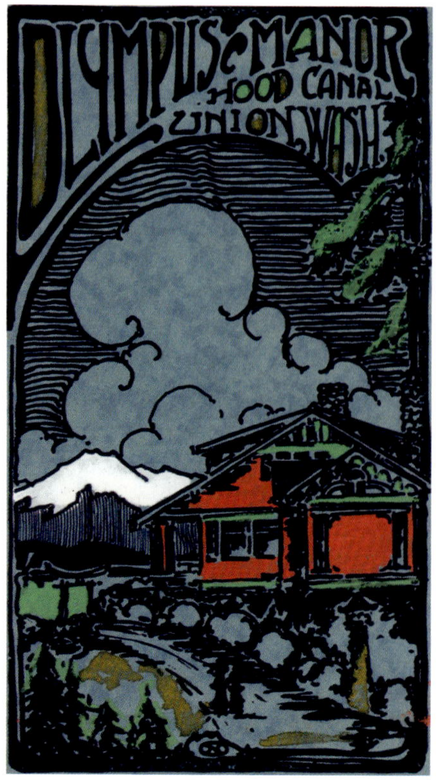

ORRE NELSON NOBLES (1894–1967), *Olympus Manor, Hood Canal, Wash.*, ca. 1924, woodblock print with hand coloring, 6 ¼ x 3 ½ in. Private collection

Outside of Seattle at Hood Canal in the Olympic Peninsula, Orre Nelson Nobles (1894–1967) created an arts oriented enclave with a main structure named Olympus Manor. The manor was the home of his parents and siblings, but by 1923 Orre had transformed it into a sixteen-room lodge with cabins available to accommodate visiting guests. Nobles had graduated from Columbia University in 1922 with the intention of having a teaching position in his native Washington State. He set up a press at the manor, and, along with assistants, created beautiful advertising cards and brochures, many of them hand colored. No fine-art prints by Nobles have surfaced.

Orre Nobles was one of several gay men involved in printmaking in the region. Tacoma's artist/illustrator Mac Harshberger (1900–1975) created magnificent Art Deco prints, drawings, illustrations, and paintings. He had a lifelong partner, Harry "Hollande" Robinson, who was also an illustrator, but mostly active as a musician and composer. Harshberger, like Nobles, made relief prints for utilitarian purposes—advertising, ex-libris bookplates, and personal cards, as well as illustrations used for Hollande's published music. He would often depict himself and his partner in comical situations like the circa 1929 linocut portraying the couple with limp wrists holding their symbolic muses of art and music. Even their cat holds his fish with a limp-wristed paw, comically undermining the stereotypes of the day.

Other activity outside of Seattle included Bellingham's Elizabeth Colborne (1885–1948). A student of Arthur Wesley Dow, Colborne had extensive training in fine art and was highly successful as an illustrator during the early decades of the twentieth century. She divided her time between New York City and Bellingham, preferring the subject matter of her home state for her artistic expression. Around 1925, Colborne began producing extraordinary color woodblock prints that she designed, carved, and printed herself. Like her contemporaries, Waldo and Corwin Chase, she lived in the wilderness to study her subjects at first hand. Colborne thoroughly submerged herself in Japanese methods like *kira-zuri*

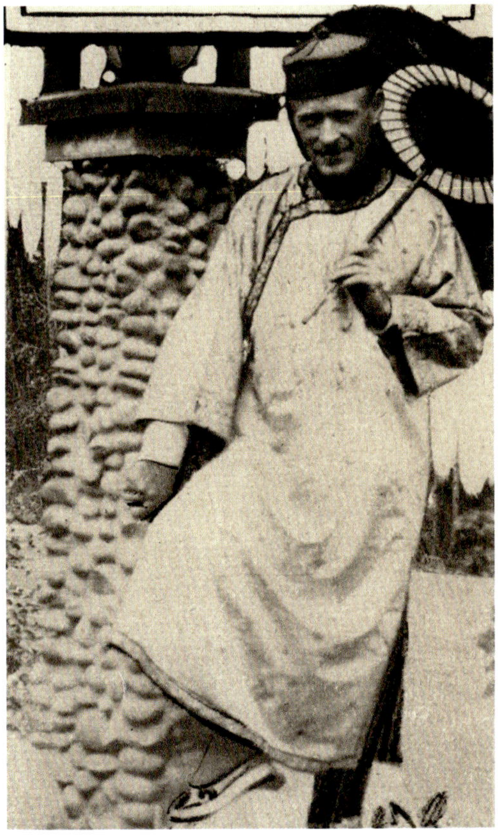

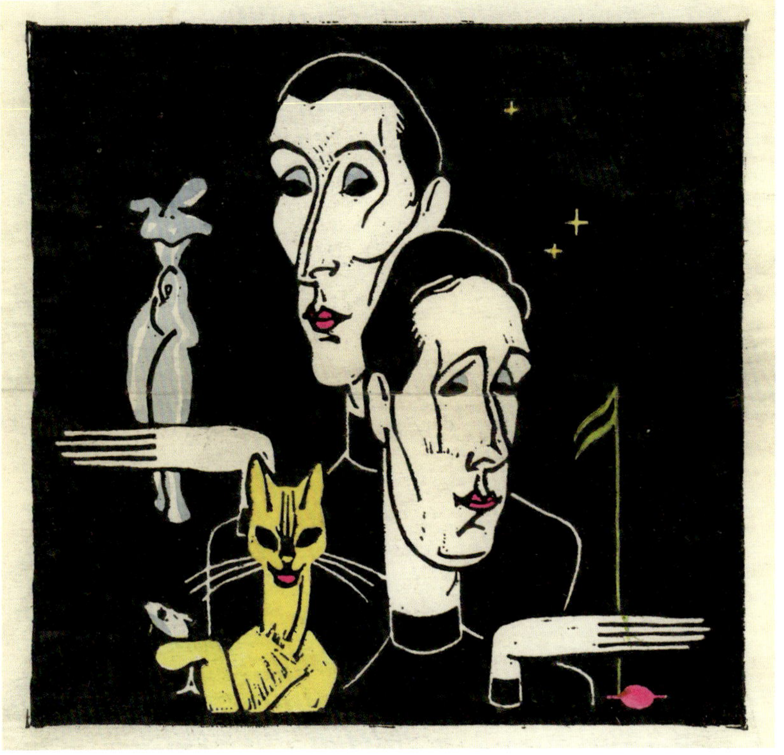

(left) ORRE NELSON NOBLES, *The Seattle Daily Times Rotogravure Pictorial Section*, June 1, 1924, p. 5. The Martin-Zambito Archive

(right) MAC HARSHBERGER (1900–1975), Christmas card, ca. 1929, color linocut with additional hand coloring, 5 ½ x 5 ½ in. Private collection

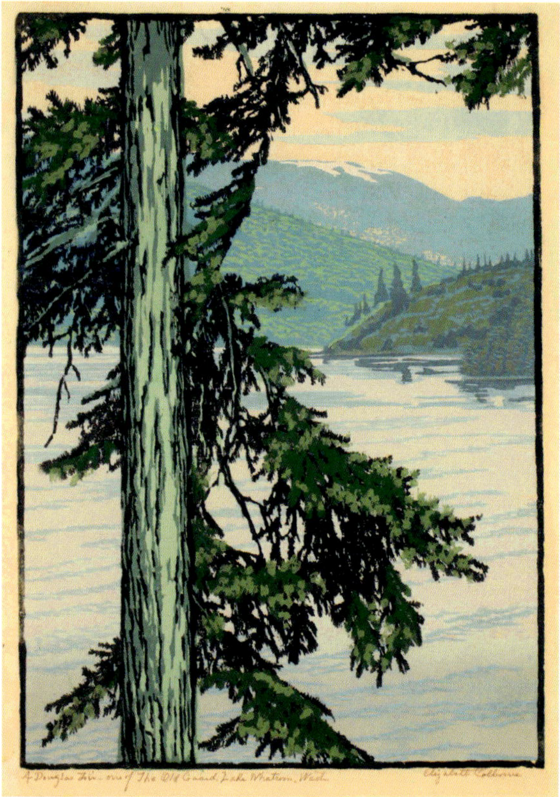

ELIZABETH COLBORNE (1885–1948), *A Douglas Fir, One of the Old Guard, Lake Whatcom, Washington*, ca. 1929, color woodblock print, 13 x 9 in. Private collection

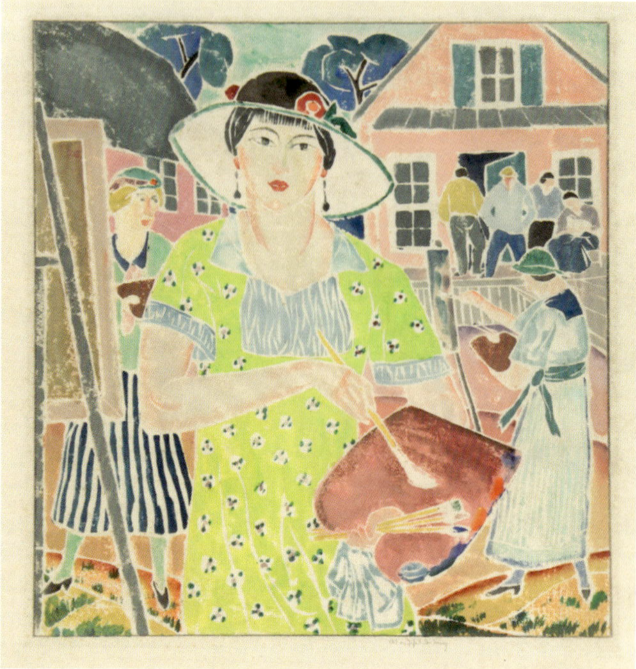

BROR JULIUS OLSSON NORDFELDT (1878–1955), *The Art Student*, ca. 1916, white line color woodblock print, 12 x 11 in. Philadelphia Museum of Art, Gift of Mrs. Bror Julius Olsson Nordfeldt, 1957, Accession no. 1957-46-3

and, like her Japanese counterparts, would sometimes add mica to her inks to give the finished print additional luster. On several of her prints she also inked the verso of certain areas to give the print a more luminous quality. Her prints were well received in New York, where she had been represented by the Argent Gallery. In 1939, the art critic for the *New York Times* stated that "Elizabeth Colborne . . . presents Western forest subjects in drawings, block prints and watercolors. This is capable and serious work, the tree and plant pictures stressing a keen sense of observation and ability in detailed arrangement."[8]

Because Colborne never married or had any descendants, much of her life story remains a mystery.[9]

As discussed earlier, the first exhibit to include white-line or "Provincetown" prints in Seattle was in 1916. The technique was an American variation on the Japanese style of color woodblock printing except that with this technique the artist only uses one block. The print is created by the carving of a *V*-shaped-groove in the block around the outlined design and repeatedly painting and printing the raised areas while the paper is tacked down at the top for proper registration. The technique has been traditionally credited to B. J. O. Nordfeldt, who apparently developed the method around 1915. A recent rediscovery of the work of Provincetown artist Edith Lake Wilkinson (1868–1957) contained two white-line prints dated 1914, suggesting that the technique had been developed earlier than previously thought.[10] Provincetown prints became very popular with teachers and students at the University of Washington School of Art. Helen Rhodes had gone to Provincetown before 1924 and learned the technique, instructing her students upon her return. Ruth Fisken also went to Provincetown to learn the technique and taught it to her students in Seattle and Spokane as well.[11]

Elizabeth Warhanik (1880–1968), one of the region's finest painters, also produced a number of Provincetown prints likely made between 1925 and 1932, although none are dated. Warhanik's descendants recalled her travels

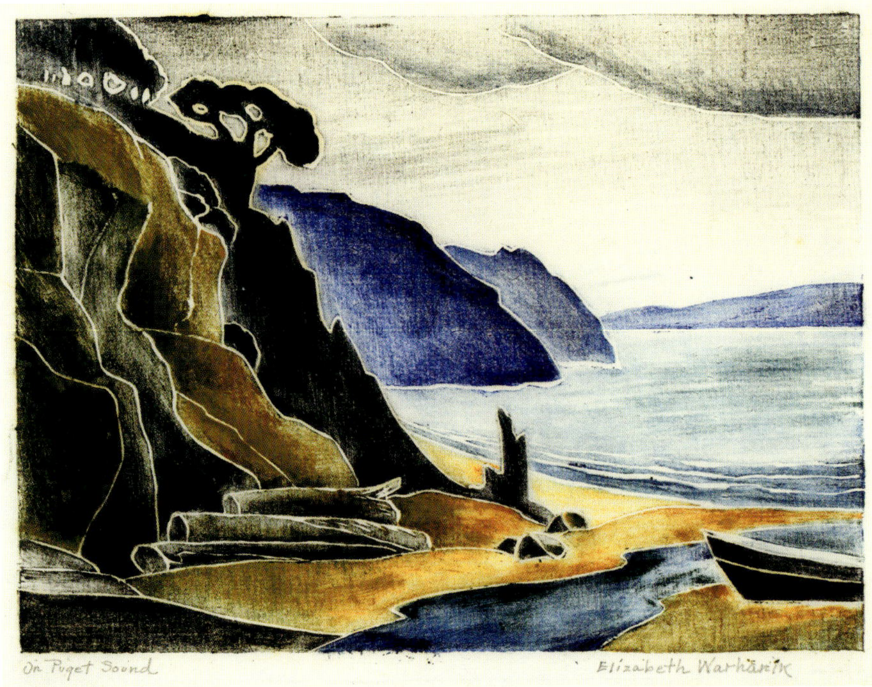

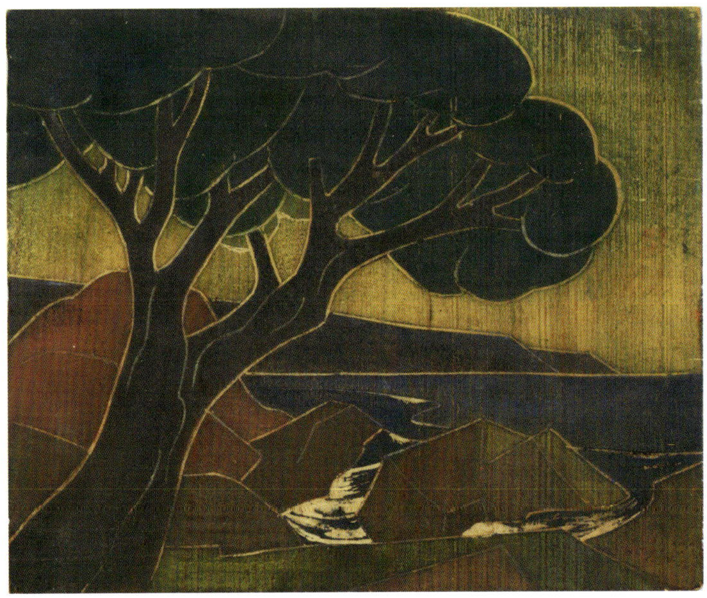

(top) ELIZABETH WARHANIK (1880–1968), *On Puget Sound*, ca. 1928, white line color woodblock print, 7 x 9 1/8 in. Private collection

(bottom) ELIZABETH WARHANIK (1880–1968), white line printing block showing incised carving of the wood and paint application before the print was pulled, 5 3/4 x 6 3/4 in. Collection of the Estate of Elizabeth Warhanik

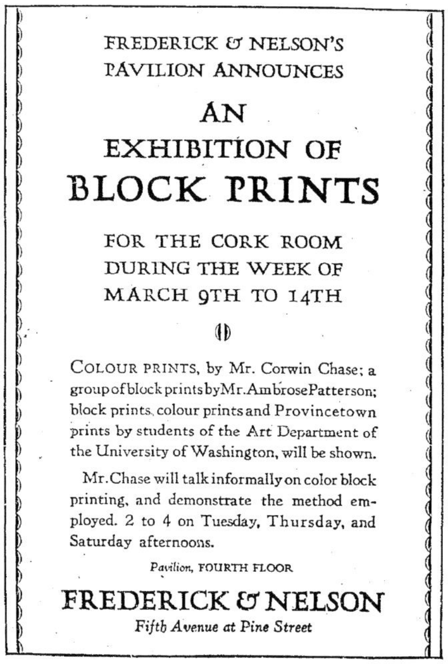

FREDERICK & NELSON'S
PAVILION ANNOUNCES

AN
EXHIBITION OF
BLOCK PRINTS

FOR THE CORK ROOM
DURING THE WEEK OF
MARCH 9TH TO 14TH

COLOUR PRINTS, by Mr. Corwin Chase; a group of block prints by Mr. Ambrose Patterson; block prints, colour prints and Provincetown prints by students of the Art Department of the University of Washington, will be shown.

Mr. Chase will talk informally on color block printing, and demonstrate the method employed. 2 to 4 on Tuesday, Thursday, and Saturday afternoons.

Pavilion, FOURTH FLOOR

FREDERICK & NELSON
Fifth Avenue at Pine Street

Exhibition announcement, *The Seattle Sunday Times*, March 8, 1931, p. 7, Courtesy of The Seattle Public Library

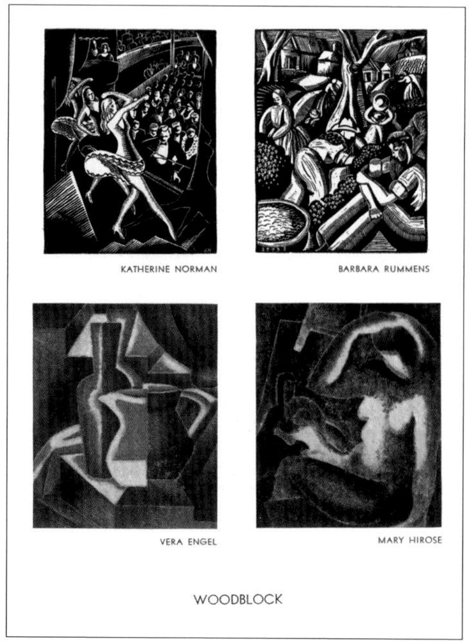

Dorothy Woempner and Kathleen Johnston, *P.S.D.: Departments of Painting, Sculpture, and Design and Department of Architecture, University of Washington*, published by Lambda Rho and Atelier, Seattle, Washington, 1932, p. 20.

to Provincetown but no dates have been verified. Her prints show her awareness of the prints of Blanche Lazzell (1878–1956), who was one of the finest printmakers in Provincetown and was included in the 1916 Seattle exhibition that Warhanik likely attended.

The Northwest Printmakers Society (NWPS) was formed in 1928 "to stimulate an interest in prints on the part of the public and to increase the activity of printmakers in the Northwest." When they held their first exhibition at the University of Washington's Henry Art Gallery in 1929, ten Provincetown prints were included, created mostly by UW students as well as by charter members Ruth Penington (1905–1998) and Josephine Hanks (dates not known).

Helen Rhodes continued her crusade to educate the public about printmaking. She gave a lecture on woodblock prints at the Seattle Art Institute in February, accompanied by a display of prints, anticipating and perhaps drumming up interest for the NWPS first exhibit in March.

In this first exhibition, several distinguished California color printmakers participated. Frances Gearhart (1869–1958) exhibited three color-woodblock prints, and William Seltzer Rice (1873–1963) showed two. Both would exhibit again over the next few years.

One of the few local venues for artists to sell their prints was established by Harry Hartman (1896–1945), whose bookstore and gallery supported graphic arts and photography. The fact that Hartman was blind did not impede his enthusiasm for the arts. The other store that consistently sold prints was the downtown studio of artist Jacob Elshin (1892–1976). Besides displaying his own handmade cards, he hired artists like Helmi Juvonen (1903–1985), who was just beginning to establish her career. Elshin also sold the cards and prints of artists including the brothers Waldo Chase (1895–1988) and Corwin Chase (1897–1988), and Lewis Carlton Ryan.

Monoprints, also called monotypes, were discussed in the local press as early as 1910, with an article in the *Seattle Daily Times* describing the process.[12] A monoprint is made by an artist who paints a design, usually using oil paint, directly onto a surface such as a glass or metal plate. A piece of paper is then placed over the painting, and the paper is carefully rubbed, transferring just one single impression (proof) of the image onto the paper—thus creating a mono (single) print. Monoprints by local artists were shown as early as 1913, when Jeanette Powell (dates not known), a Tacoma art instructor who had studied with William Merrit Chase and Robert Henri in New York, exhibited one with the Washington State Art Association.

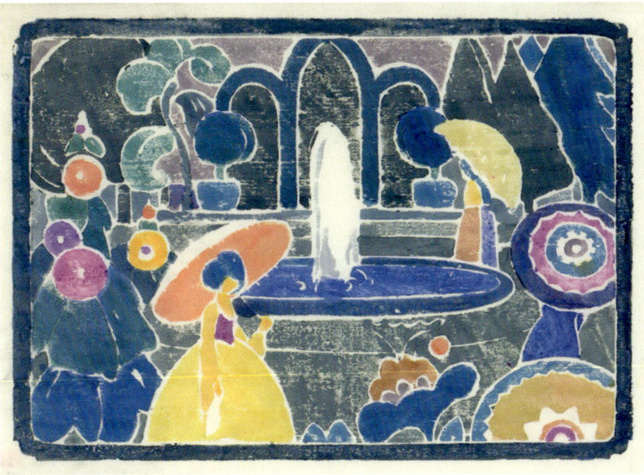

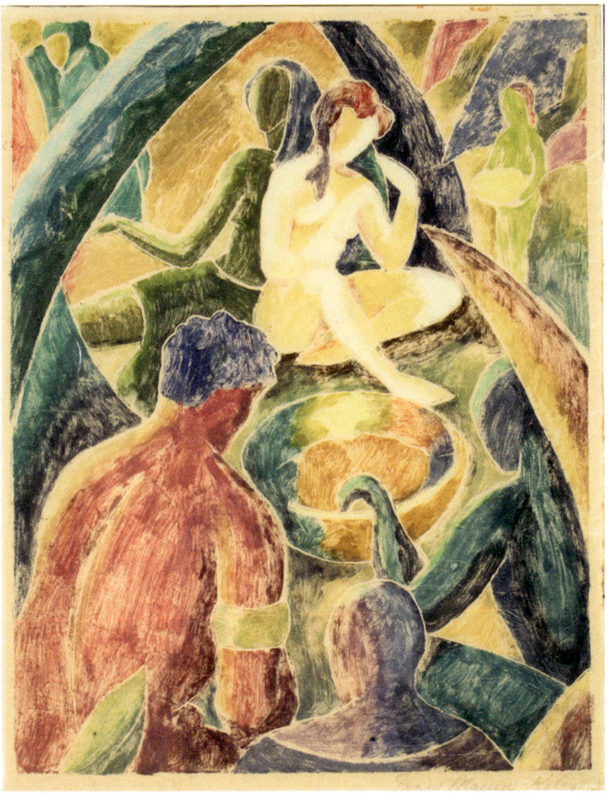

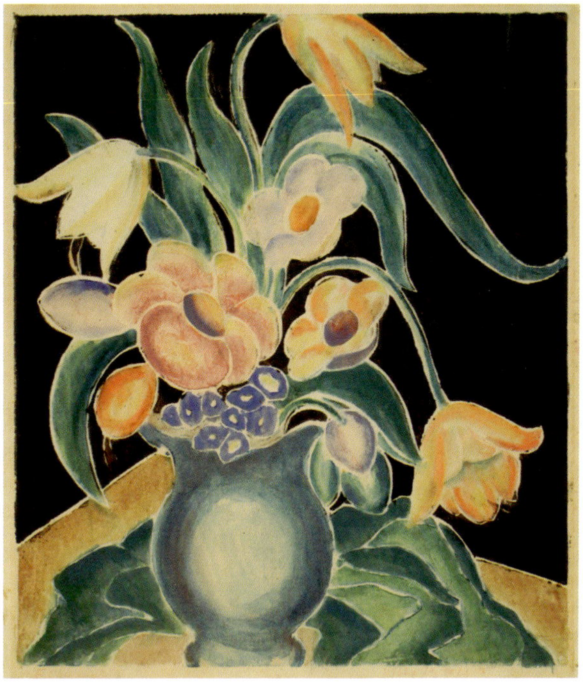

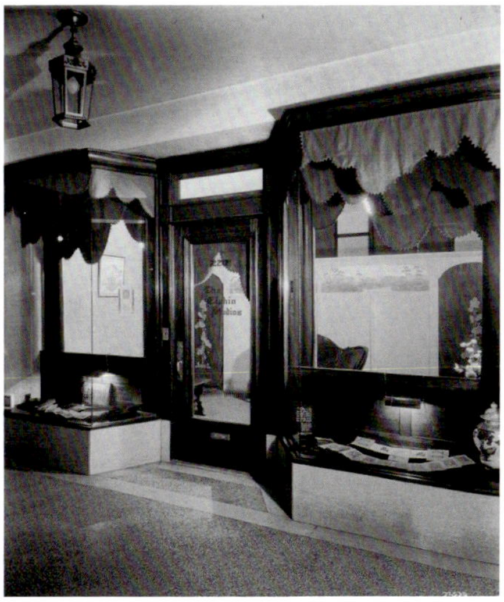

(top left) ELIZABETH A. COOPER (1877–1936), *Untitled*, ca. 1925, white line color woodblock print, 7 ½ x 10 ¼ in. Collection of the John Marshall Cooper QTIP Trust

(bottom left) IVAN MARION KELEZ (1907–1965), *Luau*, ca. 1929, white line color woodblock print, 12 x 9 in. Private collection

(top right) VIOLA HANSEN PATTERSON (1898–1984), *Flowers*, ca. 1928, white line color woodblock print, 12 x 10 in. Collection of Kji and Rebecca Kelly

(bottom right) Jacob Elshin's Studio, ca. 1925. The studio was located on the street level, unit 2207 in the White Building in downtown Seattle, 410 University Street at Fourth Avenue. The Martin-Zambito Archive. Photographer not known

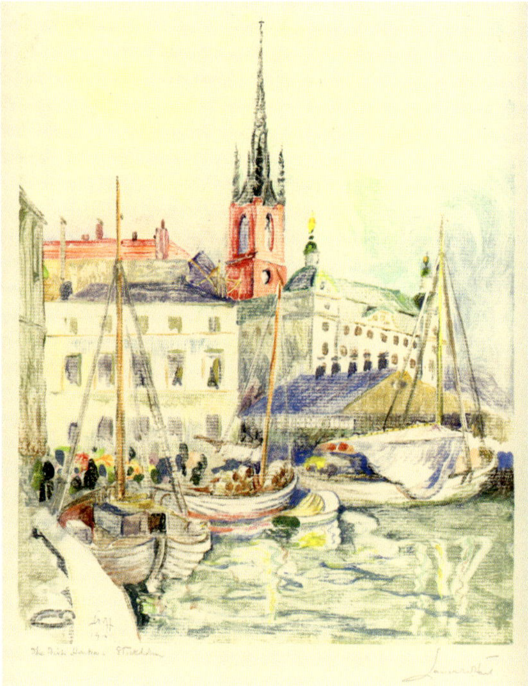

LANCE WOOD HART (1891–1941), *The Fish Harbor – Stockholm*, 1924, monoprint, 10 x 8 in. Collection of Lucy Hart

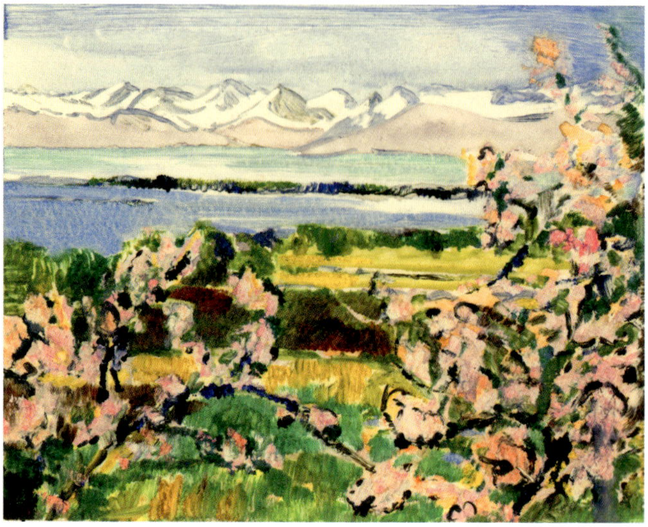

DOROTHY DOLPH JENSEN (1895–1977), Untitled, ca. 1933, monoprint, 4 7/8 x 5 7/8 in. Private collection

Other local artists occasionally produced monoprints, but only two made enough to constitute a small body of work in the medium.

Lance Wood Hart, of Aberdeen, Washington, produced monoprints as a student at the Royal Academy of Fine Arts in Stockholm, Sweden, in 1924. He continued to make them during his time in Seattle and then at the University of Oregon as Assistant Professor of Drawing and Painting. Hart was an early instructor and mentor to Robert Motherwell (1915–1991), also of Aberdeen, and may have instilled an affinity for the monoprint method in the young man, as Motherwell would later produce quite a few works in that medium during his long career.

Dorothy Dolph Jensen (1895–1977) was the first woman to produce intaglio prints in Seattle after being trained in Paris at the age of thirteen. She imported an etching press from France and used it for making prints and instructing other artists, especially women. Jensen experimented with color printmaking, making monoprints on her copper etching plates and also hand-coloring some of her drypoints, either directly or with the *à la poupée* technique of applying several ink colors to an etching plate with just one pass through the press. She undoubtedly learned this technique while a student in Paris. Jensen was one of the few local printmakers who was not affiliated with the University of Washington during that time. She was raising a young daughter during the 1920s but even with her maternal responsibilities still managed to make a significant amount of art.

University of Washington students such as Mary Erckenbrack Hennessy (1910–1992) also made prints using color ink, influenced by European modernism. Hennesy, after studying in Le Havre at Pension Jeanne d'Arc, returned to Seattle and attended UW. Her *Untitled* woodblock print, with its decorative border and dense compositional elements, appears to have been inspired by Art Deco tapestries. She later moved to California, where she became a well-known sculptor and ceramic artist.

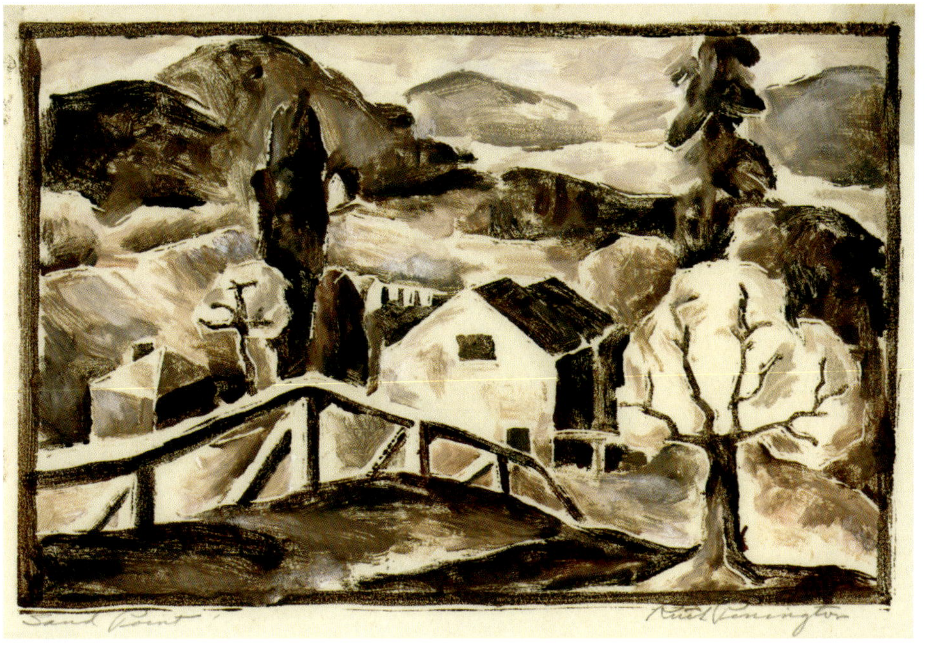

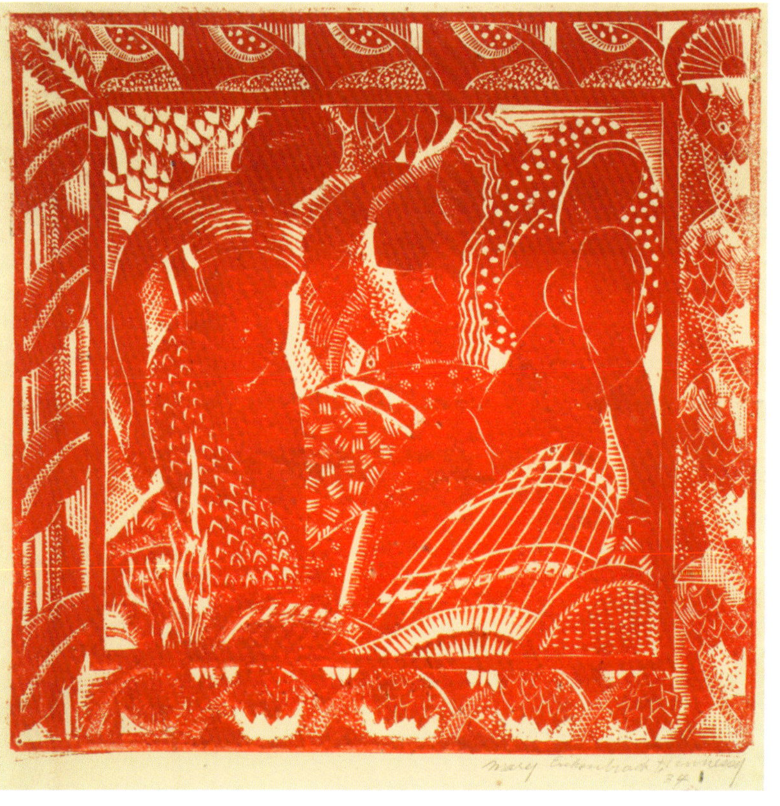

(top) RUTH PENINGTON (1905–1998), *Sandpoint*, ca. 1928, monoprint, 7 ¼ x 10 ½ in. Collection of Vera Zimmerman

(bottom) MARY ERCKENBRACK HENNESSY (1910–1992), *Untitled*, 1934, woodblock print, 10 x 10 in. Private collection

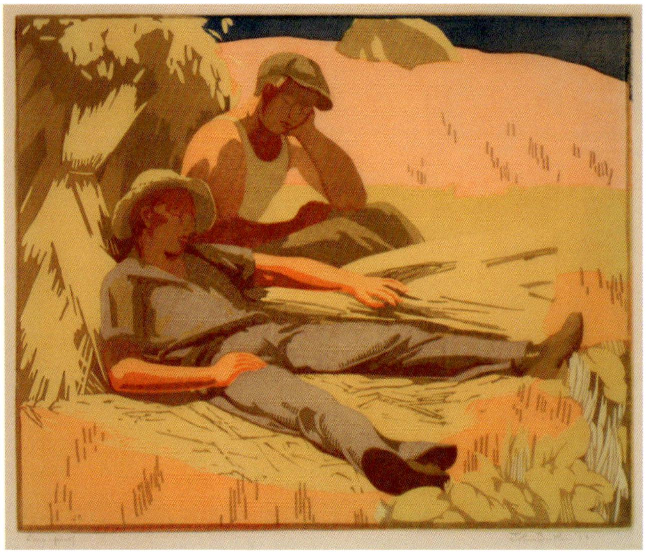

JOHN DAVIDSON BUTLER (1890–1976), *Untitled*, 1934, color linocut print, 12 5/8 x 15 in. Private collection

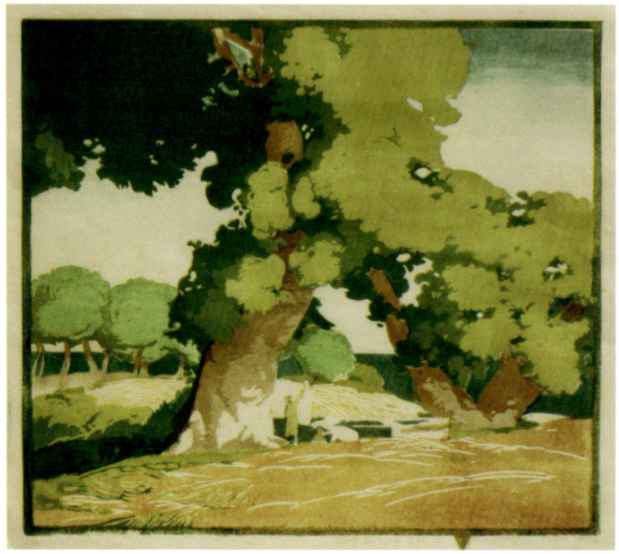

JOHN DAVIDSON BUTLER (1890–1976), *Prosphorion Plane Trees*, 1931, color linocut print, 12 3/4 x 14 in. Collection of Mark Humpal and Diane Zuhl

John Davidson Butler (1890–1976), one of Seattle's most important early artists, had been extremely successful during his early years and traveled extensively. He was on the faculty at the University of Washington during the 1920s and later produced a number of color linocuts, usually based on watercolors or oil paintings that he made while living intermittently in Europe from 1918 through 1932. Butler's untitled, French-inspired linocut depicting two harvesters resting, represents a common theme in nineteenth-century European art, and was reflective of the work of Jean-François Millet (1814–1875) and Léon Augustin Lhermitte (1844–1925)

Butler's print was compatible with the popular themes of American artists of the period who were celebrating the working man in urban and rural industries during the Great Depression. The UW art department maintained its interest in modernism as practiced by the School of Paris and informed by Japanese art, which had been so important to the teachings of Dow and Fenollosa. Ruth Penington, then on faculty at UW, and former student Frances Blakemore (1906–1997), began organizing tours to Japan in the 1930s, where Blakemore was then living. She would spend most of her life in Japan and had a profound effect on modern Japanese printmaking in the upcoming decades.

Unfortunately, most of the region's artists could not afford to eat during this time let alone travel internationally. Most relied on the small income provided by the government through President Roosevelt's New Deal art programs such as PWAP and WPA. The Washington State WPA project had a particularly good emphasis on prints and printmaking, in part due to R. Bruce Inverarity, who was head of the program for Washington State and himself a printmaker. In addition to the numerous black-and-white prints created by artists such as Fay Chong (1912–1973), Z. Vanessa Helder (1904–1968), and others, color prints were also produced. Richard Correll (1904–1990), a superb printmaker with strong social values who often

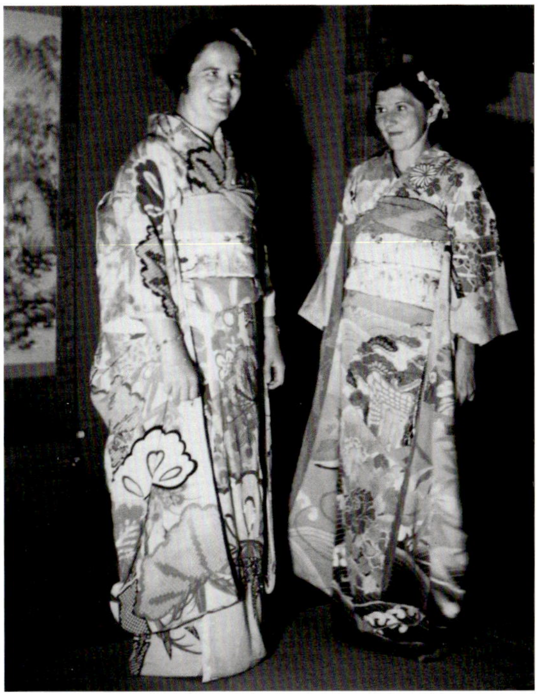

Ruth Penington (left) and Frances Blakemore in Japan, 1937. Courtesy of the Blakemore Foundation. Photographer unknown

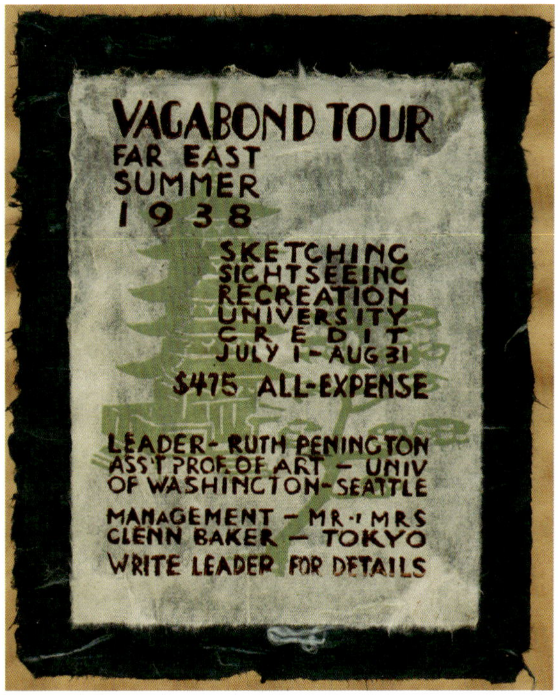

Flyer announcing a tour of Japan led by Ruth Penington under the management of Frances Blakemore (1906–1997) and her first husband, Glenn Baker. Courtesy of The Seattle Public Library

incorporated laborers in his prints, as in his *Work Rhythm* of 1937. Correll was one of several local printmakers who used an unusual technique advocated by Inverarity and others. It was called "lacquer airbrush stencil," and the prints were made exactly the way the name implies: a stencil was cut for the main design, and airbrushed lacquer paint was then sprayed through the stencil onto the paper, giving the prints a soft, luminous quality that accommodated realistic or abstract subjects. The actual stencils and printing were produced by artisans on the project, primarily Otho Raymond Barnes (1884–1960) and D. E. Macdonald (dates unknown), who worked with the artists in realizing their designs. Artists like Hans Bok (1914–1964) created prints that were traditional as well as experimental, others like Julius "Land Elk" Twohy (Two-vy-nah-auche) (1902–1986) created prints based on his Native American heritage. Twohy was an accomplished printmaker before he entered the project due to his close friendship with Dorothy Dolph Jensen, with whom he worked at the Schneiders frame shop and gallery in the early 1920s. Malcolm Roberts (1913–1990), the region's first Surrealist, was very active on the WPA program. At the time he was in a relationship with the artist Morris Graves (1910–2000), and some of his prints and paintings of that period have homoerotic content. Roberts produced several lithographs that he hand-colored for the WPA project. His print *Dance Group Variations* of 1937 reflects his work as a stage and costume designer for local dance companies, and especially for the Cornish School of the arts (now the Cornish College of the Arts). Cornish has one of the most impressive dance histories in the U.S., and Roberts's print was likely inspired by Martha Graham (1894–1991), who had a close association with the school and taught there in 1933.

The 1930s, in spite of the Great Depression, brought significant importance to the Northwest Printmakers Society. International artists such as Pablo Picasso (1881–1973), André Derain (1880–1954), Raoul Dufy (1880–1953), and José Clementé Orozco (1883–1949) all exhibited in that

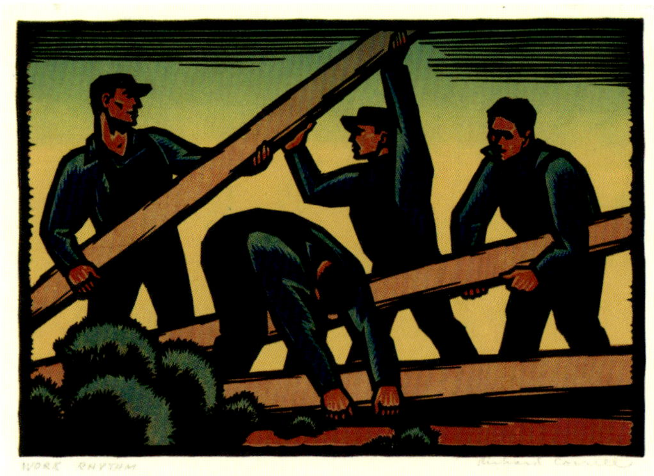

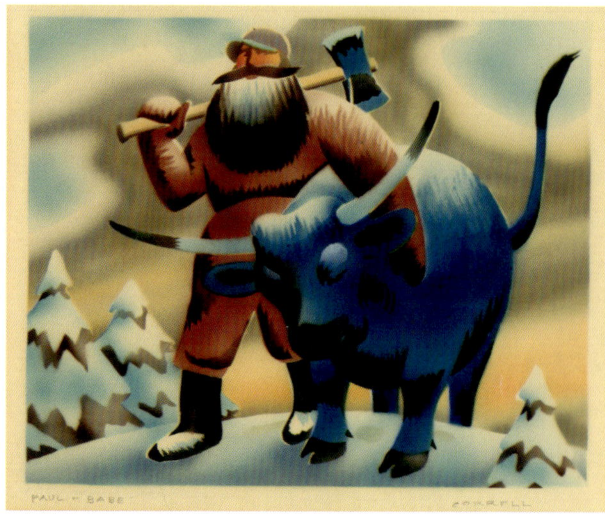

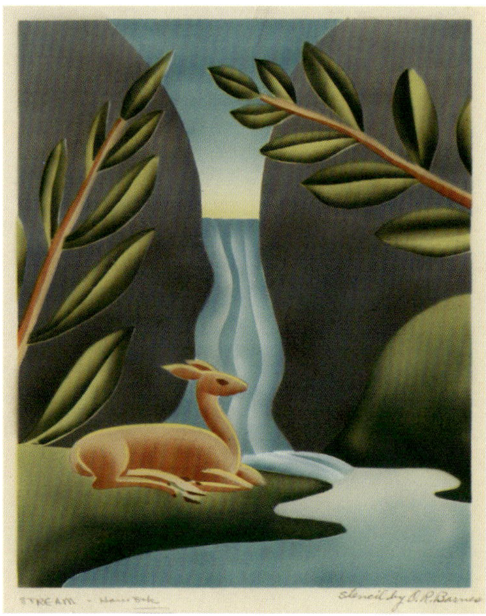

(top left) RICHARD CORRELL (1904–1990), *Work Rhythm*, 1937 (also titled *Packing Lumber*), color linocut, 9 ⅞ x 13 ¼ in. University of Washington Libraries Special Collections, Labor Archives of Washington, Richard V. Correll prints and papers, accession #5855-001 [box 4, folder 2]

(bottom left) Design by HANS BOK (1914–1964), stencil by OTHO RAYMOND BARNES (1884–1960), *Stream*, ca. 1936, lacquer airbrush stencil print, 8 ½ x 6 ¾ in. Courtesy of The Seattle Public Library

(right) RICHARD CORRELL (1904–1990), *Paul and Babe*, 1938, lacquer airbrush stencil print, 7 ½ x 10 in. University of Washington Libraries Special Collections, Labor Archives of Washington, Richard V. Correll prints and papers, accession #5855-001 [box 4, folder 2]

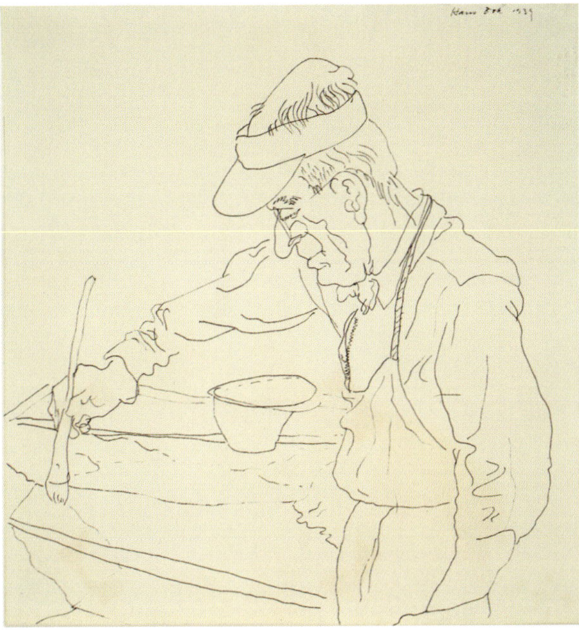

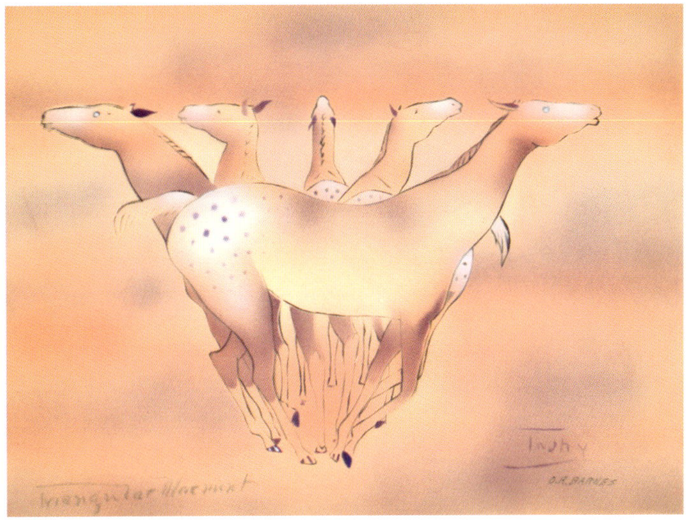

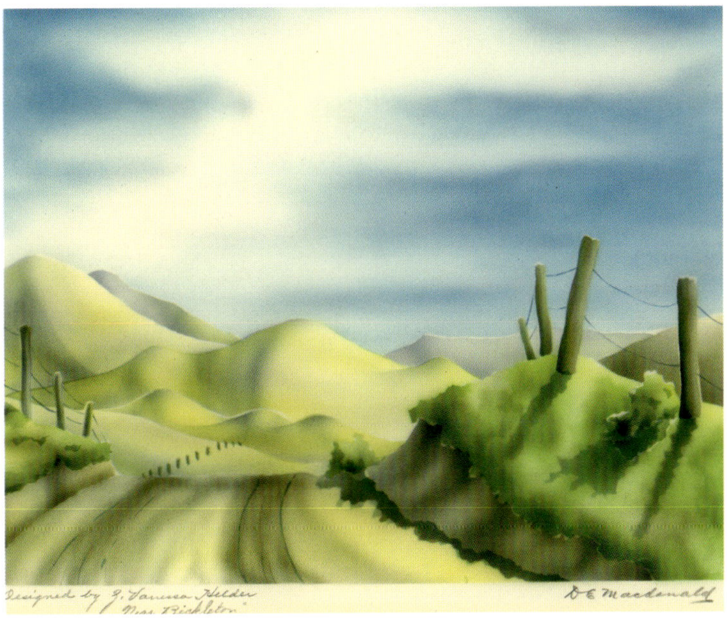

(top left) HANS BOK (1914–1964), *Barnes*, 1939, ink drawing, 12 x 11 in. Collection of Roger and Jeanna van Oosten

(top right) Design by JULIUS "LAND ELK" TWOHY (Two-vy-nah-auche) (1902–1986), stencil by OTHO RAYMOND BARNES (1884–1960), *Triangular Movement*, ca. 1935–1938, lacquer airbrush stencil print, 8 5/8 x 11 in. Henry Art Gallery, University of Washington, Seattle, Unknown donor, 69.88

(bottom) Design by Z. VANESSA HELDER (1904–1968), stencil by D. E. MACDONALD (dates not known), *Near Bickleton*, ca. 1938, lacquer airbrush stencil print, 7 x 8 5/8 in. Collection of The Kitsap Regional Library, Bremerton, Washington

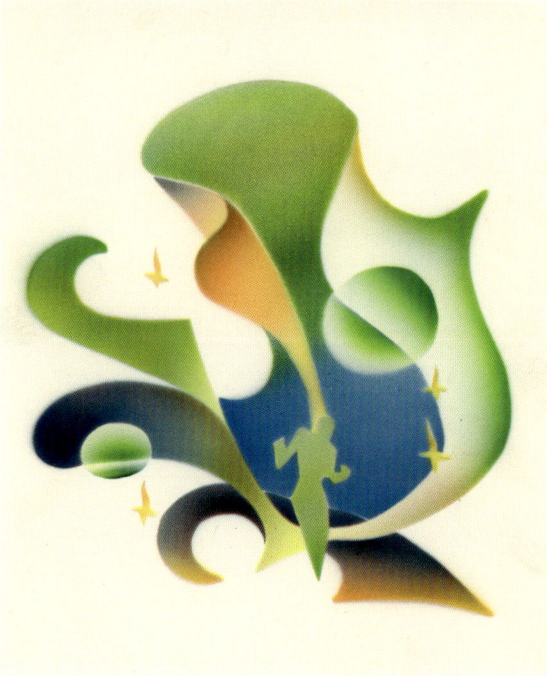

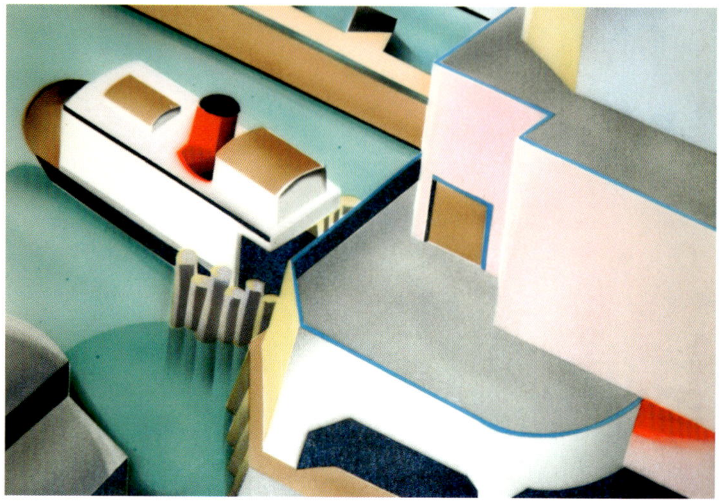

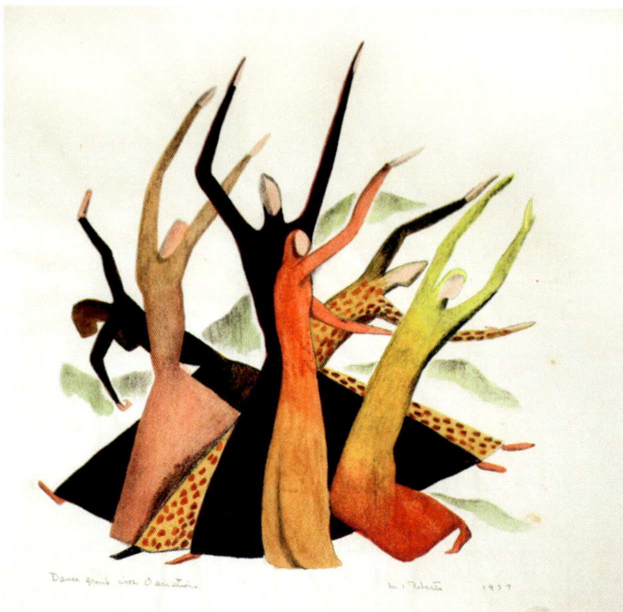

(top left) Design by HANS BOK (1914–1964), stencil by OTHO RAYMOND BARNES (1884–1960), *Moment Musicale*, 1938, lacquer airbrush stencil print, 7 x 6 ¼ in. Collection of Roger and Jeanna van Oosten

(bottom) MALCOLM ROBERTS (1913–1990), *Dance Group Variations*, 1937, lithograph with hand coloring, 12 x 10 ⅞ in. Collection of the Indiana State University Permanent Art Collection, Terre Haute, Indiana, 1943.01.177

(top right) MALCOLM ROBERTS (1913–1990), *Docking Ferry*, 1938, lacquer airbrush stencil print on cream paper, 11.032 x 8.4710 in. Commissioned through the New Deal art projects, 1945. Collection of the Newark Art Museum, Newark, New Jersey, 45.900

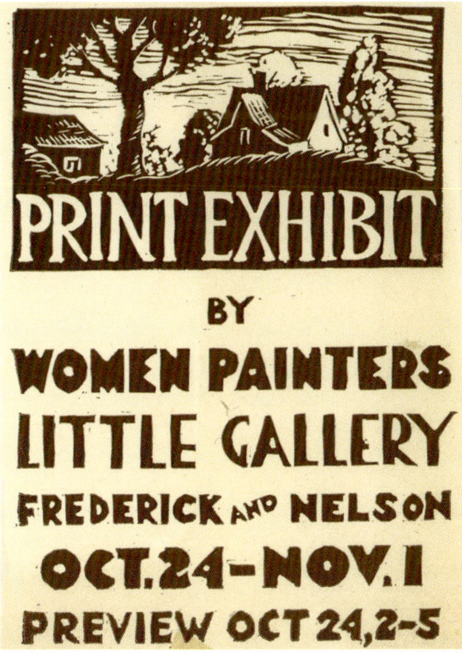

Women Painters of Washington exhibition flyer, ca. 1938. The Martin-Zambito Archive

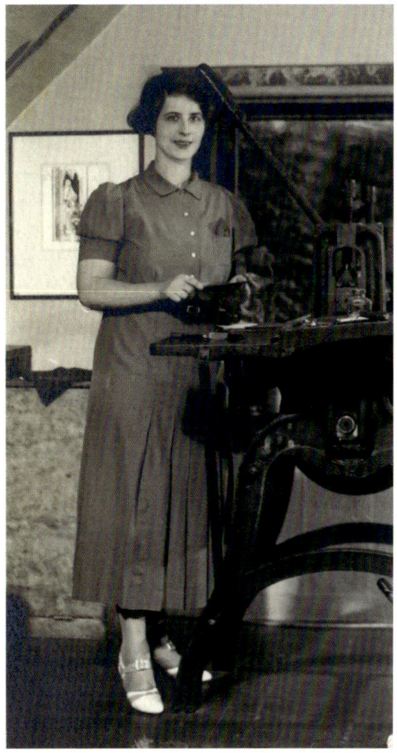

Dorothy Dolph Jensen at her etching press, ca. 1935. The Martin-Zambito Archive. Photograph by McBride and Anderson Studios, Seattle, WA

decade and allowed both the public and artists to see their work at first hand.

Another organization that advocated for regional printmaking was the Women Painters of Washington, one of the region's oldest arts organizations. Two of the group's founders were Elizabeth Warhanik and Dorothy Dolph Jensen, and their activities as printmakers assured that the medium was practiced within the organization.

Locally, most color prints were made as monoprints, color etchings, or relief prints, and used either wood or linoleum blocks. Very few color lithographs were produced until the University of Washington brought in the Mexican artist Emilio Amero (1901–1976) to establish a lithography workshop in their art department. He then went on to teach at the Cornish School and, in 1944, established a short-lived art colony outside of Seattle in the town of Carnation, famous for its dairy products and "contented cows."

Amero was a beloved figure in his Seattle classes, and his influence affected many Northwest artists including Helmi Juvonen, who studied with him at Cornish, as well as Peter Camfferman and Kenneth Auvil (1925–1999), whose lithographs display Amero's vibrant, chromatic color palette and Cubist forms. Amero remained in Seattle until he accepted a position at the University of Oklahoma in 1946, where he remained until his death in 1976.[13]

The serigraph or screen print refers to the use of a technique where inks are squeezed through stencils supported on a porous silk mesh that has been stretched across a wooden frame. This inexpensive technique was used intermittently during the WPA in Washington State as well as at the Spokane Art Center during the Depression but mostly for producing posters and advertising. Its use as a fine-art medium really escalated locally when Glen Alps (1914–1996) arrived at the University of Washington in 1945. Alps was intrigued with the medium and set out to expand its potential. His innovative work in this process won him two consecutive first-prize awards in 1951 and 1952 from the National Serigraph Society in New York. Alps was

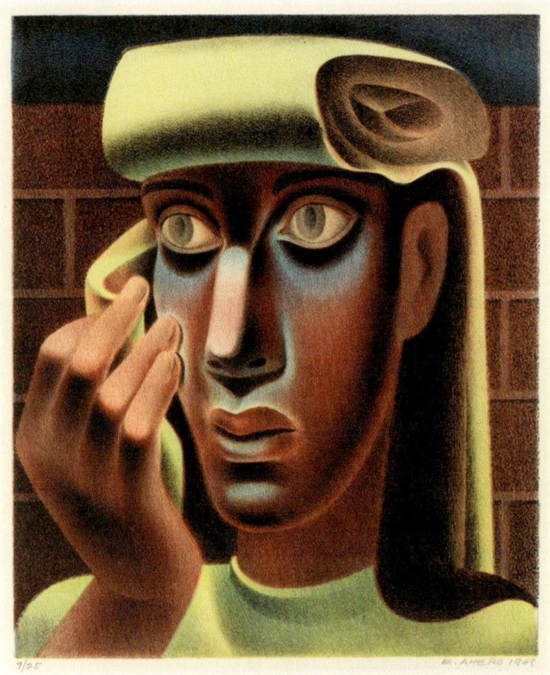

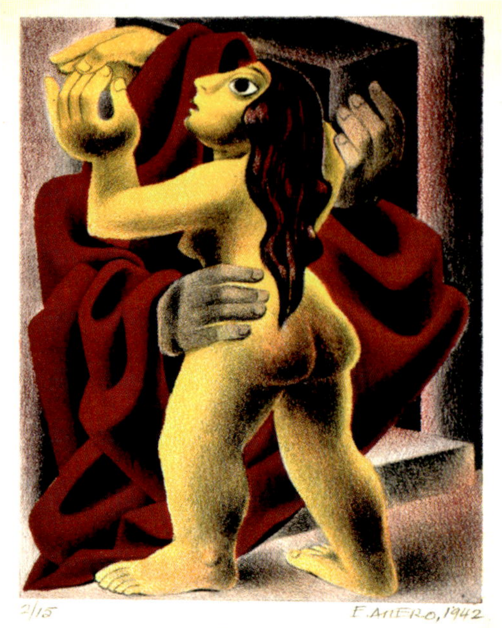

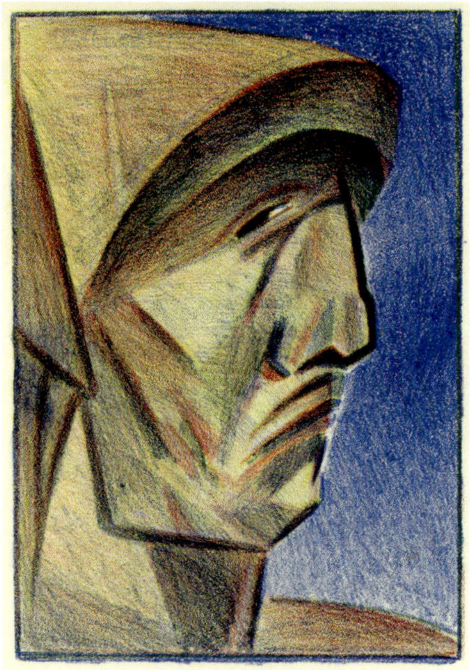

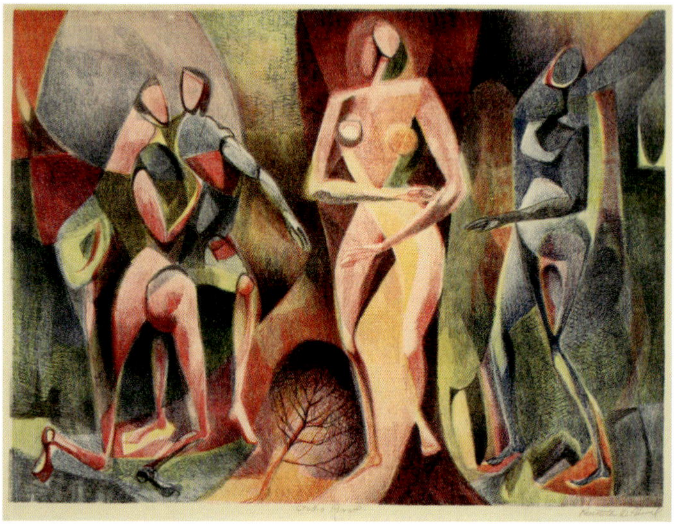

(top left) EMILIO AMERO (1901–1976), *The Gesture*, 1948, color lithograph, 12 ⅜ x 10 ⅛ in. Collection of the Seattle Art Museum, #69.218, Gift of the Northwest Printmakers Society. Photograph by Elizabeth Mann

(bottom left) PETER CAMFFERMAN (1890–1957), *Untitled*, ca. 1944, color lithograph, 10 ½ x 7 ⅛ in. Collection of Maureen Duryee

(top right) EMILIO AMERO (1901–1976), *Two Figures*, 1943, color lithograph, 8 x 6 ¼ in. Henry Art Gallery, University of Washington, Seattle, Unknown donor, FA 42.1

(bottom right) KENNETH AUVIL (1925–1999), *The Reunion*, ca. 1948, color lithograph, 12 ¼ x 16 in. Private collection

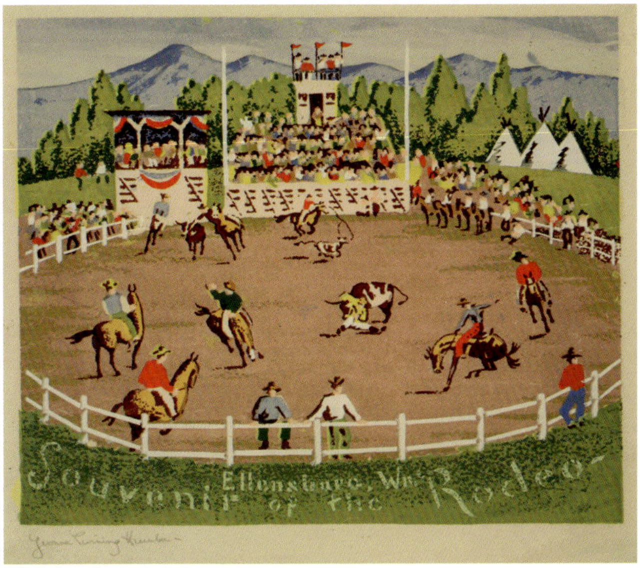

YVONNE TWINING HUMBER (1907–2004), *Rodeo*, 1946, serigraph, 12 x 14 in. Private collection

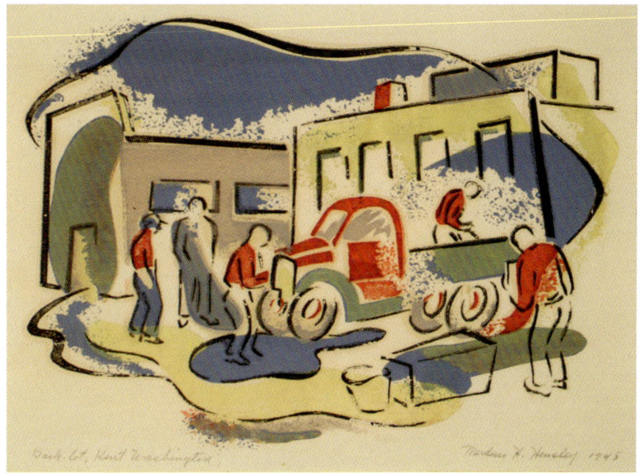

MERDECES HENSLEY (1893–1979), *Back Lot, Kent, WA*, 1948, serigraph, 8 x 11 in. Private collection

a fervent proponent of the medium and not only taught the technique in his classes at UW but offered workshops for artists associated with other groups, such as the Women Painters of Washington.

Yvonne Twining Humber (1907–2004), a prominent WPW member, took a class in screen printing with Alps in 1946 and produced several images that year. Seeking some financial returns, Humber tried marketing her prints but found no buyers. She had created one image of a rodeo from an oil painting that she had made the previous year. The subject depicts the popular rodeo at Ellensburg, Washington, that she had visited with her husband. Since her prints were not selling in Seattle, she decided to add text to the print and tried selling it as a souvenir of the event at the rodeo the following year. Much to her dismay, the rodeo crowd paid no attention to her print and she put her screen prints in her basement studio and did not revisit the process until three decades later when she actively pursued it again. Humber was only one of dozens of women who produced screen prints under Alps's guidance. Merdeces Hensley (1893–1979) was on the faculty of the UW School of Art for thirty years. She was one of the charter members of the NWPS in 1928, but only exhibited one print with the organization, a screen print titled *Back Lot, Kent, WA* of 1948.

In the 1940s the NWPS continued to maintain itself as the stalwart print advocacy group in the region. An important and influential figure in American printmaking at that time, Mauricio Lasansky (1914–2012), had established the print department at the University of Iowa by 1948. He had a long history with NWPS, first exhibiting in 1945 and consistently showed with the group through 1967, winning four purchase prizes.

Frances Blakemore, after graduating from UW, had left Seattle for Japan in 1935 to teach English for various organizations. She continued to mail her prints back to Seattle to include in the NWPS exhibitions. Because of the escalating fear of war, she left for Honolulu in 1940. In 1942,

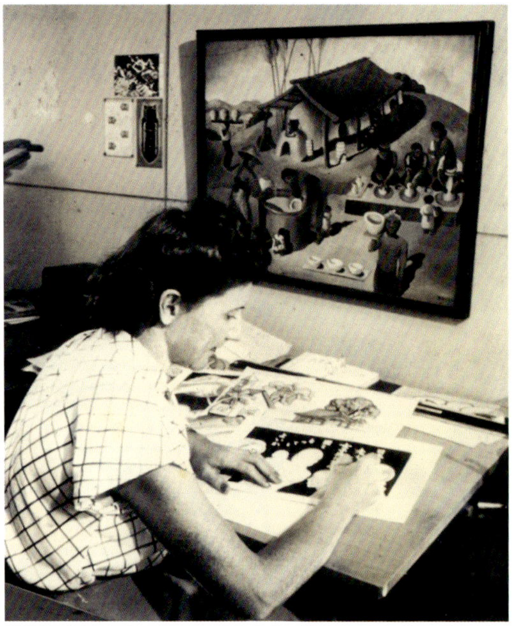

Frances Blakemore sketching a war leaflet design at the Central Pacific Operations headquarters, Honolulu, 1944. Courtesy of the Blakemore Foundation

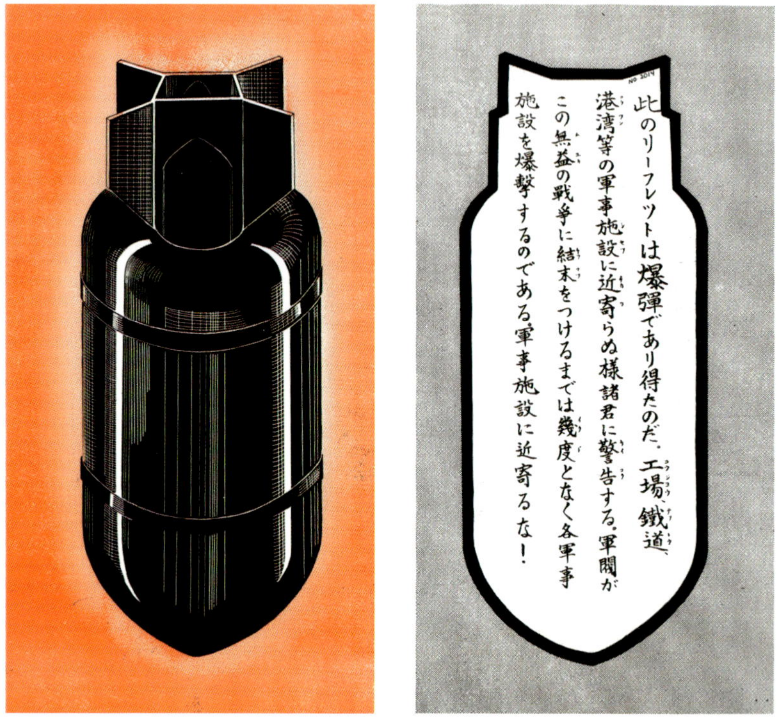

"Thought Bomb" war propaganda leaflet No. 2014, designed by Frances Blakemore, ca. 1945. This leaflet explained the American military's intention of destroying Japanese military forces and warned the general public to avoid potential target areas. Courtesy of the Blakemore Foundation

she began working for the U.S. Government in the office of censorship, screening media, especially in the area of postal censorship, and also worked with Japanese translators. She used her graphic skills in the US propaganda campaign, designing leaflets dropped by the millions over mainland Japan and Japanese forces in the Southwest Pacific. When she returned to Japan in 1946, she began working for the Civil Information and Education Section to assist the Occupation forces by designing posters and exhibitions for reorienting the Japanese citizens under their new constitution. While there, she produced probably the first technical book on Western-style screen printing in Japan. Although a type of stencil printing had existed in Japan from the twelfth century, Blakemore's activities helped popularize screen printing in Japan through her numerous students.[14]

Blakemore went on to become a champion for contemporary Japanese printmakers, and opened the Fran-Nell Gallery in Tokyo to promote their work. She was instrumental in the development of the careers of many of these artists and wrote the definitive biographical source on the subject, *Who's Who In Modern Japanese Prints*, published in 1975.

The work of two of Japan's most important members of the *Sôsaku-hanga* movement, Kiyoshi Saito (1907–1997) and Jun'ichiro Sekino (1914–1988), was beginning to be noticed and supported in Seattle. They were part of a successful group exhibition titled *Saito and His Associates* at the Seattle Art Museum in January 1955. The work of the Japanese artists of the *Sôsaku-hanga* movement differed from that of the earlier *Shin-hanga* movement, where craftsman carved and printed the blocks after the artists original design, thus removing the artist from its direct execution. The *Sôsaku-hanga* artists both conceived the design and created their prints completely by themselves, something very appealing to American artists of the time who did not have access to the traditional craftsmen who were well-known throughout Japan.

Following the success of the Seattle Art Museum show, Saito's work was exhibited at the Henry Gallery in March

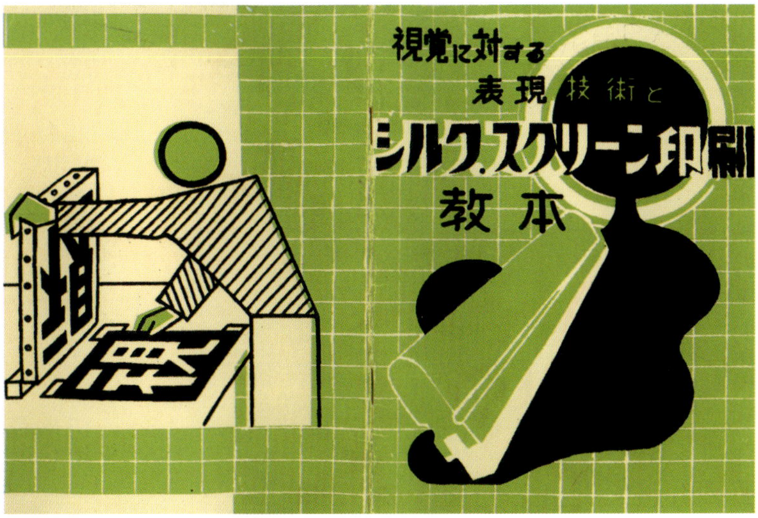

FRANCES BLAKEMORE, *Textbook: Method for Visual Expression and Silkscreen Printing*, ca. 1951. Courtesy of the Blakemore Foundation

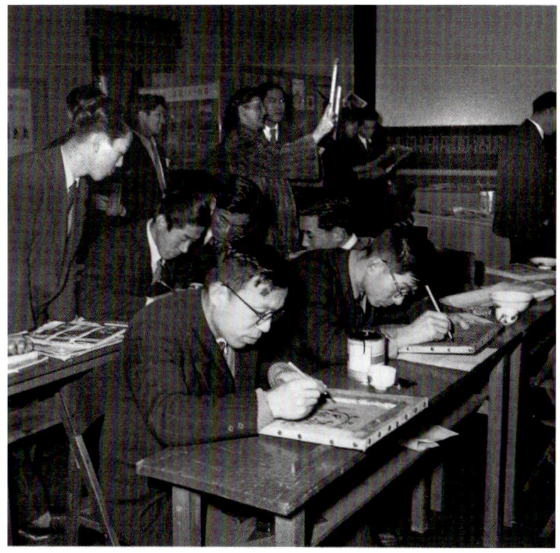

Frances Blakemore and her staff at work in the silkscreen workshop at her studio in the Radio Tokyo Building, Japan, ca. 1951. Courtesy of the Blakemore Foundation

1956, undoubtedly through the influence of Glen Alps, who was a prominent figure at the university.[15] Saito again visited Seattle the following year and gave a lecture to the Washington State Chapter of the American Institute of Architects.

Glen Alps's innovations in screen printing methods were soon eclipsed by another medium that he developed and named the "collagraph." The name was derived from the words *collage* (to paste) and *graph* (to draw). The technique consisted of pasting objects and materials to a sturdy matrix, usually Masonite, inking the collaged surface, and pulling prints from it. Alps did not discover this technique but is credited with giving it a name and popularizing its use. He used unorthodox materials like ground walnut shells, coffee, and sawdust to create varied, interesting textures.

The collagraph made its exhibition debut when Alps displayed his *Collagraph #2* with the NWPS in 1956, winning an honorable mention. The black-and-white print was actually the second collagraph that Alps had created (the first was in color and was exhibited at NWPS the following year). From then on, it became his main medium for printmaking. The term made its national debut in 1958 when Alps's *Collagraph # 12* (*Chickens*) was exhibited in the Brooklyn Museum's National Print Annual.

Alps was by then quickly developing a national and international reputation for his innovative prints. The same year that he exhibited his first collagraph he was invited to be part of a three-person exhibition, along with fellow Seattle artists George Tsutakawa (1910–1997) and Paul Horiuchi (1906–1999) at the Yōseidō Gallery in Tokyo, in September 1956. The exhibition was arranged by Kiyoshi Saito, whom Alps had recently met in Seattle, and Alps exhibited eight of his lithographs, intaglios, and screen prints.

In 1959, the Hanga Gallery opened in Seattle and became an important venue for the exhibition and sale of contemporary Japanese prints and eventually local artists as well. Their opening featured a solo exhibition of Saito's prints. That year, Sekino began exhibiting with the NWPS,

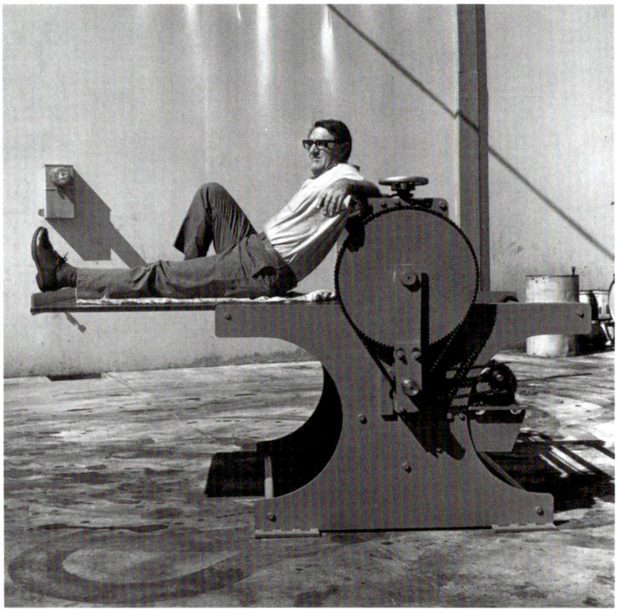

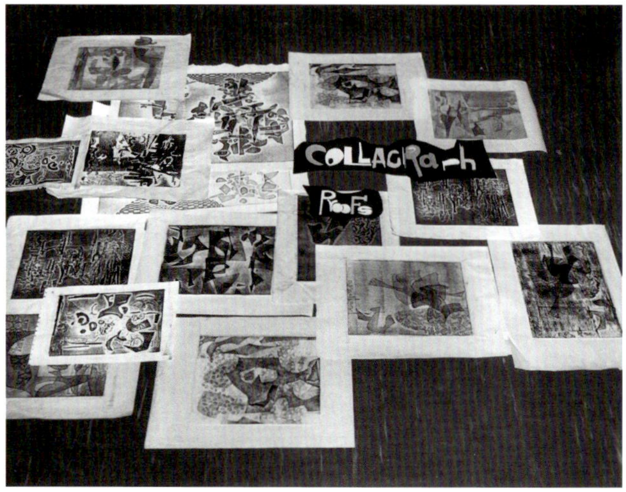

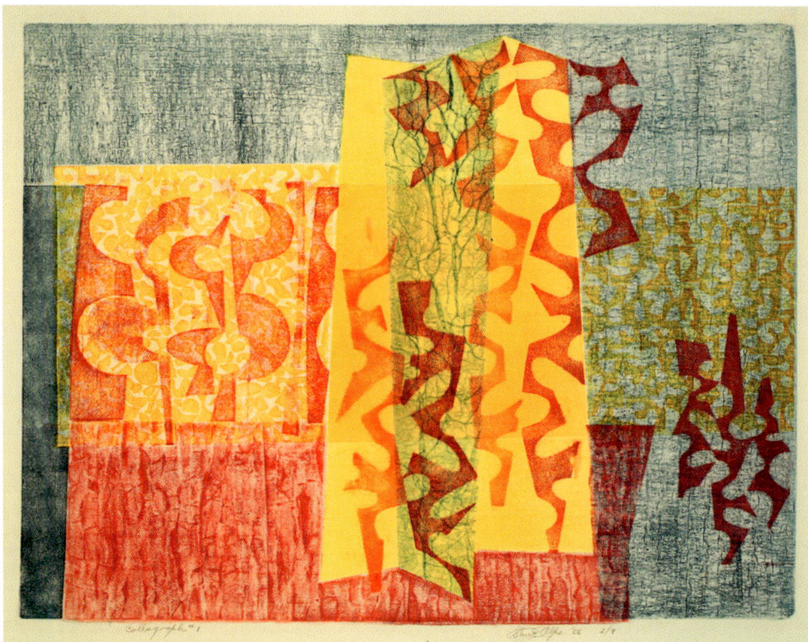

(top left) Glen Alps reclining on his press, ca. 1955, University of Washington Libraries, Special Collections, Negative No. 38041, Acc. No. 5152-002 Glen E. Alps Papers

(top right) Promotional photograph for a collagraph exhibition at the School of Art, University of Washington, ca. 1956. University of Washington Libraries, Special Collections, Negative No. # UW 38044, Acc. No. 5152-002 Glen E. Alps Papers

(bottom) GLEN ALPS (1914–1996), *Collagraph #1*, 1956, collagraph, 20 3/8 x 25 7/8 in. Private collection

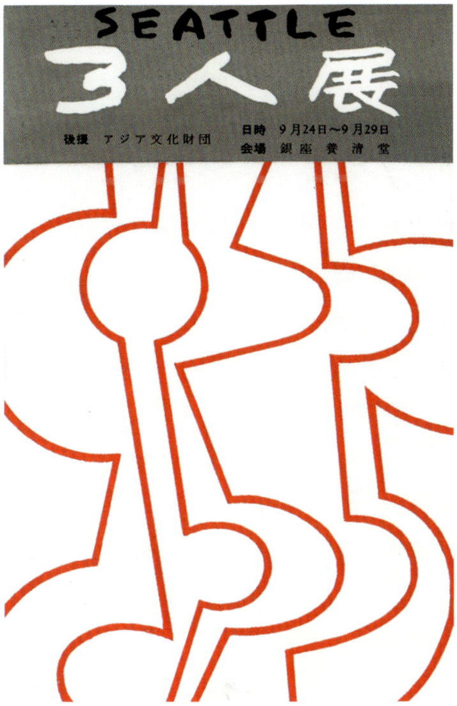

Catalogue for a three-person exhibit featuring Glen Alps, George Tsutakawa, and Paul Horiuchi, Yōseidō Gallery, Tokyo, Japan, 1956. The Martin-Zambito Archive

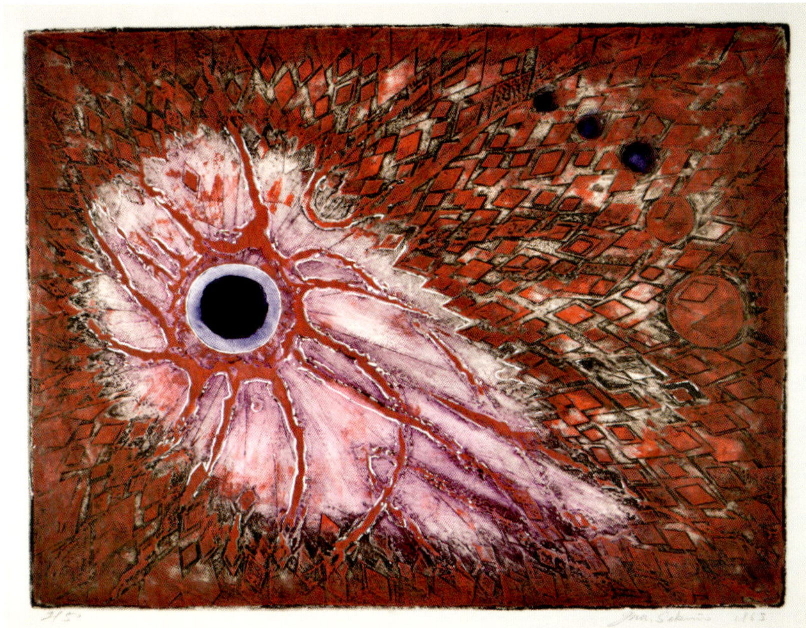

JUN'ICHIRŌ SEKINO (1914–1988), *Untitled*, 1963, collagraph, 21 ½ x 26 ½ in. Henry Art Gallery, University of Washington, Seattle, Gift of the artist, 63.24

winning a purchase prize the following year. Sekino's work was featured at the Hanga Gallery in 1962.

That year also marked the opening of Century 21, Seattle's second World's Fair. By now, the art scene in Seattle had grown immensely and the international spotlight was focused on the Northwest.

Printmaking was particularly fertile during this period because of the efforts of NWPS, Alps, and Danny Pierce (1920–2014), who was also developing a significant reputation at that time.

Saito returned to Seattle that year on a grant from the university's center for Asian Arts and spent a month making collagraphs with Alps.[16] He also gave a class in his own technique sponsored by NWPS on November 1, and the resulting collagraphs that he made with Alps were exhibited at the Henry Gallery in December.

That same year, Sekino spent two quarters as a visiting professor at UW, and like Saito worked with Glen Alps in learning the collagraph method.[17] All fifteen of the works that he created at the university are in the collection of the Henry Art Gallery.

Alps retained his friendship with the two Japanese artists for the remainder of their lives, sometimes exchanging prints and cards with them.

The other printmaker who was bringing attention to the region through his international success was Danny Pierce. His early years could not have been more inauspicious. Born in Woodlake, California, he was raised on a ranch and spent his early years sketching horses and working at the various jobs of a cowboy. Animals figure prominently in the work of both Pierce and Alps, who had been raised on a farm in Colorado. Pierce's art education was delayed until after he was drafted into the army in 1942. The following year, he married Julia Rasmussen of Kent, Washington, who was attending his war wounds as an army nurse. He went on to fight in two major battles during WWII and was awarded several medals of honor. In May of 1945, Pierce's squad liberated the death camp at Maulthausen in upper Austria. After the war, Pierce

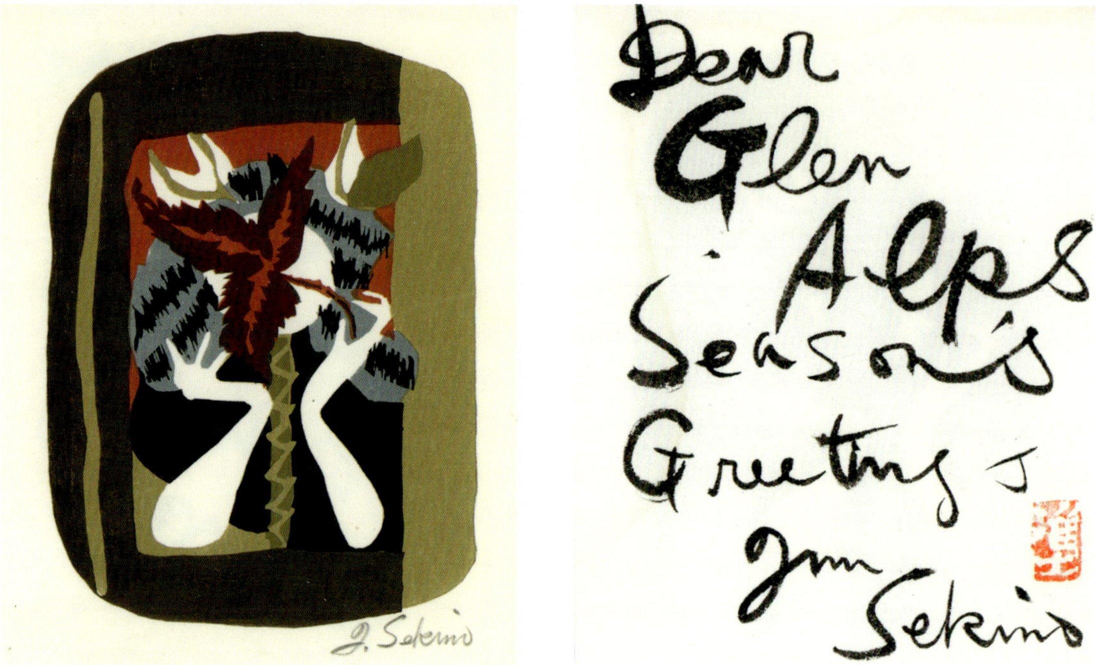

New Year's greeting card from Jun'ichirō Sekino to Glen Alps, ca. 1965. The Martin-Zambito Archive

and his wife moved to New York, where Danny continued his art education under the G.I. Bill. There he studied with prominent artists such as Max Beckmann (1884–1950), Raphael Soyer (1899–1987), Ben Shahn (1898–1969), and William Gropper (1897–1977).

Pierce accepted a teaching position at Hunter College in New York and completed a print commission for the Museum of Modern Art after exhibiting there in 1953 in a group exhibition titled *Young American Printmakers*. Later that year he and his wife left New York and moved to his wife's hometown of Kent, Washington. Pierce's earlier works mostly focused on intaglio prints influenced by his teacher and friend, Gabor Peterdi (1915–2001).

Peterdi had begun working with Stanley William Hayter (1901–1988) at Atelier 17 in Paris in 1933, and then after the war at Atelier 17, in New York. Hayter was one of the most important and influential printmakers of the twentieth century, and his influence filtered down to Pierce through Peterdi.

Pierce became a noted teacher in the Northwest, where he had taught at Seattle University; he was also director of the art department at Cornish College of the Arts. He almost always included human or animal figurative elements in his work. He originally used traditional tools to create his prints, but then discovered that dental tools were handy for fine details on his metal plates. In 1959, he and his budding family moved to Alaska where, thanks to a Carnegie Grant, he became the first artist-in-residence at the University of Alaska. The following year he founded the university's art department, the first in the state.

Pierce brought his friend Gabor Peterdi to Alaska in 1963 to lecture and work with younger printmakers and to explore the arctic terrain. Making a significant contribution to printmaking in Alaska, Pierce worked with both Native and Caucasian artists and students. While his work with Native Alaskans influenced some of his subject matter, and he appreciated Northwest Native American art forms intellectually and aesthetically, his own work remained closer

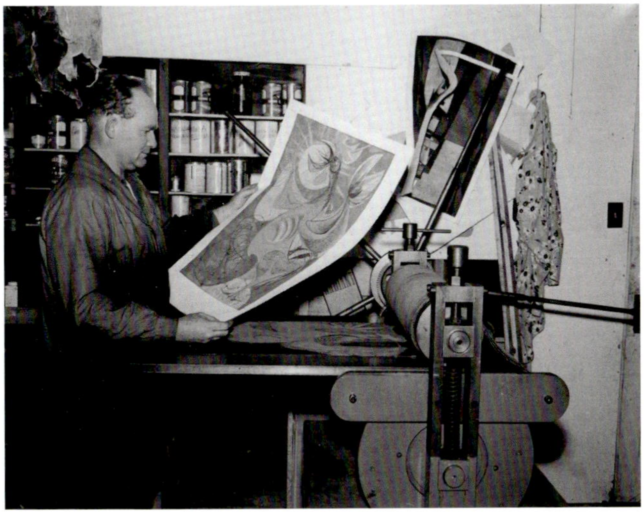

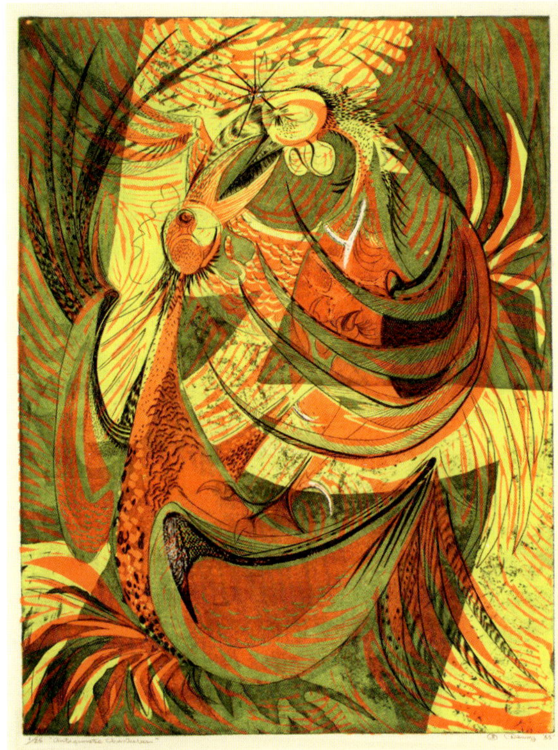

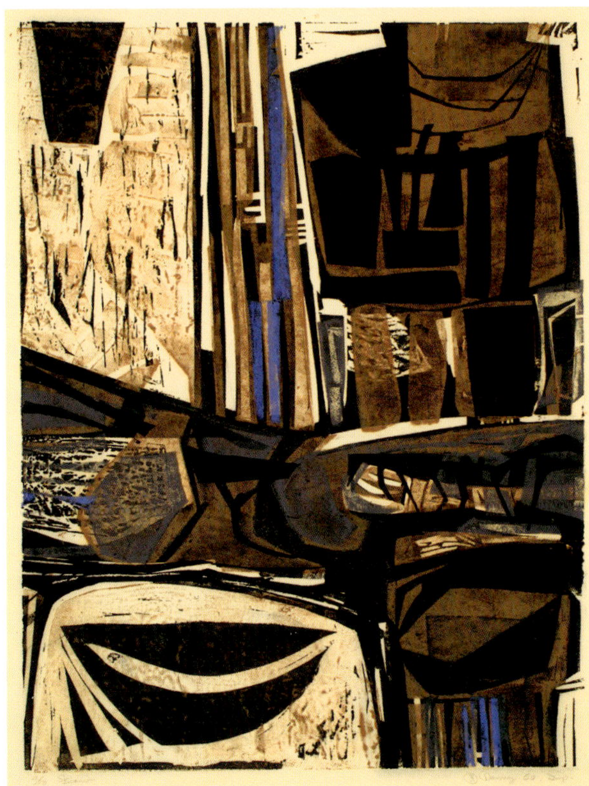

(top left) Danny Pierce at his press, ca. 1955. Courtesy of the Estate of Danny Pierce

(bottom) DANNY PIERCE (1920–2014), *Flow*, 1960, color woodblock print, 24 x 18 in. Collection of the Estate of Danny Pierce

(top right) DANNY PIERCE (1920–2014), *Antagonistic Chanticleers*, 1955, mixed intaglio print, 23 ¾ x 17 ½ in. Collection of the Estate of Danny Pierce

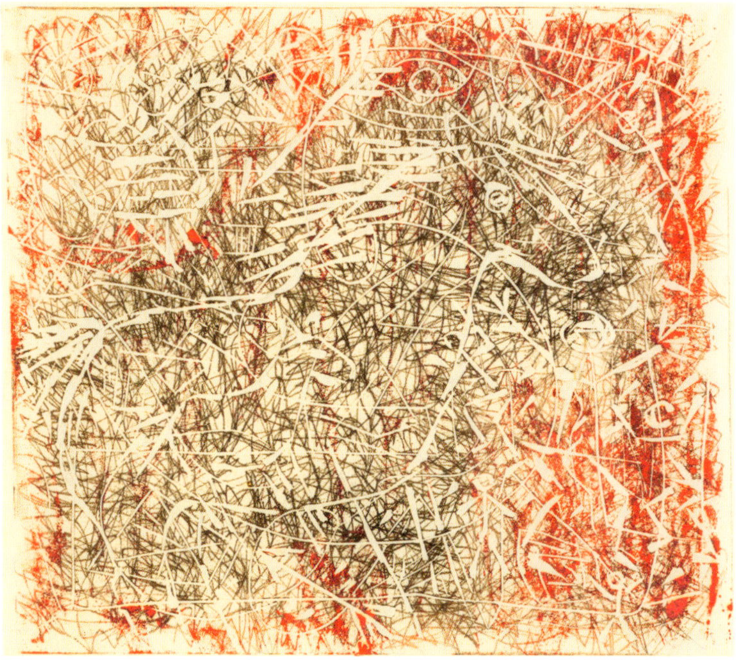

HELMI JUVONEN (1903–1985), *Pinto Pony*, ca. 1954, linocut with monoprint inking, 8 ½ x 9 ½ in. Collection of the Washington State Historical Society, C1983.2.1

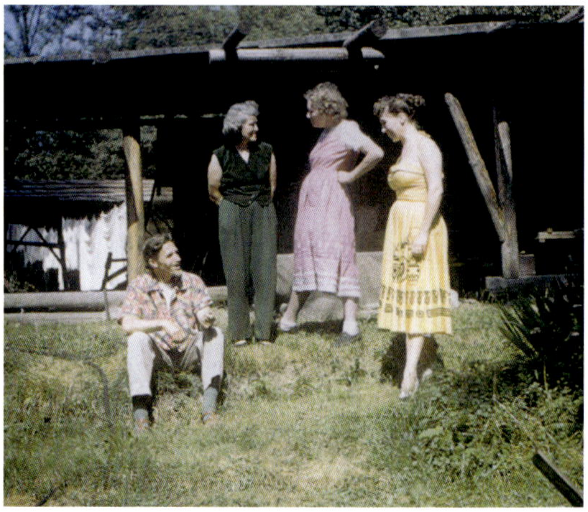

Helmi Juvonen visiting Corwin Chase at his home at Vaughn, Washington 1952. From left: Corwin Chase, Cora Chase, Helmi Juvonen, Mrs. Eijo Vesanen. Photograph by Dr. Eijo Vesanen, print collector and University of Washington Seismologist, Courtesy of Ulrich Fritzsche

to his original interest in animals and people. Pierce was a consistent exhibitor with the NWPS, where his work was shown from 1952 until 1968. He won four purchase prizes and received four honorable mentions.

One artist, however, became synonymous with the integration and synthesis of Native American culture into her work. Helmi Juvonen, the daughter of Finnish immigrants, began taking an interest in Native American culture in the 1930s after befriending Ute artist Julius Twohy in Seattle. She began accompanying him to various ceremonies, yet after their friendship dimmed she continued on her own. Helmi had begun making prints as far back as the 1920s, working with Jacob Elshin in his Seattle studio and while studying at Cornish College of the Arts. Her initial production consisted of black-and-white linocuts that had whimsical imagery and Native American references. In the early 1950s she began to experiment with color-relief prints, perhaps influenced by the color lithography course she had taken with Emilio Amero at Cornish.

Juvonen's color prints are among the most unique made in the region and possibly in the country at that time. Her process involved using her linoleum blocks as a matrix to print just as she would in black and white, but she then added localized patches of colored ink or paint directly to the block and, using a blunt pencil or stub to add pressure, transferred the inks from the block to the paper, giving the prints an unusual, abstract quality. She would sometimes expose the negative space of the design, in a way similar to the white-line method discussed earlier, giving some of the prints the appearance of primitive cave paintings. In other examples, her manic handling of the inks almost obscures the main subject matter. Helmi's prints and some of her paintings appear to be the work of a naive or folk artist which was intentional. She was actually a master draughtsman, and worked as an illustrator at the Boeing Aircraft Company during WWII, making highly detailed illustrations. Helmi courageously fought serious mental health issues throughout her life and befriended other artists and

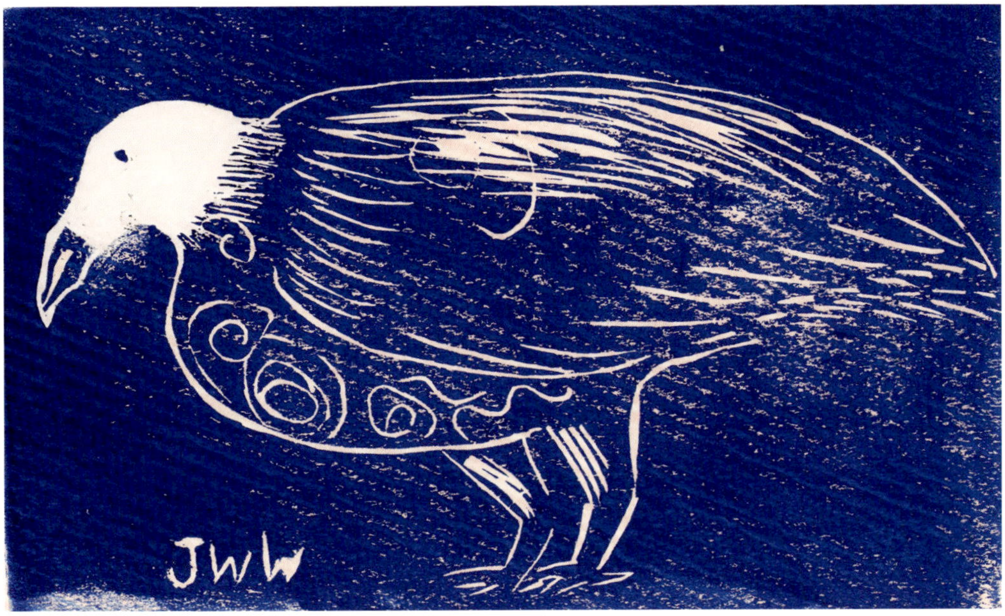

JAMES W. WASHINGTON, JR. (1909–2000), *Untitled*, ca. 1955, woodblock print, 5 x 7 7/8 in. Collection of the Family of John Matsudaira

printmakers like Waldo and Corwin Chase and Glen Alps, who admired her work and tenacity.

James W. Washington, Jr. (1909–2000), the region's only black artist to work in printmaking at that time, created relief prints that are comparable to Juvonen's in their use of simplified forms. He moved to Washington State in 1944, having previously worked primarily with drawing and painting. Although his work appears to display a simple, almost naive quality it is much more sophisticated—even if this way of working made him appear less technically adept. His paintings and prints align themselves with the aesthetic of earlier American artists such as Albert Pinkham Ryder (1847–1917) and Ralph Albert Blakelock (1847–1919), whose moody, allegorical paintings were stylistically unconventional but conveyed a powerful emotional response.

Washington began producing prints in the 1940s after befriending artist Dorothy Dolph Jensen and her frame-maker husband Lloyd Jensen (1895–1990). Lloyd, who was the region's primary frame maker, had been hand-carving beautiful designs into his frames since 1912. He and Dorothy assisted Washington, buying him tools and blocks, and providing initial printmaking instruction. Washington studied with Glen Alps as well, but never ventured into any other techniques beyond relief and screen printing.

As the 1950s progressed and into the '60s, the Northwest Printmakers Society continued to maintain its position as one of the region's most successful arts organizations. It had sustained this reputation for excellence over five decades and was still attracting both accomplished artists as well as talented newcomers like the Washington State native Chuck Close (b. 1940), who exhibited a color etching titled *Woman Seated in Doorway* with the NWPS in 1964.

The NWPS remained active until 1970, when it formally disbanded after its final exhibition. The region was in the beginning stages of a debilitating economic recession that contributed to the demise of the organization. Soon afterward, the Northwest Annuals at the Seattle Art

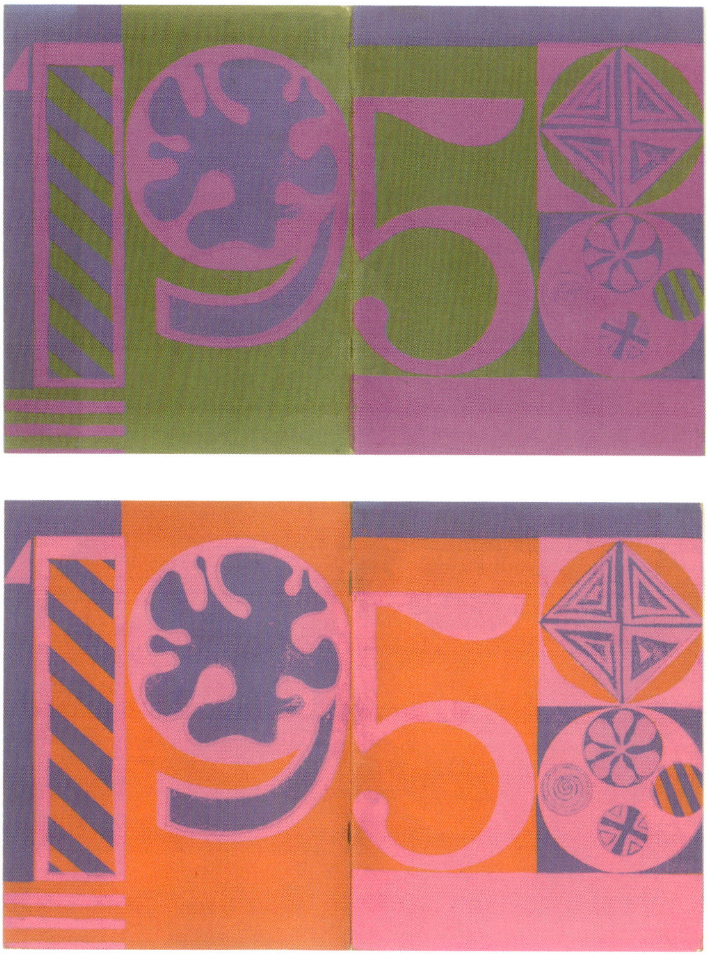

1958 Northwest Printmakers Society exhibition catalogues with variant colors, silkscreen. The Martin-Zambito Archive

Museum, which had been the leading venue for regional artists since 1914, ceased as well. Art production would be rekindled, with new museums and exhibition series in the decades to follow, as Seattle became an international leader in the world of technology.

Today it is clear that the history of color printmaking in Washington State was characterized by distinctive and significant innovations and achievements. It is my hope that, in featuring the work of the regional artists who made lasting contributions to the medium, this book will mark the beginning of a new reassessment and deeper appreciation of their contributions by scholars and art institutions throughout the country.

NOTES

1 "Late Dr. Kibbe Left Fine Accumulation of Japanese Art Specimens." *Seattle Daily Times*, April 27, 1904, p. 10.

2 "Katherine Ball Talks of Japanese Pints." *Seattle Daily Times*, October 24, 1906, p. 7.

3 "Classes in Design Have Been Formed." *Seattle Daily Times*, February 28, 1915, p. 40.

4 "With the Fine Arts Folk," *The Town Crier* [Seattle], November 11, 1916, p. 13.

5 "Prints Form New Exhibit in Fine Art Rooms." *Seattle Daily Times*, November 12, 1916, p. 63.

6 "Hyde Japanese Prints Featured." *Seattle Daily Times*, May 18, 1919, p. 7.

7 "Japanese Art Work to Be Exhibited." *Seattle Daily Times*, August 10, 1924, p. 24.

8 *New York Times*, January 22, 1939, p. 124. ProQuest Historical Newspapers, http://search.proquest.com.ezproxy.spl.org/hnpnewyorktimes/docview/102855226/61BF46FFC33B-4865PQ/1?accountid=1135 (accessed February 24, 2017).

9 For further information on Elizabeth Colborne, see David Martin, *Evergreen Muse: The Art of Elizabeth Colborne* (Bellingham, WA: Whatcom Museum, 2011).

10 "Packed in a Trunk: The Lost Art of Edith Lake Wilkinson." Documentary film, January 2015, 77 minutes.

11 Phone conversation between David Martin and Rhodes's student Frances Swift, May 24, 2002. Swift had studied with Rhodes from 1924 to 1927. She explained that Rhodes had been to Provincetown before 1924 and taught the technique in her classes at the University of Washington.

The painter/printmaker Robert O. Engard (1915–2003), in a phone conversation with David Martin on the same date, explained that Ruth Fiskin, his early art instructor, had also gone to Provincetown to learn white-line printmaking in the early 1920s.

12 "How Monotypes Are Made." *Seattle Daily Times*, April 17, 1910, p. 19.

13 The Amero information is drawn from Carl Brown Sennheim, *Emilio Amero: A Modern Master* (typed article, undated, pages not numbered, in Martin-Zambito artist files).

14 For an in-depth account of the life and career of Frances Blakemore, see Michiyo Morioka, *An American Artist in Tokyo, Frances Blakemore, 1906–1997* (Seattle, WA: Blakemore Foundation and University of Washington Press).

15 Kenneth Callahan, "Saito Ranks High in Japanese Art." *Seattle Daily Times*, January 16, 1955, p. 59.

16 Anne G. Todd, "Kiyoshi Saito Has Scenic Drive in Printmaking." *Seattle Sunday Times*, November 18, 1962, p. 37.

17 Tom Robbins, "230 Works Accepted for Northwest Annual." *Seattle Daily Times*, October 29, 1963, p. 26.

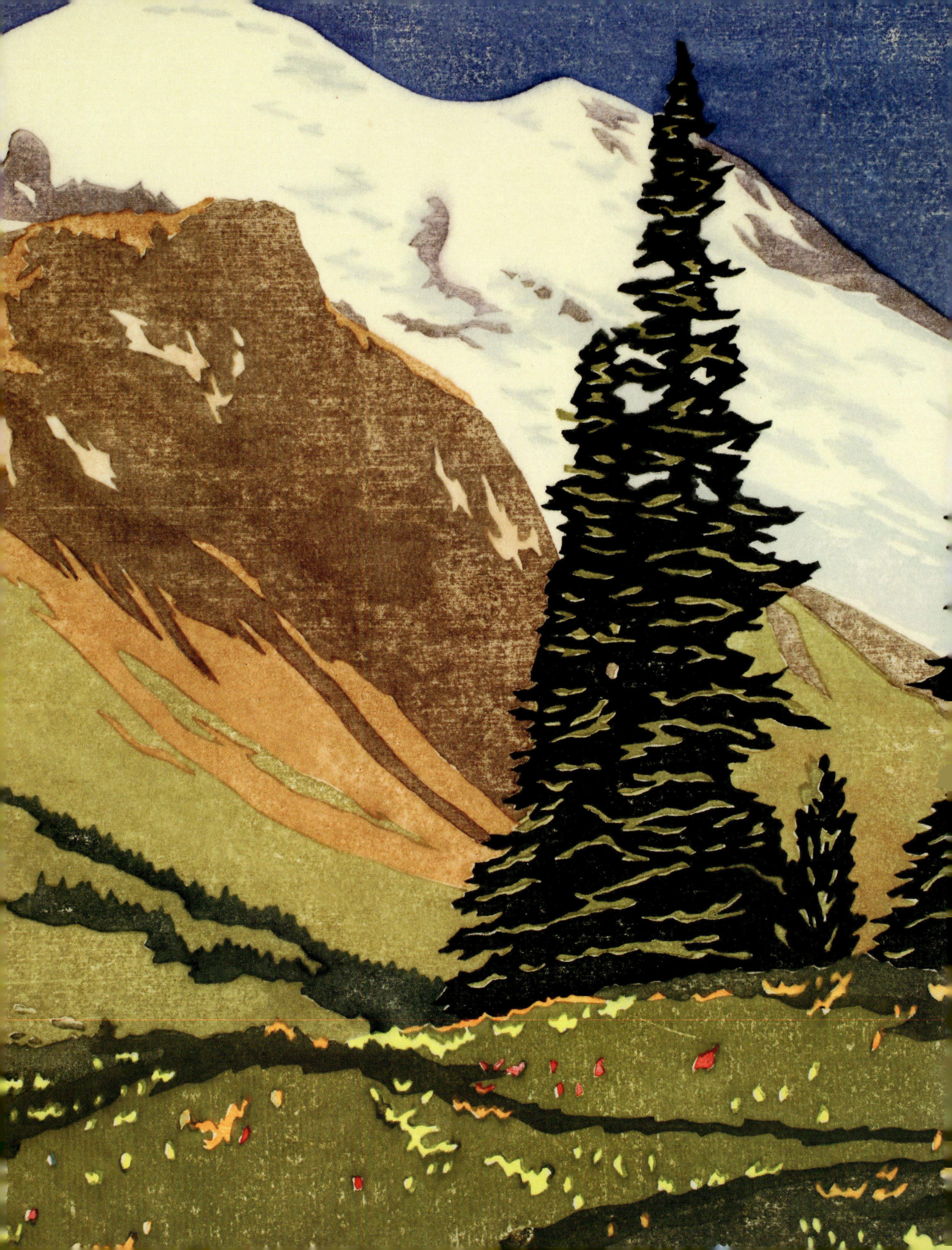

THE CHASE BROTHERS

DAVID F. MARTIN

Waldo Spore Chase (1895–1988) and Wendell Corwin Chase (1897–1988) were two of four children born to Ella Ann Ryther Chase (1872–1928) and Wendell Nye Chase (1863–1944), who married in 1891. The eldest and youngest of the children were Marjorie Chase Gilleland (1892–?) and Philip Nye "Brownie" Chase (1900–1983). Ella's mother was Olive "Mother" Spore Ryther (1849–1934), who was a legendary figure in Seattle's history. Ryther assisted the indigent population of Seattle and was especially known for her work with homeless children. Her initial organization was the Ryther Child Home, founded in 1883 to care for orphans and young wards of the state. The organization survives today as the Ryther Center for Children and Youth with a focus on serving children with severe emotional and behavioral challenges.

The Chase parents both had artistic leanings. Ella was a talented pictorialist photographer and Wendell "Pa" Chase, worked in the Arts & Crafts medium of hammered copper. Wendell supported the family as an engineer and surveyor, first setting up a practice in 1887 in Sidney, Washington (later renamed Port Orchard), and then later working for the city of Seattle. He was a prominent member of the Pacific Northwest Society of Engineers. His craft-related works were exhibited in local venues including the Seattle Craftsmen Applied Arts & Crafts Exhibition at the Seattle Art Museum in 1936.

Marjorie exerted an artistic influence on her younger brothers; she attended Pratt Institute's School of Fine & Applied Arts in Brooklyn, New York, graduating in 1915 with a diploma in Normal Art & Manual Training.[1] Upon graduating, she returned to Seattle and became the assistant to Clara P. Reynolds (1879–1961), art director for Seattle's public schools. The youngest brother, Brownie, followed in his father's technical path. After attending the University of Washington, he moved to Olympia, Washington, and worked on the ground planning for the construction of the State Capitol Building complex, completed in 1928. He later moved to Washington, DC, for employment in the engineering field. Shortly after NATO was formed in 1949, he moved to Italy, living near Verona, where he worked as a cartographer for the organization. He died in Italy in 1983.

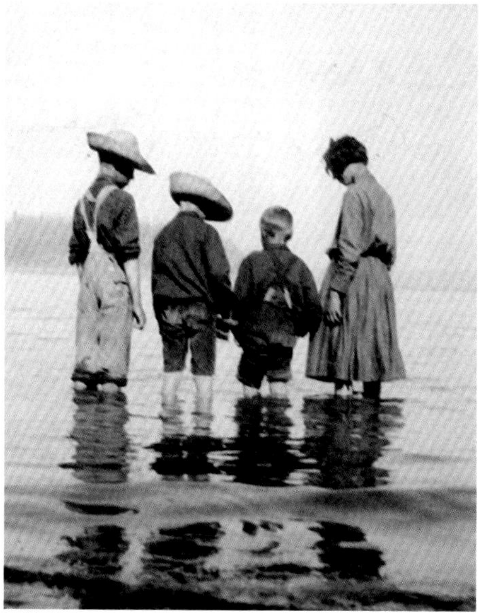

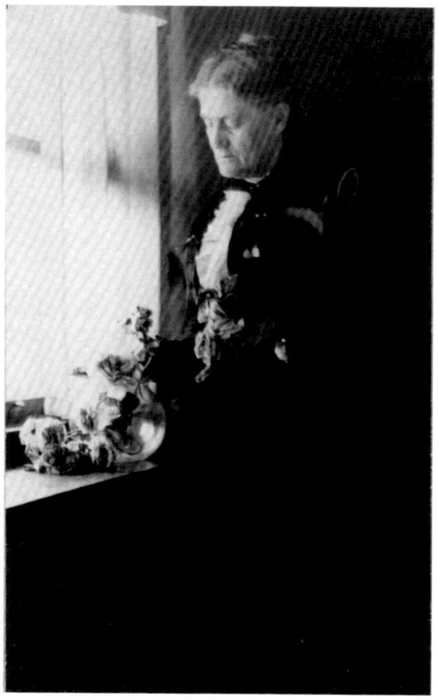

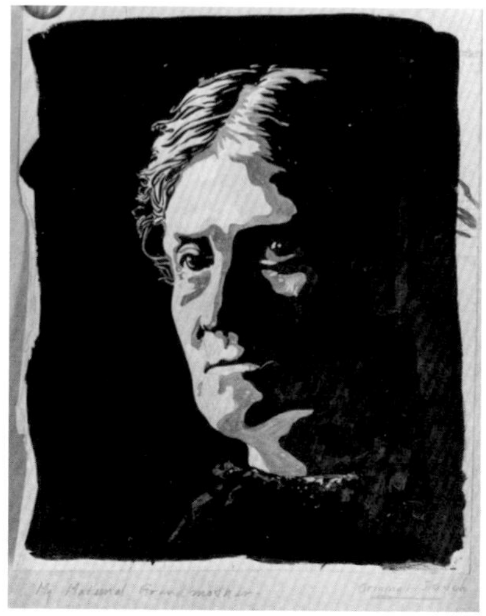

(left) The children of Wendell Nye Chase and Ella Ryther Chase. From left: Waldo, Corwin, Philip, and Marjorie. Courtesy of Florence Gilleland Schieve

(center) Olive "Mother" Ryther, ca. 1910, as photographed by her daughter, Ella Ryther Chase. Courtesy of Florence Gilleland Schieve

(right) WALDO S. CHASE, *My Maternal Grandmother* (Mother Ryther), photograph of a sketch by Waldo S. Chase (original ca. 1926). Photograph by Henry Blocher

Henry Blocher, "My Maternal Grandmother," *Lewis & Clark Digital Collections*, http://digitalcollections.lclark.edu/items/show/5465 (accessed 5-18-2017). Courtesy of Lewis & Clark College Aubrey Watzek Library Special Collections & Archives

The Chase family enjoyed hiking and camping and took every opportunity to savor the region's natural beauty. On one occasion, Mrs. Chase documented the family's 1914 trip to Mount Rainier in a series of personal notes that chronicled the adventures of her husband and growing children. Waldo graduated from Queen Anne High School in 1915, and Corwin graduated the following year in 1916. Waldo held various jobs, including streetcar conductor, and was leaning toward a career in teaching. Corwin wanted to be an architect and landed an entry position with the Seattle firm of Patterson & McDowell as a draftsman. Under the influence of their parents, they were both enthralled by nature and set out to explore the rugged Northwest terrain on their own. With conventional careers looking less attractive, Corwin merged his love of the outdoors with a new profession when he became secretary of the Cooperative Campers, leading amateur camping expeditions around Mount Rainier and other areas of the Cascade range.

Waldo had a vague interest in education as a profession and began teaching school in 1923 at the Skokomish Indian reservation. Because of his unorthodox teaching methods and allowing the children to wander around unrestricted, he was dismissed and returned to Seattle the following year. With both brothers interested in pursuing their artistic instincts, they attempted to turn art production into a viable way to make a living. Corwin had learned photography from his mother and began producing numerous photographs of Northwest landscapes. According to his biography, he was trying to market his photographs and when they failed to create much interest he thought that they might be more appealing if he hand-colored them. Unhappy with the results, he and Waldo considered making color woodblock prints in the Japanese manner as an alternative to the pale tinted photographs. Together they began the study of color printmaking by using a contemporary instructional book: *Wood-block Printing* by Frank Morley Fletcher, first published in 1916. Waldo purchased the necessary equipment and they set out to conquer this new medium.

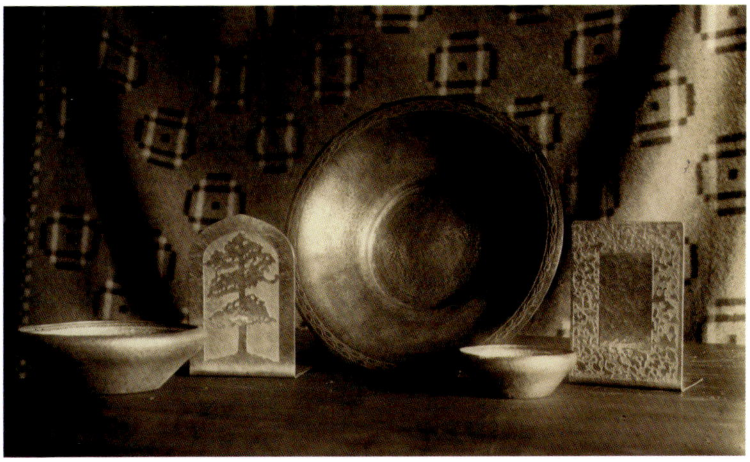

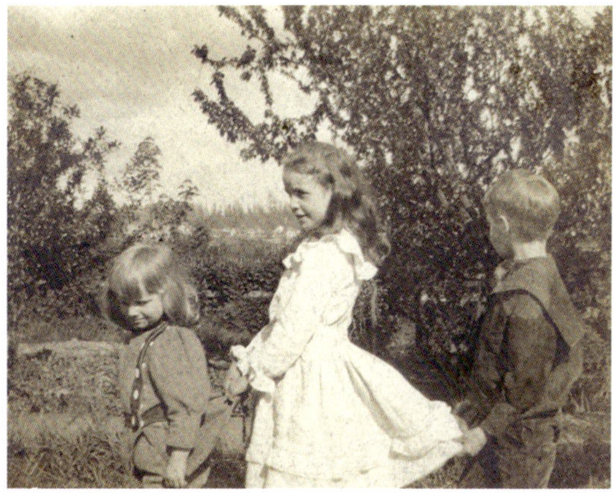

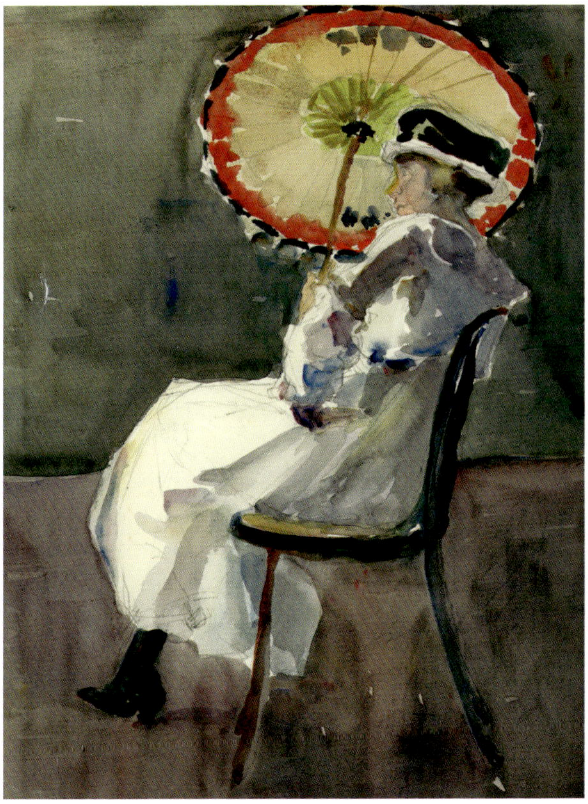

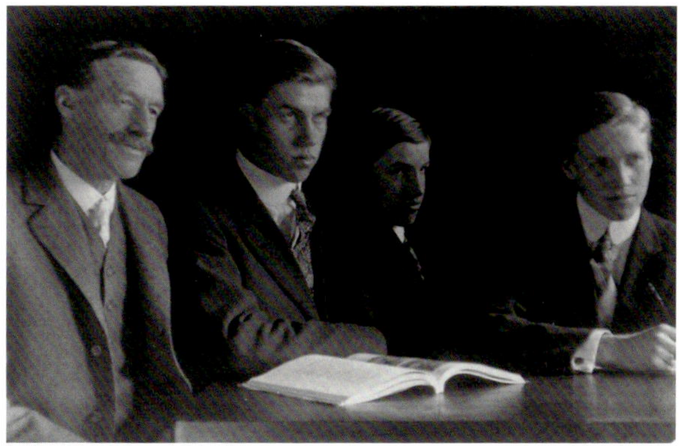

(top left) Hammered copper objects created by Wendell Nye Chase, ca. 1925. Courtesy of Florence Gilleland Schieve

(bottom left) MARJORIE CHASE (1892–). Untitled, 1917, watercolor. Collection of Florence Gilleland Schieve

(top right) Corwin, Marjorie, and Waldo Chase, ca. 1900. Courtesy of Florence Gilleland Schieve

(bottom right) Wendell N. Chase with sons Waldo, Philip, and Corwin, ca. 1912. Courtesy of Florence Gilleland Schieve

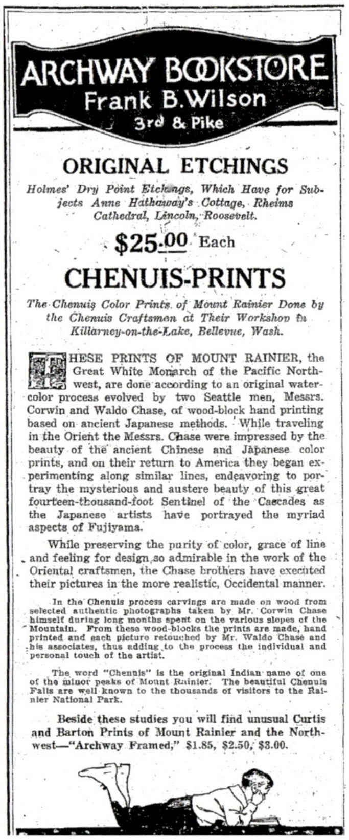

ARCHWAY BOOKSTORE
Frank B. Wilson
3rd & Pike

ORIGINAL ETCHINGS

Holmes' Dry Point Etchings, Which Have for Subjects Anne Hathaway's Cottage, Rheims Cathedral, Lincoln, Roosevelt.

$25.00 Each

CHENUIS-PRINTS

The Chenuis Color Prints of Mount Rainier Done by the Chenuis Craftsmen at Their Workshop in Killarney-on-the-Lake, Bellevue, Wash.

THESE PRINTS OF MOUNT RAINIER, the Great White Monarch of the Pacific Northwest, are done according to an original water-color process evolved by two Seattle men, Messrs. Corwin and Waldo Chase, of wood-block hand printing based on ancient Japanese methods. While traveling in the Orient the Messrs. Chase were impressed by the beauty of the ancient Chinese and Japanese color prints, and on their return to America they began experimenting along similar lines, endeavoring to portray the mysterious and austere beauty of this great fourteen-thousand-foot Sentinel of the Cascades as the Japanese artists have portrayed the myriad aspects of Fujiyama.

While preserving the purity of color, grace of line and feeling for design so admirable in the work of the Oriental craftsmen, the Chase brothers have executed their pictures in the more realistic, Occidental manner.

In the Chenuis process carvings are made on wood from selected authentic photographs taken by Mr. Corwin Chase himself during long months spent on the various slopes of the Mountain. From these wood-blocks the prints are made, hand printed and each picture retouched by Mr. Waldo Chase and his associates, thus adding to the process the individual and personal touch of the artist.

The word "Chennis" is the original Indian name of one of the minor peaks of Mount Rainier. The beautiful Chenuis Falls are well known to the thousands of visitors to the Rainier National Park.

Beside these studies you will find unusual Curtis and Barton Prints of Mount Rainier and the Northwest—"Archway Framed," $1.85, $2.50, $3.00.

Advertisement for Archway Bookstore, featuring *Chenuis* prints. *Seattle Daily Times*, December 7, 1924. Courtesy of The Seattle Public Library

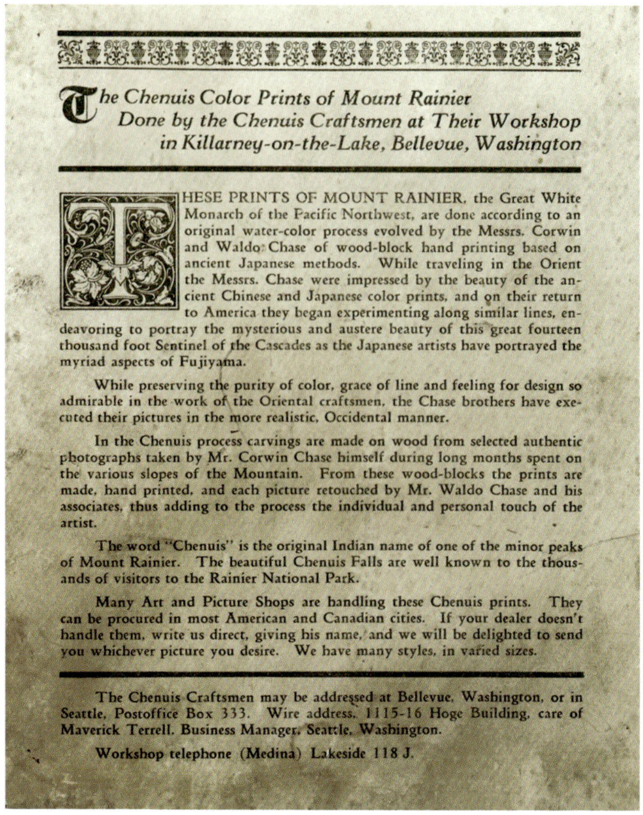

The Chenuis Color Prints of Mount Rainier Done by the Chenuis Craftsmen at Their Workshop in Killarney-on-the-Lake, Bellevue, Washington

THESE PRINTS OF MOUNT RAINIER, the Great White Monarch of the Pacific Northwest, are done according to an original water-color process evolved by the Messrs. Corwin and Waldo Chase of wood-block hand printing based on ancient Japanese methods. While traveling in the Orient the Messrs. Chase were impressed by the beauty of the ancient Chinese and Japanese color prints, and on their return to America they began experimenting along similar lines, endeavoring to portray the mysterious and austere beauty of this great fourteen thousand foot Sentinel of the Cascades as the Japanese artists have portrayed the myriad aspects of Fujiyama.

While preserving the purity of color, grace of line and feeling for design so admirable in the work of the Oriental craftsmen, the Chase brothers have executed their pictures in the more realistic, Occidental manner.

In the Chenuis process carvings are made on wood from selected authentic photographs taken by Mr. Corwin Chase himself during long months spent on the various slopes of the Mountain. From these wood-blocks the prints are made, hand printed, and each picture retouched by Mr. Waldo Chase and his associates, thus adding to the process the individual and personal touch of the artist.

The word "Chenuis" is the original Indian name of one of the minor peaks of Mount Rainier. The beautiful Chenuis Falls are well known to the thousands of visitors to the Rainier National Park.

Many Art and Picture Shops are handling these Chenuis prints. They can be procured in most American and Canadian cities. If your dealer doesn't handle them, write us direct, giving his name, and we will be delighted to send you whichever picture you desire. We have many styles, in varied sizes.

The Chenuis Craftsmen may be addressed at Bellevue, Washington, or in Seattle, Postoffice Box 333. Wire address, 1115-16 Hoge Building, care of Maverick Terrell, Business Manager, Seattle, Washington.

Workshop telephone (Medina) Lakeside 118 J.

Advertising label for *Chenuis* Prints, 1925. The Martin-Zambito Archive

In 1924, they were living together in the attic of a store near the Carbon River entrance to Mount Rainier in the coal-mining town of Fairfax, Washington. Being in close proximity to the landscapes that they wanted to portray in their prints was the main reason for their choosing to stay in such an obscure location.

Their first attempts at printmaking were quite successful. With only two images created, they began marketing their work under the collaborative allonym, *Chenuis* "the original Indian name of one of the minor peaks of Mt. Rainier." Their statement is romantically exaggerated, since neither brother ever visited the "Orient" as their advertisements proclaimed. Their first print, *Mirror Lake*, was based on Corwin's photograph of Mount Rainier as seen from Indian Henry's Hunting Ground. Creating the print required the use of seven blocks for the color separations, and the images were printed in a small edition of ten. To get more variety while using the same blocks, they changed the watercolor-based inks to create a nocturnal image of the same view. Their second attempt, simply titled *Mt. Rainier*, was based on a photograph of the mountain overlooking Lake Washington from Seattle. This time, eighty proofs were pulled in the hopes of finding a market for them. These first two prints were a collaboration between the brothers, but the printing of the blocks became so frustrating for Corwin that he decided they would function more productively if he carved all of the blocks while Waldo took on the arduous task of mixing the paints and printing the proofs. This system worked out well, and for the next three years it became their standard practice. Waldo's main color theories were based on *The Atlas of the Munsell Color System*, first published in 1913. The system used charts to measure hue (pure color without tint or shade), chroma (strength of the pigment color), and value (the range from light to dark).

Waldo made an intense study of color theory while Corwin perfected his carving. These two prints were the only ones produced in 1924.

The prints were displayed in a variety of Seattle's retail

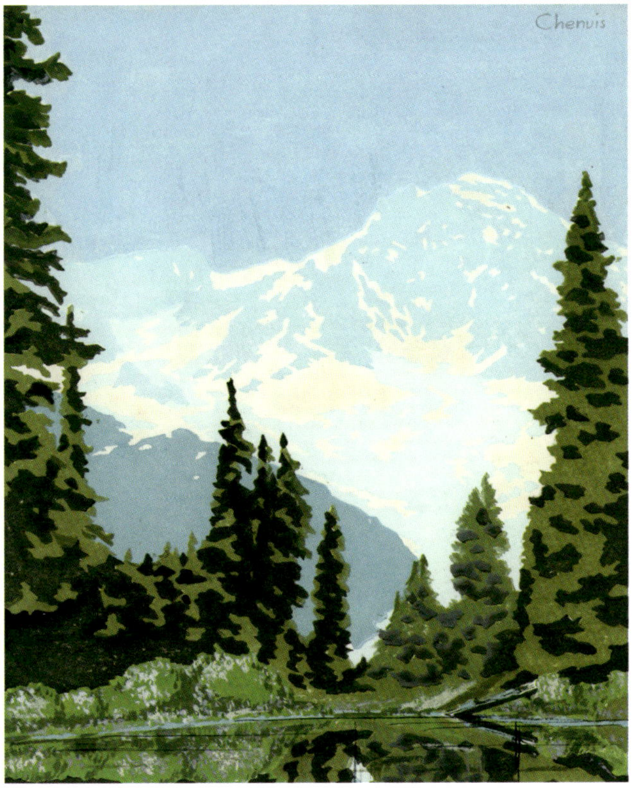

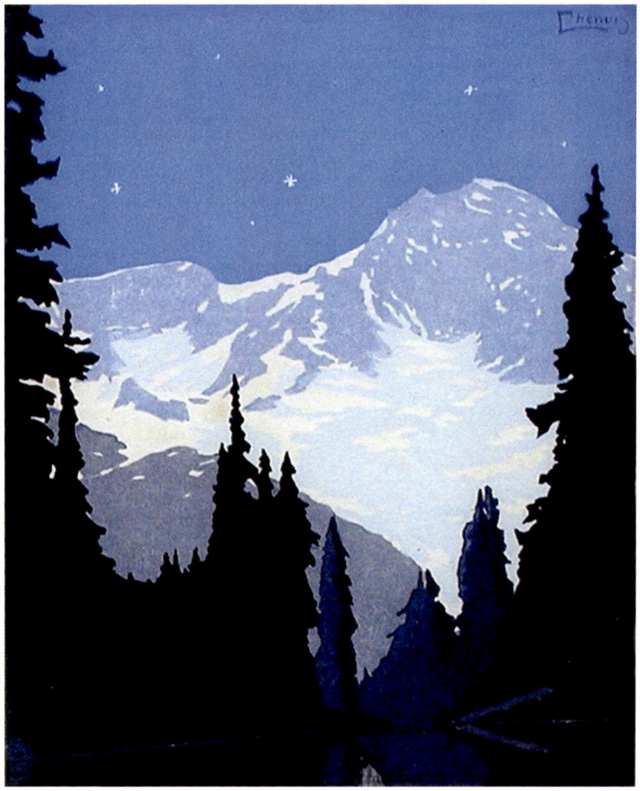

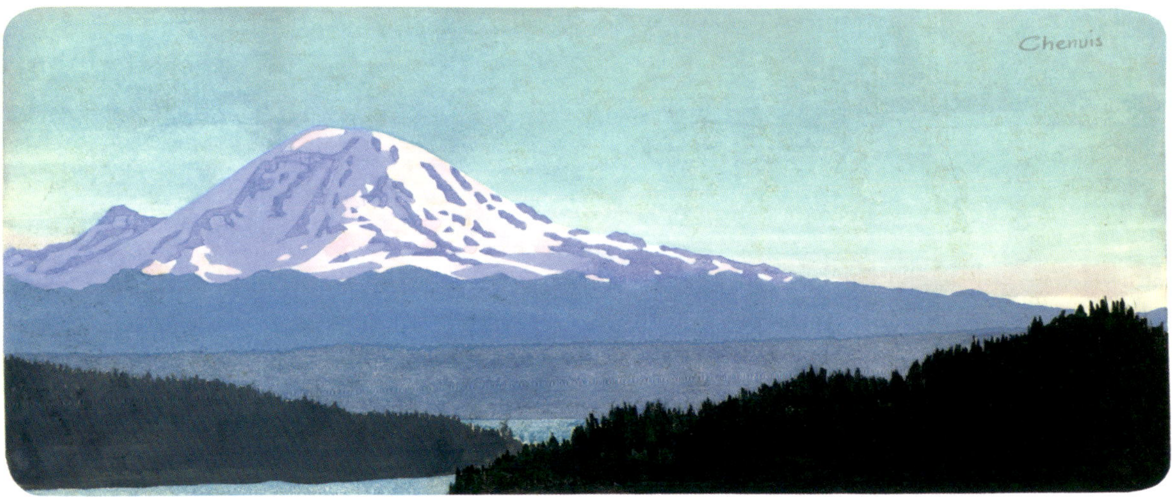

(top left) *Chenuis: Mirror Lake*, 1924, color woodblock print, 10 x 8 in. Private collection

(bottom) *Chenuis: Mt. Rainier*, 1924, color woodblock print, 5 ½ x 13 ¼ in. Private collection

(top right) *Chenuis: Mirror Lake*, 1924, color woodblock print, 10 x 8 in. Collection of Florence Gilleland Schieve

These two prints illustrate how the brothers used the same blocks with different inking to achieve a variety of effects, including daylight and nocturnal depictions.

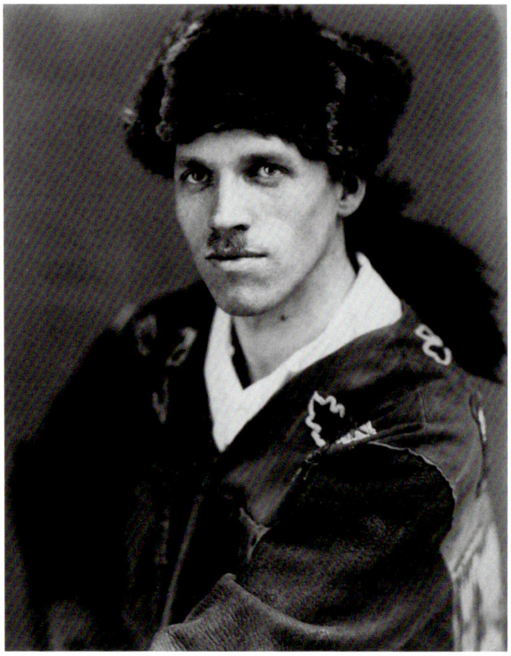

W. Corwin Chase, ca. 1926. The Chase Place Collection. Photographer unknown

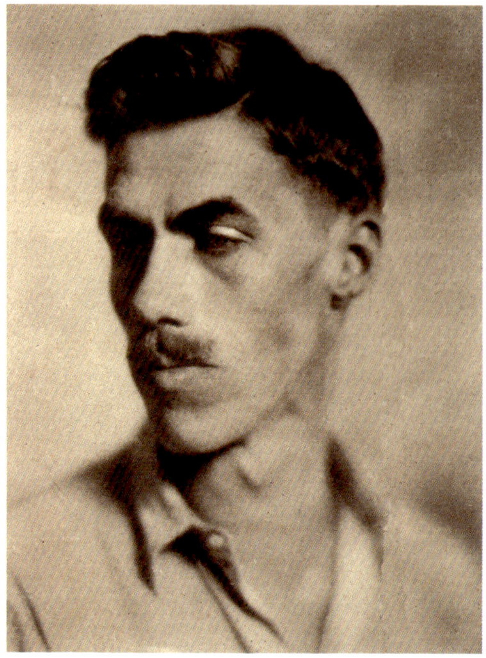

Waldo Chase, 1926, after a portrait study by Leonid Fink. Reproduced in *The Seattle Times* rotogravure pictorial section, October 24, 1926, page 3. The Martin-Zambito Archive

stores although no sales were made. While on a camping trip to Glacier Basin in Mount Rainier National Park, however, they met members of The Mountaineers, a group of outdoor enthusiasts who were naturally drawn to the familiar subject matter depicted in the prints. They received positive encouragement that validated their objective, and sold their first two prints to two prominent members of the group: University of Washington Professor Edmond S. Meany (1862–1935), and Heinie Loss, an early climber of Mount Rainier. They also discovered another useful way of drawing interest to their prints. Explaining the mysterious methods they employed for creating them could serve as a way to impress the female members of The Mountaineers. For promotional purposes and perhaps as a way to ignite some future dating prospects, they gave away some of the proofs to the admiring women.[2]

Soon, the brothers began living in a small cabin at Beaux Arts Village near the Seattle suburb of Bellevue by Lake Washington. Here they produced a limited number of prints, relying once again on using variations of the watercolor inks to give a variety of effects with the same blocks, thus increasing sales possibilities with reduced effort. While their aesthetic impulse was not compromised by the need to make a living, they used their printing skills for commercial work as well, as seen in an extant advertisement for the Kitsap Dairy company. In the winter of 1926–27, the brothers were approached by the developer of the new Hotel Georgia, currently near completion in nearby Vancouver, BC. They were to produce 320 woodblock prints, one for each room in the luxury hotel, along with three large oil paintings for the common areas, all for the sum of $1500. They accepted the commission and were allowed to stay in the rooms of the hotel to complete the work before the grand opening. With most of the prints completed, albeit with a quickly escalating resentment between them and the hotel developer, they were evicted two weeks before the opening and took off on their bicycles for the long trek back to their studio on Lake Washington.[3]

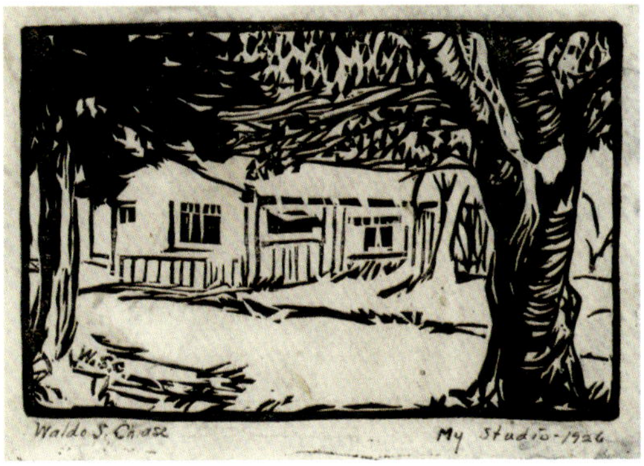

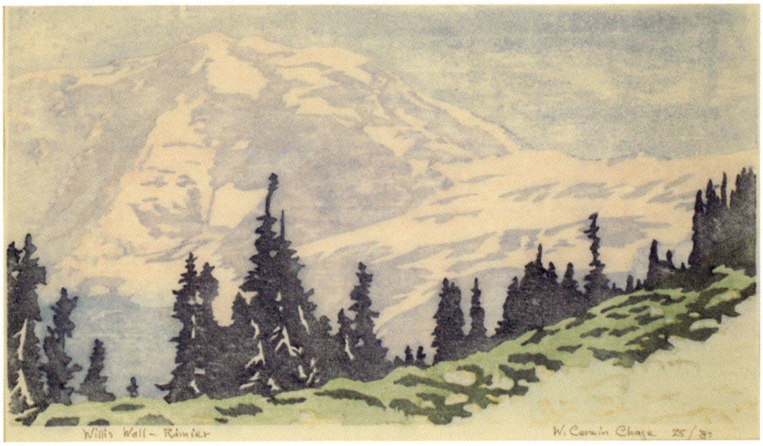

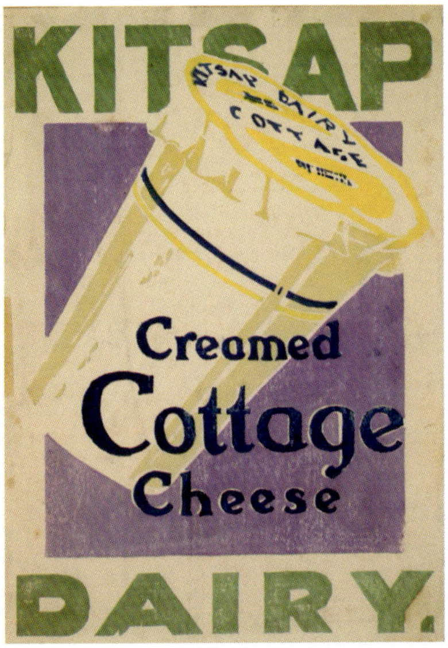

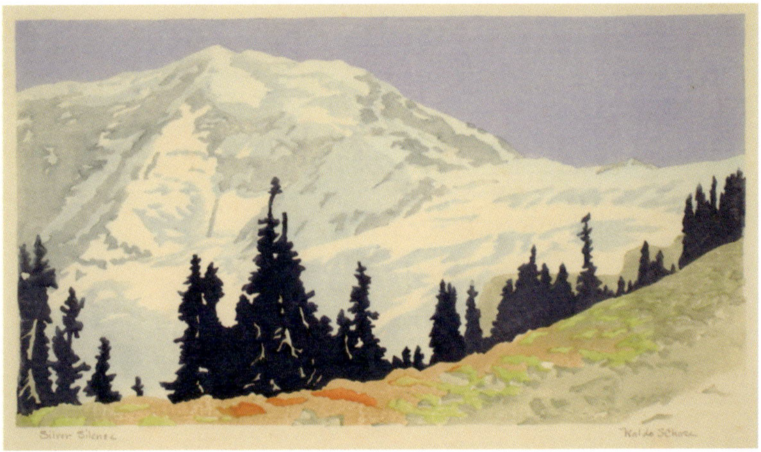

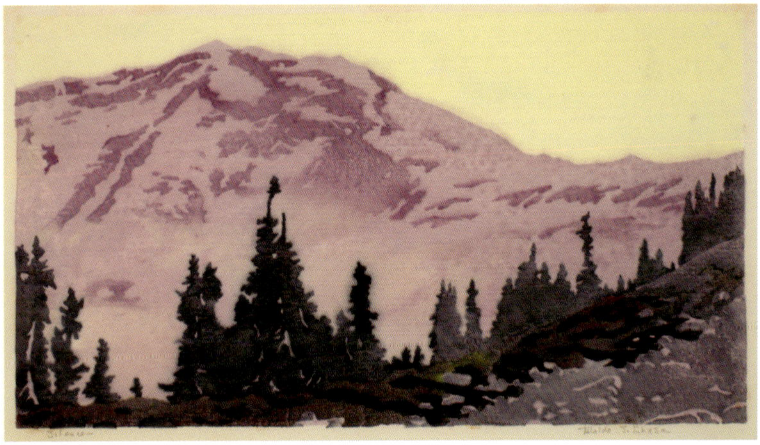

(top left) WALDO S. CHASE: *My Studio*, 1926, woodblock print, 4 ½ x 6 ½ in. Private collection.

Inscribed: *"This is one of the first little places where I lived and worked – (1925–1927) at the color block printing – two years of color study and experiments – this is near Beaux Arts – East of Seattle – The last print of this block – to me most rare."*

(bottom left) WALDO S. CHASE, Kitsap Dairy Creamed Cottage Cheese, ca. 1926, color woodblock print, 14 x 9 in. Private collection

(top right) W. CORWIN CHASE, *Willis Wall*, 1925, re-struck 1987, color woodblock print, 7 ½ x 13 ⅛ in. The Chase Place Collection

(center right) WALDO S. CHASE, *Silver Silence*, 1925, color woodblock print, 7 ½ x 13 ¼ in. Private collection

(bottom right) WALDO S. CHASE, *Silence*, 1925, color woodblock print, 7 ½ x 13 ¼ in. Collection of John Impert

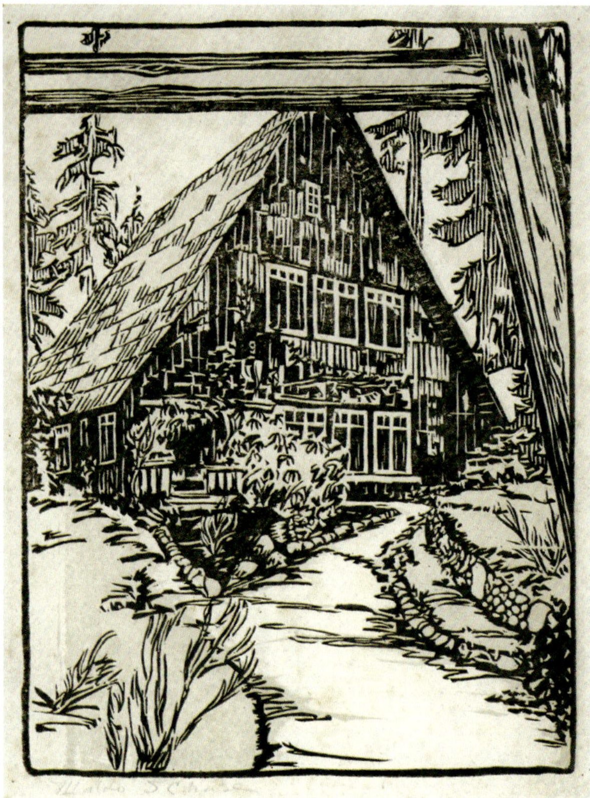

WALDO S. CHASE, *Studio, Beaux Arts on Lake Washington*, 1927, woodblock print, 9 ¼ x 6 ⅞ in. Private collection

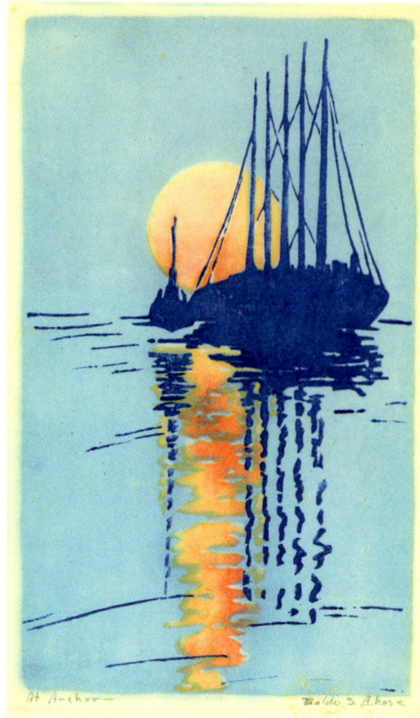

WALDO S. CHASE, *At Anchor*, ca. 1927, color woodblock print, 7 ½ x 4 ¼ in. Private collection

By 1927, the brothers were living in a larger studio in Beaux Arts. In May of that year, they decided to move into the wilderness to explore nature first hand as the main inspiration for their print production. They began identifying as primitive or "savage occidentals" in an effort to reject the conventions of society and live independently as close to nature as possible. They erected what was the first of numerous tepees that they would live in for various lengths of time throughout their lives, both together and separately. They had a twelve-foot-high tepee constructed and then settled at Irish Creek Camp near Mount Rainier National Park to align their art with the natural setting.

The large tepee accommodated both brothers with two sleeping mats around a central fire pit. Clothing, art materials, and food supplies were stored in chests within the perimeter of the tepee. They were not totally without modern conveniences, however. Waldo had a Model T that was used for transportation, hauling, and getting food staples from markets. But by being mainly out in the wilderness, away from distractions, the brothers were able to produce a substantial number of prints in various sizes until the end of the year. Then it became time to emerge from the tepee and make an effort to market their prints. They did this by offering displays and lectures to various arts groups and women's organizations in Seattle. On November 15, Corwin gave a talk on "The Oriental Art of Making Wood Cuts" for the Fine Arts Department of the Seattle Federation of Women's Clubs.[4] He also had a selection of his prints on display at Barker Brothers, a deluxe furniture store in Los Angeles.

Although both brothers made good efforts, Corwin was more suited to the task of lecturing and promoting their work, as Waldo was more philosophical and introspective. Corwin was more of an extrovert, with an energetic demeanor and charismatic good looks.

By 1928, the Japanese artist Yamagishi Kazue (1883–1966) had arrived in Seattle to teach a class in the traditional technique of making color prints. He was in the process of making a world tour under the auspices of the Japanese

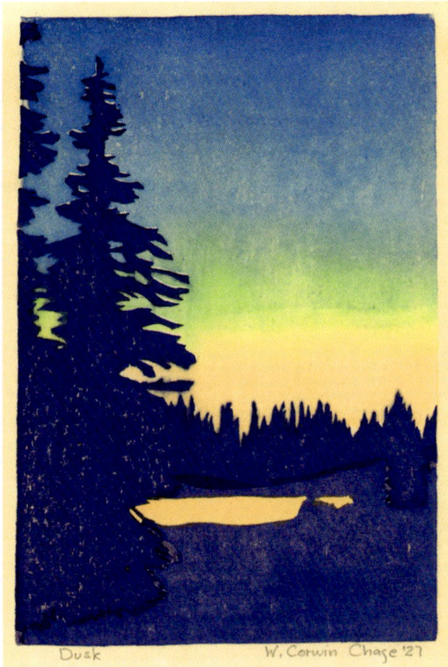

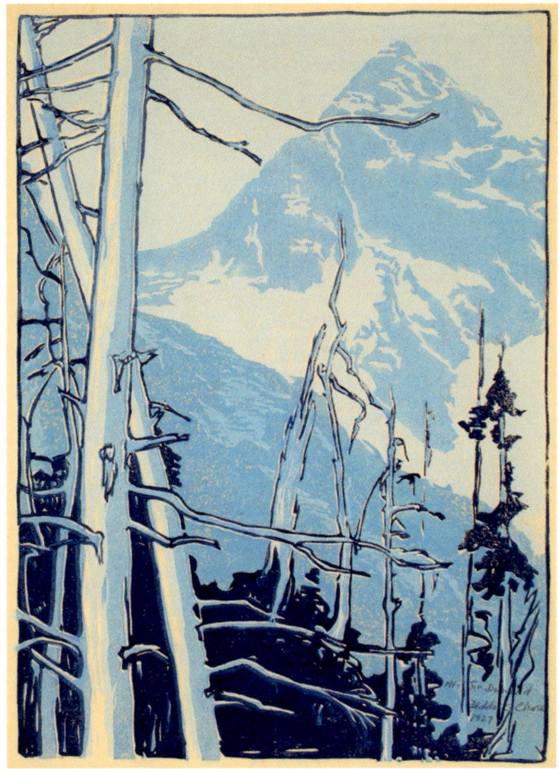

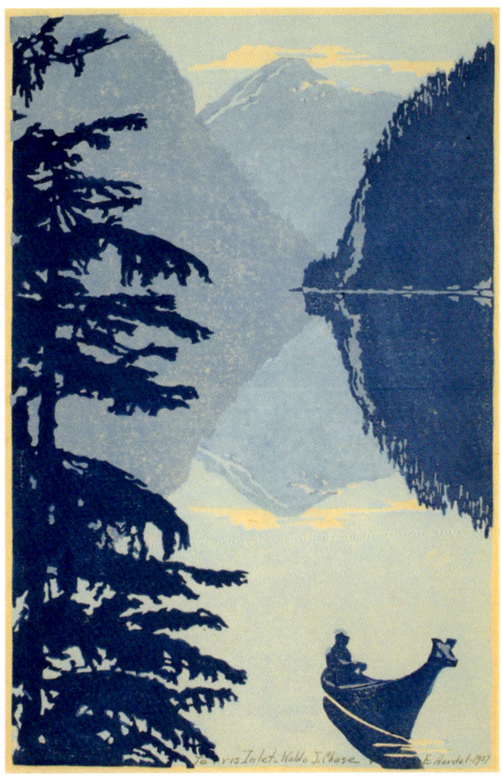

(top left) W. CORWIN CHASE, *Dusk*, 1927, 7 x 4 ½ in. Private collection

(top right) WALDO S. CHASE, *Mt. Sir Donald*, 1927, color woodblock print, 13 ½ x 9 ½ in. Collection of John Impert

(bottom) WALDO S. CHASE and EDWIN AARDAL (1910–1988), *Jervis Inlet*, 1927, color woodblock print, 12 ½ x 7 ¾ in. Collection of John Impert

This proof credits seventeen-year-old Ed Aardal as collaborator with Chase. Aardal went on to have an illustrious career as an animator with the Walt Disney Studios.

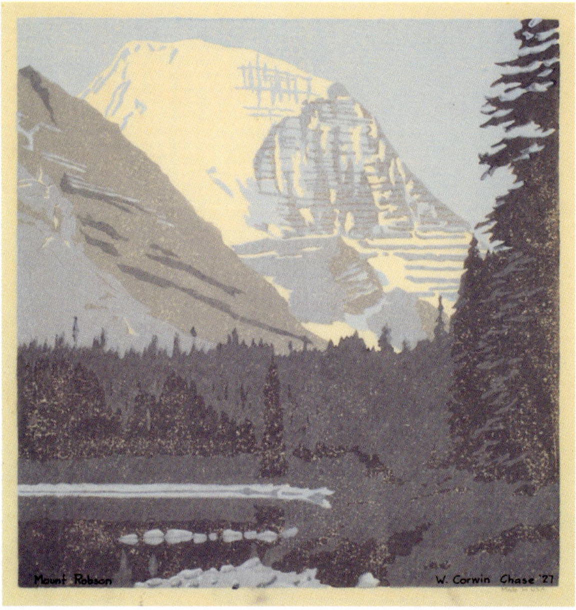

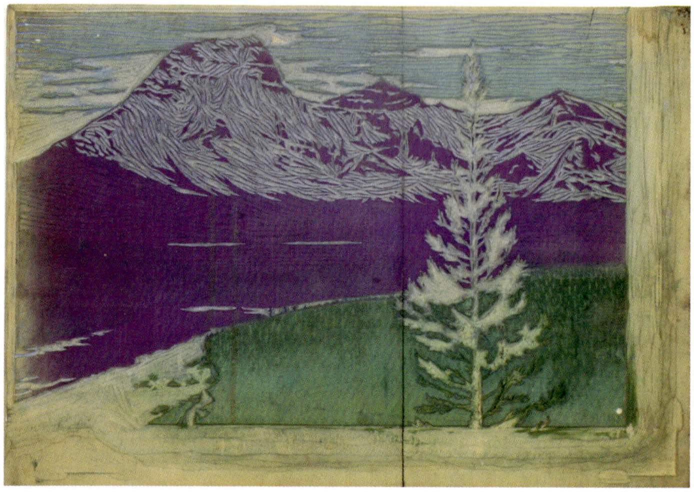

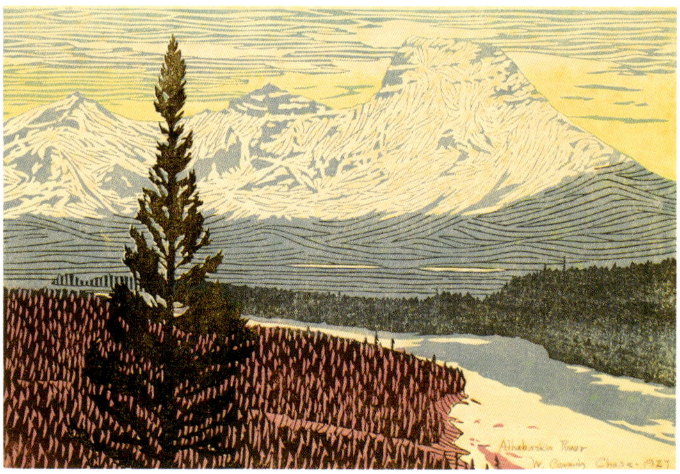

(top left) W. CORWIN CHASE, *Mount Robson*, 1927, color woodblock print, 10 x 9 3/8 in. Collection of John Impert

(top right) W. CORWIN CHASE, Printing block for *Athabaska River*, 1927, 8 1/4 x 12 in. The Chase Place Collection

(bottom) W. CORWIN CHASE, *Athabaska River*, 1927, color woodblock print, 8 1/4 x 12 in. The Chase Place Collection

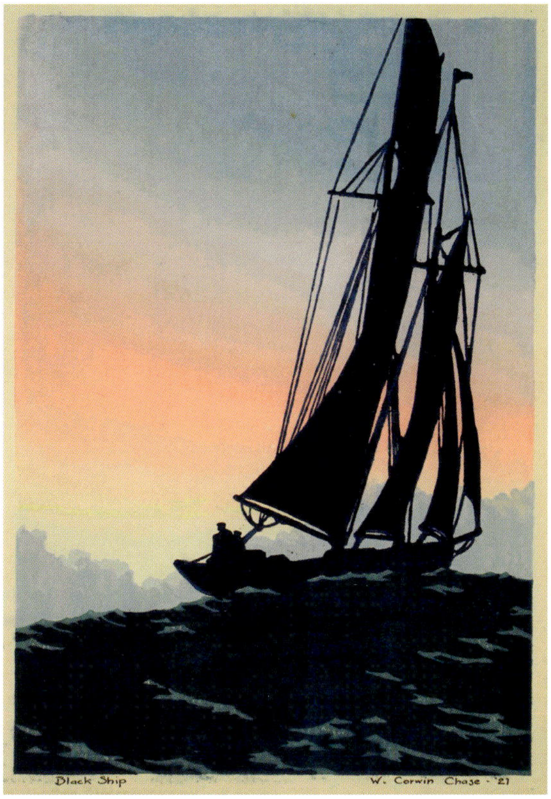

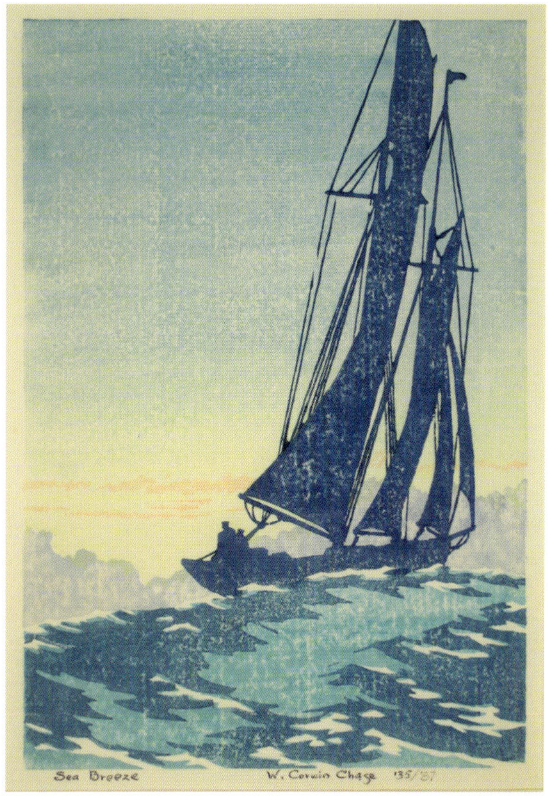

W. CORWIN CHASE, *Black Ship* (also titled *Sea Breeze*), 1927, color woodblock print, 11 ¾ x 7 ⅞ in. Collection of John Impert

W. CORWIN CHASE, *Sea Breeze*, 1927, 1935, re-struck 1987, color woodblock print, 11 ¾ x 7 ¾ in. The Chase Place Collection

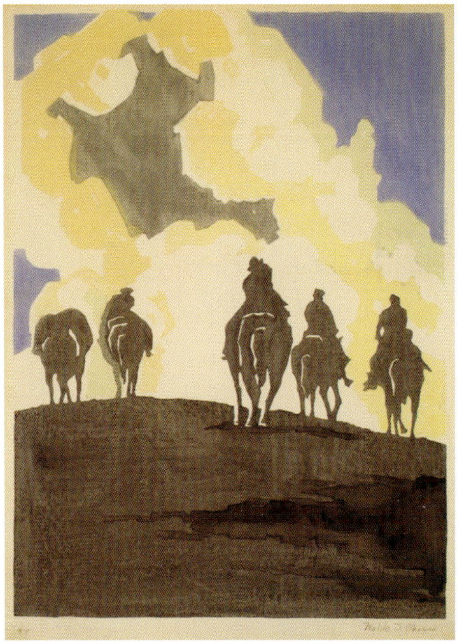

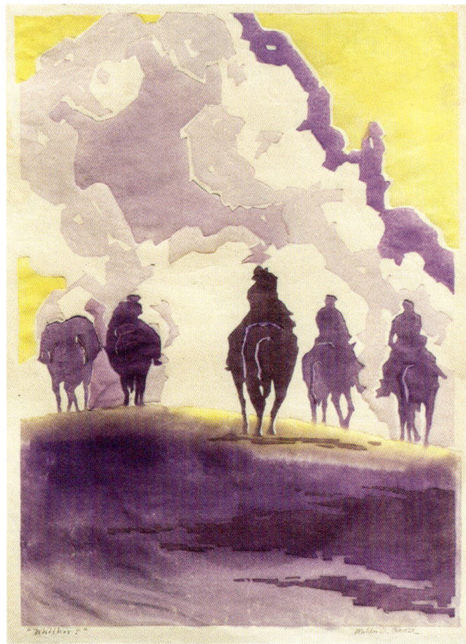

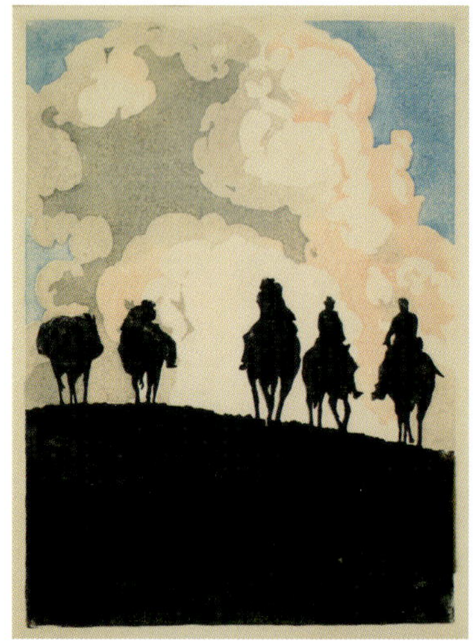

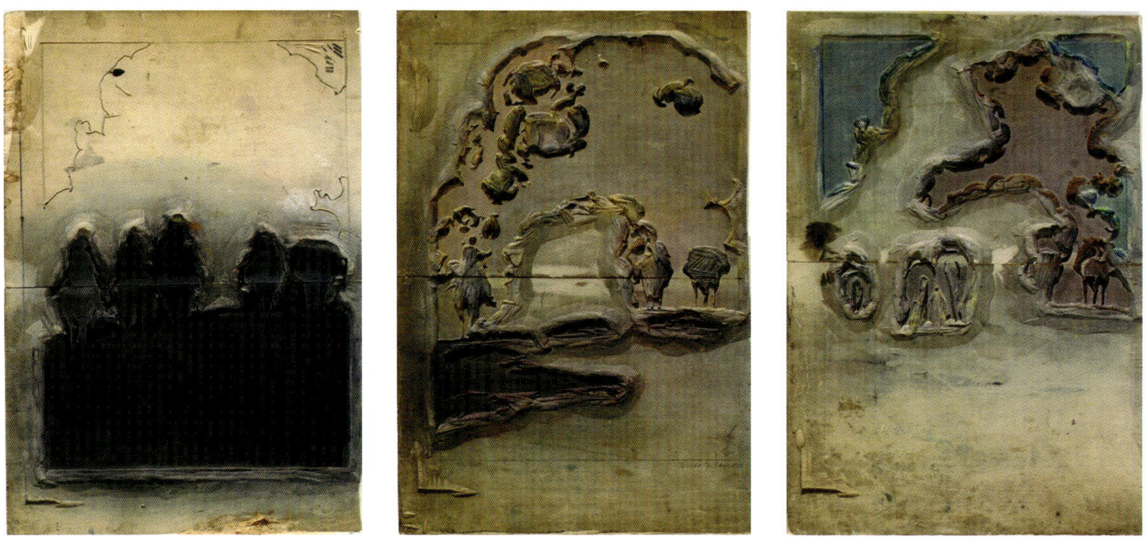

(top left) WALDO S. CHASE, *Whither*, 1927, color woodblock print, 18 ¼ x 13 in. Collection of John Impert

(top center) WALDO S. CHASE, *Whither*, 1927, color woodblock print, 18 ¼ x 13 in. Collection of Neil Collins

(top right) WALDO S. CHASE, *Whither*, 1927 (smaller version), color woodblock print, 12 x 8 ⅛ in. Collection of John Impert

(bottom) WALDO S. CHASE, three printing blocks for smaller version of *Whither*, 1927. Private collection

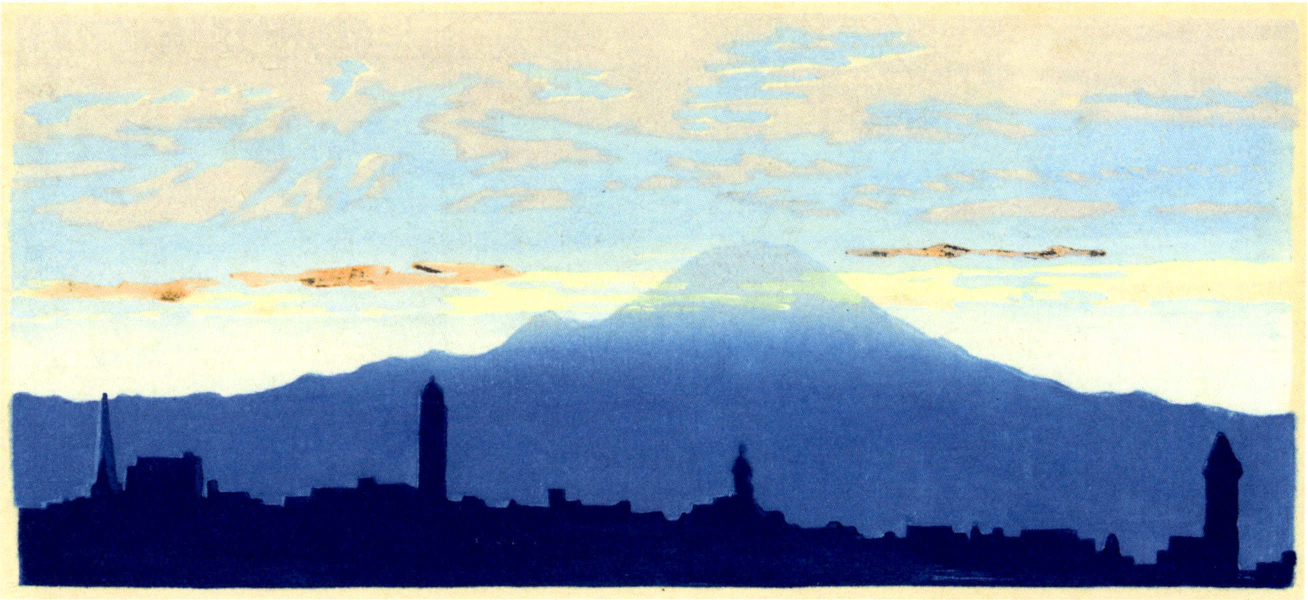

WALDO S. CHASE, *Seattle Skyline*, 1927, color woodblock print, 5 x 11 in.
Collection of John Impert

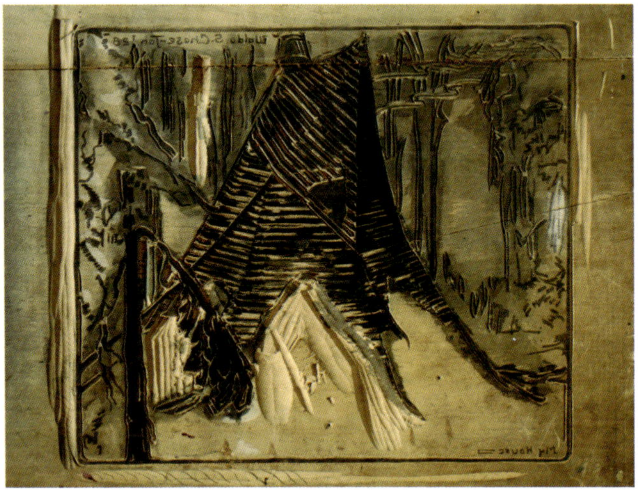

YAMAGISHI KAZUE (Japanese 1883–1966), printing block for *My House*, 1928, design by Waldo S. Chase. Private collection

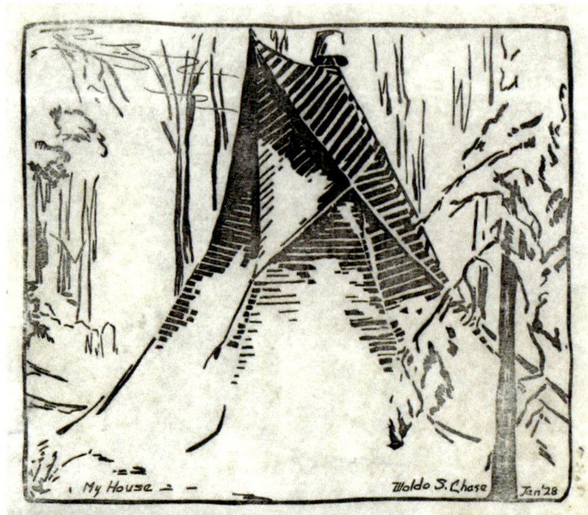

YAMAGISHI KAZUE *My House*, 1928, woodblock print, carved and printed by Yamagishi Kazue after a design by Waldo S. Chase, 6 ¾ x 7 1/5 in. Private collection

Ministry of Education. His mission was to go around the world to learn western-style contemporary art methods as well as promoting the traditional Japanese printing technique. His first stop was in San Francisco in 1926. He then went on to give a class at the University of California at Berkeley before arriving in Seattle. The brothers attended the local class, along with their friend Robert Bruce Inverarity (1909–1999) and other regional printmakers. Yamagishi visited their primitive lair out in the wilderness. He must have been impressed by their dedication to living such a basic existence in service to their art. He carved a block after a drawing that Waldo made of his tepee and pulled one proof in January 1928.[5] A few months later, Yamagishi was the guest of members of the Seattle Camera Club, the most prominent internationally known art group in Seattle at that time. The members were mostly Issei photographers with extremely impressive reputations. Besides promoting photography as a fine art through their local exhibitions, the SCC members educated the public by writing about Japanese art and literature in their biweekly publication, *Notan*. Their welcoming of Yamagishi to the region was recorded in 1928.

> On March 9th we held our 38th monthly meeting at Gyokkoken Cafe. There were 18 in attendance with Mr. Kazuye Yamagishi, Japanese wood-engraver and painter as our guest. He recently came from Japan and is expecting to tour this country and then to travel through Europe. His purpose is to learn the foreign method of wood-engraving and to find foreign subjects to develop the plan he has for his future work. He showed us about 30 woodcuts of his own making. His first work is somewhat different from the ordinary Japanese genre-pictures both in subject and technique. He explained many things about Japanese woodcuts.[6]

By March of 1928, the brothers returned home to pursue more sales, setting up their tepee in a vacant lot near their parent's house at 2120 Warren Avenue on Seattle's Queen Anne Hill. They had stopped working collaboratively by this time, with each designing, carving, and printing their own subjects. By August, the brothers became restless and headed across Puget Sound to Bremerton, Washington, on a

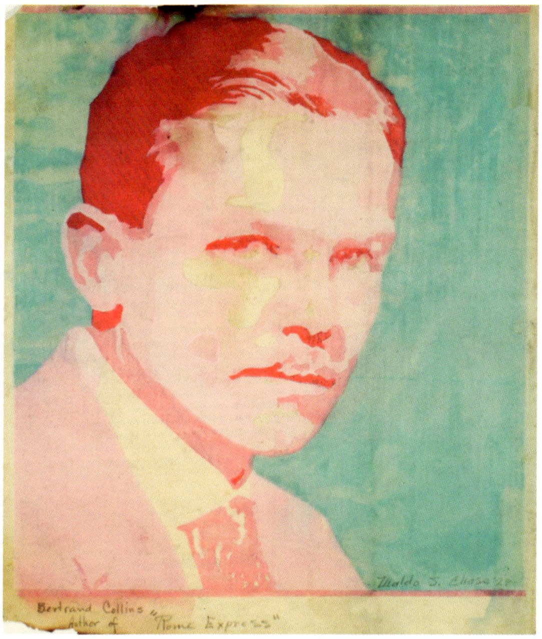

WALDO S. CHASE, *Bertrand Collins, Author of Rome Express*, 1928, color woodblock print, 14 ¼ x 12 in. Private collection

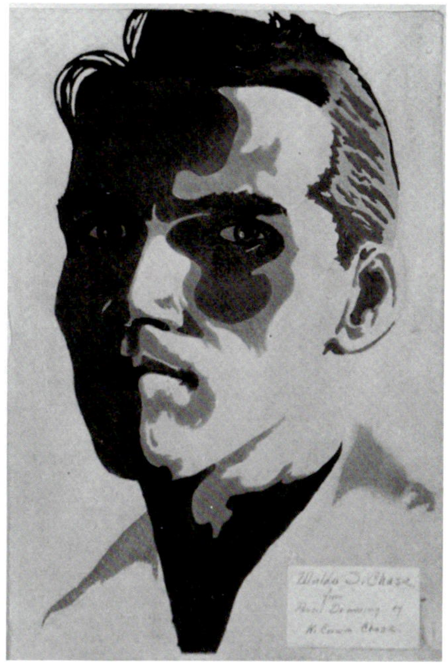

WALDO S. CHASE, photograph of a color woodcut made by Waldo Chase after a self-portrait of his brother Corwin (original ca. 1928) Photograph by Henry Blocher

Henry Blocher, "Waldo S. Chase," *Lewis & Clark Digital Collections*, http://digitalcollections.lclark.edu/items/show/5453 (accessed 5-18-2017). Courtesy of Lewis & Clark College Aubrey Watzek Library Special Collections & Archives

ferry with their tepee protruding from the car. They initially set up camp on the Skokomish Reservation, followed by campsites near Union, Clam Bay, and finally at Maples Camp, between the Sinclair Inlet and Hood Canal in Washington State.

Although both brothers preferred to work in isolation, they realized that they needed to participate to a degree in the local arts community. In September 1928, Waldo exhibited an untitled oil painting in the 14th Annual Exhibition of Northwestern Artists sponsored by the Seattle Fine Arts Society, at that time the region's most prominent venue. Both brothers began to develop good reputations in the art circles of the city while maintaining their peripatetic life throughout the region.

During this time, the brothers were frequent guests of their friend Orre Nelson Nobles (1897–1967), a wildly creative gay man who was the proprietor of Olympus Manor on Hood Canal. The Manor attracted creative artists of many disciplines from Seattle and Tacoma as well as national visitors, and became a nexus for nontraditional and individual cooperative living. Nobles, like the brothers' sister Marjorie, had graduated from Pratt Institute, he in 1922 from the School of Fine and Applied Arts with a diploma in "Teaching Training in Art."[7]

In 1928, Waldo created several woodblock print portraits of frequent visitors to Olympus Manor, including the writer Bertrand Collins (1893–1964), whose novel *Rome Express* was based on the life of Seattle heiress Guendolen Carkeek Plestcheeff (1892–1994). The print is highly unusual for a color print of that era. Its bold contrast of warm pink colors against the cool turquoise background and the subject's graphically realistic likeness now invite comparison with Andy Warhol's society portraits that would become cultural icons some forty years later. Wealthy local arts advocates like Plestcheeff and Tacoma's Erna Tilley (1887–1982) patronized the artists and were also drawn to their uninhibited lifestyles and bohemian disregard for tradition. The brothers were now maturing, yet neither had developed any significant relationships with women. Living out in the wilderness for most of the year may have decreased their chances of meeting someone special—or, perhaps because of their independent natures, they

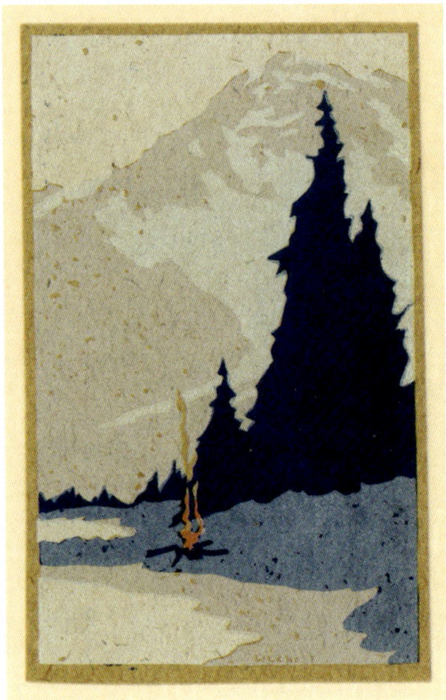

W. CORWIN CHASE, *Untitled*, ca. 1928, color woodblock print, 5 x 3 in. Collection of Thomas H. Wake

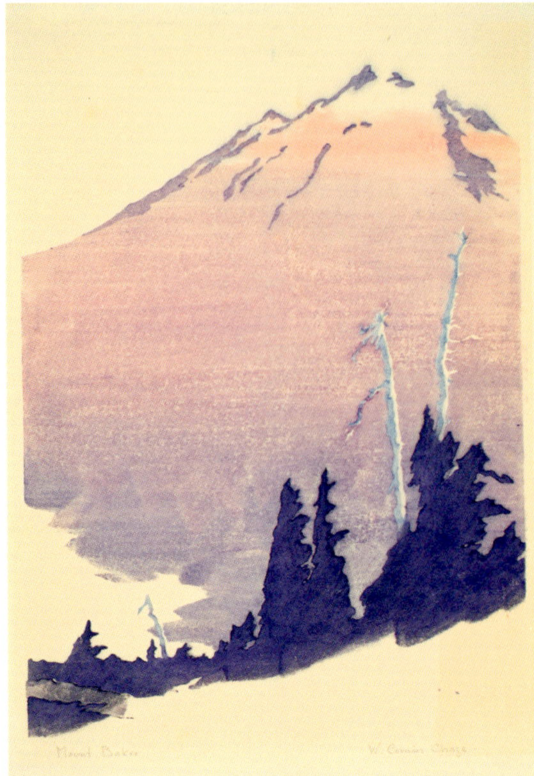

W. CORWIN CHASE, *Mount Baker*, ca. 1928, color woodblock print, 11 ½ x 8 ¼ in. Collection of John Impert

likely didn't have the urge to enter a conventional marriage or have children. In his memoir, Corwin wrote about falling in love with a woman twice his age (he was thirty-one at the time). The woman was divorced and had grown children but he pursued her with fervor. The relationship was not successful and he returned to the wilds with Waldo, renting a cabin nearby.

Corwin became increasingly more connected to his natural habitat and reveled in his self-identity as untamed and unrestrained. He wrote, "In this seclusion, I could give unlimited vent to my perpetual urge to enjoy the pleasures of nakedness."[8]

As a photographer, Corwin likely attended the popular international pictorialist photography exhibitions sponsored by the Seattle Camera Club. He apparently learned of the work of the Austrian Pictorialist Rudolf Koppitz (1884–1936), whose photographs had been exhibited with SCC and were reproduced in art journals of the period. Koppitz, like Corwin, was also uninhibited and featured his own nude body in a number of his photographic studies. Corwin had obviously seen his 1923 self-portrait showing him throwing a large rock into an abyss and used the photo as inspiration for an untitled work circa 1929.

Corwin had developed a long friendship with photographer/printmaker Virna Haffer (1899–1974), herself a member of the SCC, who grew up in the utopian society of Home, Washington, near Tacoma. Home residents were unorthodox, both politically and socially. They believed in exercising personal freedoms in living their lives. This included nontraditional sexual expression and unapologetic nudity. In late 1929, Haffer created a series of nude photographic studies of Corwin after she painted his body with concentric blue circles and depicted him as he envisioned himself, the unfettered wild man with aesthetic war paint. Corwin was enamored with the writings of Walt Whitman and would quote his famous passage from Section 52 of his poem "Song of Myself" in *Leaves of Grass*:

> I too am not a bit tamed—I too am untranslatable,
> I sound my barbaric yawp over the roofs of the
> world.

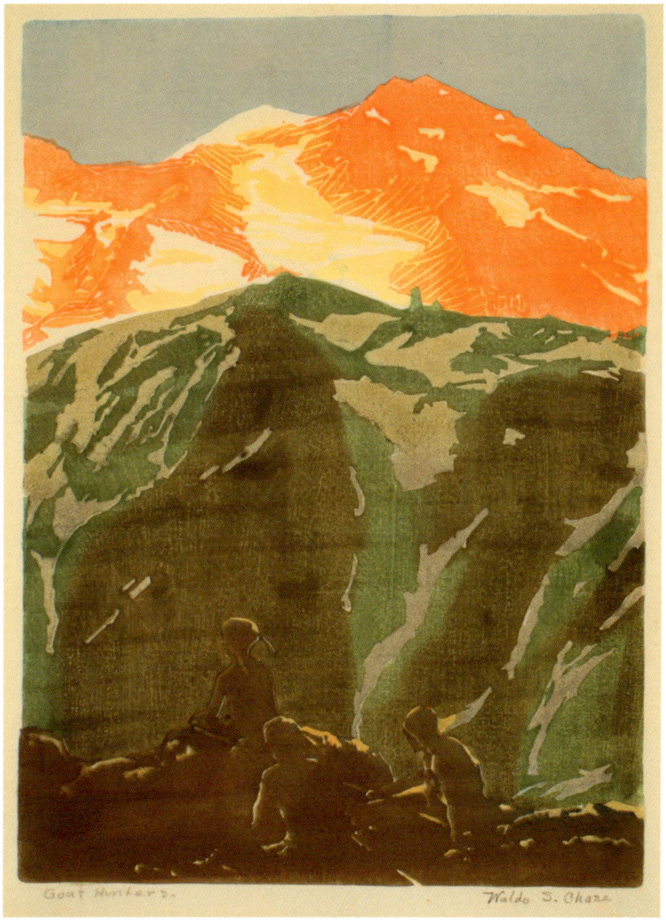

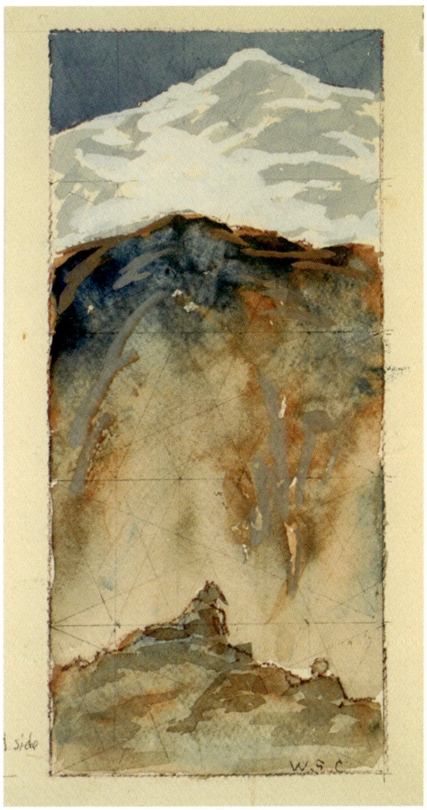

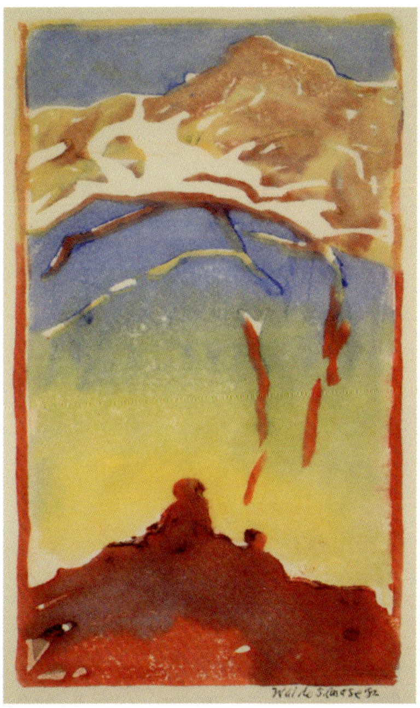

(top left) W. CORWIN CHASE, *Elephant Butte*, 1928, color woodblock print, 13 5/8 x 10 7/8 in. The Chase Place Collection

(top right) WALDO S. CHASE, *Goat Hunters*, ca. 1928, color woodblock print, 17 1/2 x 12 1/2 in. Collection of John Impert

(bottom left) WALDO S. CHASE, perspective study for *Goat Hunters*, ca. 1928, gouache and graphite, 12 3/4 x 5 1/2 in. Collection of John Impert

(bottom right) WALDO S. CHASE, *Goat Hunters*, 1982, color woodblock print, 8 1/4 x 4 5/8 in. Collection of John Impert

Waldo Chase made this small version of his earlier print to give away to his friends.

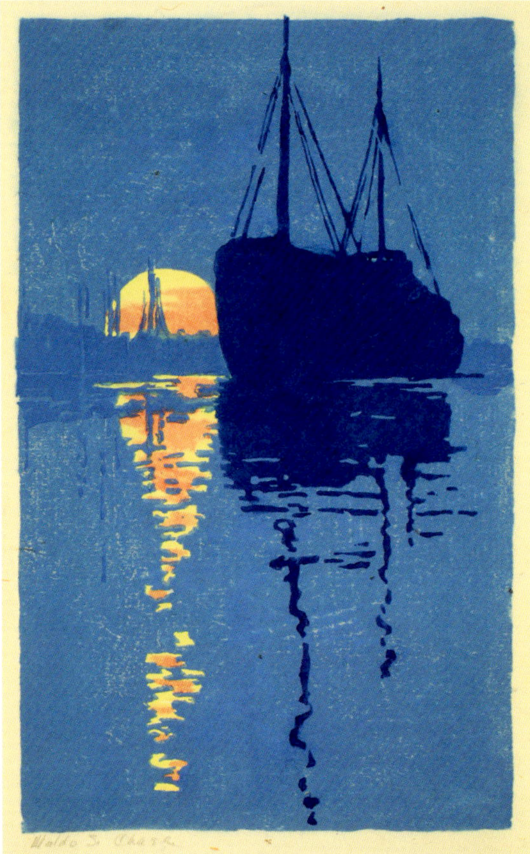

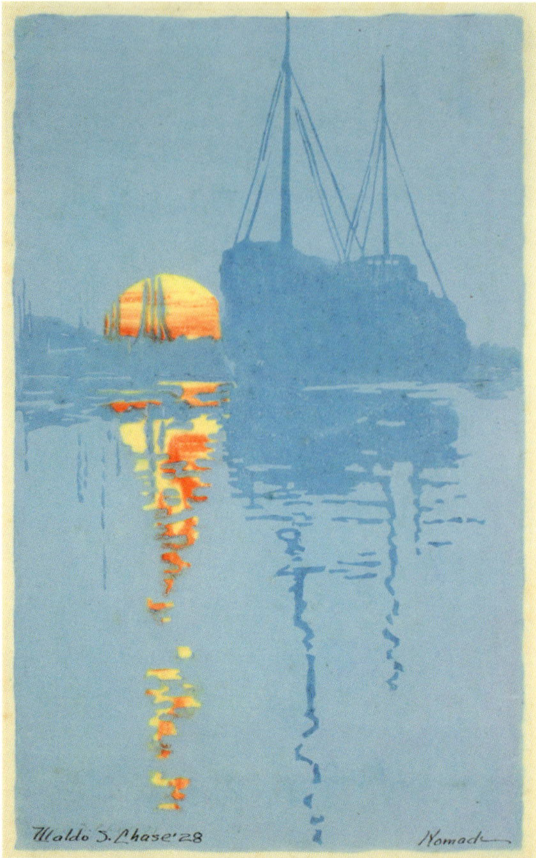

Waldo S. Chase '28
Nomad

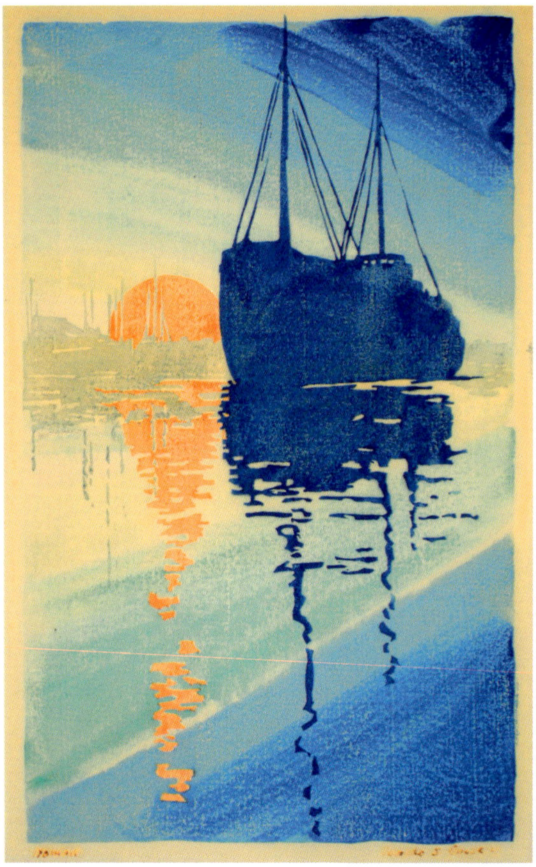

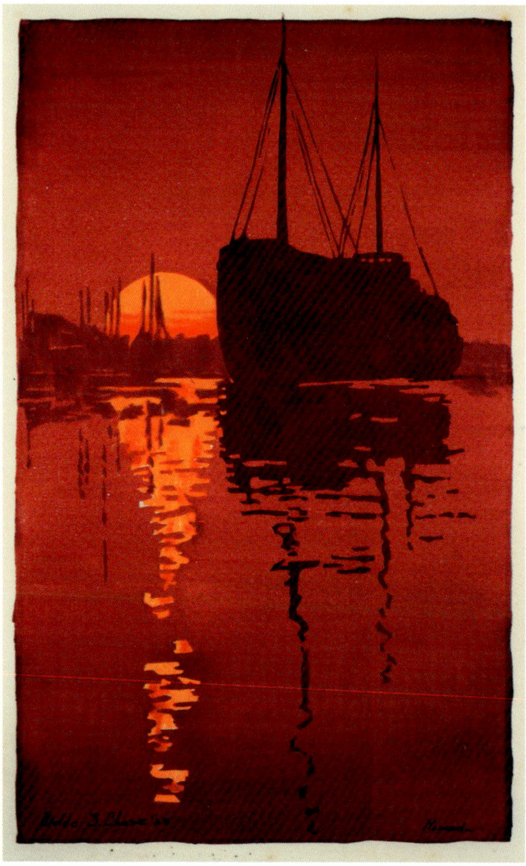

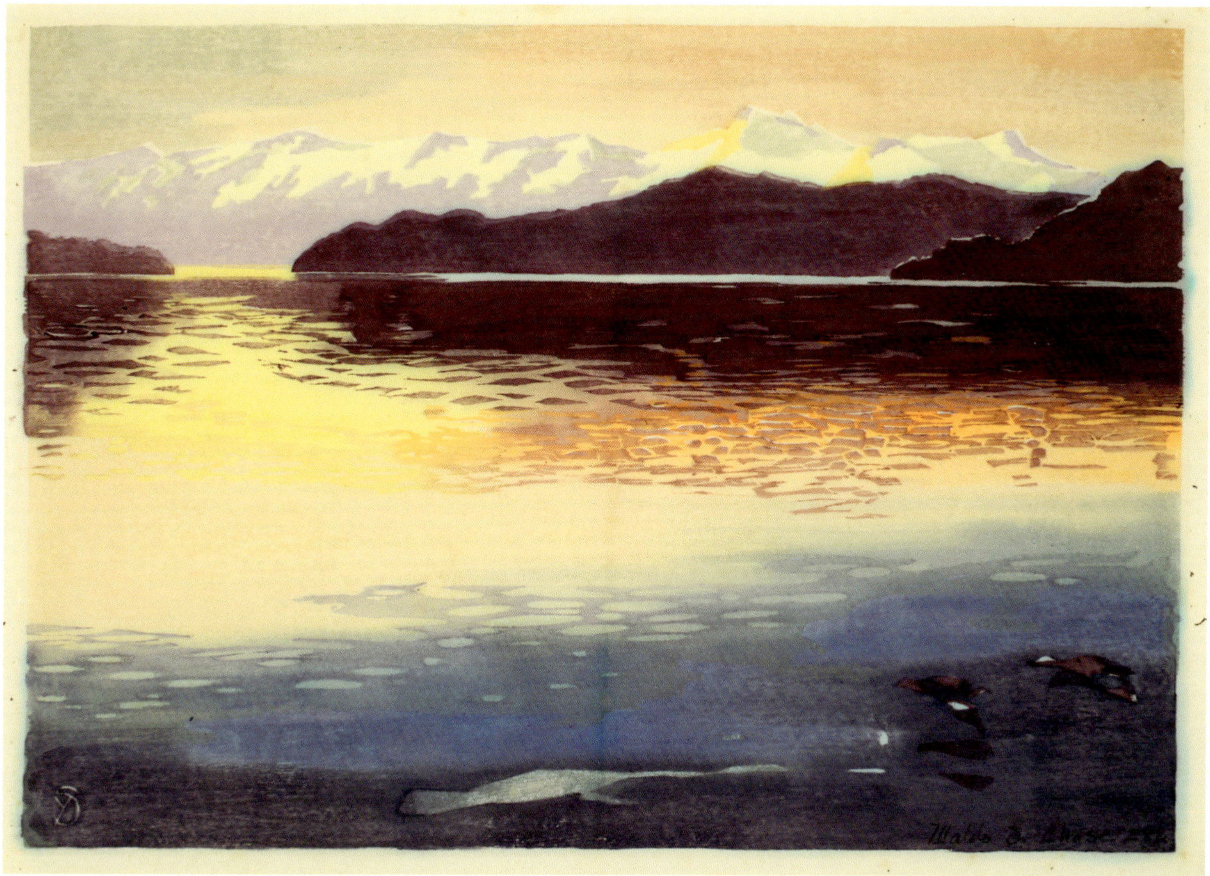

(opposite page, top left) WALDO S. CHASE, *Nomad*, 1928, color woodblock print, 12 ¼ x 7 ¼ in. Collection of John Impert

(opposite page, top right) WALDO S. CHASE, *Nomad*, 1928, color woodblock print, 12 ¼ x 7 ¼ in. Private collection

(opposite page, bottom left) WALDO S. CHASE, *Nomad*, 1928, color woodblock print with areas of monoprint inking, 12 x 7 ¼ in. Collection of John Impert

(opposite page, bottom right) WALDO S. CHASE, *Nomad*, 1928, color woodblock print, 12 ¼ x 7 ¼ in. Private collection

(above) WALDO S. CHASE, *Seymour Narrows*, 1928, color woodblock print. 10 x 14 in. Private collection

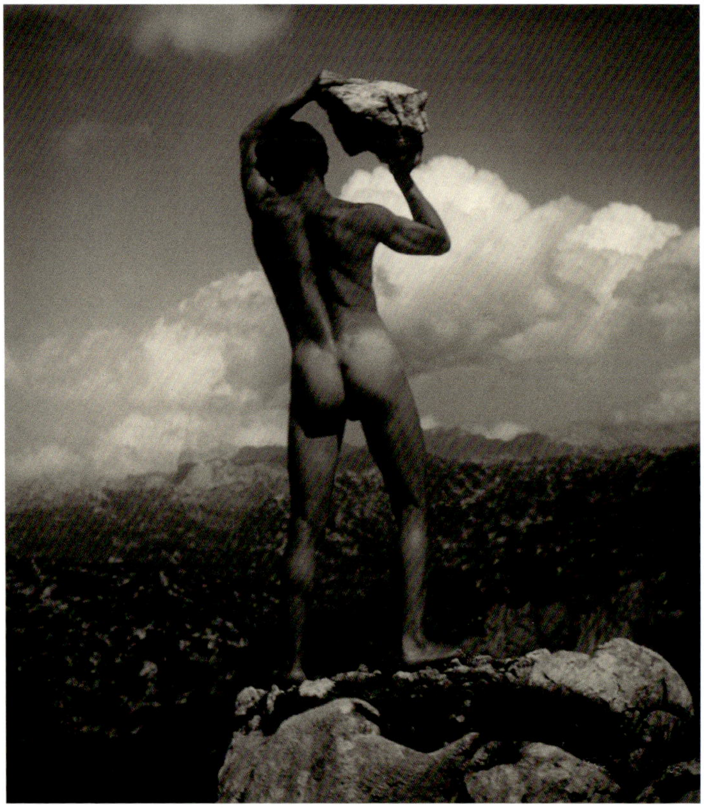

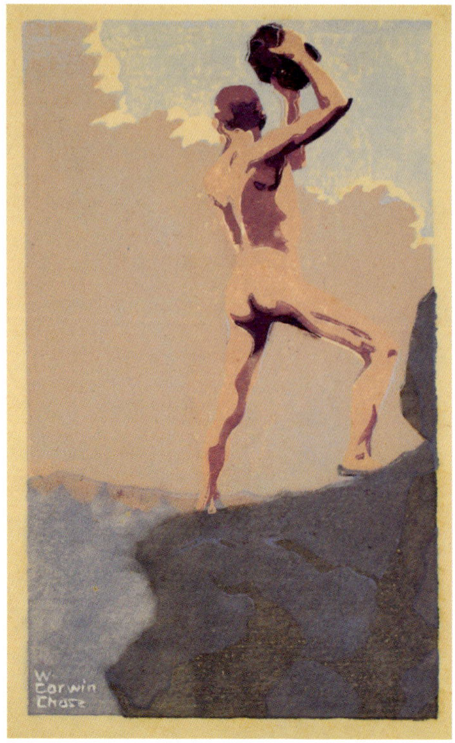

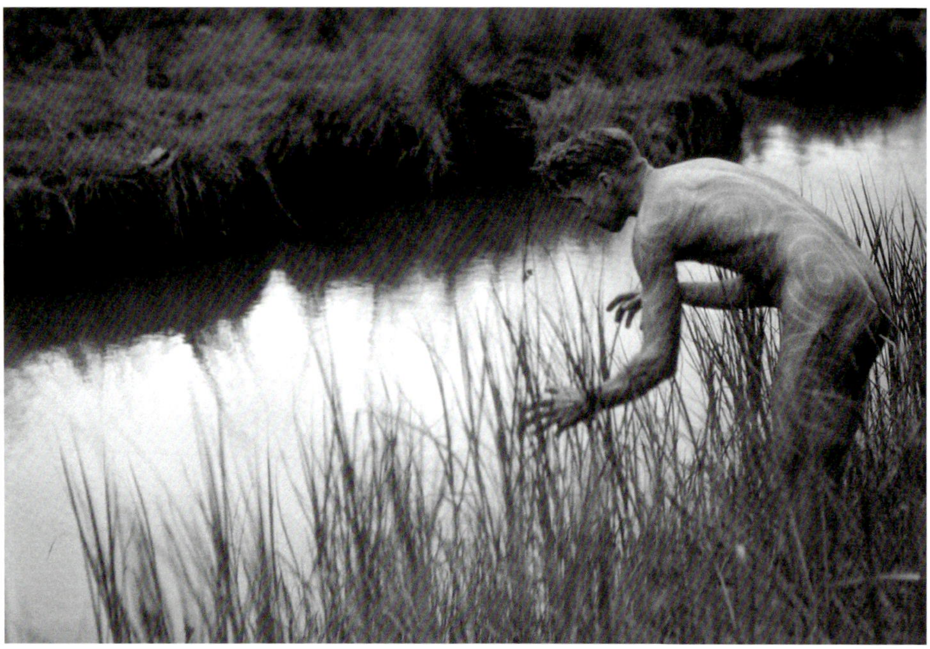

(top left) RUDOLF KOPPITZ (Austrian, 1884–1936), *The Stone-Thrower* (self portrait), 1923, gelatin silver print, 10 x 8 in. Copyright: Courtesy Galerie Johannes Faber, Austria

(bottom) VIRNA HAFFER (1899–1974), Corwin Chase, 1929, Scanned from the original negative. Collection of the Washington State Historical Society, gift of the estate of Virna Haffer 1974.35.1145.9. Scanned file restored by Tod Gangler

(top right) W. CORWIN CHASE, *Untitled*, ca. 1928, color woodblock print, 8 ¾ x 5 in. Collection of John Impert

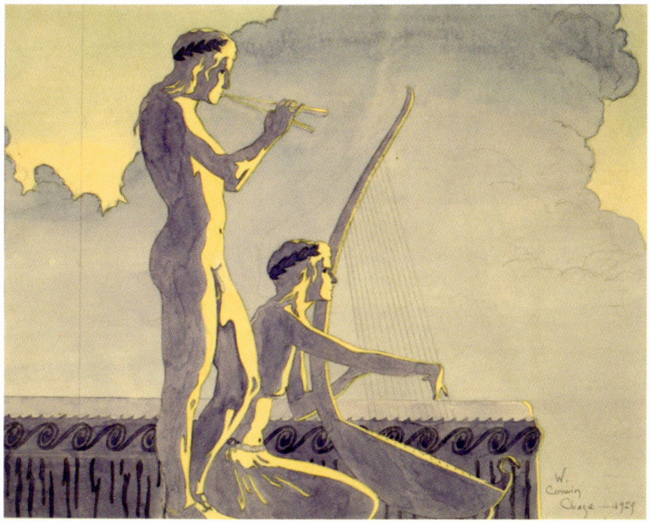

W. CORWIN CHASE, Study for *Orpheus*, 1929, watercolor, 11 ½ x 14 5⁄16 in. The Chase Place Collection

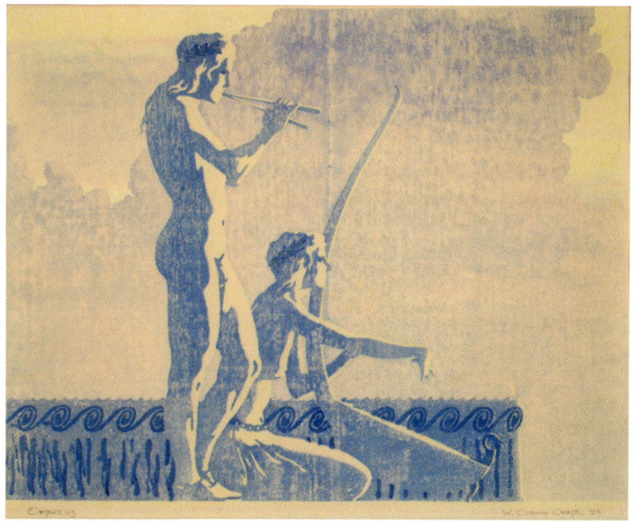

W. CORWIN CHASE, *Orpheus*, 1929, color woodblock print, 11 ½ x 14 5⁄16 in. The Chase Place Collection

Corwin's love of the human figure was now starting to be reflected in his subject matter. This can be seen in his watercolor and woodblock print titled *Orpheus* of 1929. Perhaps the inclusion of nude figures inspired Waldo's print titled *Clallam*, from the same period. This print incorporates the nude silhouette of a young woman sitting in a Chinook-style canoe. The canoe depicted in the print was the cedar dugout moored at Olympus Manor on Hood Canal. Orre Nobles had brought the vessel from Tatoosh Island on the Olympic Peninsula and incorporated it into his multicultural manor. The canoe is depicted again in Waldo's 1927 print *Jervis Inlet,* and once more in the 1934 print, *Ko-Ko-Bish*.

Returning to his preference for landscape subjects, Corwin reflected on the need for creating some new challenges in his work.

> I had resolved in my mind some changes in my method of printing. The largest set of blocks I had ever made were all ready for the first trial print. This design was an alpine landscape about seventeen by twelve inches: a picture of Mount Rainier with the pink afterglow of sunset, seen from Spray Park. There were some thirty colors, requiring twenty-nine blocks, and it had taken a solid month to carve. I now proposed to print this most difficult design by means of my revised method. It took me four days to prepare the thirty required colors in covered bottles, to print samples of these colors on small strips of paper comparing them carefully with the original design and with each other. The fifth day came and all was made ready. This was to be my largest print. I was working in my big tepee for the first time and the idea was to do it in the Japanese fashion, not on a high table, but close to the floor. So I sat on a cushion and worked on the tops of chests, in front and on either side of me. The printing paper, a Japanese hand-made (Hosho) paper, was cut to size and dampened (the night before) evenly with

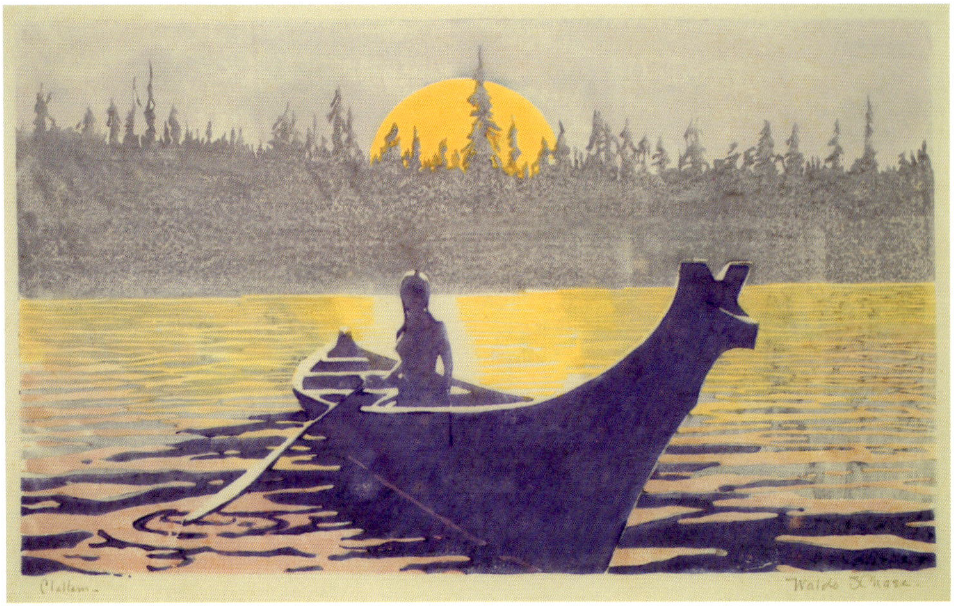

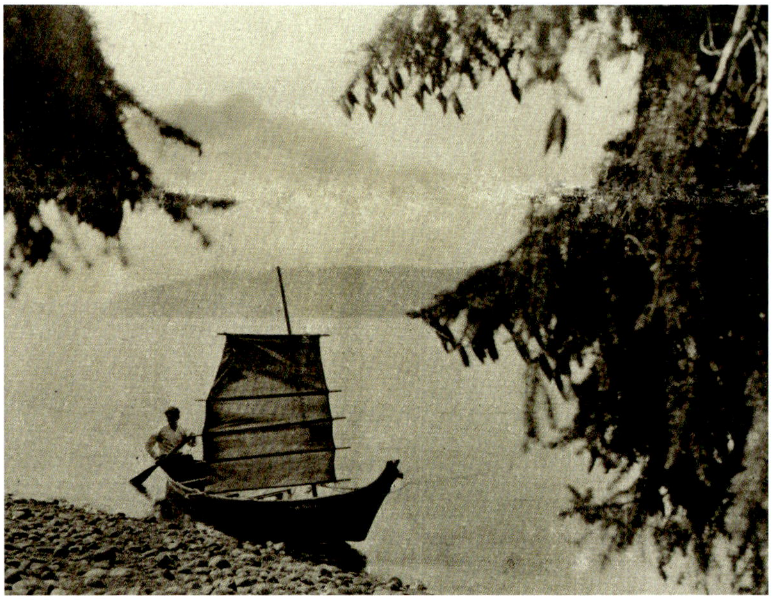

(top) WALDO S. CHASE, *Clallam*, ca. 1929, color woodblock print, 8 x 13 in. Collection of John Impert

(bottom) Orre Nobles in the dugout used for at least three of the Chase brothers prints. Nobles sometimes equipped the canoe with a Japanese Junk style sail, reflecting his interest in merging cultures. *The Seattle Daily Times* photogravure pictorial section, June 1, 1924. The Martin-Zambito Archive

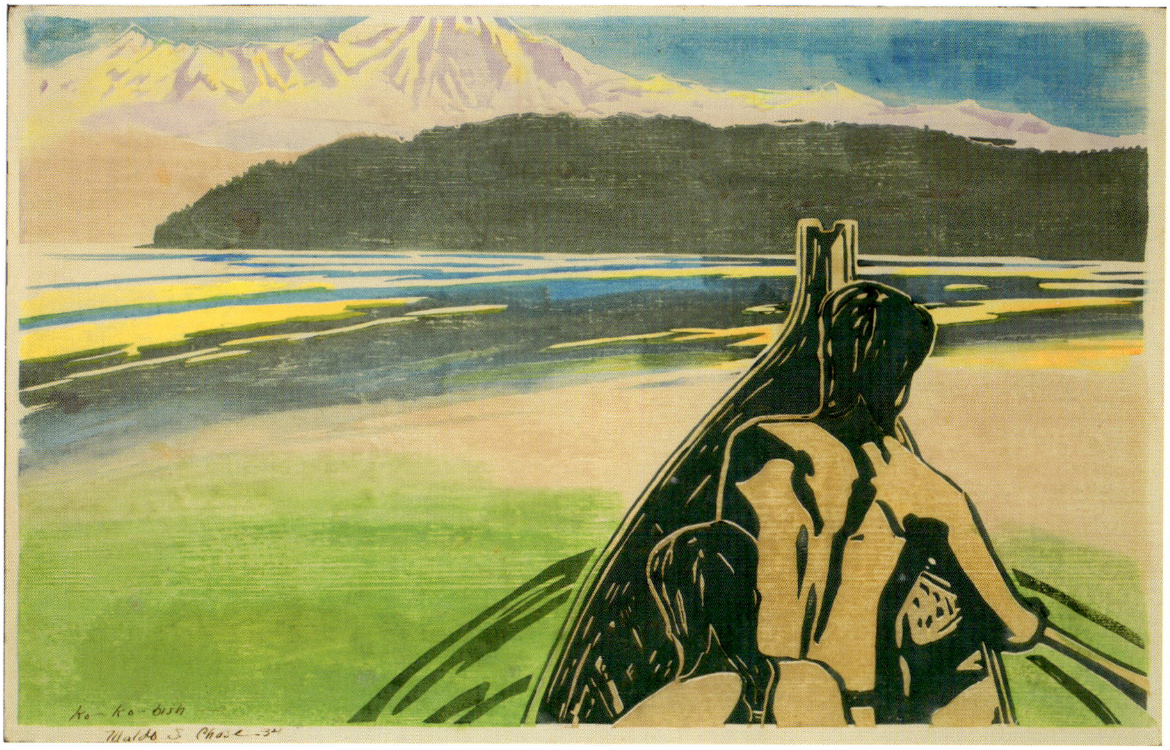

WALDO S. CHASE, *Ko-Ko-Bish*, 1934, color woodblock print, 12 ½ x 19 ½ in.
Collection of John Impert

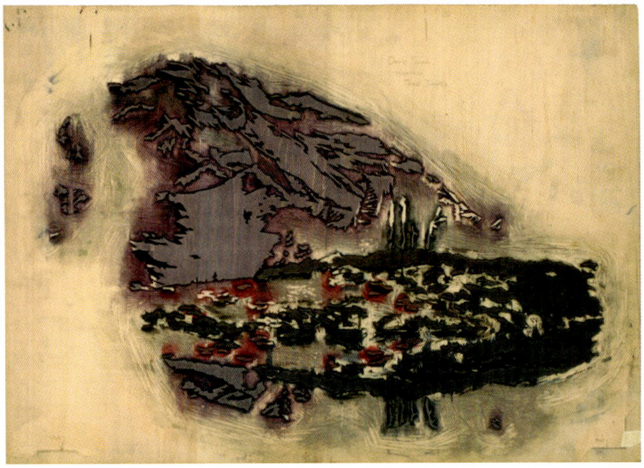

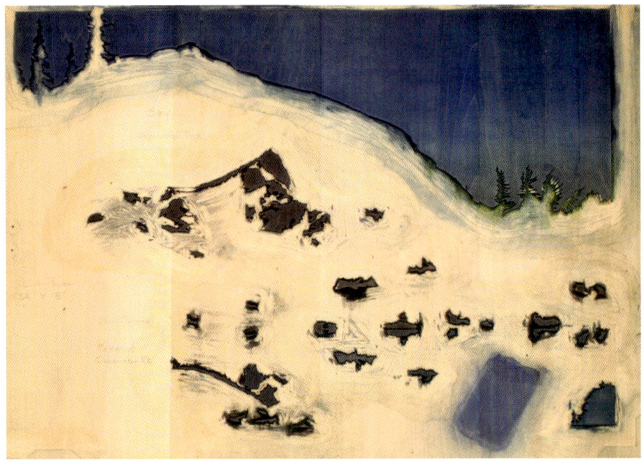

Two of the twenty-nine blocks used to create the print *Tak-Hoo-Ma*, 1929. The Chase Place Collection

> a sponge and placed between two pieces of glass to remain in a uniformly damp condition. I prepared the rice paste of a creamy consistency, using a finely ground rice flour. I assembled blocks, "damper" (or dampener) paints, water, brushes, sponge, Saturday Evening Post sheets to protect the back of the print while being rubbed with the baren. The pressure of printing is applied with the baren by rubbing; no printing press is needed . . . The print was titled "Tak-hoo-ma", a variation of Ta-co-bish or Duck-a-bish, all Indian names for the great volcanic mountain that dominates the Puget Sound landscape.[9]

With their technical skill refined and with mounting recognition, the brothers continued to promote their work and give demonstrations throughout the region. Corwin's work was featured at the F. Denks Art Gallery at 157 West 57th Street in New York City and then, just weeks after the stock market crash in October 1929, Waldo had a solo exhibition of watercolors and prints at the Seattle Art Institute. During the run of the popular exhibition, he gave demonstrations and lectures, but the economic situation was beginning to spiral downward. Waldo persevered and had his work shown in two prominent venues in the early years of the Depression. The first was held at Harry Hartman's Bookstore in downtown Seattle in 1930. Hartman was a remarkable force in Seattle's cultural history. Besides offering books, he consistently exhibited graphic arts and photography and also brought national traveling print exhibitions to town. The store regularly featured the Chase brothers' prints over the years as well. The fact that Hartman was blind made his business and support all the more intriguing.

In 1932, Waldo held another exhibition, this time at the Women's Century Club in Seattle, an alliance of professional women who supported important social causes and the arts.

The new decade would usher in several changes into the brother's lives. In 1930, as Corwin was living in his

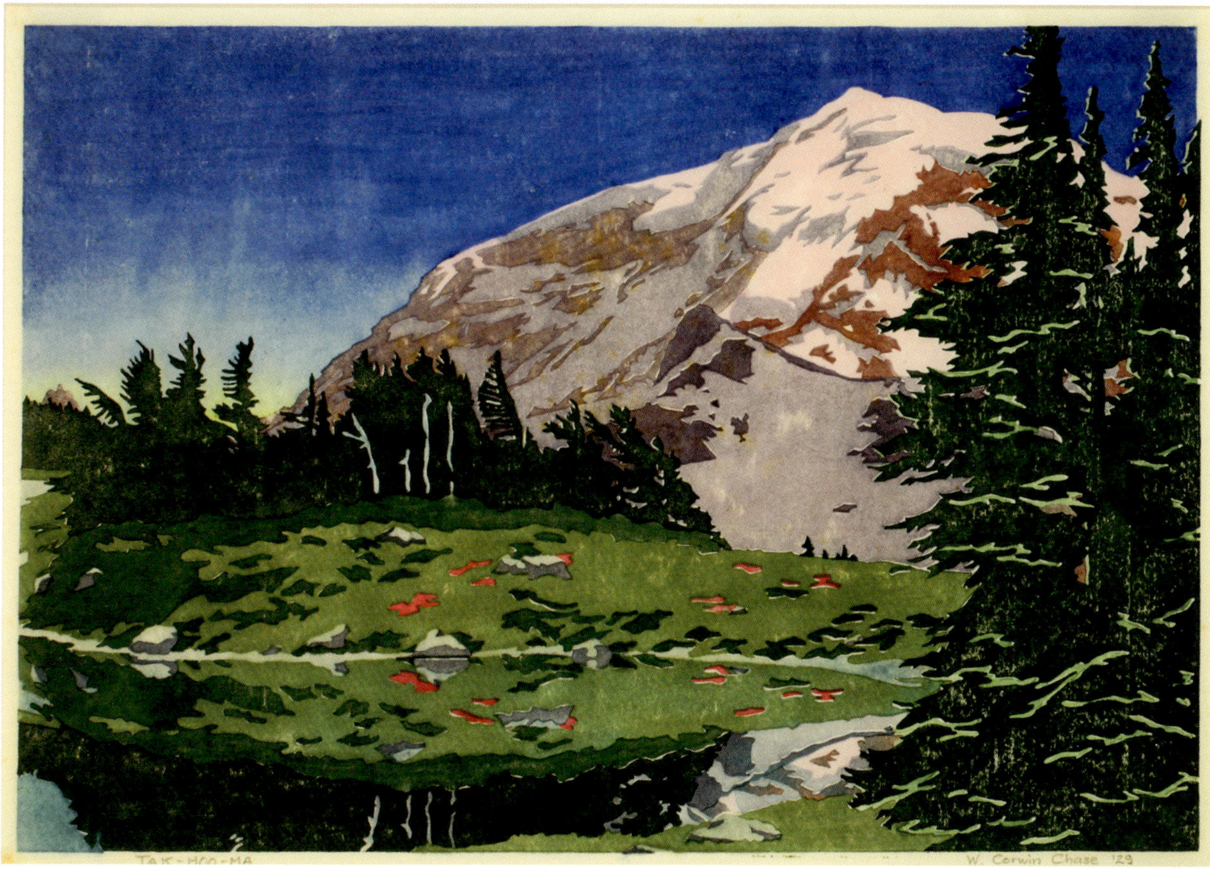

W. CORWIN CHASE, *Tak-Hoo-Ma*, 1929, color woodblock print,
11 15/16 x 16 9/16 in. The Chase Place Collection

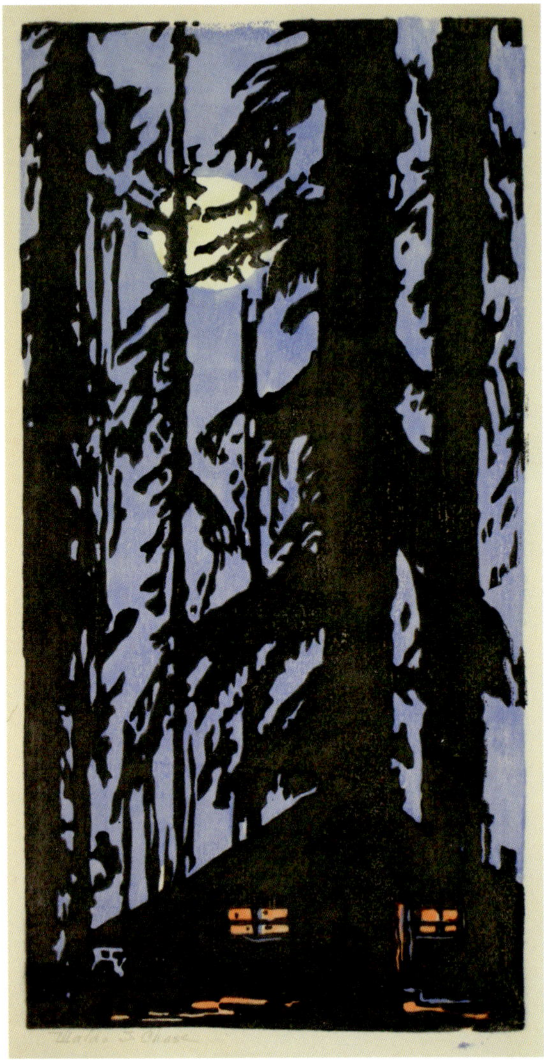

(left) WALDO S. CHASE, Untitled, ca. 1929, color woodblock print, 15 x 7 ¼ in. Collection of John Impert

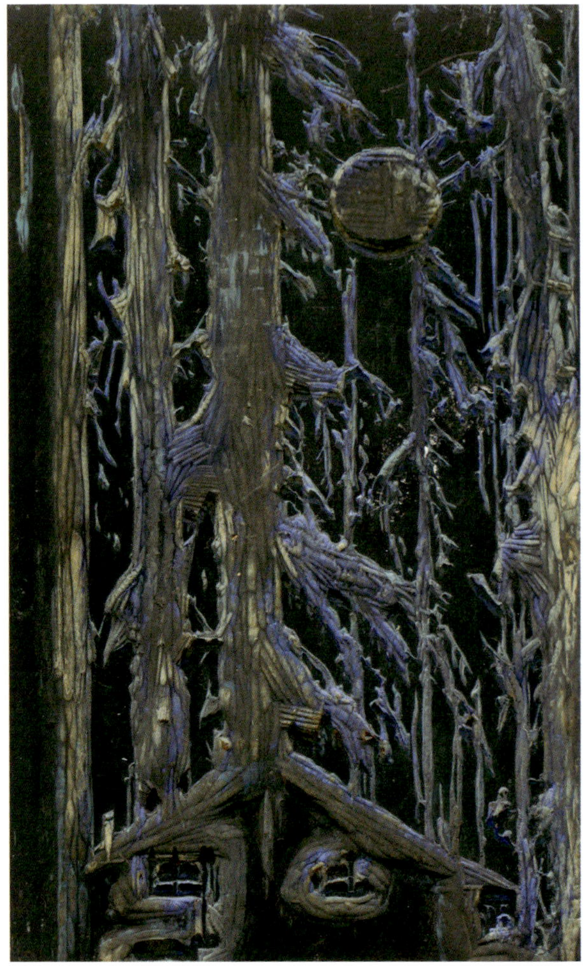

(right) One of the blocks used to create the untitled ca. 1929 print by Waldo Chase.

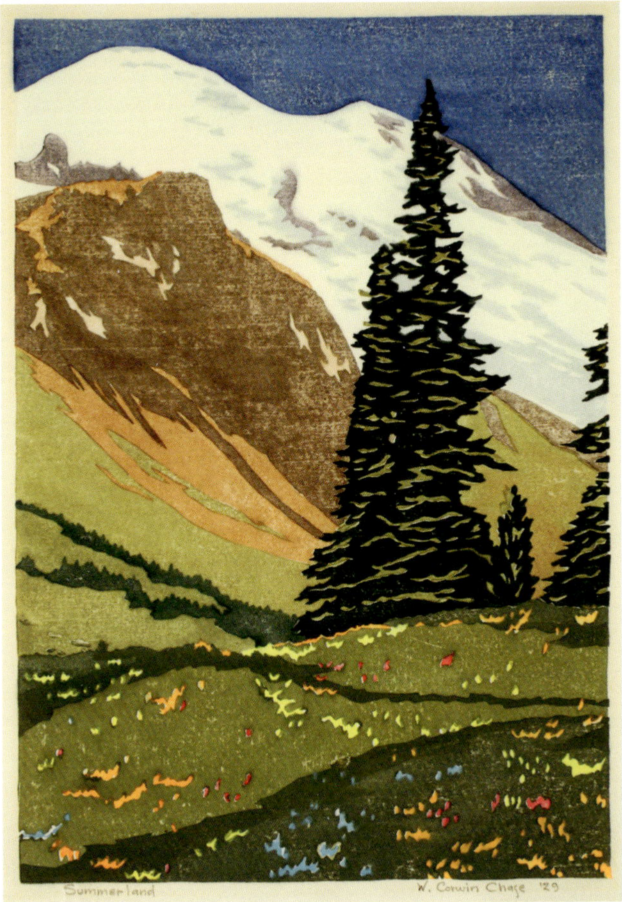

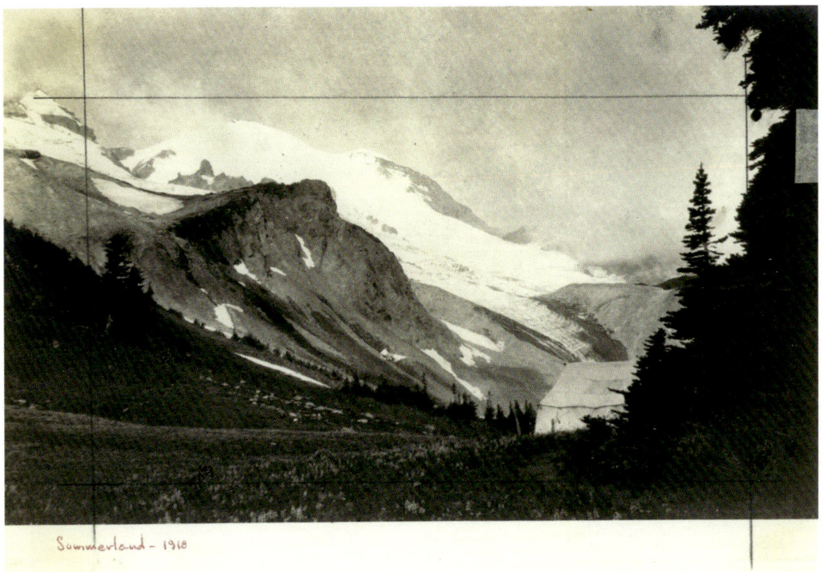

(top) W. CORWIN CHASE, *Summerland*, 1929, color woodblock print, 12 ½ x 8 ⅜ in. Private collection

(bottom) Corwin Chase's photograph of Summerland near Mount Rainier from 1918, used as the basis for his 1929 print. The Chase Place Collection

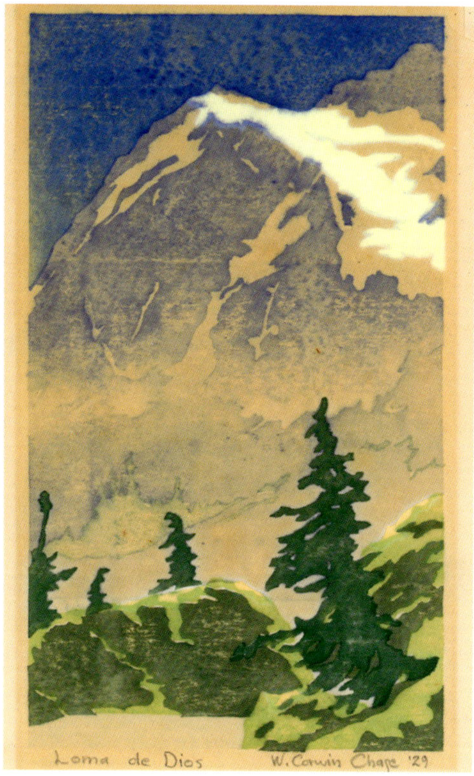

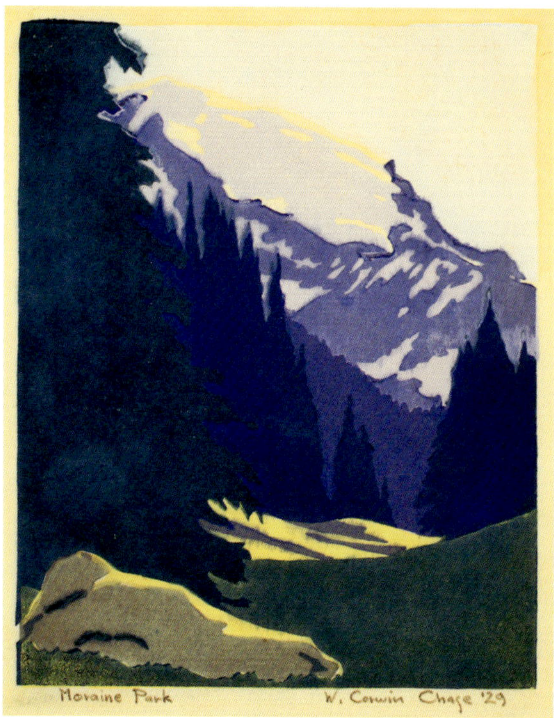

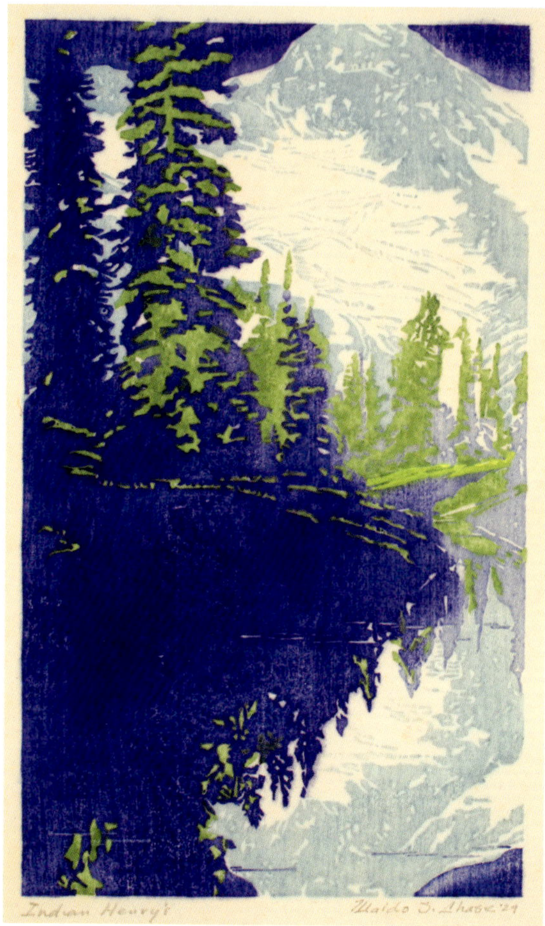

(top left) W. CORWIN CHASE, *Loma de Dios*, 1929, color woodblock print, 8 x 4 ½ in. Collection of Thomas H. Wake

(bottom left) W. CORWIN CHASE, *Moraine Park*, 1929, color woodblock print, 6 ⅝ x 5 in. Collection of John Impert

(right) WALDO S. CHASE, *Indian Henry's*, 1929, color woodblock print, 12 ½ x 7 in. Private collection

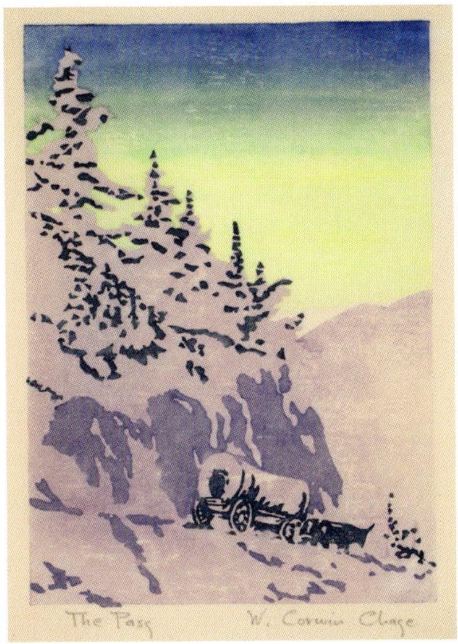

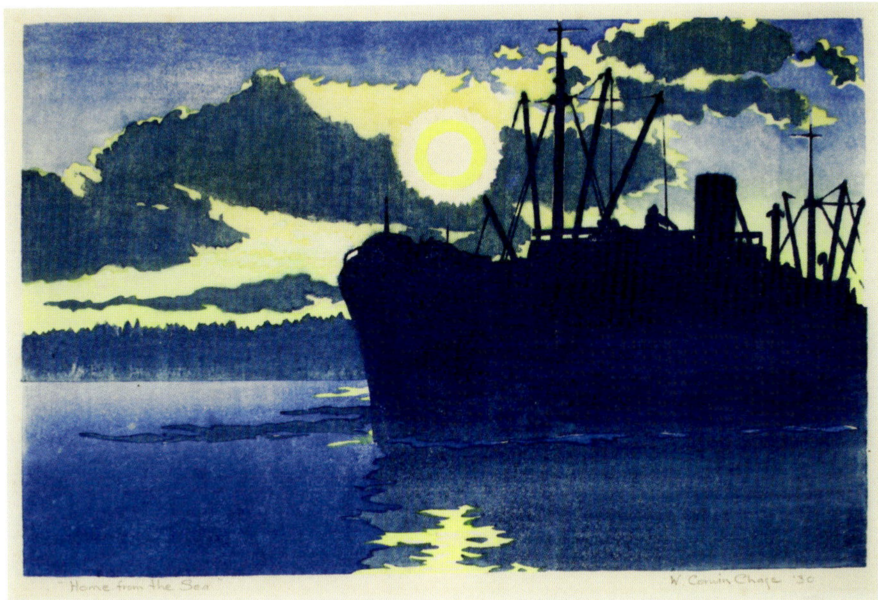

W. CORWIN CHASE, *The Pass*, 1930, color woodblock print, 6⅞ x 4⅝ in. Collection of John Impert

W. CORWIN CHASE, *Home From the Sea*, 1930, color woodblock print, 8 x 12¼ in. Collection of John Impert

tepee at Portage Point, he was commissioned to create a woodblock frontispiece for the book *North-Westward* by T. M. Pelly, published by Lowman & Hanford Co., the Seattle art store that had sold their work for years. The print, titled *The Pass*, ignited a contentious battle between Pelly, Corwin, and the publisher. Although he fulfilled his commission, it was not without great difficulty. The experience would cause Corwin to dismiss any other future commissions.

He returned to the tepee that he had set up at Twanoh State Park and had a few unsuccessful, short-lived relationships. Frustrated, he spent the summer at Olympus Manor, where Waldo had set up his tepee and was creating prints that their friend Orre helped them sell. Waldo and a friend began promoting camping tours of the region where tepees would be set up and the attendants would be guided by the "Vagabond Artist." Corwin, meanwhile, met a free-spirited young woman named Dorothy "Dot" Blodgett and they were married by the end of the year.

Following their marriage, Corwin and Dot moved temporarily to Hawaii. Corwin continued to make prints and was invited to have a solo exhibition at the Honolulu Academy of Arts in 1931. When Corwin and his wife returned to Seattle in 1933, he and Waldo became involved with President Roosevelt's New Deal art program, under the Public Works of Art Project (PWAP). This government-sponsored program paid artists to produce work that could be used for hospitals, schools, libraries, and other public buildings. The brothers primarily used their older blocks, which they reprinted, with the exception of a few Hawaiian subjects made by Corwin during his recent stay.

One of Corwin's outstanding prints, *Summerland*, was part of a large national exhibition of PWAP art held at the Corcoran Gallery in Washington, DC, in the spring of 1934.

The brothers continued to live in cabins and tepees on the Hood Canal near Union, Washington. They built their homes entirely by hand with fir poles and hand-split cedar shakes.

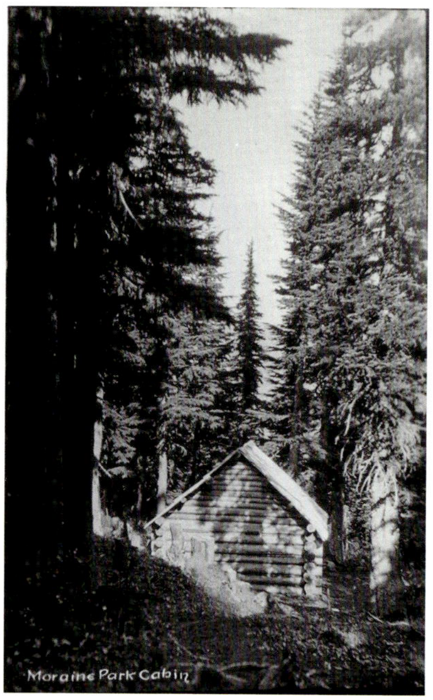

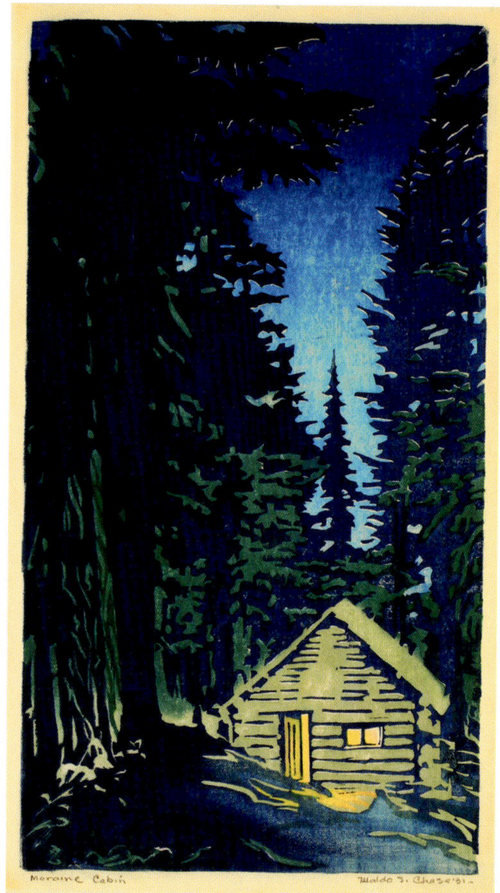

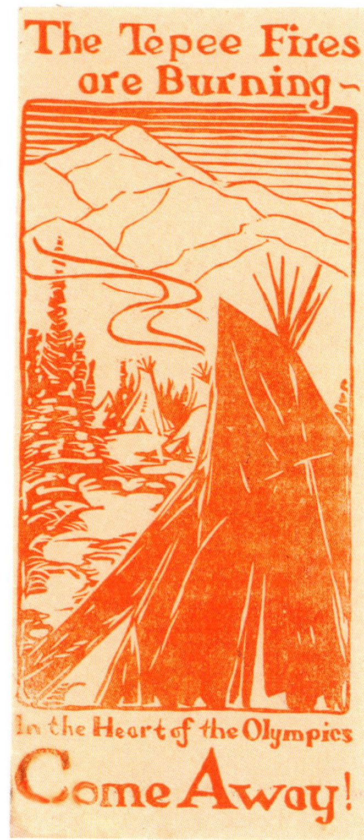

(left) W. CORWIN CHASE. *Moraine Park Cabin*, 1929, gelatin silver print, 5 x 3 ⅛ in. Private collection

(center) WALDO S. CHASE, *Moraine Cabin*, 1931, color woodblock print, 14 x 7 ⅜ in. Collection of the Len Braarud Estate

(right) WALDO C. CHASE, *The Tepee Fires Are Burning*, 1930, promotional brochure for camping tour led by Waldo Chase and Don Norlin, The Martin-Zambito Archive

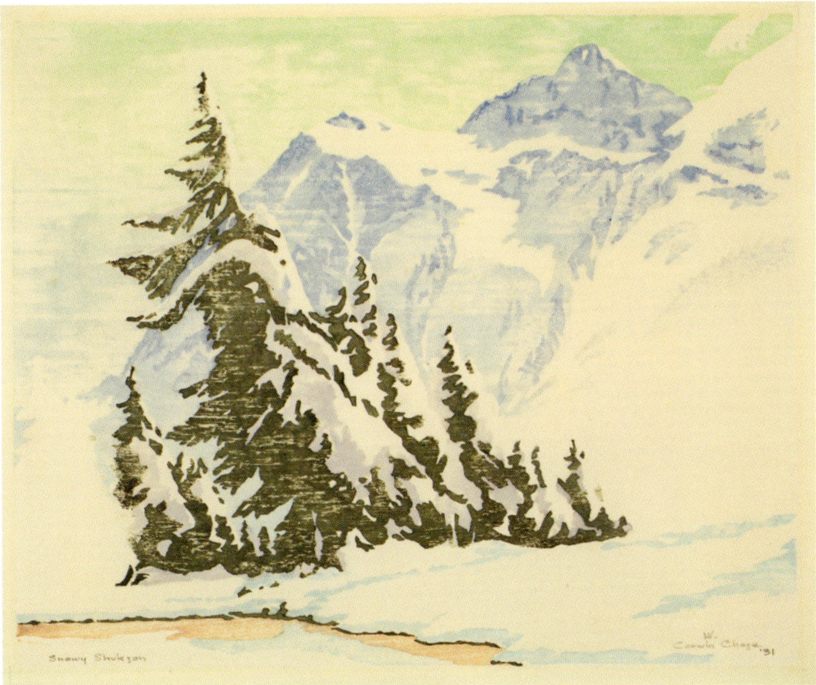

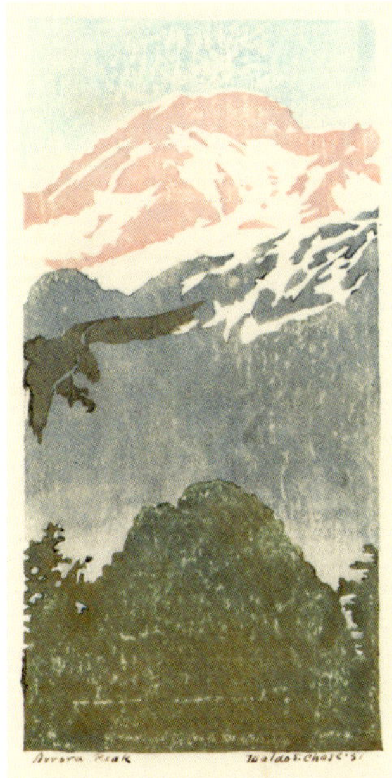

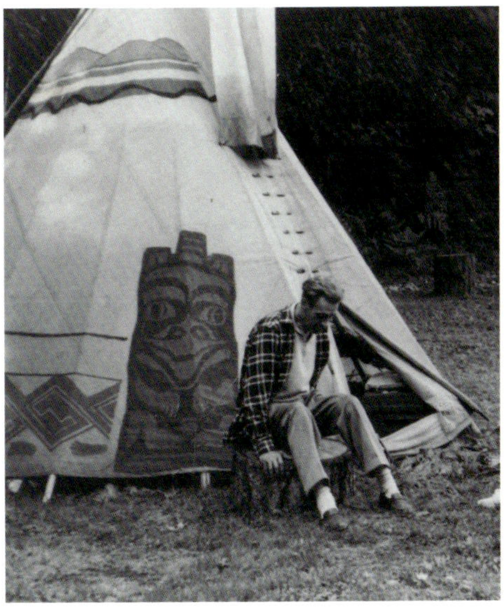

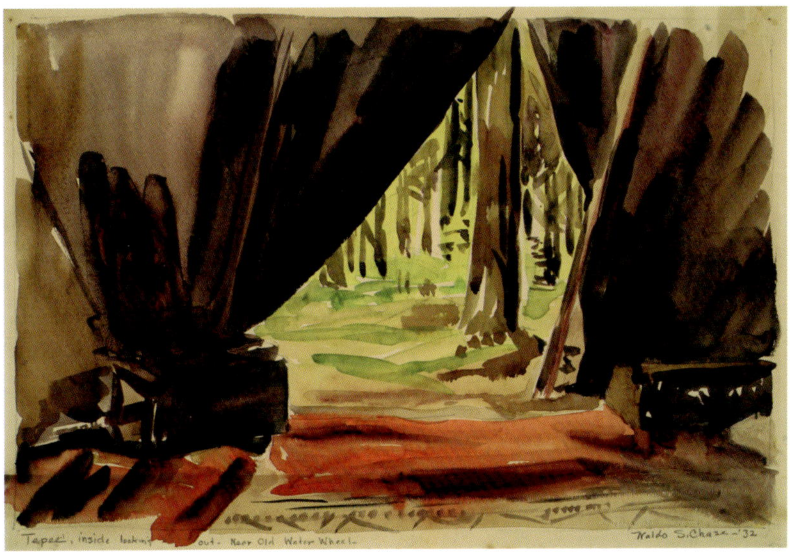

(top left) W. CORWIN CHASE, *Snowy Shuksan*, 1931, color woodblock print, 10 3/4 x 13 in. Collection of Thomas H. Wake

(bottom left) Waldo Chase by his tepee, ca. 1950. Photographer unknown. The Martin-Zambito Archive

(top right) WALDO S. CHASE, *Aurora Peak*, 1931, color woodblock print, 7 1/2 x 3 5/8 in. Private collection

(bottom right) WALDO S. CHASE, *Tepee, Inside Looking Out – Near Old Water Wheel*, 1932, watercolor, 10 x 14 in. Private collection

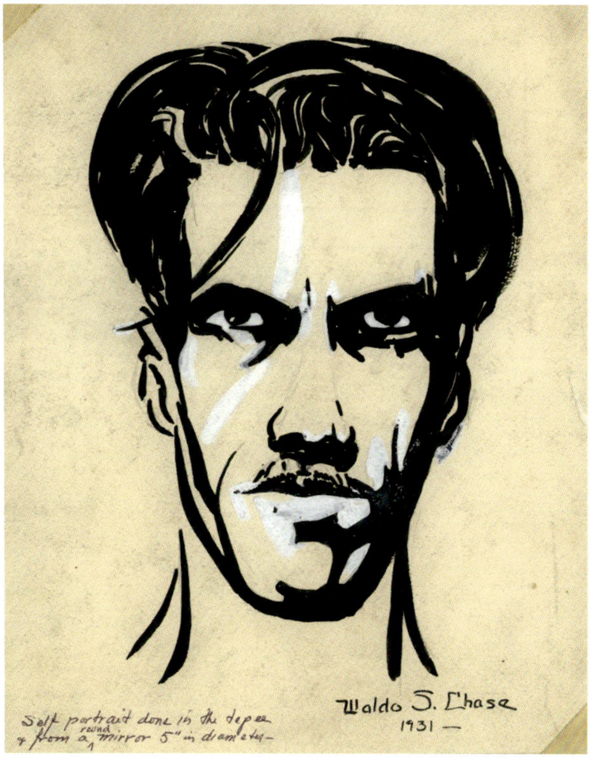

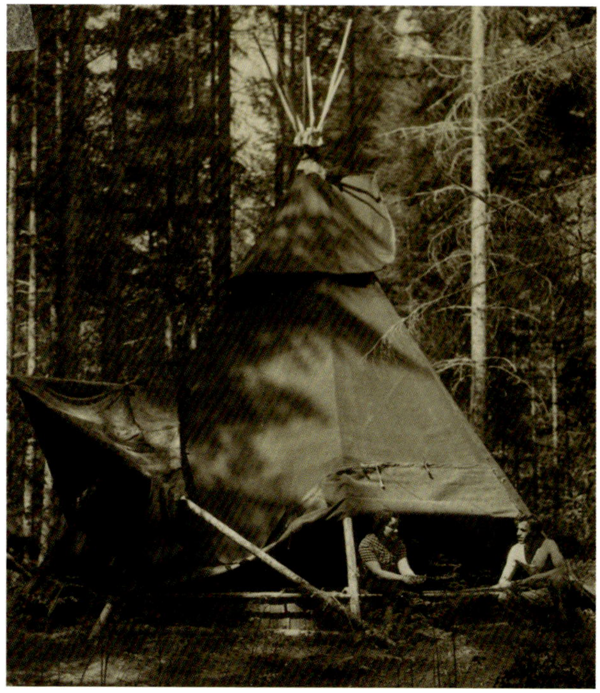

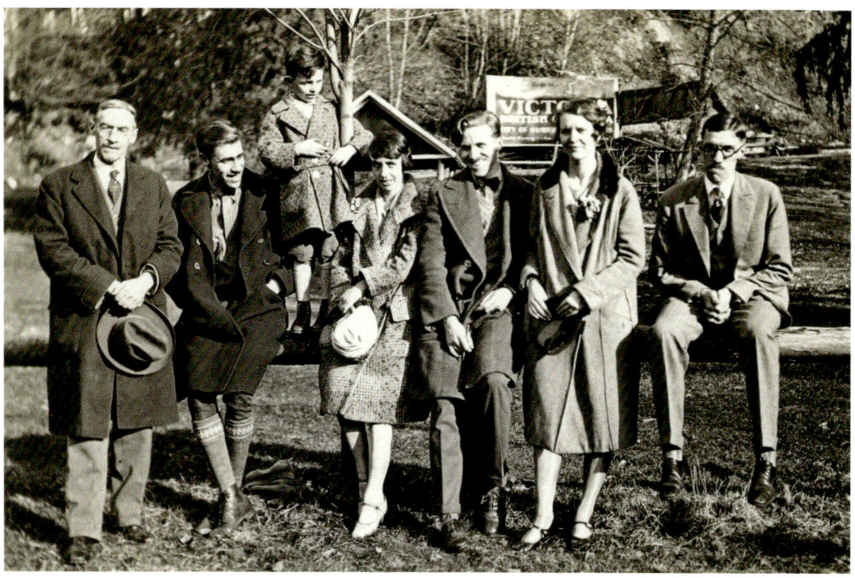

(top left) WALDO S. CHASE, *Self Portrait Done in the Tepee from a Round Mirror 5" in Diameter*, 1931, ink and gouache, 11 x 8½ in. Private collection

(top right) Corwin Chase and his wife Dorothy by his tepee, ca. 1935. Photograph courtesy of the Chase Place Collection

(bottom) Chase family photo, ca. 1935. From left: Wendell "Pa" Chase, Waldo Chase, Carter Gilleland (Marjorie's son) Marjorie Chase Gilleland, Corwin Chase, Corwin's wife, Dorothy "Dot" Chase, and Philip "Brownie" Chase. Courtesy of Florence Gilleland Schieve

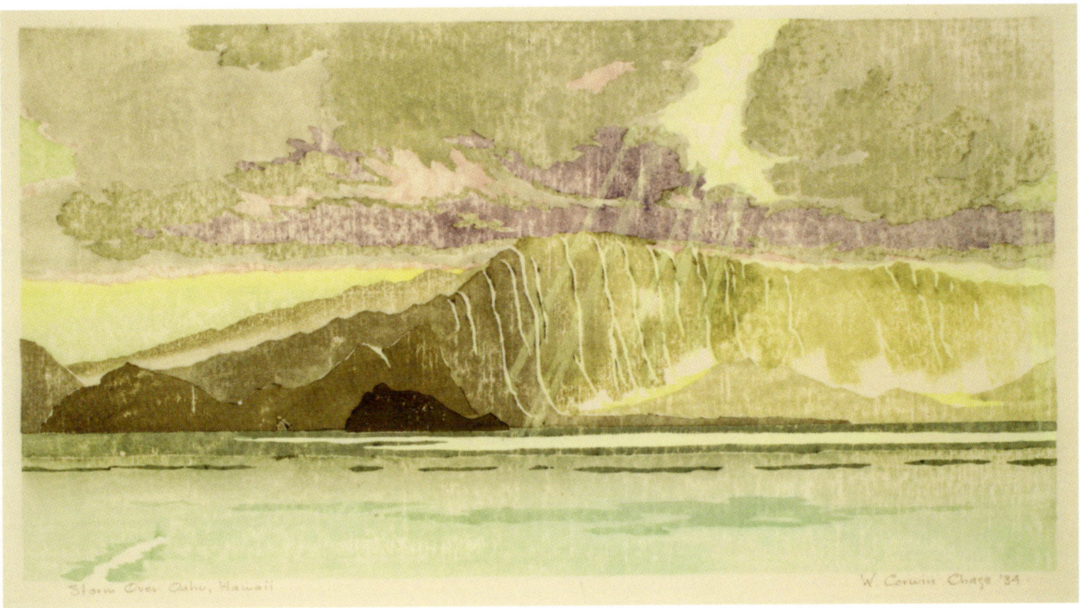

W. CORWIN CHASE, *Storm over Oahu, Hawaii*, 1934, color woodblock print, 7 ½ x 13 ⅞ in. Collection of John Impert

In 1935, Waldo married Helen Chard Engell of Olympia in "a primitive ritual midst towering fir trees of Hood Canal. . . . After the fire has been lighted by a child, wedding guests will be escorted to the circle of the blaze and there witness the ritual."[10] By the following year, both brothers were divorced. Although Corwin's breakup was amicable, Waldo's was far different. He would joke to his friends that there was a reason why his wife's name had "Hell" in it. He never remarried.

As the decade progressed, the brothers' print production began to decline drastically. Instead, they began working in other media like oil, pastel, and watercolor, while maintaining a simple existence with very little income. Corwin had a solo exhibition in 1936 at the Art Barn in Salt Lake City, Utah, and later at Seattle's Frederick & Nelson department store in 1938. Waldo continued to work and teach, but his output was diminishing.

When the United States' involvement in WWII began, the repercussions on the brothers' lives would be significant.

The Japanese papers and materials that had previously been easily accessible were no longer available, banned because of the war. Corwin joined the Army Air Corps Air Transport Command as a photographer, while Waldo, always a pacifist, became a conscientious objector, disdaining any type of violence and warfare. He joined Seattle's Church of the People, a nondenominational assembly that included members of all races and ages who were progressive both politically and socially. In 1942, he created a series of seven murals for the church and designed the accompanying brochure. He joined the Civilian Public Service Camps as artist-in-residence at the Waldport and Cascade Locks camps, both in Oregon. The camps were set up by the U.S. Government to offer an alternative for conscientious objectors who wanted to participate in contributing to society during the war years without engaging in military duty. He would also visit the Tule Lake Relocation Center in the Klamath Falls Basin in northern California, just south of the Oregon border, to teach art and craft related skills to the Japanese American internees.[11]

Waldo's life choices were not well received by his father who wrote about him in a 1944 letter to his daughter Marjorie:

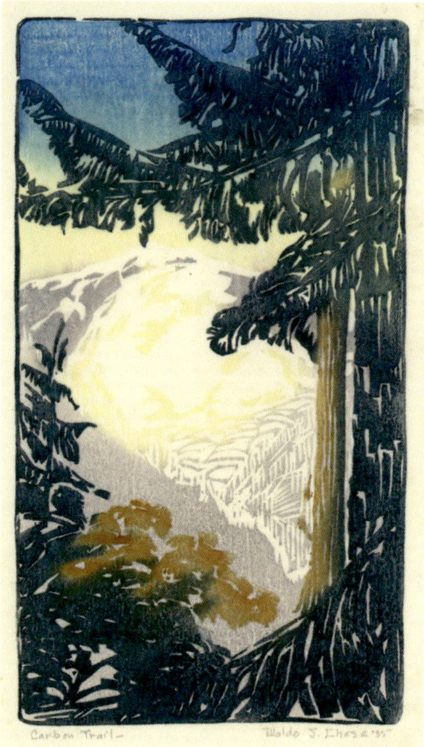

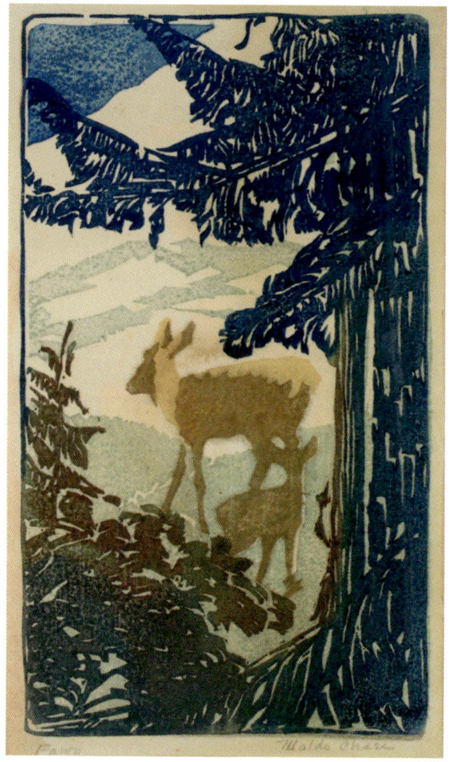

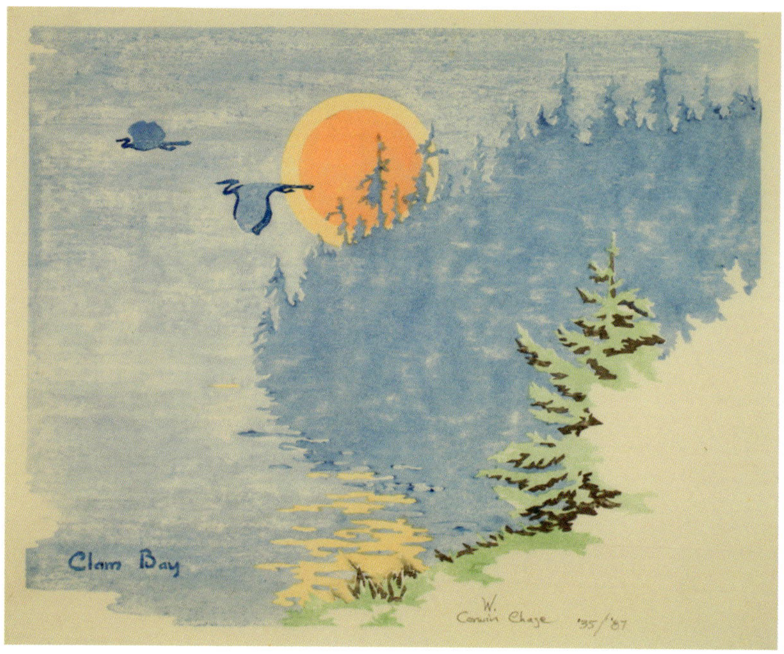

(top left) WALDO S. CHASE, *Carbon Trail*, 1935, color woodblock print, 8 ½ x 4 ¾ in. Private collection

(bottom) W. CORWIN CHASE, *Clam Bay*, 1935, re-struck in 1987, color woodblock print, 10 ½ x 12 ½ in. Collection of John Impert

(top right) WALDO S. CHASE, *Fawn*, ca. 1936, color woodblock print, 8 ⅝ x 4 ¾ in. Collection of John Impert.

For this proof, Waldo Chase utilized the block for *Carbon Trail* and carved additional blocks to include the fawns and changes to the background.

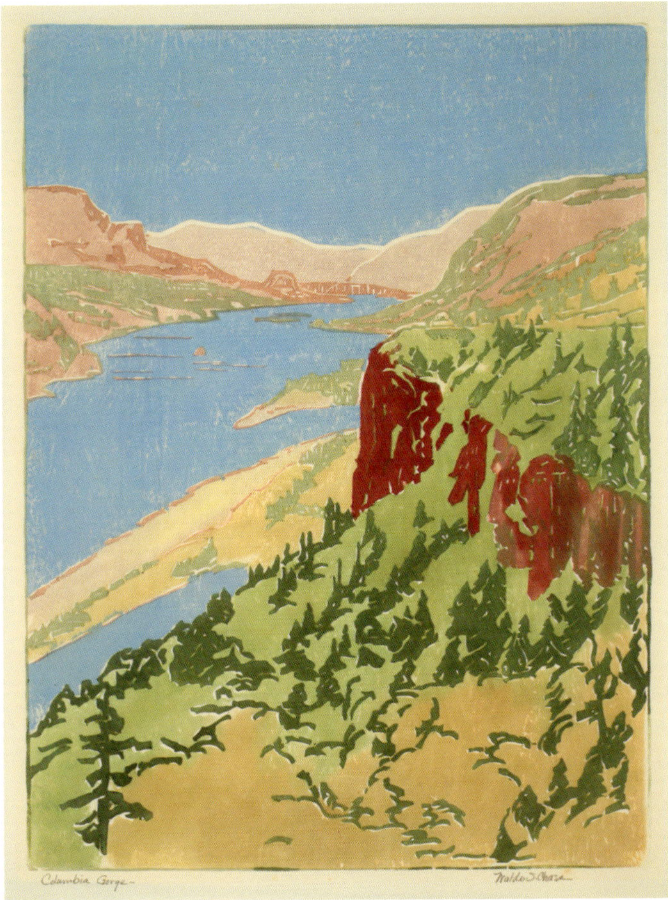

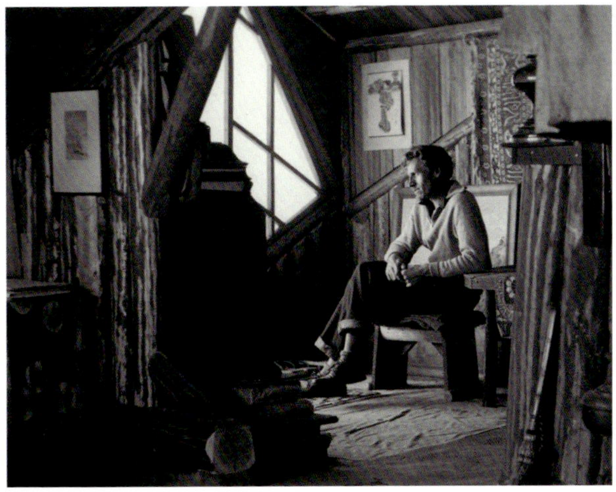

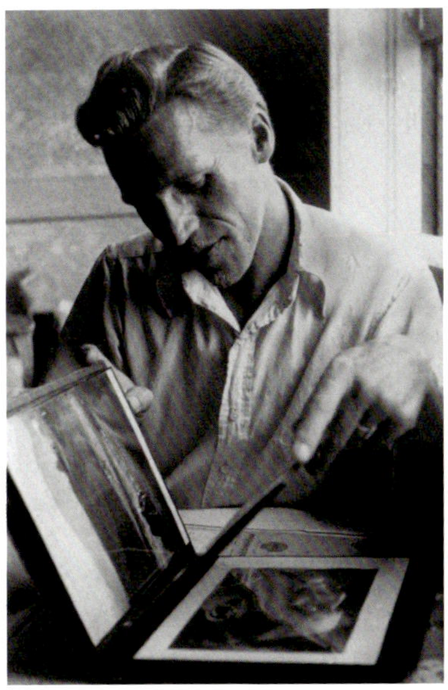

(top left) **WALDO S. CHASE**, *Columbia Gorge*, ca. 1940, color woodblock print, 14 ½ x 10 ½ in. Collection of Thomas H. Wake

(top right) Corwin Chase in his home, ca. 1940. Courtesy of Florence Gilleland Schieve. Photographer unknown

(bottom) Corwin Chase, ca. 1940. The Chase Place Collection. Photographer unknown

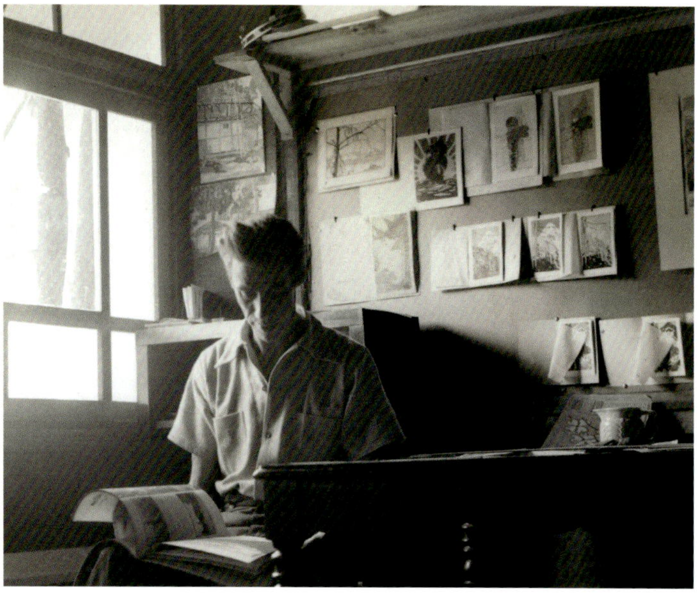

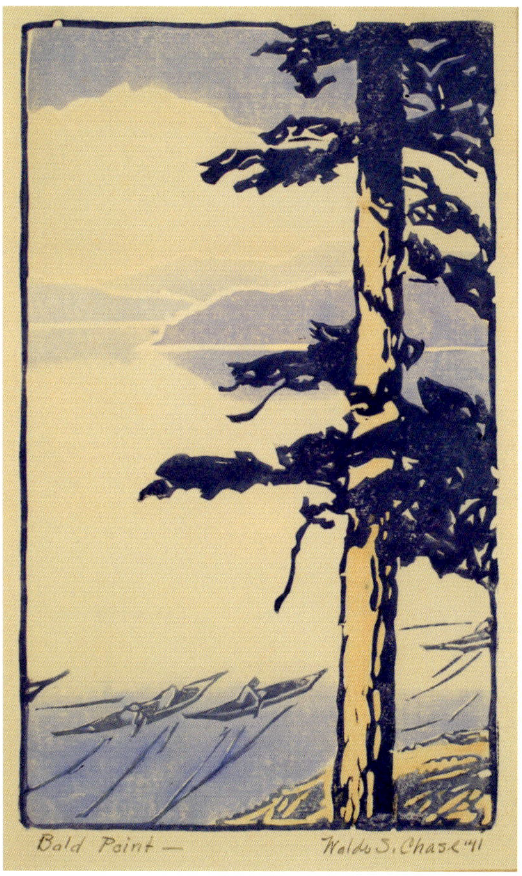

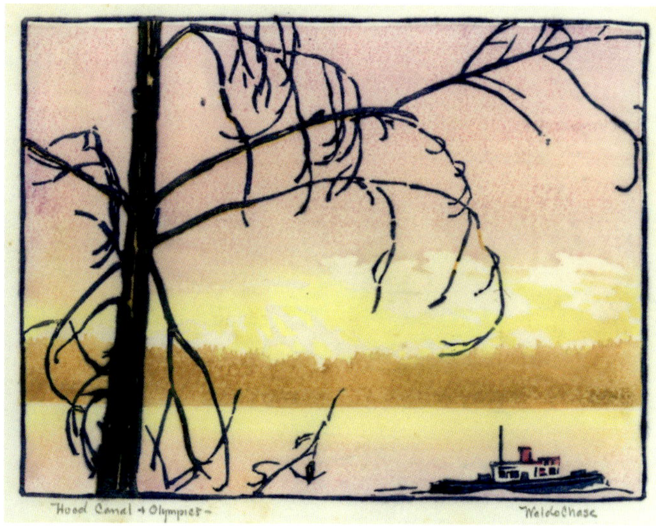

(top) Waldo Chase in his home, ca. 1940. Courtesy of Florence Gilleland Schieve. Photographer unknown

(bottom left) WALDO S. CHASE, *Bald Point*, 1941, color woodblock print, 10 ⅛ x 6 in. Collection of Thomas H. Wake

(bottom right) WALDO S. CHASE, *Hood Canal & Olympics* (also titled *Rose Point – Hood Canal*), printed in 1941 from a block carved in 1935, color woodblock print, 6 x 7 ⅝ in. Collection of John Impert

Waldo Chase Explains His and His Brother's Printing Process in 1938

This process of color printing is derived from the most primitive methods. It was first worked out in China and about 700 AD was taken to Japan.

With the help of Morley Fletcher's book [*Woodblock Printing*, 1916], my brother Corwin and I felt our way thru the first steps of the process. Later by much trial and error and a little Japanese artist I mastered the technique. The whole thing can be done on an ordinary table as there is no press. The design is first worked out in full on paper, then a tracing is made of all shadows and outlines. This tracing is then turned over and glued down to the surface of block number one. Then the light parts are carved away. When this block is complete the surface is inked, impressions are rubbed off and used as guides in the carving of the following color blocks, hence this first block is called the Key Block. For the wood I have used holly from Louisiana, poplar and Alaska cedar. In the carving outfit there are only about six tools—gouges, V tools, Skew tools.

In printing the soft Japanese paper takes the impression best of any. Made of rice stalks, it has strength, body, and is soft and absorbent. It must be sized with a thin solution of gelatin and alum, dried and damped again before printing. The finest quality of transparent water colors are dissolved in rice water, and used to coat the blocks in printing. The block is laid face up on the table, the color is brushed on the raised part of the block with a small, square brush. Then the top sheet of rice paper is taken from under the glass which keeps it damp, and placed on the colored surface. The position of the sheet on the block is fixed by two grooves carved in the margin, called registration marks. The pressure is applied with a small rubbing device called a baren. It is about the size and shape of a doughnut without the hole and covered with sea grass matting to make it soft and smooth. This baren is moved around in a circular motion, and as the paper absorbs the color it shows through on the back. In this way, one can tell how it is progressing, as to amount of color, value, etc. Dark colors require two impressions, and several colors can be applied to different parts of the same block. Thus the hand print takes on an individuality that is not possible with the machine process.

Finally the prints are laid out to dry, pressing and mounting completes the ancient Oriental method of color printing.

My brother Corwin who is also a printmaker, and I were mountaineers before we made prints. Thru our many trips to the local mountains, mainly to explore with an eye for beauty, spots where we could live, we became artists at camping, and hence could live with our skills. We absorbed our lessons in color and form from nature. When winter came we retired to our cabin, designed and carved our blocks, criticized and helped each other as we were unable to afford the usual art schooling. Our designs have leaned toward the Representative rather than the Interpretive manner up to this time, 1938.

At first we worked together, but we soon found that it was necessary for each to execute his own design as personal impressions vary in many subtle ways and are impossible to transmit in words.

Unpublished descriptive letter provided by Florence Gilleland-Schieve

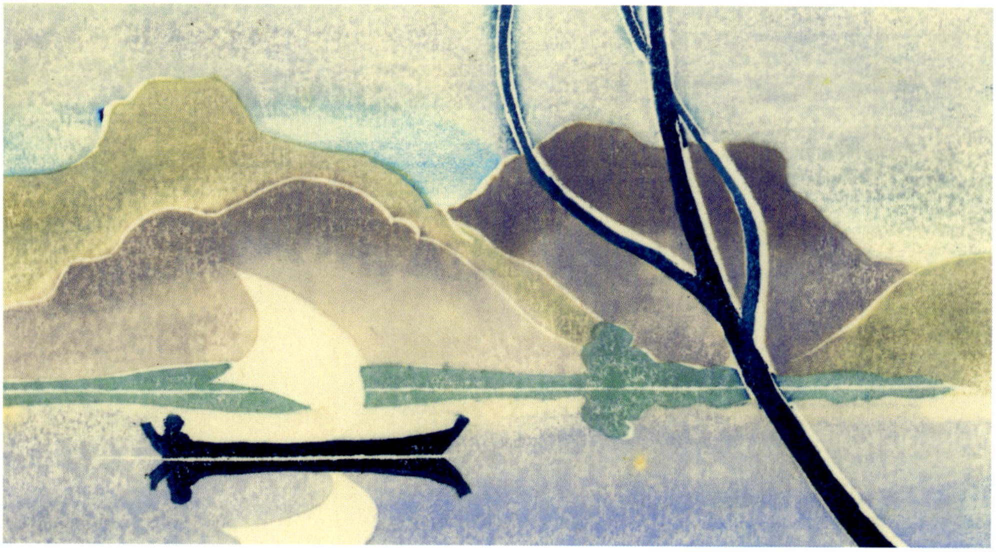

C. WILLARD SWANBERG (1923–1998), *Dewatto*, 1941, white line color woodblock print, 3 7/8 x 6 7/8 in. Private collection

Swanberg was one of Waldo's students and created this print at the age of eighteen. Swanberg went on to be a very successful commercial artist in Seattle.

> Some of the things Waldo has written are good reading up to a certain point. Where he should give credit to Divine Mind he looks forward to accomplishment through a cooperative of human endeavor. Tries to convert friends to his line of thought instead of allowing them to "Work out their own Salvation." In the letter to you he appears to see those "who close their eyes to unpleasant developments incurring much danger of having a house "afire" to extinguish" Waldo forgets that he has written in his "Man's Struggle For Freedom" (which he wrote explaining the murals he made for the walls of the Church of the People) that what he see's in others is Himself – a different expression of the saying that man quietly discerns his own faults in others (or thinks he does). So he will have to be on his guard against "unpleasant developments" hence after.[12]

Mr. Chase had urged Waldo to pursue his teaching credentials for future economic security. He failed to see how his son's current situation would benefit him as he was soon approaching fifty. His father died shortly after the letter was written.

Waldo continued working with the Church of the People. One interesting project that they funded was the development of a model cooperative farm that was started in 1943 at Deer Park near Spokane to assist Japanese American citizens who were removed from the Tule Lake Relocation Center. The farm experiment also included other minorities in a successful cooperative interracial experience.

After the war, the brothers continued to maintain their love of nature. Corwin met Cora Gingrich Cormier (1898–1983) and they married in 1946. Cora was the perfect partner for Corwin. She was as much of an independent spirit as he was, knew a great deal about natural food and plants, and was an accomplished writer. They settled near Juanita, Washington, in a hand-crafted home studio that Corwin had built in 1937.

By the late 1940s, American art had begun to focus on abstraction, and the style of realistic art produced by

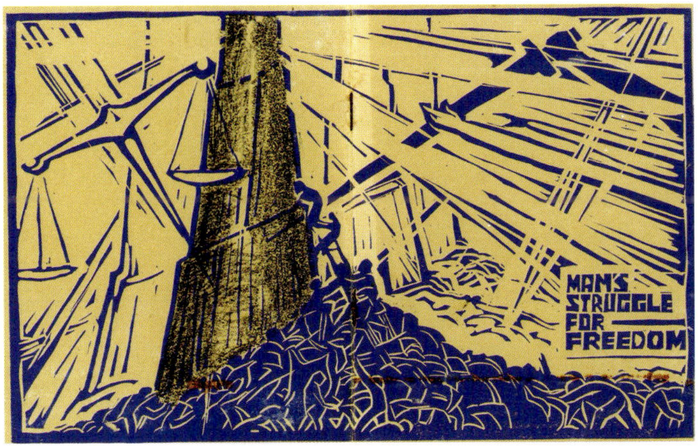

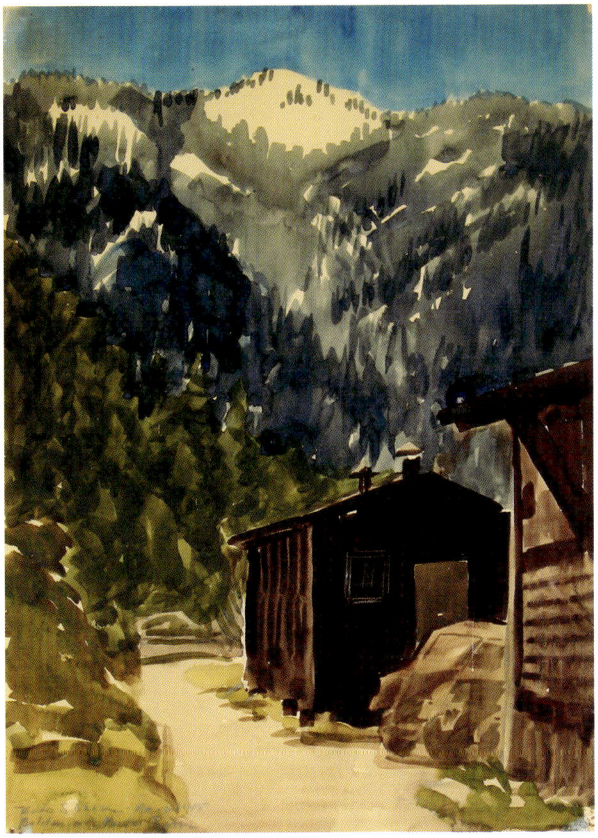

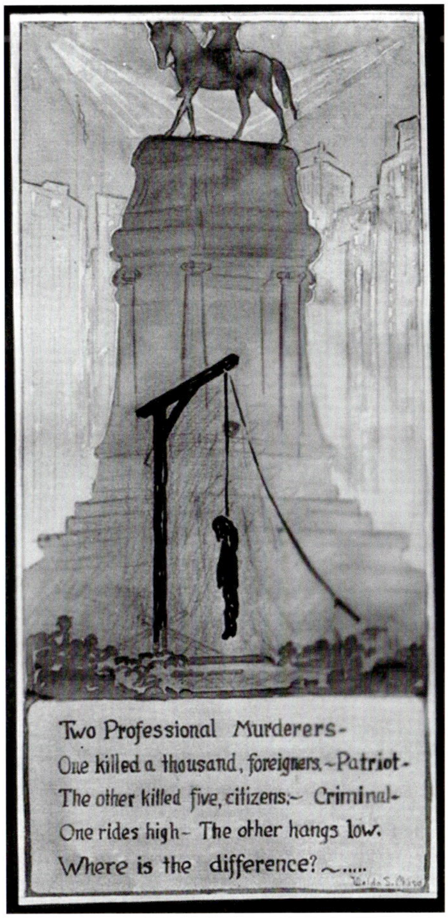

(top left) WALDO S. CHASE, *Man's Struggle For Freedom*, 1943. Woodblock cover and guide describing the seven mural panels Chase designed and executed for The Church of the People, Seattle, 7 3/8 x 5 1/4 in. The Martin-Zambito Archive

(bottom left) WALDO S. CHASE, *Belden, On the Feather River*, 1945, watercolor, 20 x 14 in. Private collection.

Waldo Chase painted this depiction of the Belden, California, Public Service Camp during his time at the CPS camps in Oregon.

(right) WALDO S. CHASE, *Two Professional Murderers*, photograph of a drawing by Waldo S. Chase. Photograph by Henry Blocher

Henry Blocher, "Two Professional Murderers," *Lewis & Clark Digital Collections*, http://digitalcollections.lclark.edu/items/show/5462 (accessed 5-18-2017). Courtesy of Lewis & Clark College Aubrey Watzek Library Special Collections & Archives

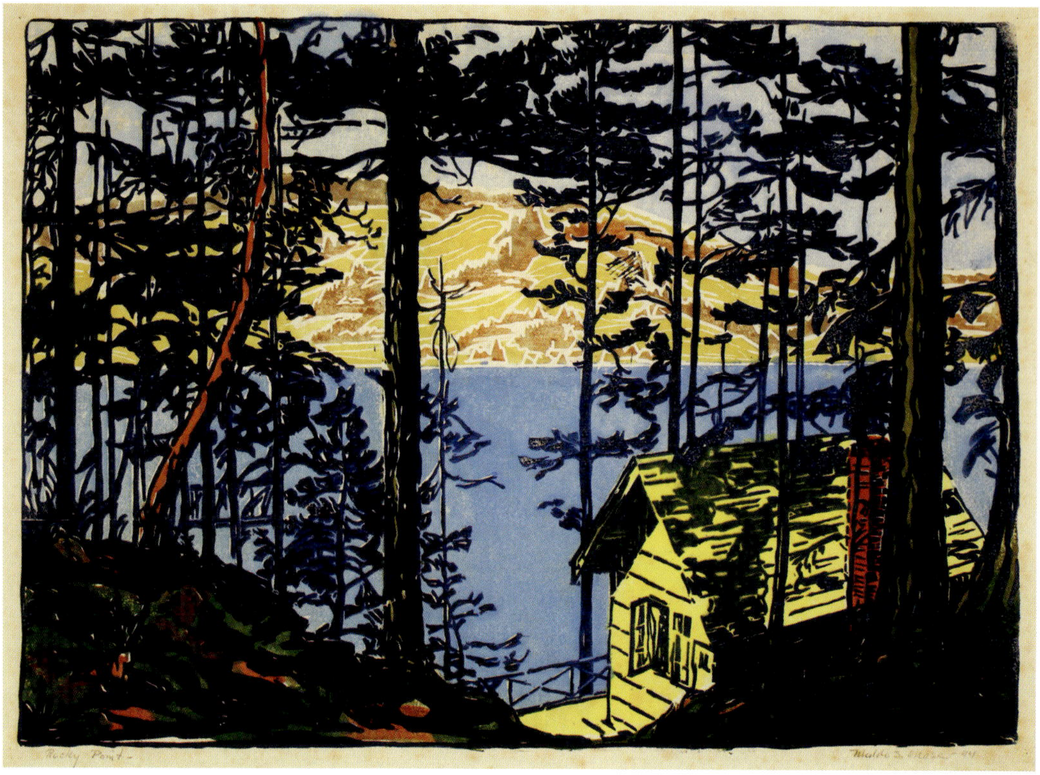

WALDO S. CHASE, *Rocky Point*, 1944, color woodblock print, 13 3/8 x 18 in. Private collection

In this print, Waldo Chase successfully combined the standard relief blocks with an additional white line block used for the background landscape.

the brothers was beginning to fall out of favor, especially in regional art circles. The Chase brothers were never able to adapt to these changes, and so their production and exhibitions throughout the 1950s slowly dwindled almost to a halt. But Corwin was once again inspired by his sister Marjorie, who had by then become a very fine weaver. He tried his hand at it with great success and added this skill to his creative repertoire.

The 1960s brought a great deal of change into American society. The ethos of many young Americans at that time reflected that of the Chase brothers' lifestyle some fifty years earlier. Getting back to the garden was the goal of the Woodstock generation, but the Chase brothers had never left it. The sixties counterculture embraced the creation of hand-crafted, utilitarian items; tie-dyed and other nontraditional clothing, and healthier eating habits through organic foods, which were all becoming increasingly adopted by the mainstream. Cooperative communes and farms presented an alternative for those who could not function in a divisive urban environment. Waldo and Corwin were ahead of their time in this respect, and it did not go unnoticed by the many young people who surrounded them.

In 1968, Waldo had made a trip to Hawaii to visit friends while attending a Quaker summer camp. He was inspired by the natural beauty of the islands and produced several watercolors and drawings during his time there.

At the end of that year he wrote a letter describing a nostalgic impulse he had experienced and shared it with his old friend, Walter Fullaway. "Something strange happened to me in my 73rd year. First, I have not made a real block print for 26 years, I mean carved and printed [the] Japanese way."[13] He went on to describe a new color woodblock print that was based on an earlier watercolor depicting Mount Christie in the Olympic range. This was the first print he had made since 1942.

Corwin continued to produce art but turned to oil painting, pastel, watercolor, and weaving. He had solo exhibitions locally at the Washington State Historical Society in 1964 and at the Tacoma Public Library in 1969. He would also make a few additional prints in the next few decades.

By 1970, Waldo and his cabin in Union, Washington,

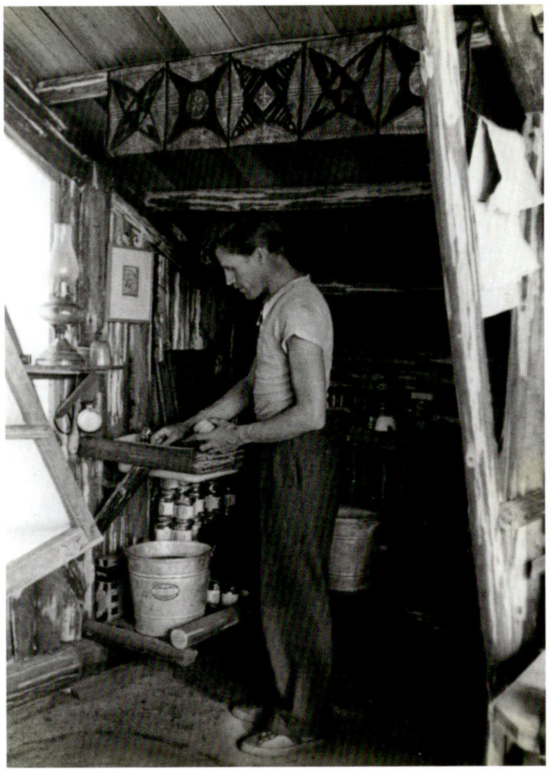

Corwin Chase in his home studio, ca. 1940. The Chase Place Collection. Photographer unknown

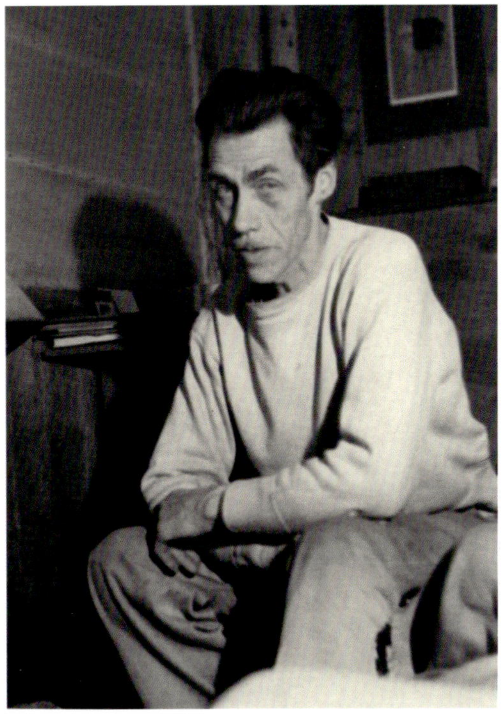

Waldo Chase in his home, 1950. The Martin-Zambito Archive. Photographer unknown

had become a mecca for the local counterculture and especially attracted younger men in transitional phases of their lives. That year, one of these young men, Joe Morosco, met Waldo and ended up staying on the property for the remainder of Waldo's life. Joe and his friends became Waldo's caretakers, often taking the older man out hiking and climbing with a keen ear for the senior's sage advice.

Waldo noticed that there was a renewed interest in graphic art at that time. Many of the counterculture images had borrowed from the Art Deco and Art Nouveau movements as well as the stylized realism of the Arts & Crafts movement. His regular printmaking days were long over but he became nostalgic enough to learn something about the fate of his earlier prints.

In 1970 he wrote to Walter Fullaway:

> There was an auction here lately of household goods. An old print of mine was sold for $7.50. The one who bought it showed it to me . . . I offered to buy the print – the tall one with dark trees and a cabin. I suggested $10. – No Deal! $25. — No Deal! Then she said $100. No less. So I am in the position of not being able to buy my own prints . . . Of course it don't mean that all the old prints (out of print blocks destroyed) are worth $100. Each. But it means that a few who know my stuff and value it might like to own certain prints.

He also remembered that "A shop in Sitka, Alaska had 16–20 prints since 1934" for which he had never been paid.

He went on to describe his print production in the same letter:

> From 1925 to 1942 – Twenty-five subjects each with a set of blocks and 9 portraits. After 1942 a gap of twenty-five years when I made paintings and no prints. Then in 1968, made carving and prints for the Mt. Christie from my painting made on the spot. I could give you more information as I recall the whole story of 20 years of moving 14 times – Lake

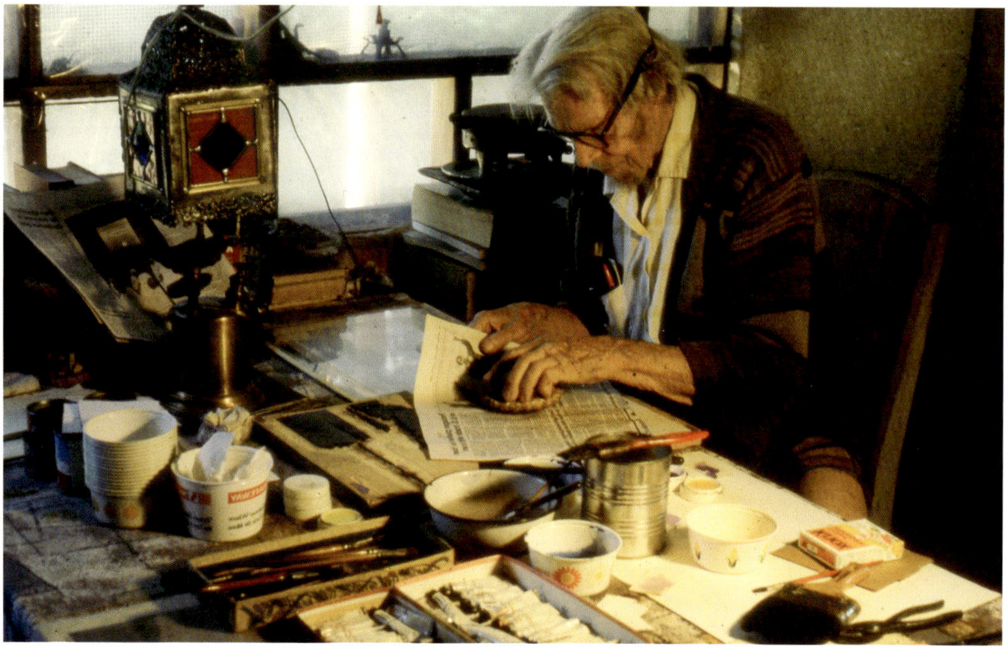

Corwin Chase in 1987 at age ninety printing some of his early blocks.
Courtesy of Rivkah Sweedler

> Washington, Mt. Rainier Carbon River, then across the sound, Clam Bay; Maples Camp; Doc. Edby's; Orre's beach; tepee in summer; and Dalby's cabin in winter, always carving or printing, 800–900 prints in all.[14]

The following year he wrote again to Fullaway,

> The lady at the store (waterwheel) sold out or had 5 blockprints – (3 of mine and 2 of Corwin's) and is offering them for sale for $1000. A couple women came to look at them. But when they saw the price – changed their direction and came to my place and got one of my later prints for $25. Instead of $200. It's a funny feeling to see something you created used that way as a means for speculation. It certainly does the artist no good.
>
> In 1927, Corwin and I put 320 prints in the (then) New Georgia Hotel in Vancouver, BC. That is 43 years ago. After 20 years or so the pictures in the rooms were changed and the prints disposed of. So 200 of mine are floating about Vancouver somewhere.[15]

In 1973, Waldo decided to accept the invitation of his friend Dorothy Jessup to exhibit his watercolors, prints, and oils created during the past thirty years in a makeshift exhibition space at her home in Hood Canal. It was to be his last.

Waldo retreated into his world of young friends, stayed home and baked bread, read constantly, and delved deeper into philosophy. He had been especially fascinated with the writings and broadcasts of the philosopher Jiddu Krishnamurti (1895–1986), whose philosophies he embraced. One quote in particular had special resonance for him: "The significance is that your consciousness is the consciousness of all humanity because you suffer, you are anxious, you are lonely, insecure, confused, exactly like others, though they live ten thousand miles away."[16]

Corwin, on the other hand, had a wife who was an extraordinary woman and the two shared a fulfilling life together. She wrote numerous publications, including a biography of Mother Ryther and a guide to naturally foraged edibles titled *The Weed Eaters Cook Book*.[17] Returning to college at an advanced age when she was 84, she became the oldest graduate of the University of Washington in 1982. At that time Corwin and Cora were still occasionally sleeping in their tepee. She died the following year, suffering a stroke on

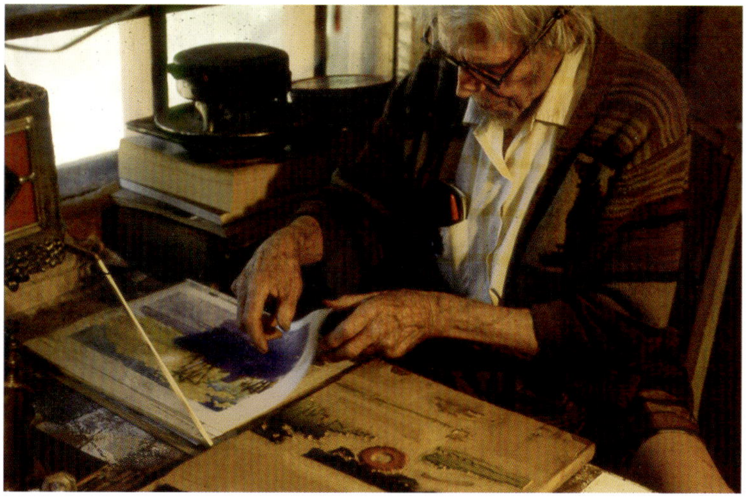

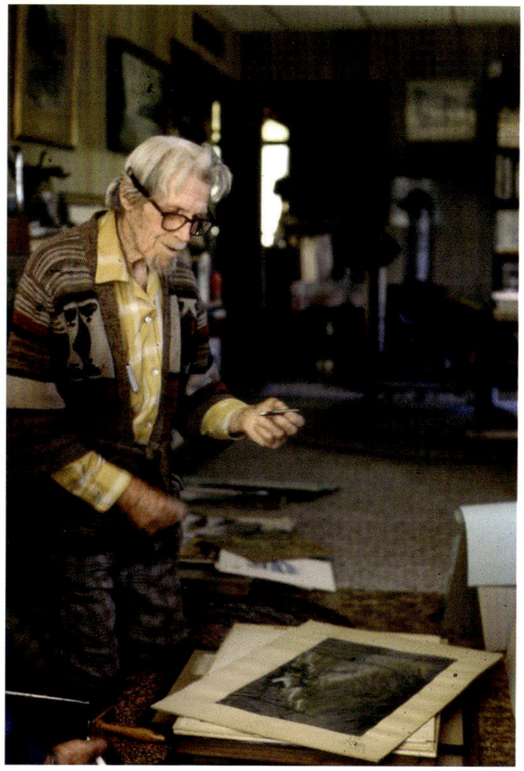

an airplane on her way home from an International Platform Association meeting in Washington, DC.

Waldo wrote to his niece Florence on November 21, 1986:

> Corwin now since Cora is not there to do the cleanup, seems very careless, he's rather deaf. I worry about him. I'm sure he'd give anything if some capable nurse would burst in once a month or week and clean up the whole place including himself. He has written a couple of books and is now writing another. My or our best memories are about trips together around Mt. Rainier and one or two into the Olympics. Otherwise, our way of thinking, etc., is very different.[18]

In fact, Corwin did have a group of younger friends who gathered around him, including Cora's grandchildren. His friend Rivkah Sweedler and others assisted him with reprinting some of his older blocks for an exhibition at Seattle's Mia Gallery in 1987. The exhibition, titled *Northwest Naturalists*, featured several prints that Corwin himself printed with some assistance at the age of 90. They are marked with the original date of the carving of the block and the year 1987 to distinguish them as a later printing. Sweedler recalled that when Corwin wasn't able to locate gelatin to size the papers, he substituted strawberry flavored jello causing the paper to have a slight pink hue.

Waldo had suffered several health problems by then and had been in a care facility after hip surgery. After healing, he returned to his cabin in Union. In April of that year, Waldo nearly lost his life in a devastating fire in his home. With the care of his neighbors and the local community he received immediate assistance, including food, clothing, and even new dentures provided by his dentist. Taking it in stride, he told a reporter that what he really needed was "a good dictionary and art supplies."[19]

Waldo recounted the conflagration to his niece Florence:

> March 26th awakened 3:00 a.m. by fire in the ceiling going fast. I tried to fight it with water. Joe came in saw it was hopeless carried me to next door neighbors – fire department volunteers came in time to save wood shed 30' away. Now I'm sleeping at Joe's place and quite comfortable – he cooks and cleans – shops and all and has some help – State sends nurses to check and bath. Joe is the hero in this situation. Imagine yourself caring for and waiting for

> an old tough one who refuses to die . . . All together I am quite content – I sleep a lot and still read Krishnamurti.[20]

A few weeks later, he wrote his final letter to Florence:

> As for me, life is not much fun – with all the limitations, no walks in the woods which were so important. Hearing almost gone – have one hearing on right with aid which works poorly. In a group, its chatter, no clear words. Eyes very weak. Read with only one, the left eye.[21]

Waldo died on April 7, 1988, at the age of ninety-three, followed eight months later by Corwin at the age of ninety-one.

NOTES

1 Marjorie's education information was provided by Marcia Approo, Assistant Registrar, Pratt Institute Records, Brooklyn, New York, in email correspondence, February 24, 2017.

2 W. Corwin Chase, *Tepee Fires* (Burley, WA: Coffee Break Press, 1981), 62.

3 Chase, *Tepee Fires*, 75–80.

4 *Seattle Daily Times*, November 13, 1927, p. 66.

5 The information on Yamagishi Kazue was derived from several sources, including notes from my telephone conversation with Robert Bruce Inverarity on October 18, 1991. Inverarity explained that he attended the class following his graduation from high school. He was a friend of the Chase brothers and they often had Yamagishi visit their studio. Inverarity remembered a few women in the class as well but couldn't recall their names.

Additional information on Yamagishi was obtained from the *San Francisco Chronicle*, February 15, 1927, p. 3, and from email correspondence with art historian Chiaki Ajioka, September 2 and 16, 2015.

6 *Notan*, Bulletin of the Seattle Camera Club [Seattle, WA], April 9, 1928.

7 The information on Orre Nobles was provided by Marcia Approo, Assistant Registrar, Pratt Institute Records, Brooklyn, New York, in email correspondence, February 24, 2017.

8 Chase, *Tepee Fires*, 35.

9 Chase, *Tepee Fires*, 47.

10 *Seattle Daily Times*, October 7, 1934, p. 12

11 *Seattle Daily Times*, April 13, 1935, p. 35.

12 Letter from Wendell Chase to Marjorie Gilleland, Seattle, July 19, 1944. Courtesy of Florence Gilleland Schieve.

13 Letter from Waldo Chase to Walter and Alice Fullaway, Christmas 1968. The Martin-Zambito Archive.

14 Letter from Waldo Chase to Walter and Alice Fullaway, Christmas 1968. The Martin-Zambito Archive.

15 Waldo Chase to Walter Fullaway, April 27, 1971. The Martin-Zambito Archive.

16 Jiddu Krishnamurti, *The Network of Thought: Authentic Report of Talks in 1981 In Saanen, Switzerland, and Amsterdam, Holland* (Madras, India: Krishnamurti Foundation India, 1982), Chapter 1, First Public Talk, Saanen July 12, 1981, from a note hand-copied by the artist in a letter to his niece.

17 See Cora G. Chase, *The Weedeater's Cook Book: How to Identify and Make Tasty Dishes of Common Weeds* (Salt Lake City, UT: 1978).

18 Waldo Chase to Florence Gilleland Schieve, November 21, 1986. Courtesy of Florence Gilleland Schieve.

19 Ed Binder, "Community Rallies to Aid Waldo." *Union* (newspaper), April 9, 1987. Union, Washington.

20 Waldo Chase to Florence Gilleland Schieve, January 13, 1988. Courtesy of Florence Gilleland Schieve.

21 Waldo Chase to Florence Gilleland Schieve, February 11, 1988. Courtesy of Florence Gilleland Schieve.

ARTIST BIOGRAPHIES

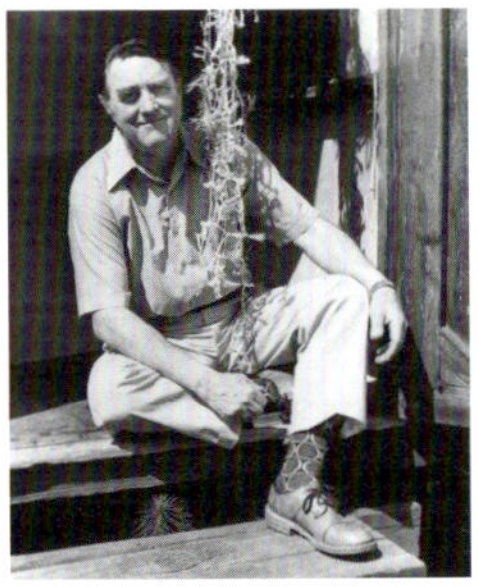

GLEN ALPS 1914–1996

Glen Earl Alps was born in Loveland, Colorado. He received his BA in Education from Colorado State College in 1940 and taught school in Greeley, Colorado, and Wichita, Kansas, before moving to Seattle in 1945. That same year he began teaching printmaking at the University of Washington, eventually becoming head of the department until his retirement in 1984. Under Alps's direction, the department became one of the most respected institutions for printmaking in the United States and internationally.

He received an MFA in 1947 from the School of Art, University of Washington, and that same year studied with Mauricio Lasansky (1914–2012) in a summer course at the University of Iowa. The following year he had an exhibition of his serigraphs, etchings, lithographs, and woodcuts at Eastern Michigan University, and in 1949 at the University of Detroit, the Henry Art Gallery at the University of Washington, and the University of Oregon Museum of Art.

Alps made several important contributions in the field of printmaking. These include the naming and development of the "collagraph" process, as well as the concept of the burnt-lacquered plate and the "vitreograph," which utilizes a glass plate as the matrix. The collagraph became a mainstream printmaking technique practiced throughout the world. His innovative work in the serigraph process won him two consecutive first prize awards in 1951 and 1952 from the National Serigraph Society in New York.

During the 1950s, his reputation as an important printmaker extended to receiving international acclaim. For several decades, he exhibited in most major print exhibitions throughout the United States, Europe, and Japan. In 1956, he was part of a three-person exhibition with fellow Seattle artists George Tsutakawa (1910–1997) and Paul Horiuchi (1906–1999) at the Yōseidō Gallery in Tokyo. In 1961, Alps completed a series of sixteen lithographs during a fellowship grant at the Tamarind Workshop in Los Angeles.

In addition to his work in the field of printmaking, Alps was also an accomplished painter, sculptor, and craftsman. During his life, he received more than a hundred solo exhibitions and was included in numerous important exhibitions. His work is included in many of the world's leading museum collections.

Glen Alps continued to create and develop experimental processes in his Seattle studio until his death in 1996.

Photo: Glen Alps, circa 1960. Courtesy University of Washington Libraries, Special Collections Division, negative # UW 38043, Acc. No. 5152-002, Glen E. Alps Papers. Photographer unknown

SOURCES

The Martin-Zambito Archive

Baro, Gene. Introduction. In *Glen Alps, Retrospective: The Collagraph Idea, 1956–1980*. Seattle: University of Washington Press, 1980 (for an exhibition at the Bellevue Art Museum, Bellevue, Washington).

Special Collections of The Seattle Public Library, Artists Scrapbooks.

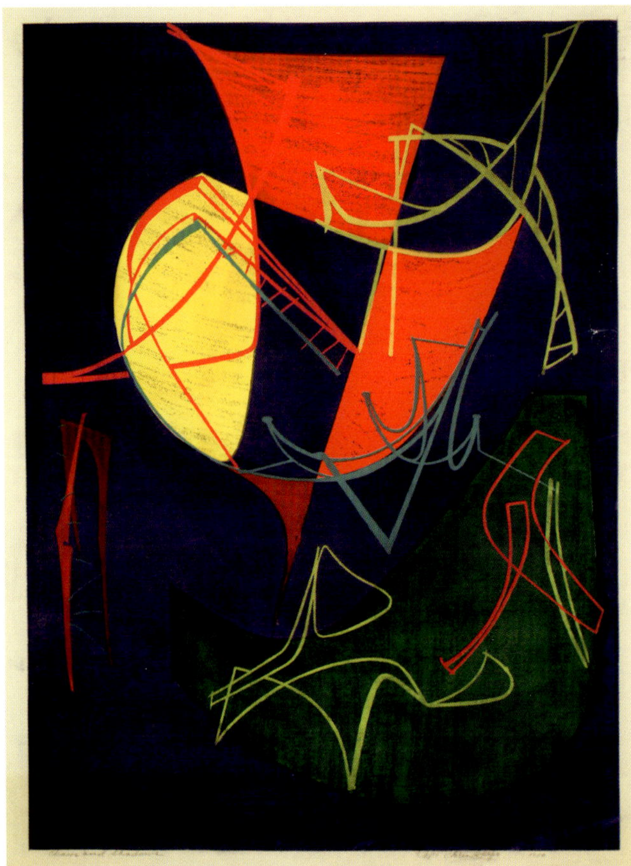

Chairs and Shadows, 1950, serigraph, 28 ½ x 20 in. Private collection

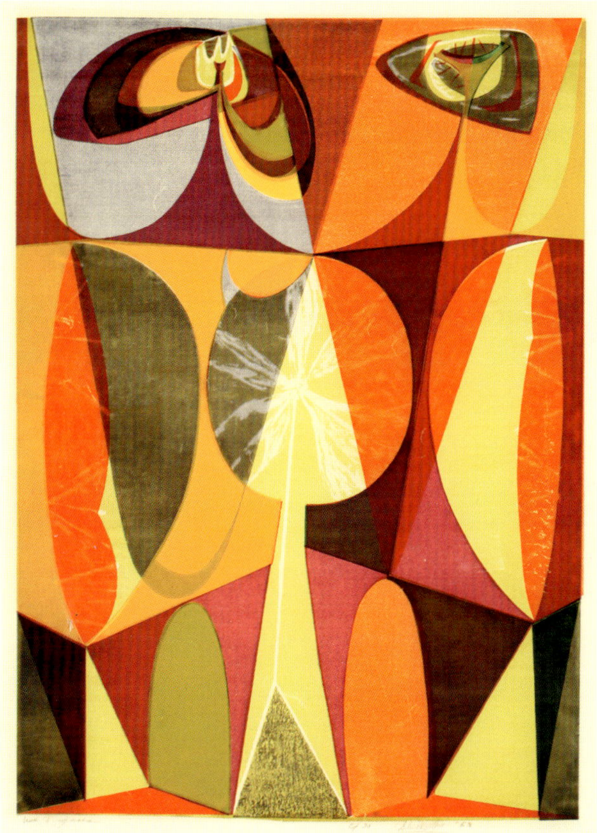

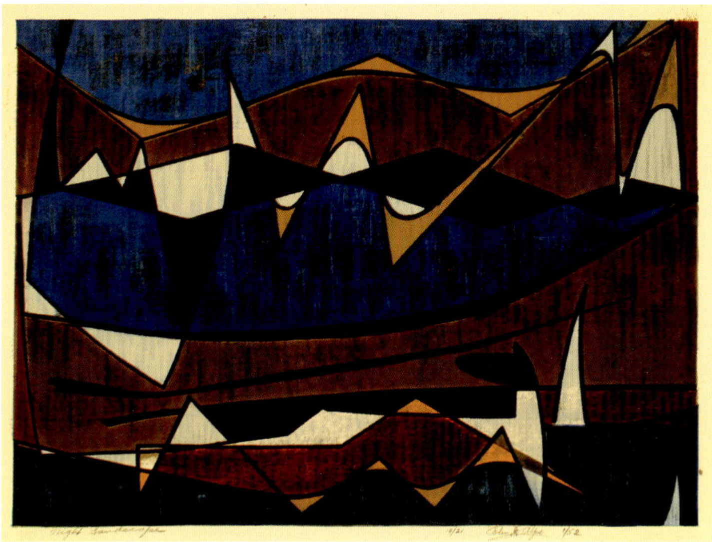

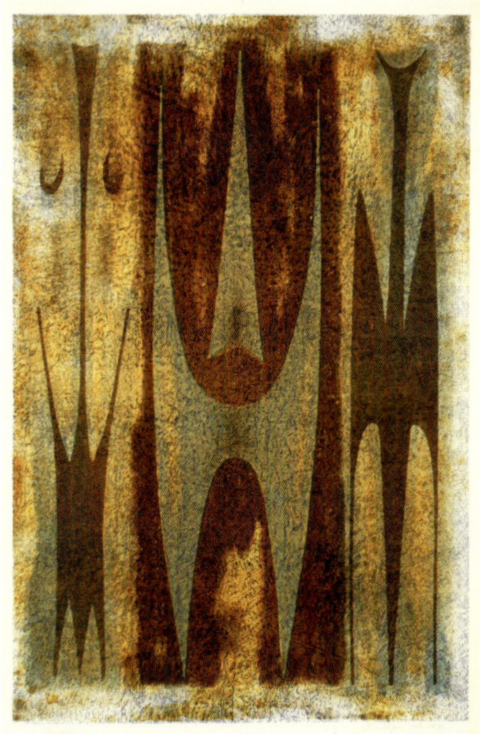

(above left) *Two Figures*, 1953, serigraph, 28 x 19 3/8 in. Private collection

(top right) *Night Landscape*, 1952. serigraph, 19 1/2 x 26 in. Private collection

(bottom right) *Mirage*, 1952, color lithograph, 27 1/4 x 17 3/8 in. Private collection

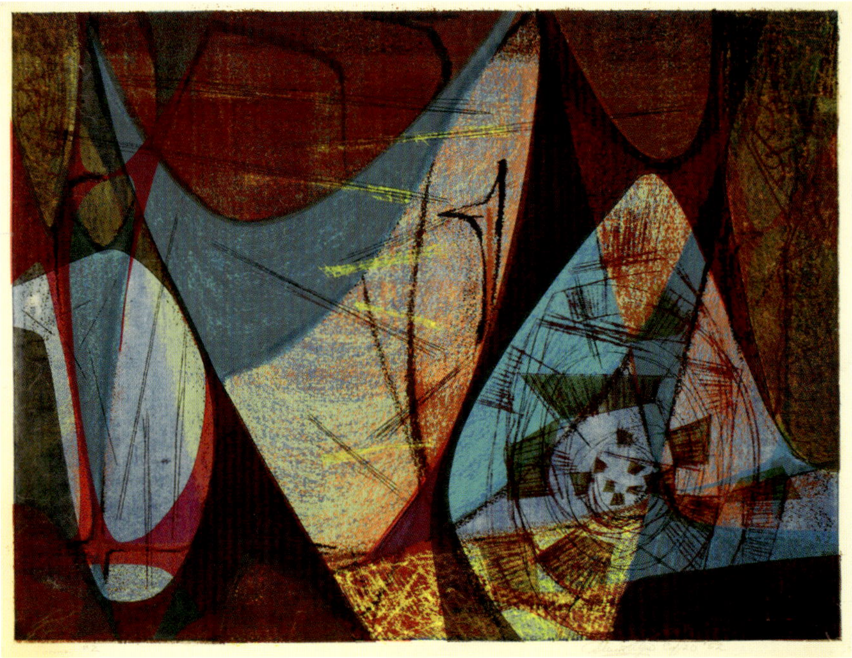

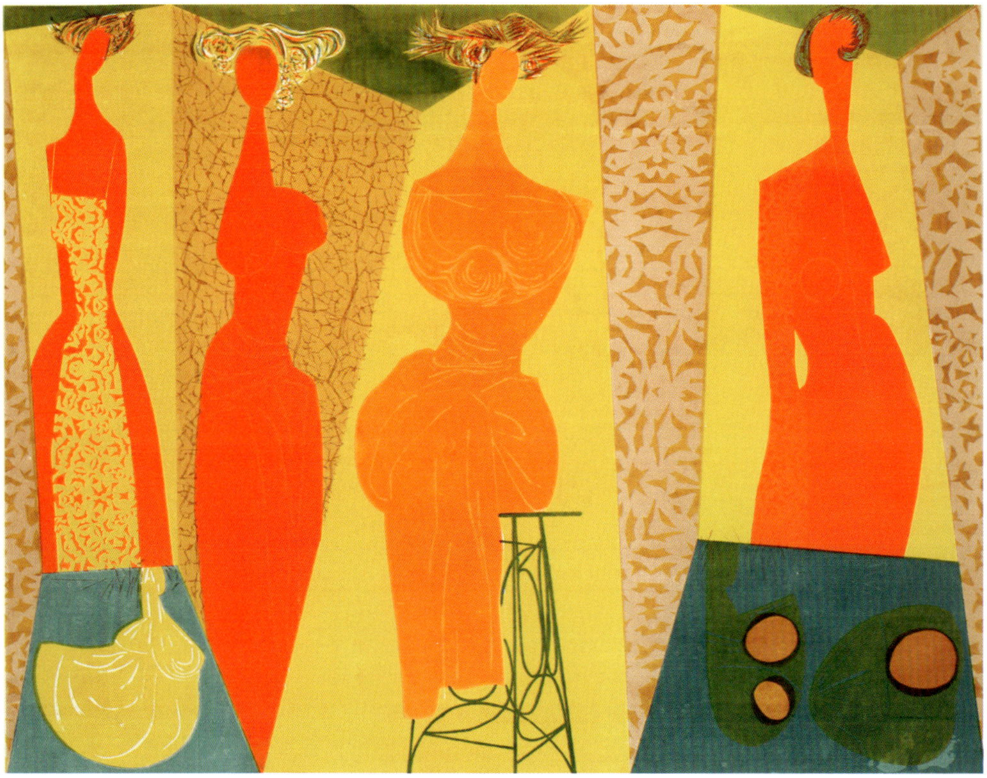

(top) *Forms # 2*, 1952, serigraph, 20 x 26 in. Private collection

(bottom) *Figures*, 1954, serigraph, 30 x 37 in. Private collection

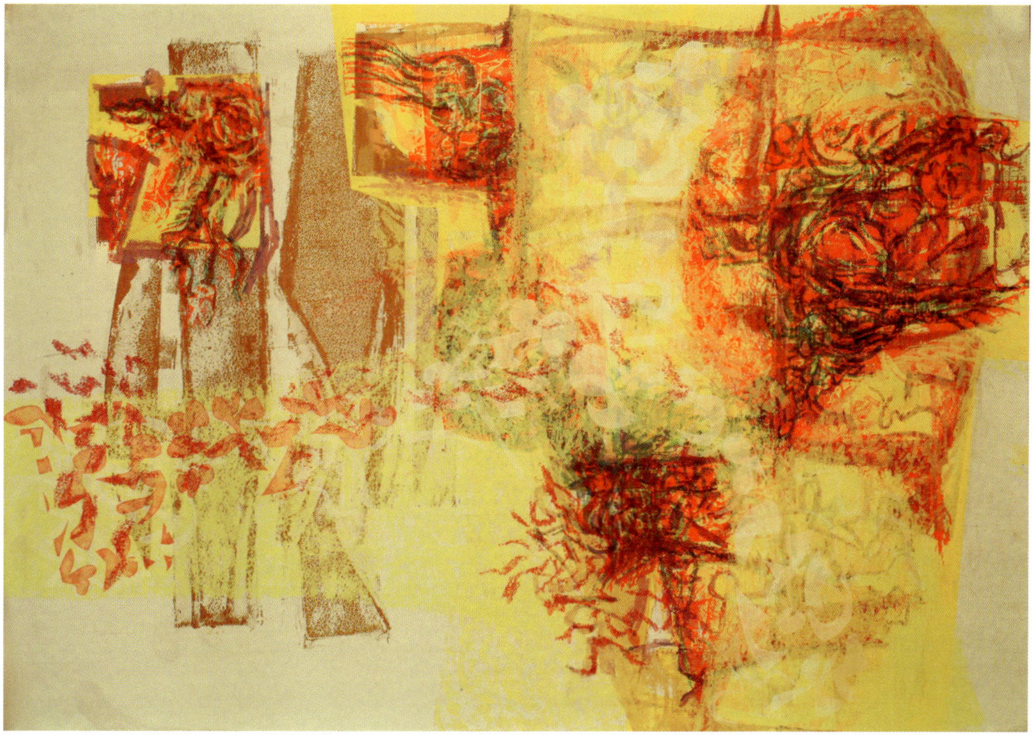

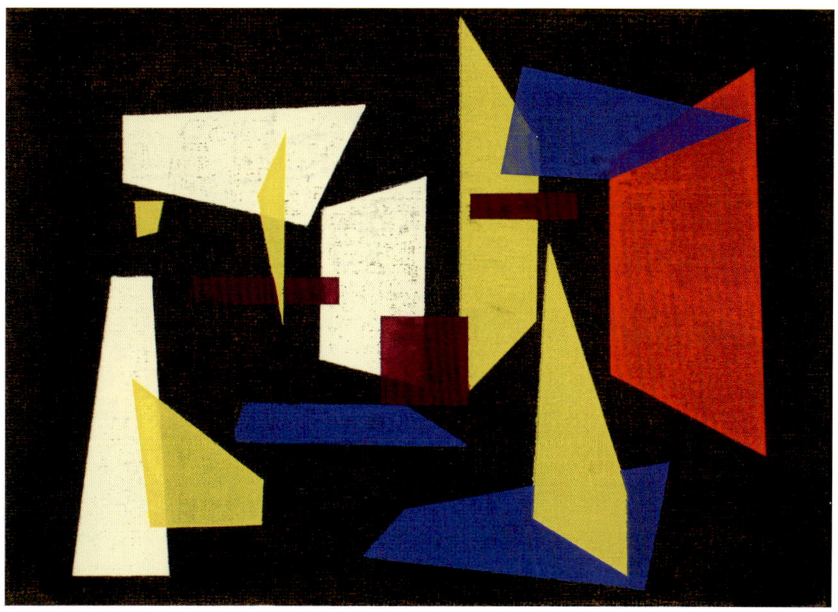

(top) *White Space*, 1958, serigraph, 32 x 41 in. Private collection

(bottom) *Geometric Space*, 1948, serigraph, 16 ½ x 23 in. Private collection

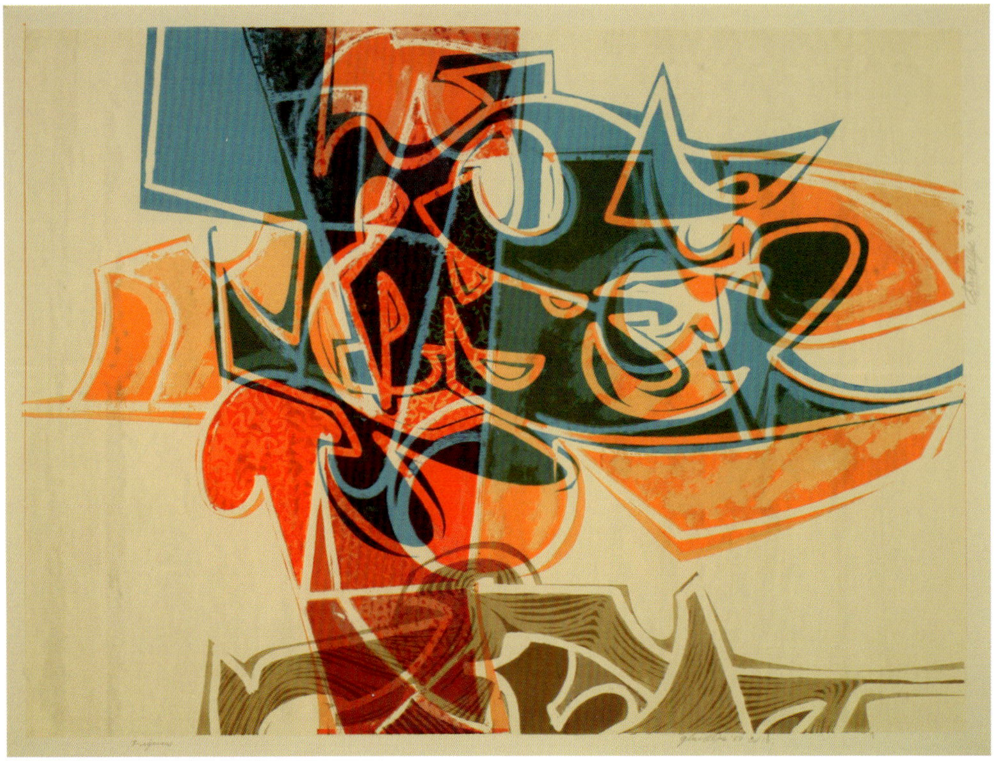

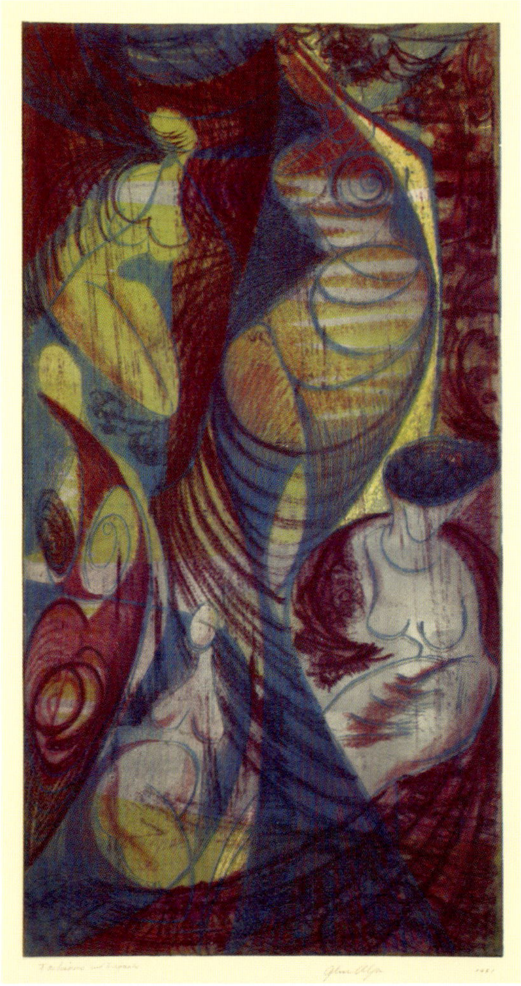

(top) *Figures*, 1959. serigraph. 21 x 27 ½ in. Private collection

(bottom) *Fashions and Figures*, 1951, color etching, 23 ½ x 12 in. Private collection

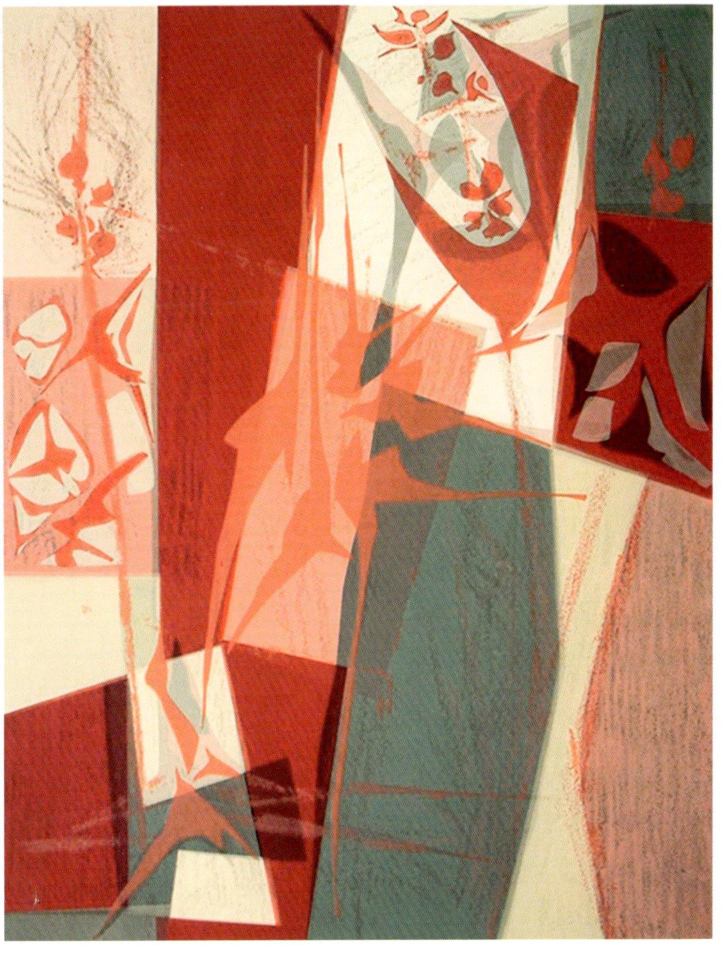

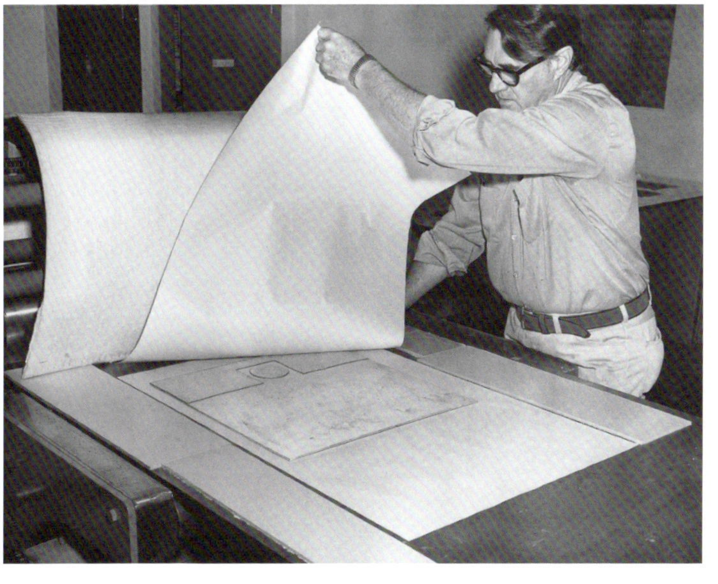

(top) *Hollyhocks*, 1958, serigraph, 25 ½ x 19 in. Private collection

(bottom) Glen Alps printing a collagraph plate, ca. 1960. University of Washington Libraries, Special Collections, Negative #38040, Acc. No. 5152-002 Glen E. Alps Papers.

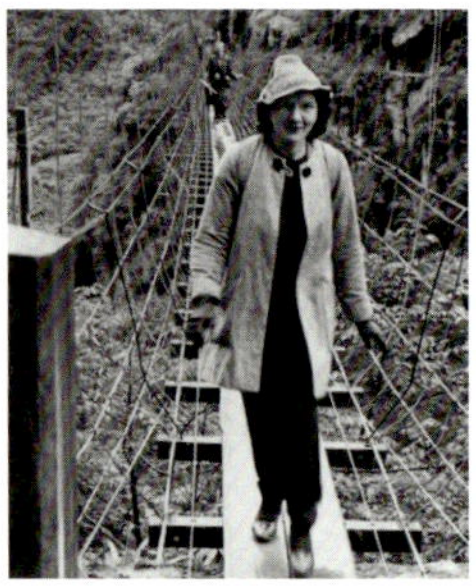

FRANCES BLAKEMORE 1906–1997

Frances Lee Wismer was born in Pana, Illinois. She and her family moved to Spokane in 1910 and later to Mabton, Washington. In 1925, she attended the University of Washington, where she studied with Walter Isaacs (1886–1964) and Helen N. Rhodes (1875–1938). To assist with her difficult financial situation, Frances worked at many jobs such as art instructor, designer, and even as an apple packer.

She was included in the first exhibition of the Northwest Printmakers Society in 1929 where she won her first of two purchase prizes.

In 1935, she married Glenn Baker and went with her new husband to Japan. Once settled, she held several positions in various fields and drew weekly sketches for *Japan News Week*. Over the next few years she executed murals and worked in the commercial art field. During this period, she sent proofs of her latest prints to be exhibited in the Northwest Printmakers exhibitions. By 1938, Frances was concerned about the charged political climate in Japan as she and her husband were regularly interrogated by the Japanese military police. In 1940, Frances left Tokyo for Honolulu; her husband joined her later. She immediately began working again, creating commercial illustrations and illustrating children's books over the next few years. In 1941, Frances witnessed the bomber planes flying across the sky before the strike on Pearl Harbor. In 1942, she began working for the U.S. Government in the office of censorship, screening media for any type of potential conflicts of leaked information. She worked for the propaganda campaign designing leaflets dropped by the millions over mainland Japan and Japanese forces in the Southwest Pacific. In 1946, she divorced her husband and, after a brief visit to Seattle, returned to Tokyo. She began working for the Civil Information and Education Section to assist the Occupation forces by designing posters and exhibitions for reorienting Japanese citizens under their new constitution. During this time she met Thomas Blakemore (1915–1994), an American attorney practicing in Japan, whom she consulted about purchasing property in Tokyo. Mr. Blakemore was an important figure in postwar Japanese legal history and the two fell in love. They were married in 1954.

Frances Blakemore became a champion of contemporary Japanese printmakers and opened the Fran-Nell Gallery in Tokyo to promote their work. She was instrumental in the development of the careers of many of these artists and wrote the definitive biographical source on the subject, *Who's Who in Modern Japanese Prints*, published in 1975.

Frances and Thomas Blakemore returned to Seattle in 1988. She died there in 1997. Their foundation continues to support important Arts and Language Grants.

Photo: Frances Blakemore in Formosa, ca. 1937. Courtesy of the Blakemore Foundation. Photographer unknown

SOURCES

Morioka, Michiyo. *An American Artist in Japan, Frances Blakemore, 1906–1997*. Seattle: The Blakemore Foundation and University of Washington Press, 2007.

Frances Blakemore archival materials, The Blakemore Foundation, Seattle.

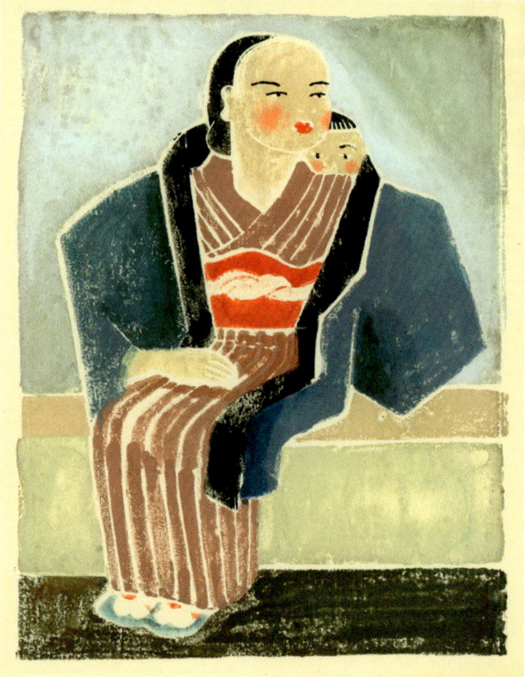

Far Eastern Madonna, 1939, white line color woodblock print, 9:½ x 7 in. Private collection

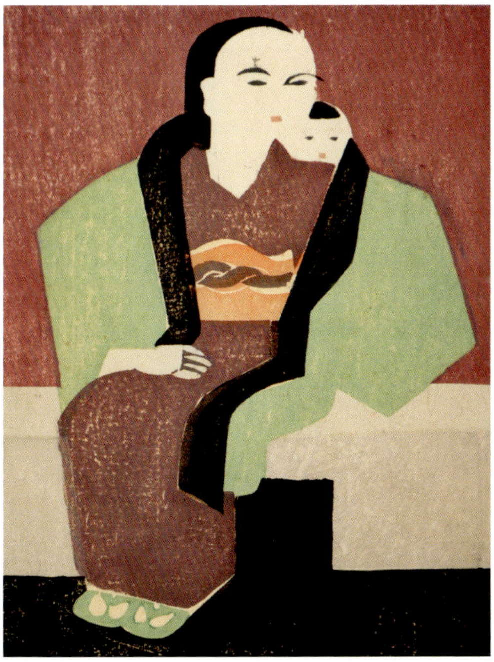

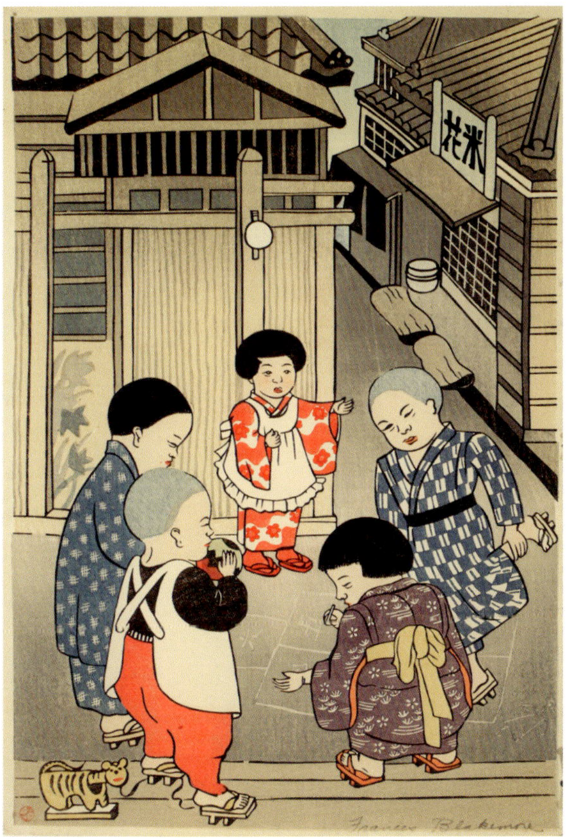

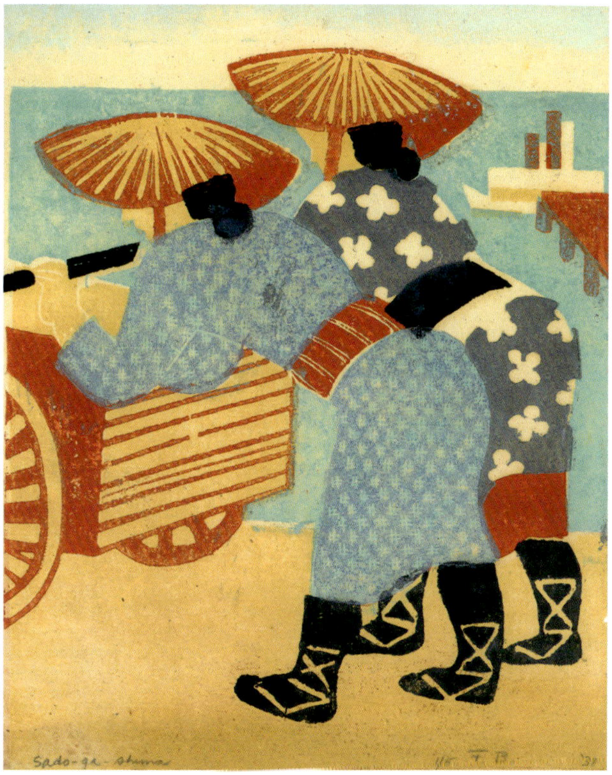

(top) *Far Eastern Madonna*, 1939, color woodblock print, 9 ½ x 7 in. Henry Art Gallery, Frances and Thomas Blakemore Collection, FA 96.79

(bottom left) *Children Playing on the Street*, ca. 1937, color woodblock print, 13 ½ x 8 ⅞ in. Watanabe Publisher. Private collection

(right) *Sado-ga-shima*, 1938, color woodblock print, 10 x 7 ¾ in. Private collection

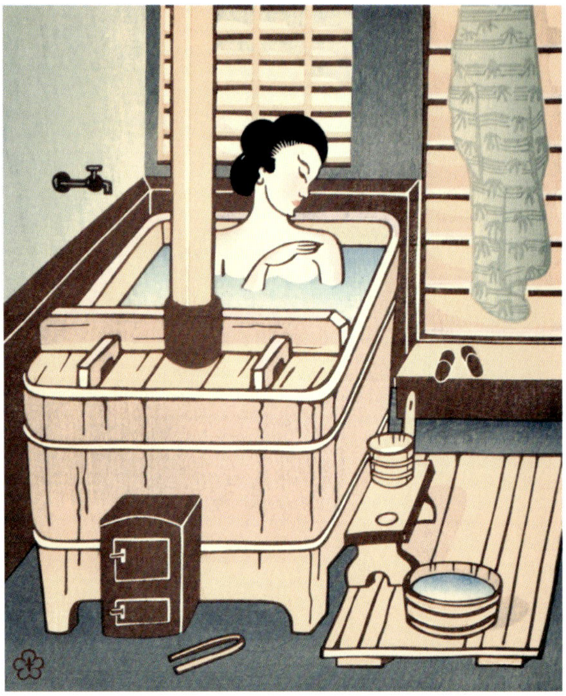

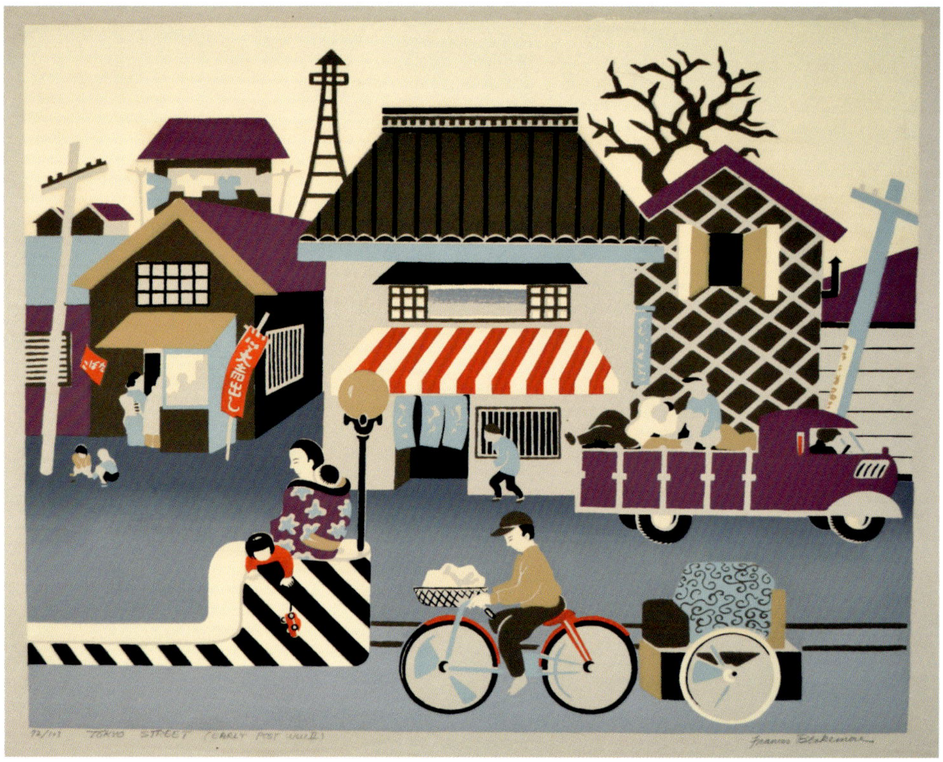

(top) *Japanese Bath*, 1937, color woodblock print, 10 ¾ x 8 ⅞ in. Watanabe Publisher. Henry Art Gallery, Frances and Thomas Blakemore Collection, FA 96.78

(bottom) *Tokyo Street*, early 1950s, serigraph, 18 ⅛ x 22 ½ in. Henry Art Gallery, Frances and Thomas Blakemore Collection, FA 96.79

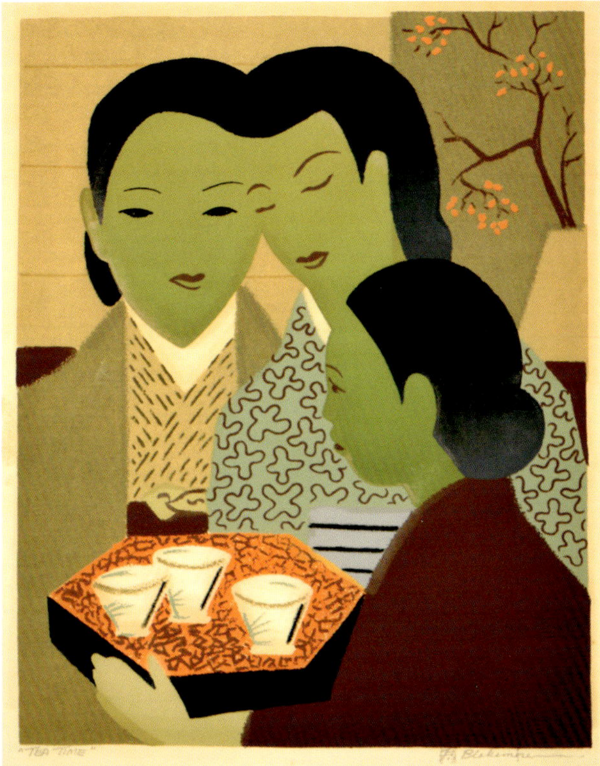

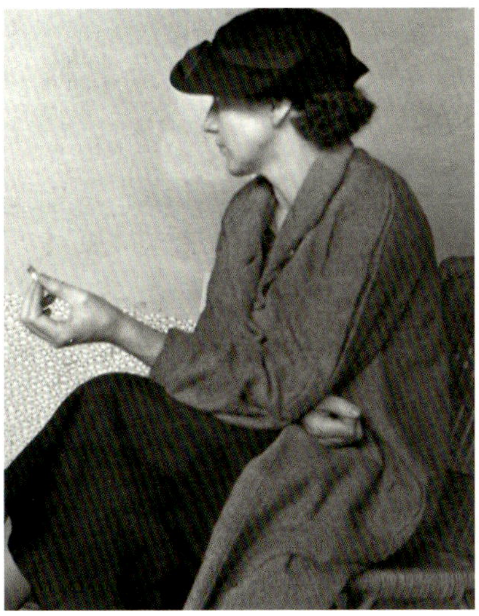

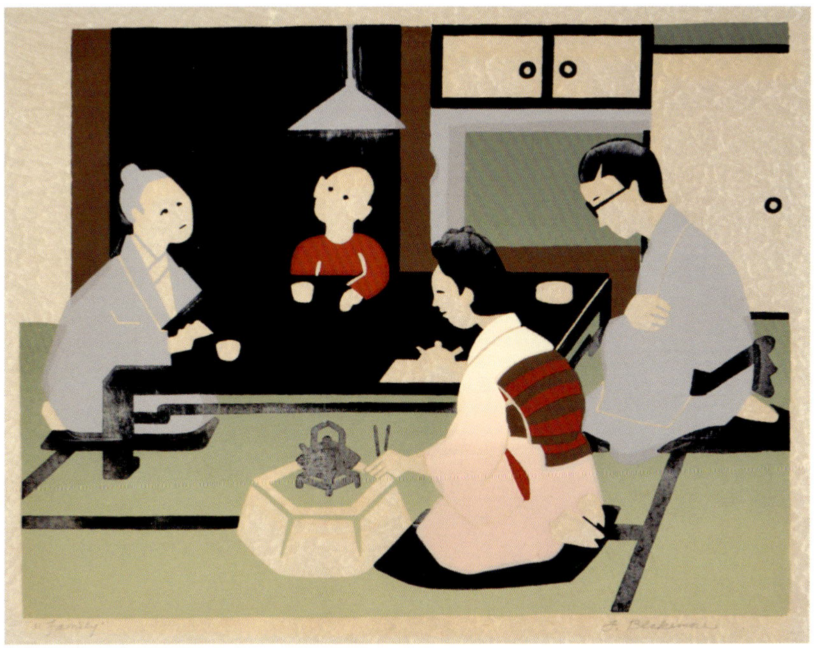

(top) *Tea Time*, late 1950s, serigraph, 17 ⅛ x 13 in. Henry Art Gallery, Frances and Thomas Blakemore Collection, FA 96.90

(bottom left) Frances Blakemore, ca. 1938. Courtesy of The Blakemore Foundation

(bottom right) *Family*, early 1950s, serigraph, 13 x 16 ¾ in. Henry Art Gallery, Frances and Thomas Blakemore Collection, FA 96.88

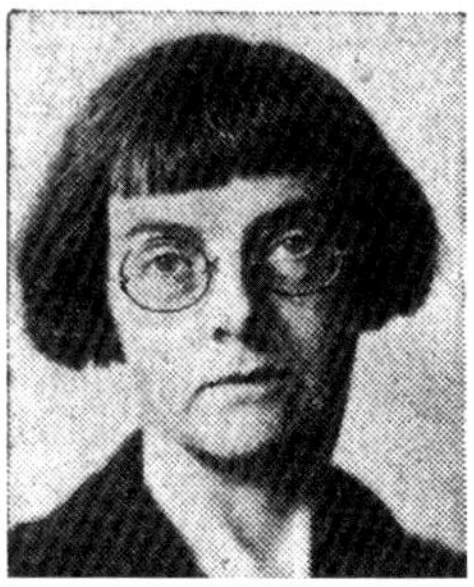

ELIZABETH COLBORNE 1885–1948

Painter, printmaker, and illustrator, Elizabeth Aline Colborne was born in Chamberlain, South Dakota, the middle child of three girls. She was particularly attached to her father, a successful civil engineer whose skillful mechanical renderings fascinated the young child and initiated her interest in drawing.

After the premature death of her parents in 1892 and 1893, she went to live with her maternal aunt in Bellingham, Washington, separating her from her two sisters. After finishing high school in 1903, she attended Pratt Institute in Brooklyn, New York, where she studied with Arthur Wesley Dow (1857–1922). For the next three years, she studied landscape painting with Rockwell Kent (1882–1971) at Monhegan Island, Maine; with Robert Henri (1865–1929) in New York; etching with Charles Mielatz (1864–1919) at the Art Students League, and William Meyerowitz (1887–1981) at the National Academy of Design.

Around 1907, Colborne began working for the Decorative Designers of New York City creating cover designs, end papers, and illustrated pages for books. Over the next few decades, she became nationally known for her numerous illustrations in children's books and other domestically oriented publications.

In the early years of her career, she would often divide her time between New York, where she lived with her younger sister, and Bellingham, where she taught art to children and young adults.

In the fine-art field, Colborne was initially known for her etchings, but none of these works have surfaced. Luckily, a handful of highly detailed conte crayon drawings of trees and vegetation of the Northwest have survived and are in the collection of the Whatcom Museum in Bellingham. She eventually returned to the Northwest and began creating color woodblock prints for which she received national recognition. None of these works are dated but they were likely initiated around 1925 after her study of block-printing methods with Allen Lewis (1873–1957) the previous year. The subject matter reflected her deep love of nature, focusing on the unique landscapes and vegetation of her adopted home. Colborne often went into the rainforests of Washington State to study and observe the trees and flora first hand. She printed a number of color woodblock prints during her activity on the Washington State Public Works of Art Project in 1933, but the blocks were likely cut in previous years.

Colborne also worked in watercolor, tempera, and gouache, and revived the *cliché verre* photo-etching technique, naming her prints "Sun Etchings." Using this technique, she produced greeting and holiday cards that she sold locally and nationally.

Colborne was represented in New York by several prominent art galleries, where images of the Northwest landscape were of special interest to the East Coast audience. In 1939, she became a member of the National Association of Women Artists.

Although she had recognition in New York, Colborne never exhibited with or joined any of the prominent Seattle arts organizations. Despite the high quality and unique subject matter of her work, she never participated in any known national print exhibitions. She was, however, given a few smaller exhibitions in Bellingham in the 1930s, and in 1940 she was given a solo exhibition at the Seattle Art Museum.

During WWII, she worked as a technical illustrator for the Boeing Company before being diagnosed with breast cancer. She died in Seattle in 1948.

Photo: Elizabeth Colborne, ca. 1930. Scanned from Colborne's obituary photo in the *Bellingham Herald*, Tuesday Feb 24, 1948, p. 14, column 2. Scan provided by The Bellingham Public Library. Photographer unknown

SOURCE

Martin, David F. *Evergreen Muse: The Art of Elizabeth Colborne.* Bellingham, WA: Whatcom Museum; Seattle: University of Washington Press, 2011.

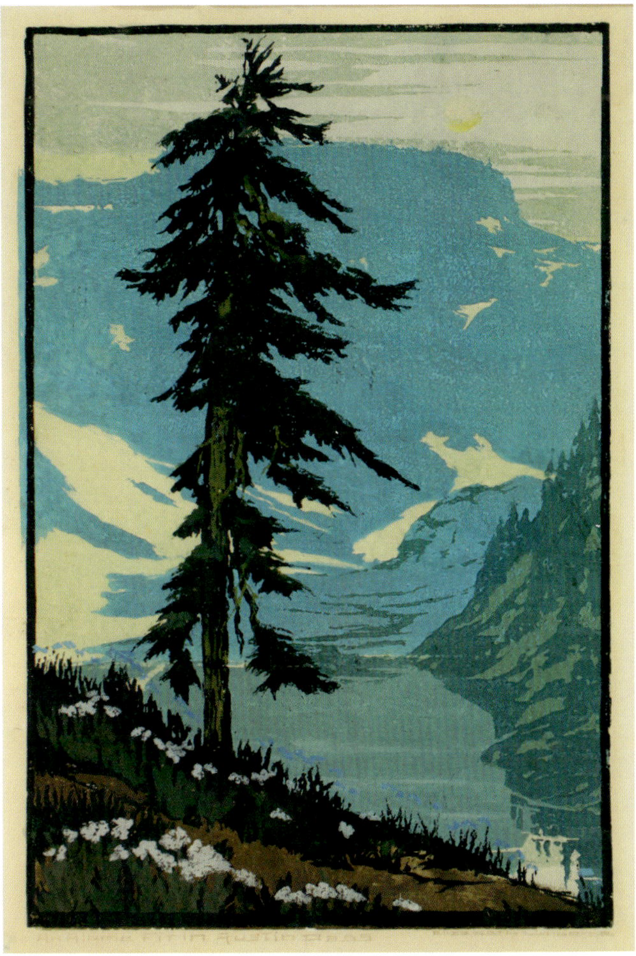

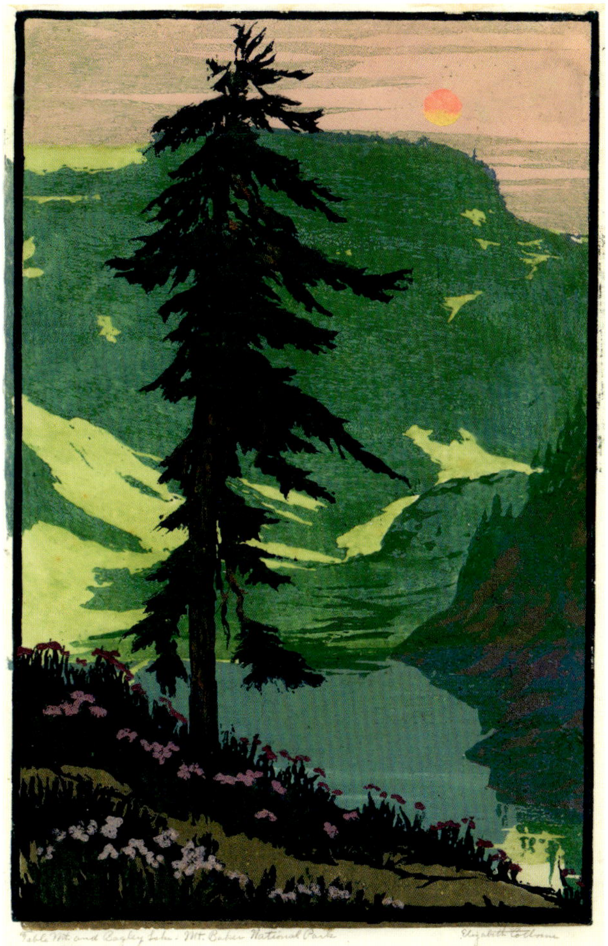

(left) *An Alpine Fir in Austin Pass*, ca. 1928, color woodblock print, 14 ¼ x 9 in. Private collection

(right) *Table Mountain and Bagley Lake, Mount Baker National Park*, ca. 1928, color woodblock print, 14 ¼ x 9 in. Whatcom Museum, Gift of the Bellingham Public Library, 1976.62.6.

In this proof, Colborne used the same blocks from *An Alpine Fir in Austin Pass* to create a completely different atmospheric effect by using different colored inks.

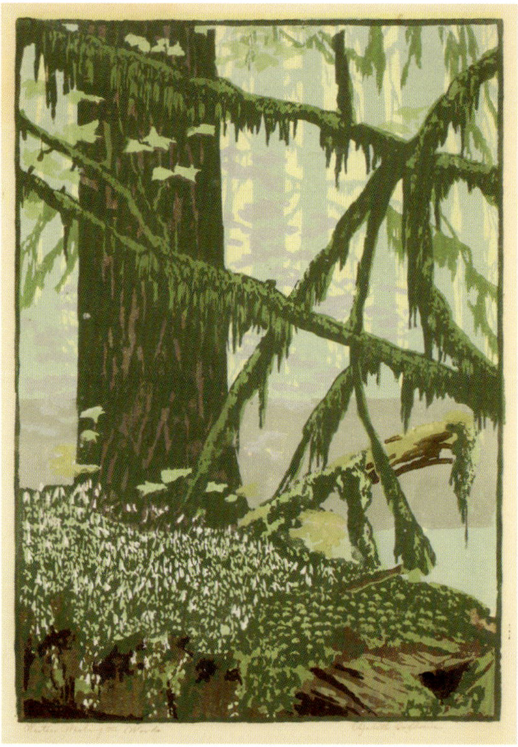

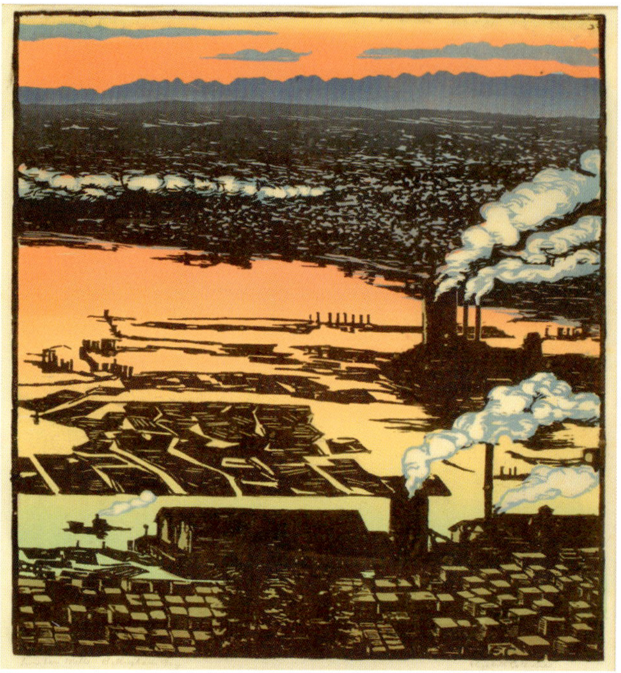

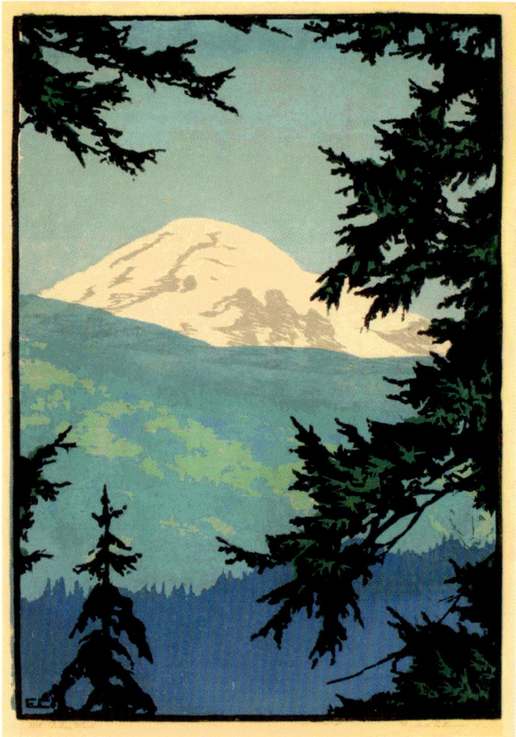

(top) *Western Washington Woods*, ca. 1933, color woodblock print, 13 ¼ x 9 in. Collection of Thomas H. Wake

(bottom left) *Mount Baker, Washington*, ca. 1928, color woodblock print, 13 x 9 in. Private collection

(bottom right) *Lumber Mills, Bellingham Bay*, ca. 1933, color woodblock print, 11 ¾ x 10 ½ in. Private collection

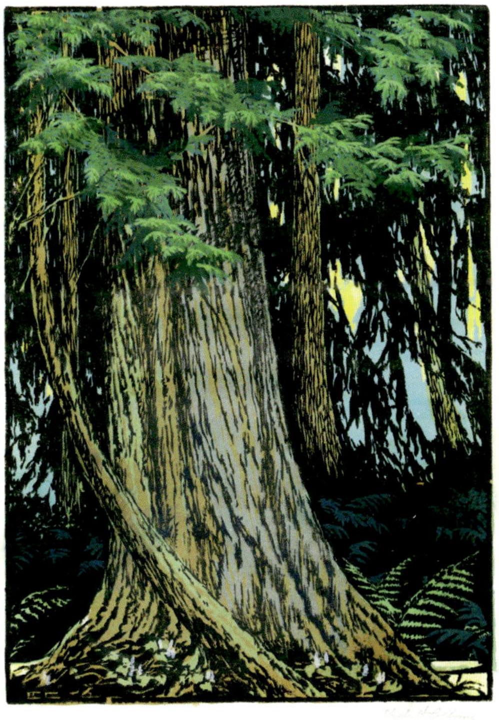

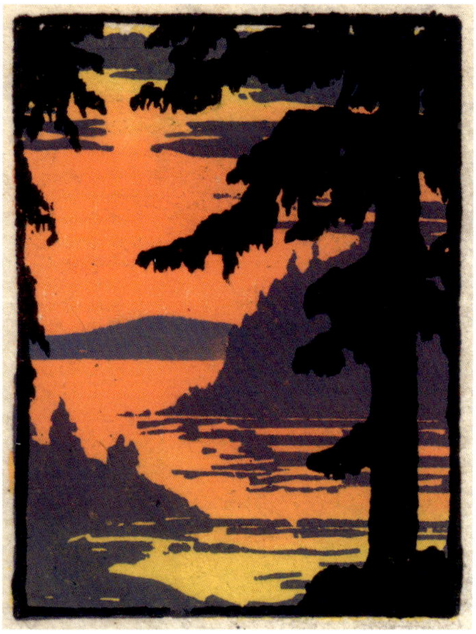

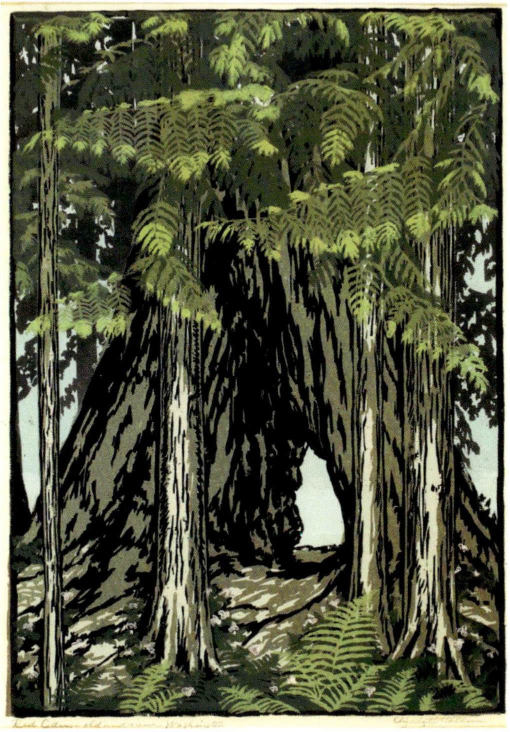

(top left) *Cedar Swamp*, ca. 1932, color woodblock print, 13 x 9 in. From the Collection of the Two Red Roses Foundation

(bottom) *Red Cedars—Old and New, Washington*, ca. 1930, color woodblock print, 13 x 9 in. Private collection

(top right) Untitled, ca. 1925, color woodblock print, 3 3/8 x 2 5/8 in. Whatcom Museum, Gift of the Bellingham Public Library, 1976.62.53

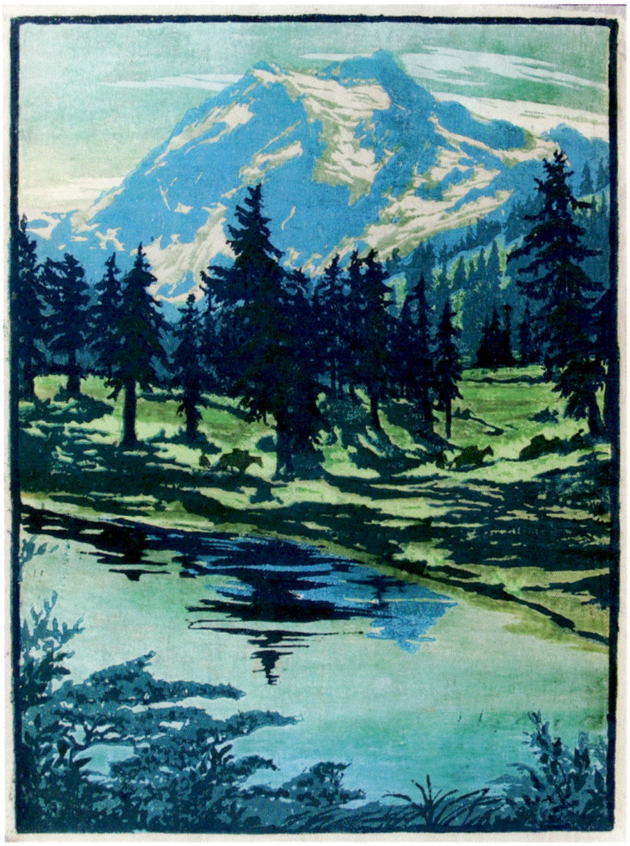

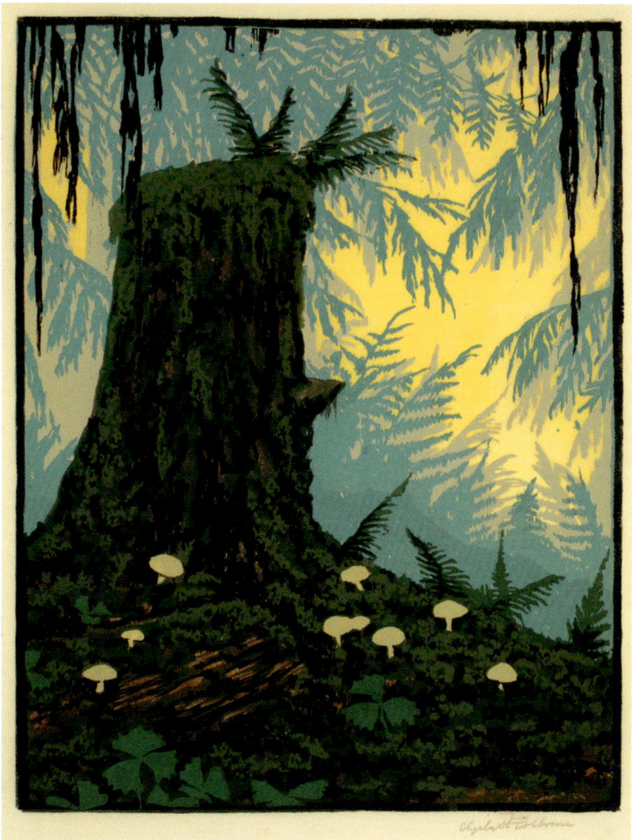

(left) *Mount Shuksan, Washington*, ca. 1928, color woodblock print, 12 ½ x 9 in. Whatcom Museum, Gift of Irene Rosser 1989.9.1

(right) *In the Rainforests of Washington*, ca. 1933, color woodblock print, 12 ¼ x 9 in. Private collection

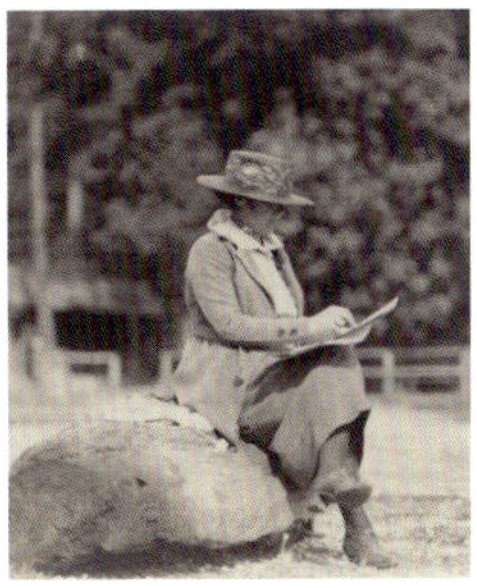

ELIZABETH A. COOPER 1877–1936

Elizabeth Ann Marshall Cooper was born in Nottingham, England. In 1882, she moved to San Francisco with her parents and later attended the Mark Hopkins Art Institute in San Francisco (now the San Francisco Art Institute). She met John H. Cooper, of Dracott, England, whose family had also relocated to San Francisco. Before moving to Seattle in 1915, she and her husband had two sons. Beginning in 1917 she attended the University of Washington where she studied with Walter Isaacs (1886–1964), Eugenie Worman (1871–1944), and others who nurtured her interest in European modernism. She would return to study intermittently at UW until 1934 but never received a degree. Like many women artists of her generation, her formal education was interrupted to raise children.

Cooper became a highly regarded painter, printmaker, and craftsman in Seattle during the 1920s and '30s. In the early 1920s, she designed and made rugs, ceramic tiles, and other utilitarian objects in bold, exuberant patterns. She exhibited in all of the major regional venues and was a member of Women Painters of Washington and the Northwest Printmakers Society, where her print *The Picnic* won a purchase prize in 1930.

Cooper was a member of the prominent Group of Twelve, an association of modernist artists in Seattle that included some of the major regional painters of the period, including Morris Graves (1910–2001), Ambrose Patterson (1877–1966), and Kenneth Callahan (1905–1986). She assimilated such modern movements in art as European Post-Impressionism, Cubism, and German Expressionism, then not commonly known in the Northwest art scene of that period.

She died in Seattle at the age of fifty-nine of cancer.

Photo: Elizabeth A. Cooper, circa 1930. Courtesy of the John Marshall Cooper QTIP Trust. Photographer unknown

SOURCES

The Martin-Zambito Archive

Special Collections of The Seattle Public Library, Artists Scrapbooks.

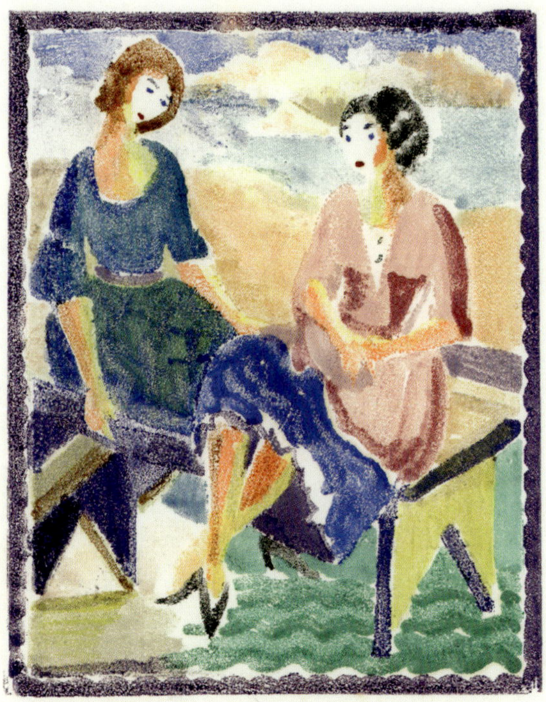

(left) *Friends*, ca. 1925–1929, white line color woodblock print, 8 ½ x 6 ½ in. Collection of the John Marshall Cooper QTIP Trust

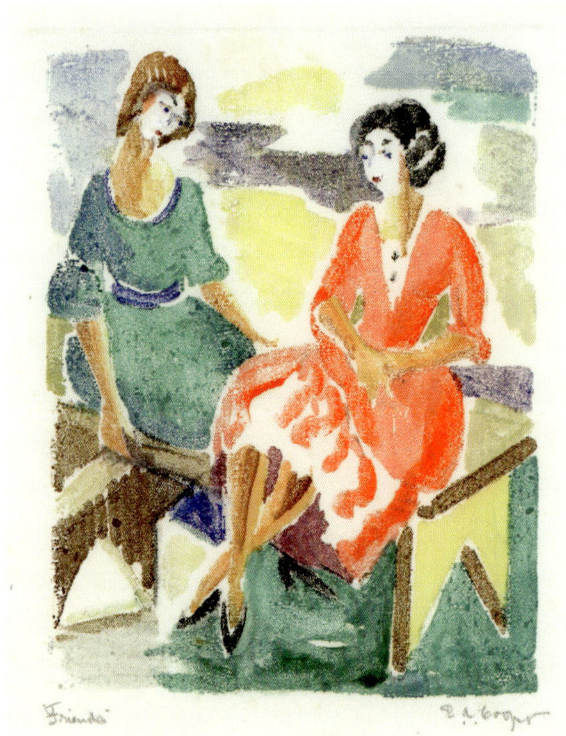

(right) *Friends*, ca. 1925–1929, white line color woodblock print, 8 ½ x 6 ½ in. Collection of the John Marshall Cooper QTIP Trust

These proofs illustrate the variety of effects created by using different colored inks and brushwork on the same block.

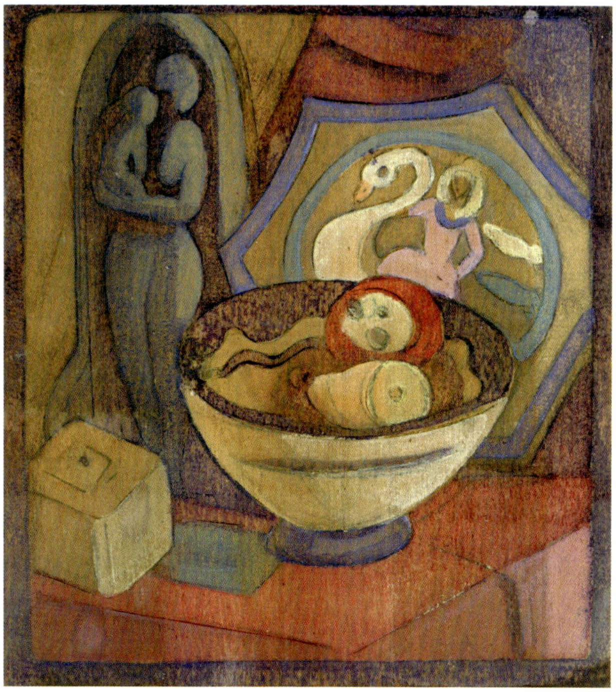

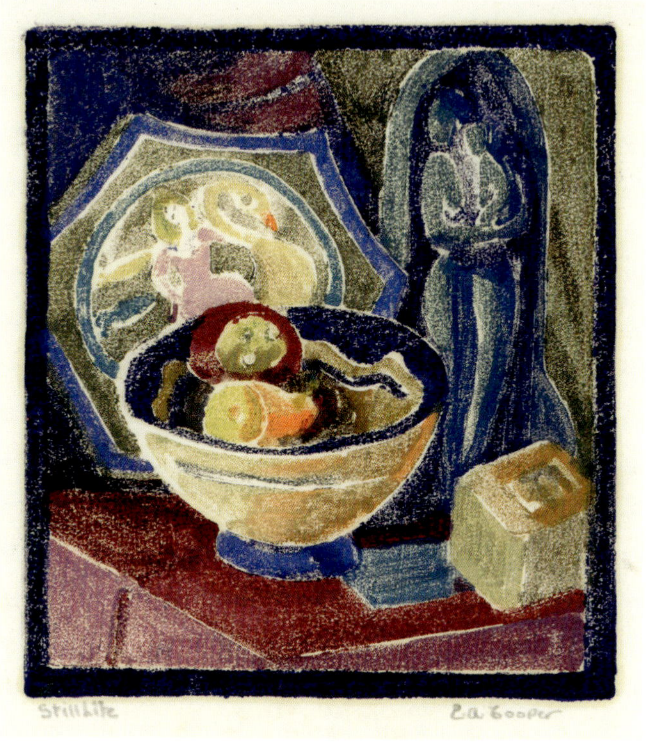

(left) Printing block used to create *Still Life* in the plate to the right, Collection of the John Marshall Cooper QTIP Trust

(right) *Still Life*, ca. 1925–1929, white line color woodblock print, 6 ½ x 5 ½ in. Collection of the John Marshall Cooper QTIP Trust

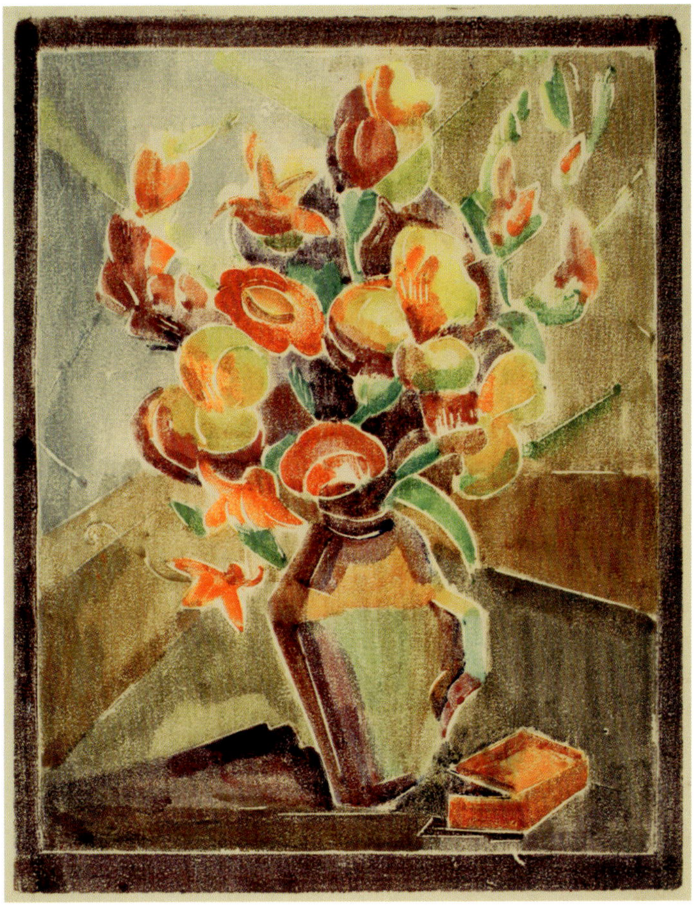

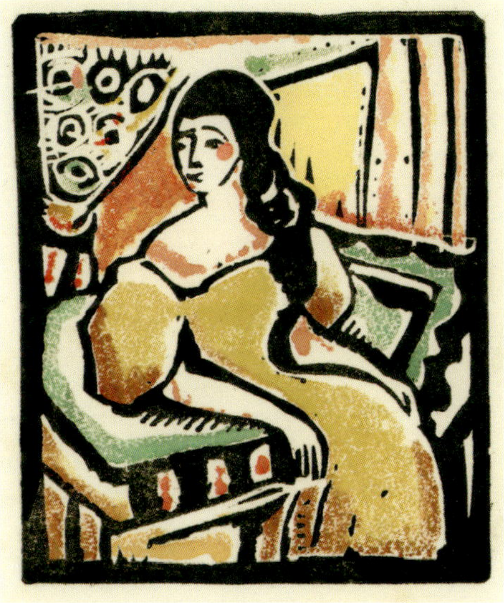

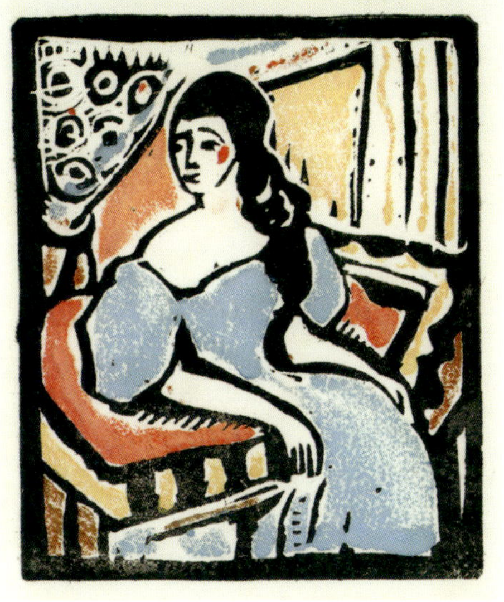

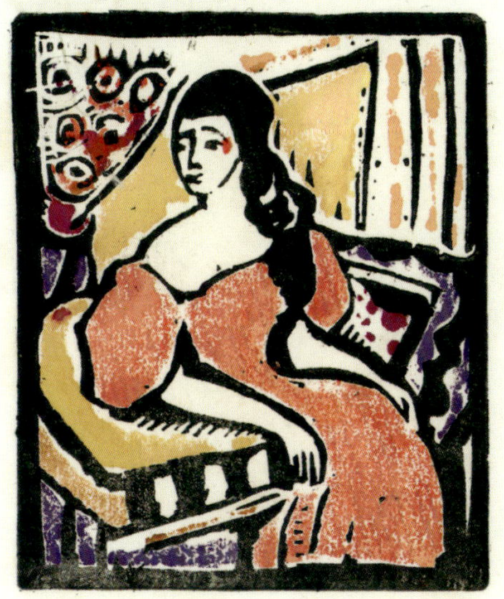

(top left) Untitled, ca. 1925–1929, white line color woodblock print, 12 x 9 in. Collection of the John Marshall Cooper QTIP Trust

(right) Untitled, ca. 1925–1929, linocuts, 6 ½ x 5 ½ in. each. Collection of the John Marshall Cooper QTIP Trust

Three proofs from the same block using a variety of applied ink colors.

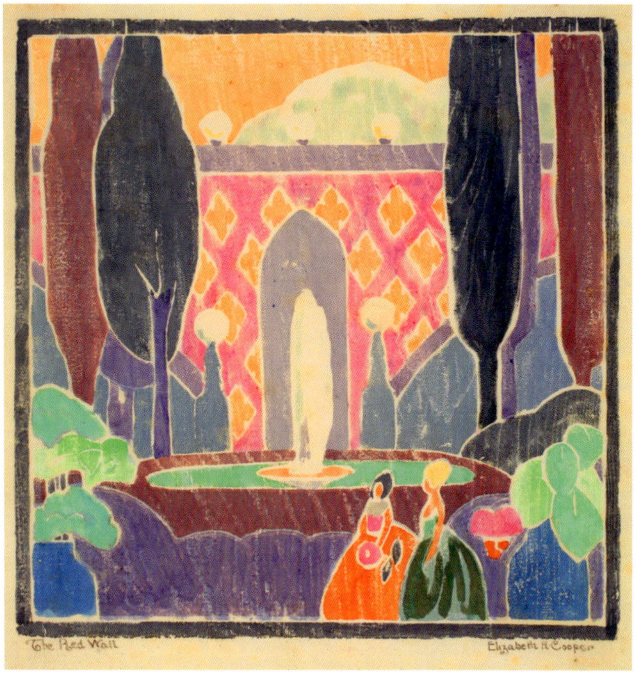

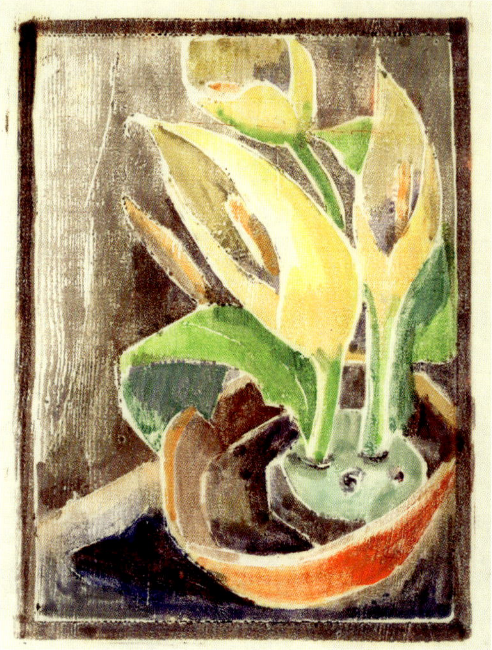

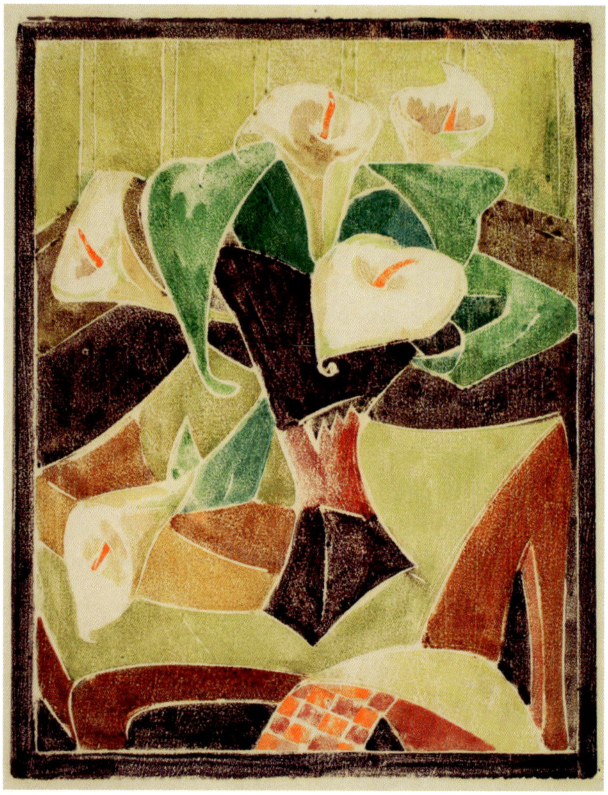

(top) *The Red Wall*, ca. 1925–1929, white line color woodblock print, 12 x 11 5/8 in. Collection of the John Marshall Cooper QTIP Trust

(bottom left) Untitled, ca. 1925–1929, white line color woodblock print, 9 1/4 x 6 3/4 in. Collection of the John Marshall Cooper QTIP Trust

(bottom right) Untitled, ca. 1925–1929, white line color woodblock print, 12 x 9 in. Collection of the John Marshall Cooper QTIP Trust

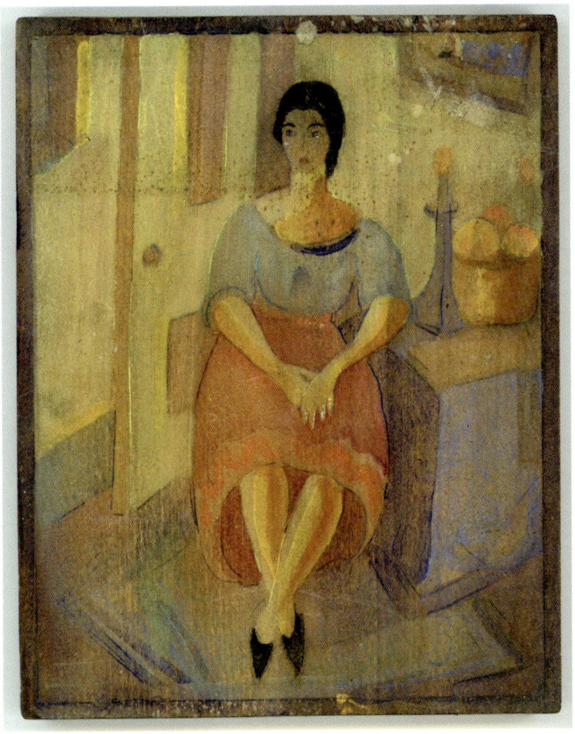

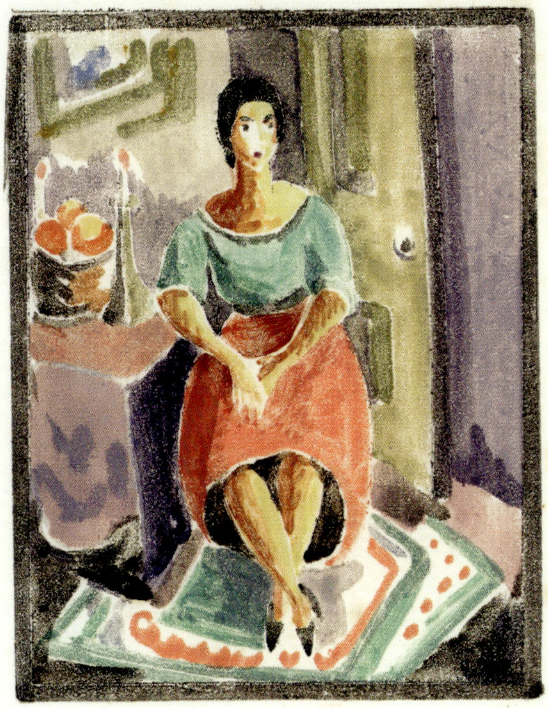

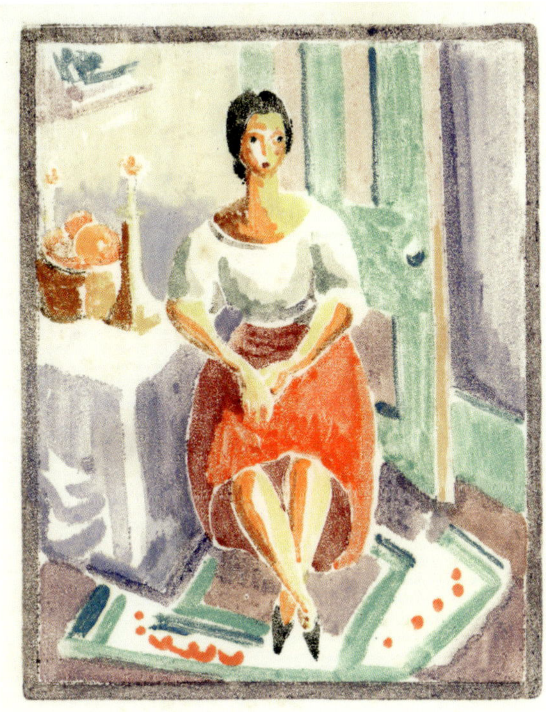

(top left) printing block for *The Yellow Room*, ca. 1925–1929

(top right) *The Yellow Room*, ca. 1925–1929, white line color woodblock print, 8 ½ x 6 ½ in.

(bottom) *The Yellow Room*, ca. 1925–1929, white line color woodblock print, proof with different colored inking, 8 ½ x 6 ½ in.

All from the Collection of the John Marshall Cooper QTIP Trust

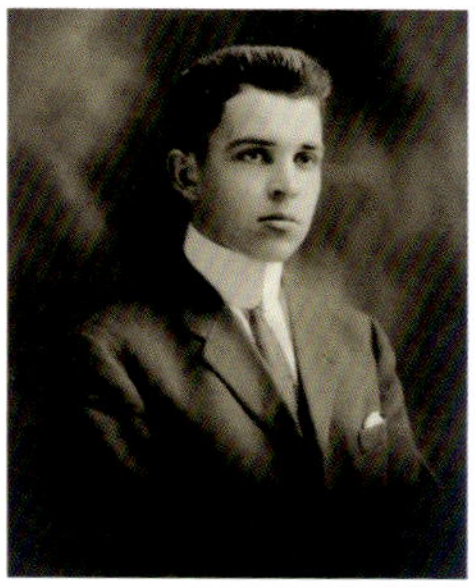

LANCE WOOD HART 1891–1941

Born Alanson Wood Hart in Conway, Kentucky, Hart relocated to Aberdeen, Washington, with his mother and two siblings after the death of his father in 1899. From childhood, he displayed an advanced talent in drawing and watercolor. As a young adult, he received his professional training at the Art Institute of Chicago (1912–1916) and the Royal Academy of Fine Arts in Stockholm, Sweden, from 1923 to 1925, where he also taught from 1931 to 1932.

Hart was president of the Art Students League of Chicago in 1913 and secretary of the Independent Society of Artists in 1915.

He was active in regional theater productions as an actor, writer, and stage designer, both in Aberdeen and Chicago.

Early in his career, Hart established an impressive reputation in the Northwest arts community both in Washington State and Oregon. He began exhibiting his work in Seattle with the Fine Arts Society in 1919, where he won first prize in watercolor.

From 1925 through 1931, Hart lived and worked in Seattle, making a living by producing decorative murals and designs for public buildings and private homes. Among his outstanding achievements are the interior and exterior designs and decorations of St. Joseph Catholic Church in Seattle. In 1928, he married Clare Blake, an art student attending the Cornish School, and they later had two daughters.

In 1931, Hart relocated to Eugene, Oregon, to accept a position as Assistant Professor of Drawing and Painting at the University of Oregon. During this time he won the respect and admiration of his fellow art professors and became a beloved and influential instructor. Hart exerted a significant influence on the Aberdeen-born artist, Robert Motherwell (1915–1991) with whom he shared a lifelong friendship.

In 1940, he was selected to complete a mural for the Treasury Department Section of Fine Arts for the U.S. Post Office in Snohomish, Washington. This mural, entitled *The Construction of a Skid Road in the Eighties*, is now housed at the Snohomish City Hall.

Other murals produced by Hart include works for the Moose Lodge, Aberdeen, Washington, of 1921 (destroyed); The Savoy Alley Club and the Grand Theater, both in Aberdeen (both destroyed); The Town Club, Portland, Oregon (extant); and the University of Oregon Art Building, 1932–33 (extant).

Lance Hart is the author of *Observation Technique in Figure Drawing*, The Valley Press, Eugene, Oregon, 1938.

Photo: Lance Wood Hart, ca. 1916. Courtesy of Lucy Hart. Photographer unknown

SOURCES

The Martin-Zambito Archive

Lucy Hart and Lisa Hart Guthrie

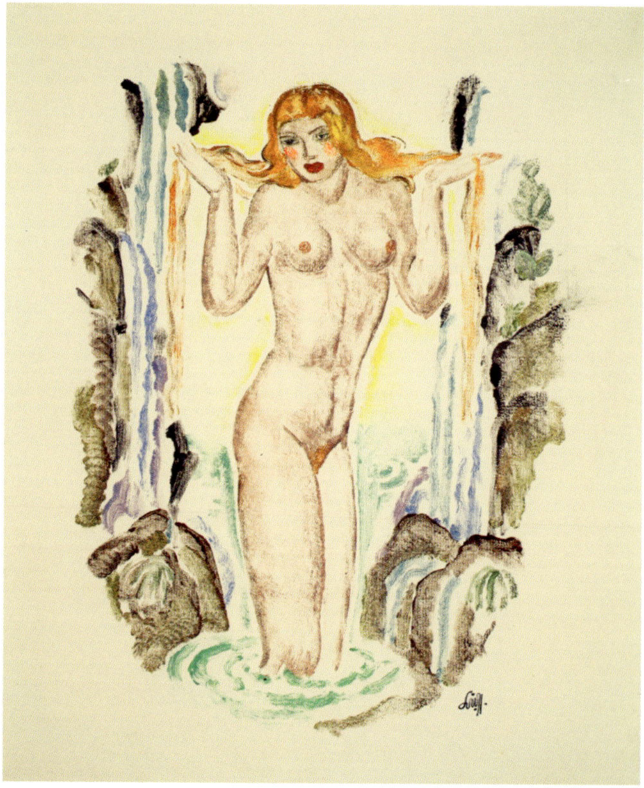

Untitled, ca. 1925, monoprint, 14 x 10 in. Private collection

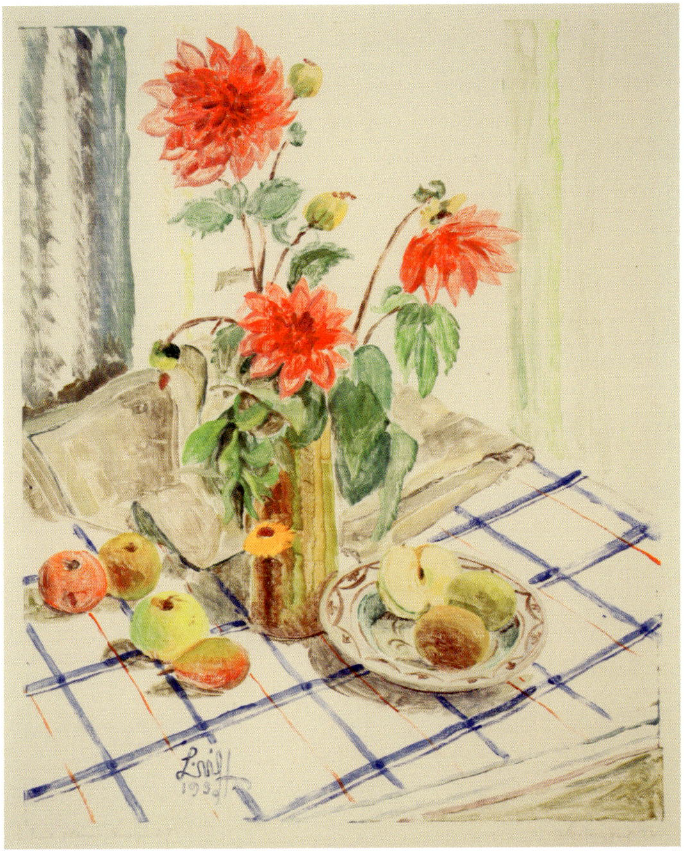

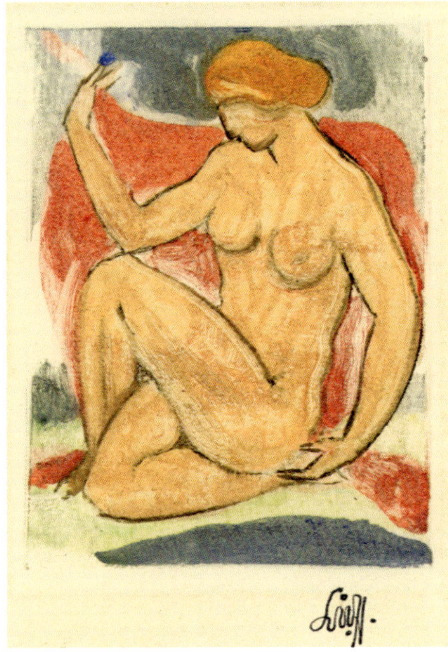

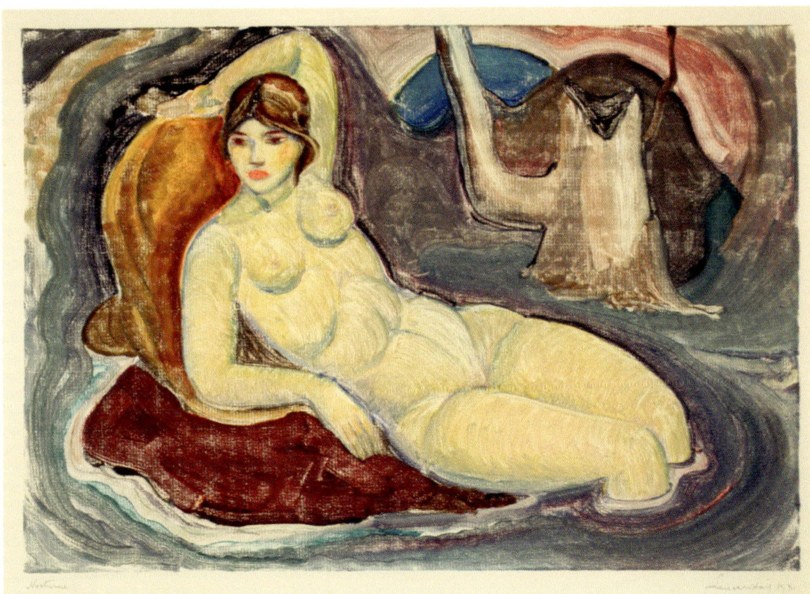

(top left) *Fruit and Flower Arrangement*, 1930, monoprint, 17 ½ x 14 in. Private collection

(top right) Untitled, ca. 1925, monoprint, 4 ½ x 3 ¼ in. Private collection

(bottom) *Nocturne*, 1931, monoprint, 14 x 10 in. Private collection

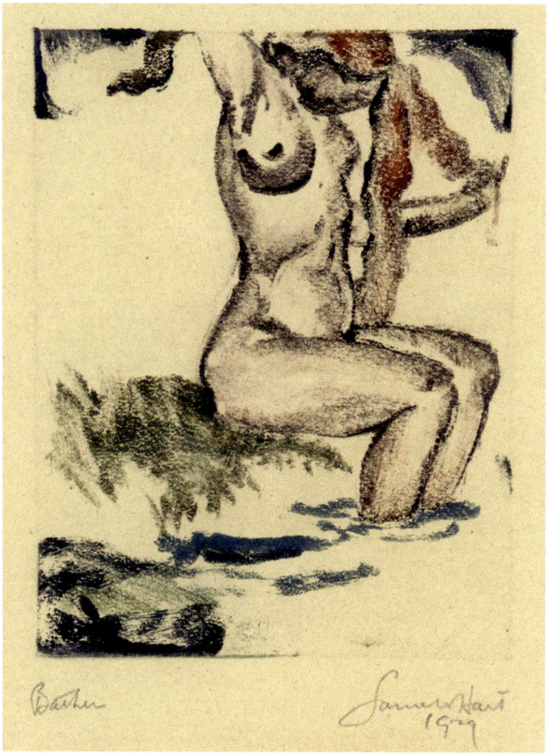

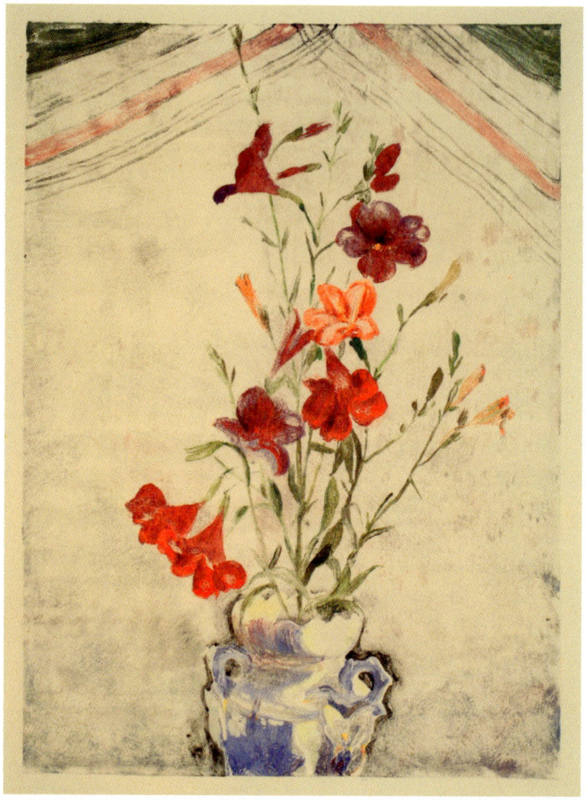

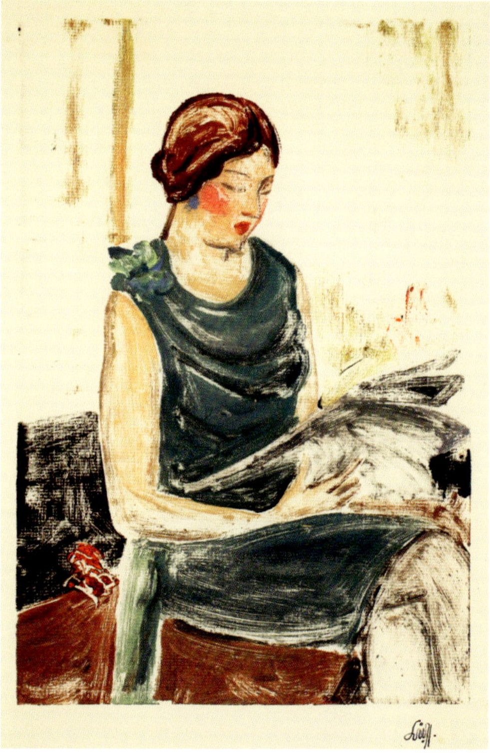

(top left) *Bather*, 1929, monoprint, 14 x 10 in. Private collection

(bottom) Untitled, ca. 1928, monoprint, 12 x 7 ¾ in. Private collection

(top right) *Salpiglossis*, 1929, monoprint, 13 ¾ x 9 ¾ in. Private collection

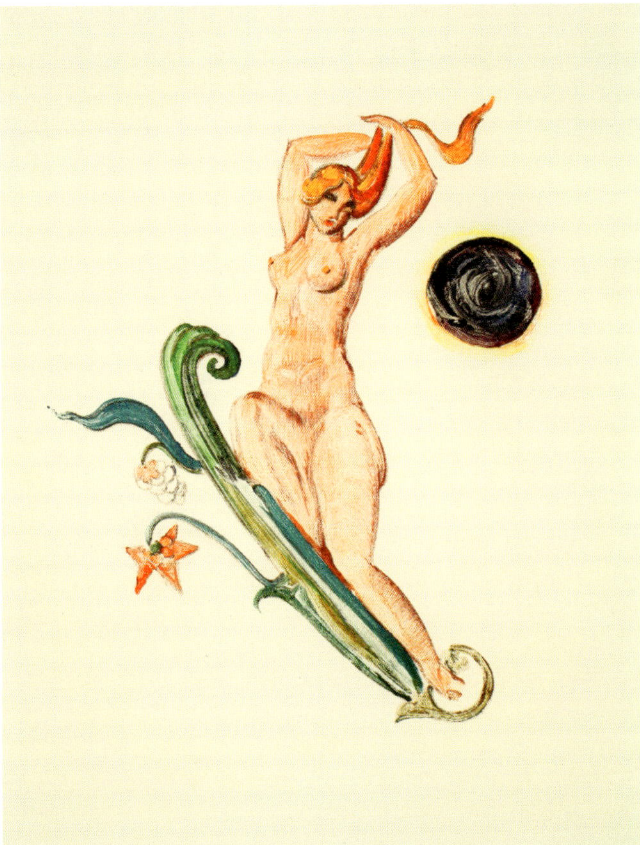

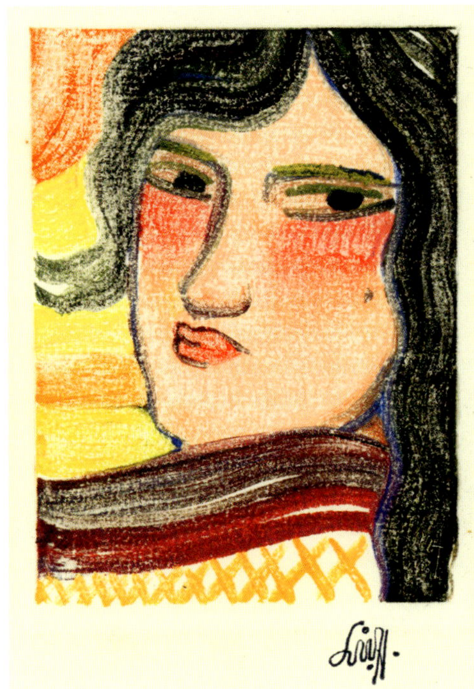

(left) *Fantasy Sketch*, 1930, monoprint, 14 x 9 ¾ in. Private collection

(right) *Decoration*, ca. 1928, monoprint, 4 ⅝ x 3 ¼ in. Private collection

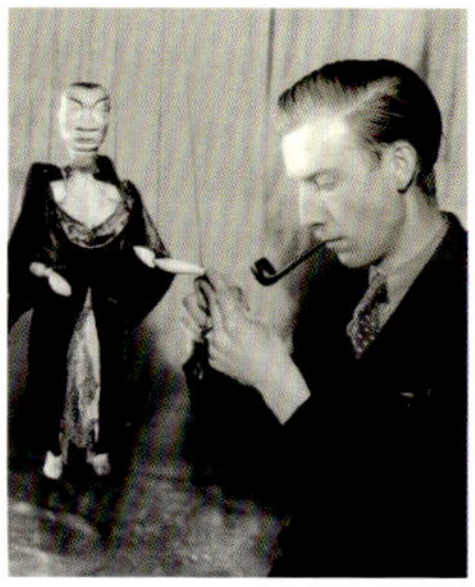

ROBERT BRUCE INVERARITY 1909–1999

R. Bruce Inverarity was born and raised in Seattle. He attended Cornish College of the Arts in the 1920s and was one of Seattle's earliest modernists. During his time at Cornish, he shared an apartment with Mark Tobey (1890–1976), who was then an instructor at the school until departing for Europe, leaving Bruce to take over his classes. Printmaking figured prominently in Inverarity's early work. He produced etchings and intaglio prints as well as color and black and white blockprints. His passionate affinity for Northwest Coast Native American design was fostered by his father, Duncan Inverarity (1868–1949). The senior Inverarity had moved to Seattle in 1883 from New Zealand. He was an attorney, theatrical entrepreneur, photographer, and lover of Native American culture. In 1899, he was part of the Harriman Alaska expedition, assisting photographer Edward S. Curtis (1868–1952), as well as creating his own body of work in the medium.

In 1927, Bruce attended a class in printmaking in Seattle by the visiting Japanese artist Yamagishi Kazue (1883–1966). He became so proficient in the medium that he published an instructional booklet in 1930. He also taught puppetry at the University of Washington Division of Drama and worked with famed puppeteers Blanding Sloan (1886–1975) and Ralph Chesse (1900–1991). He became the Director of the Washington State Federal Art Project and later an Art Director of Sales for the Boeing Aircraft Company. During WWII, he worked for the U.S. Navy where he organized a research center on camouflage that developed models and plans for the 13th Naval District as well as a training program for the Seabees. He later worked for the U.S. Navy as an official naval war artist and after the war, in 1946, he earned his undergraduate degree from the University of Washington. In 1947, he earned his Masters Degree and, in 1948, his Ph D from Fremont University in Los Angeles, California.

His 1937 oil painting, *Northwest Pacific Forms, Haida* was selected for exhibition in *American Art Today* at the 1939 New York World's Fair. As a printmaker and watercolorist, he exhibited in many cities throughout the United States and Canada. Inverarity, like his father, became an extremely talented photographer, and produced an important body of work in that medium. As an author he published *A Manual of Puppetry* (1936), *Masks and Marionettes of the Northwest Coast Indians* (1940), *Moveable Masks and Figures of the North Pacific Coast Indians* (1941), *Northwest Coast Indian Art* (1946), and articles on puppet construction and block printing as well as writings on museum design and anthropology. He was widely known for his classic book, *Art of the Northwest Coast Indians*, originally published in 1950. The book was the culmination of years of ethnological study and documentation of the various Northwest Indian tribes he visited and studied at first hand.

After his retirement in 1975, Inverarity sold his vast collection of Northwest Coast Native American artifacts to the British Museum. In his final years, he spent much of his time caring for his ailing wife. He died in La Jolla, California in 1999.

Photo: R. Bruce Inverarity, circa 1928. University of Washington, Special Collections Division, R. Bruce Inverarity Collection. Photographer unknown

SOURCES

The Martin-Zambito Archive

Special Collections of The Seattle Public Library, Artists Scrapbooks.

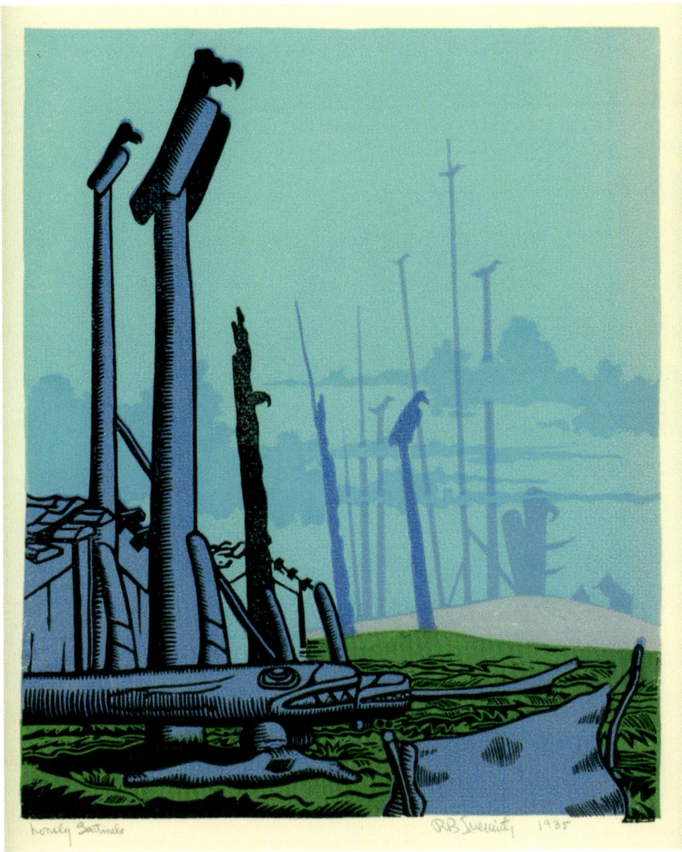

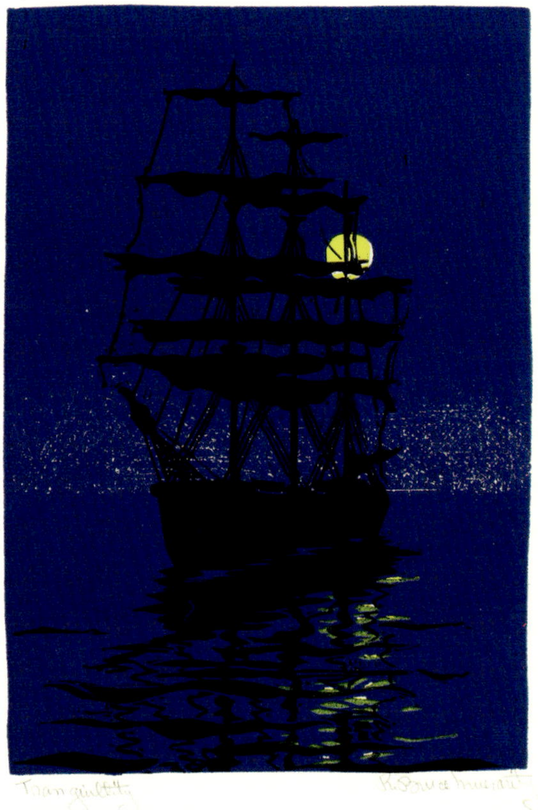

(left) *Lonely Sentinels*, 1935, color linocut, 9 x 6 in. Collection of Neil Collins

(right) *Tranquility*, ca. 1928, color linocut, 9 x 6 in. Collection of Neil Collins

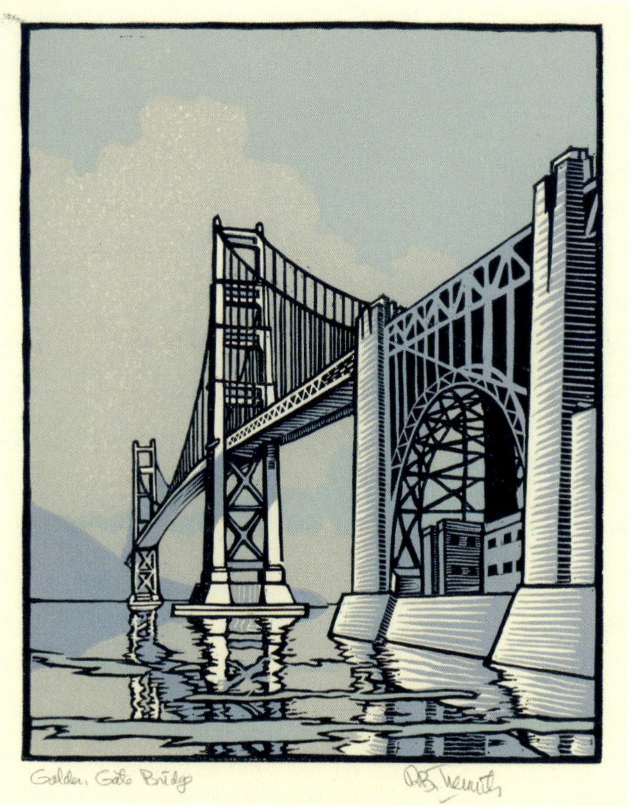

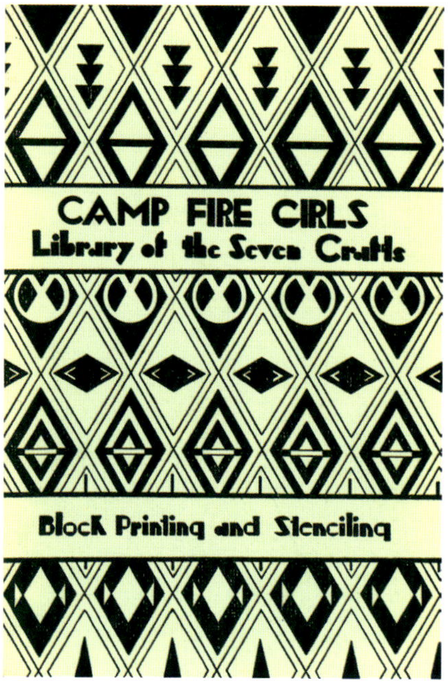

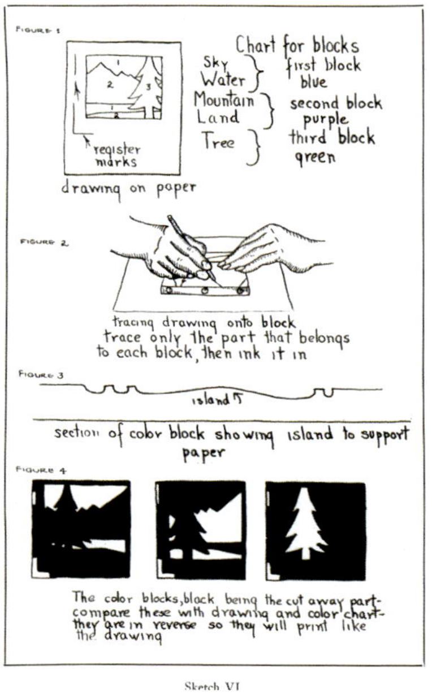

(top) *Golden Gate Bridge*, ca. 1938, color linocut, 8 ¾ x 7 in. Collection of Neil Collins

(bottom left) *Camp Fire Girls Library of the Seven Crafts: Block Printing and Stenciling*, by Robert Bruce Inverarity. The Campfire Outfitting Co., New York, ca. 1930. Courtesy of the Martin-Zambito Archive

(bottom right) Page 16 from *Camp Fire Girls Library of the Seven Crafts: BlockPrinting and Stenciling*, by Robert Bruce Inverarity

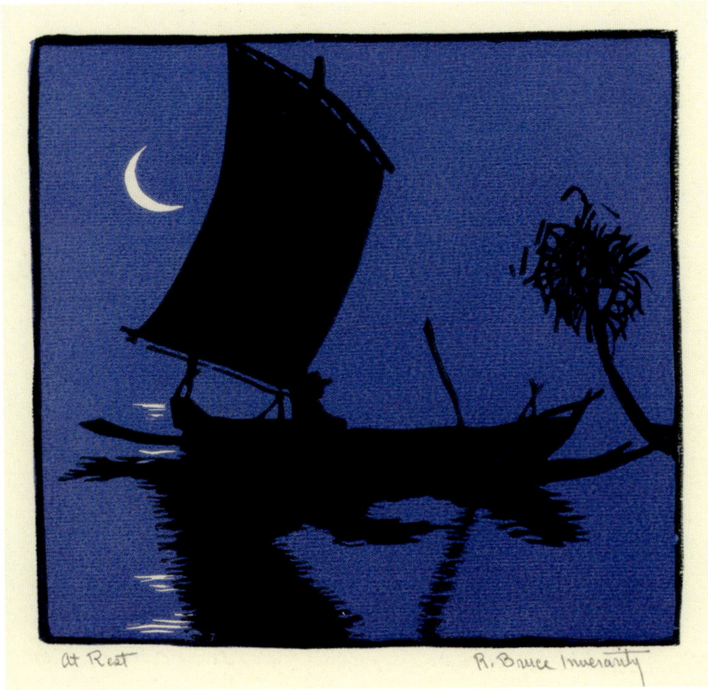

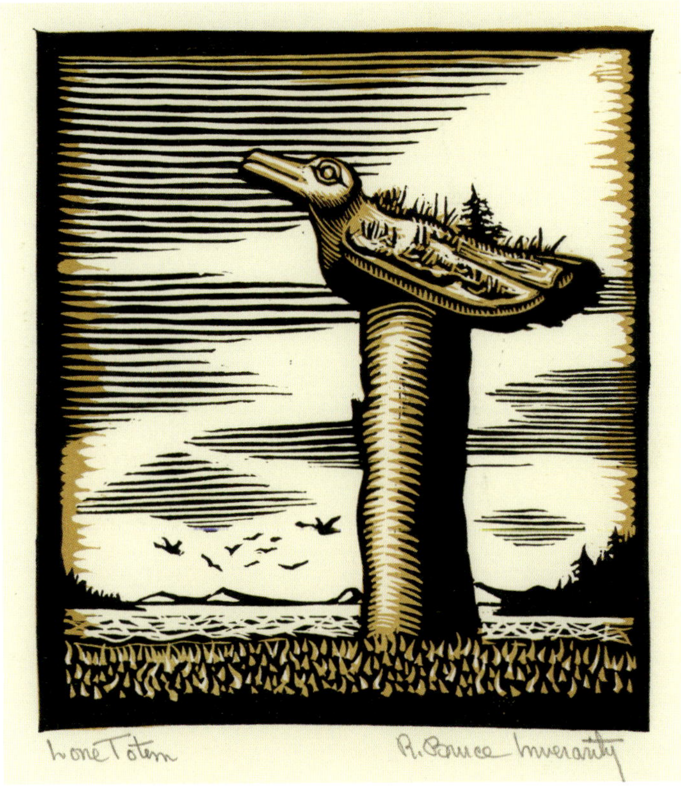

(left) *At Rest*, ca. 1928, color linocut, 6 ⅛ x 6 ⅜ in. Private collection

(right) *Lone Totem*, ca. 1928, color linocut, 6,⅛ x 6 ⅜ in. Collection of Lindsey and Carolyn Echelbarger

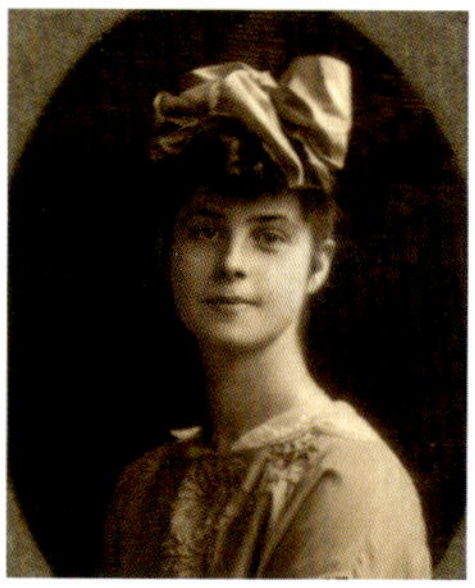

DOROTHY DOLPH JENSEN 1895–1977

Painter/printmaker Dorothy Dolph Jensen began her study of art at a very young age. Born in Forest Grove, Oregon, to a prominent pioneer family, her grandfather was the U.S. Senator from Oregon, Joseph N. Dolph (1835–1897), and her mother was a well-known character actress, Augusta Armstrong Dolph (1872–1929). Dorothy began her education at a convent in Europe at the age of twelve and remained there for two years. While in Europe, she began art studies in Antwerp, Belgium, and then in Paris with Emmanuel Hannaux (1855–1934) and Jean-Paul Laurens (1838–1921) at the Académie Julian in Paris. At the Académie, she learned how to produce etchings at the age of thirteen.

Returning to the Northwest in 1914, Jensen moved to Seattle before attending the Portland Art School, where she studied with Harry Wentz (1876–1965) and Sidney Bell (1888–1964).

Dorothy met Lloyd E. Jensen (1895–1990) while they were working together at the Schneider Art Gallery in Seattle around 1917. Lloyd was in the process of becoming the region's finest frame-maker, and Dorothy was working in the application of gold leafing. Following their marriage in 1919 she would remain in Seattle permanently, becoming one of the city's most highly respected artists, and Lloyd the region's major frame-maker.

Having retained her initial interest in printmaking, Jensen imported a large etching press from Paris around 1920. She was one of only a few local artists working in intaglio methods in the 1920s and '30s. Jensen experimented with various types of color printmaking. She made color monotypes using etching plates, colored some of her etchings and drypoints *à la poupée*, and also used hand coloring with water-based paints.

A founding member of the Women Painters of Washington in 1930, Dorothy Dolph Jensen was also a charter member of the Northwest Watercolor Society and an early exhibitor and longtime member of the Northwest Printmakers Society.

Photo: Dorothy Dolph Jensen, 1916. Courtesy of the Martin-Zambito Archive. Photograph by Edward Curtis Studio

SOURCES

Martin, David F. *A Fluid Tradition: The Northwest Watercolor Society at 75*. Seattle: University of Washington Press, 2015.

Martin, David F. *An Enduring Legacy: Women Painters of Washington, 1930–2005*. Seattle University of Washington Press, 2005.

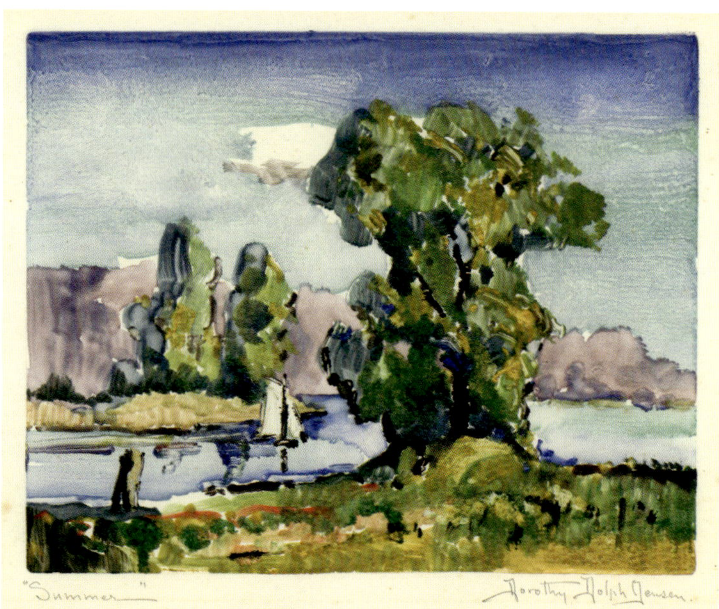

Summer, ca. 1932, monoprint, 4¾ x 6 in. Collection of Thomas H. Wake

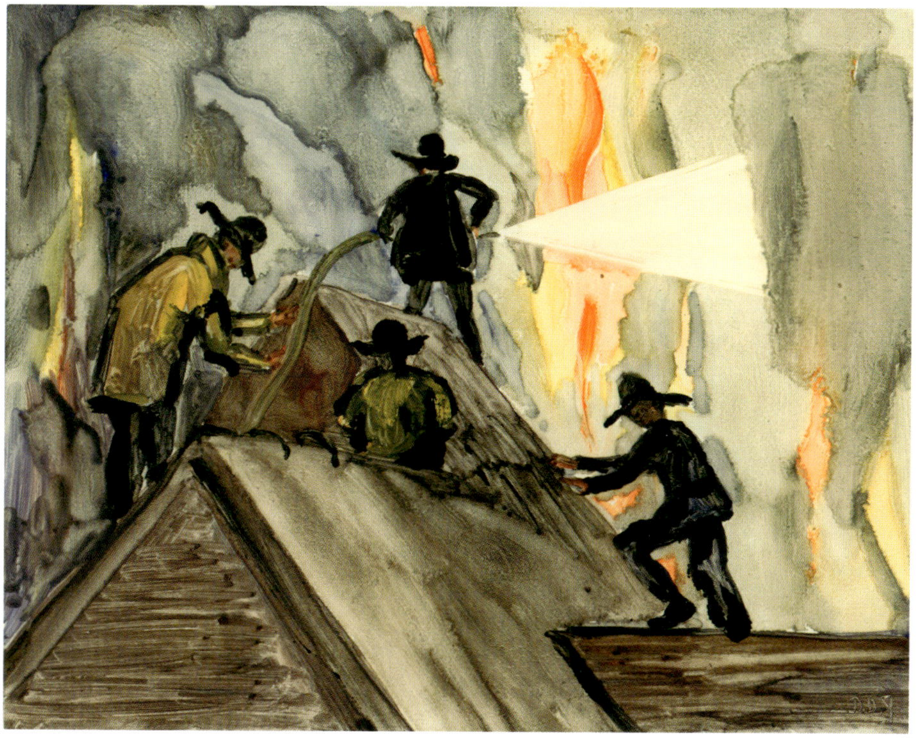

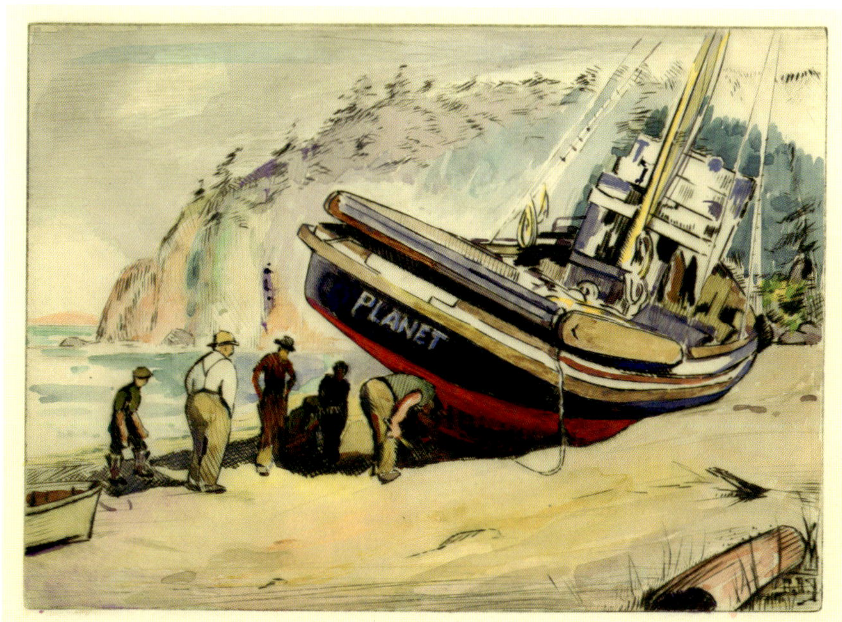

(top) Untitled, ca. 1935, monoprint, 8 ⅛ x 9 ¾ in. Private collection

(bottom) *The Planet Aground*, ca. 1935, drypoint with watercolor, 5 ½ x 7 ⅜ in. Private collection

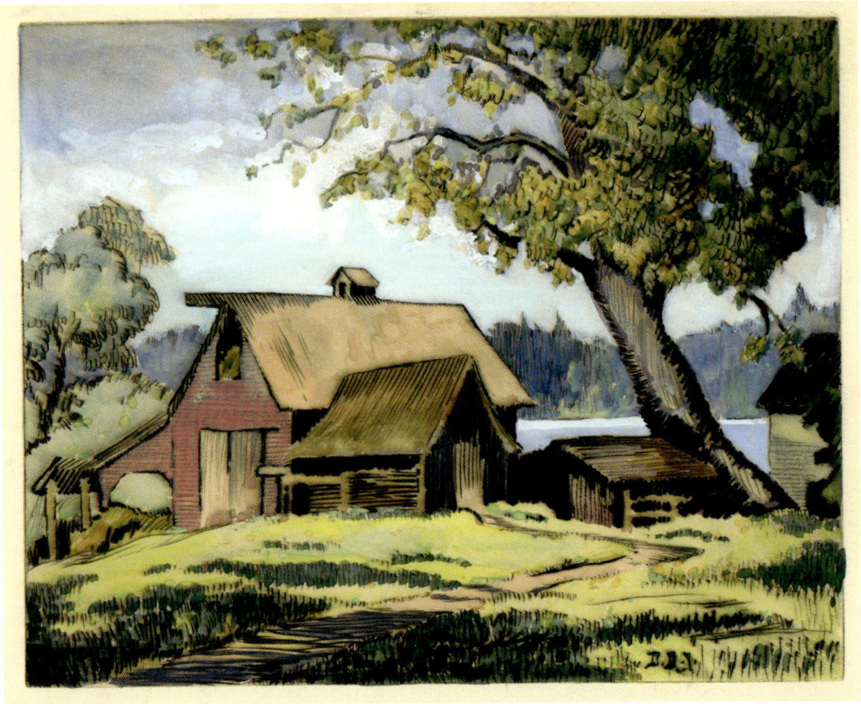

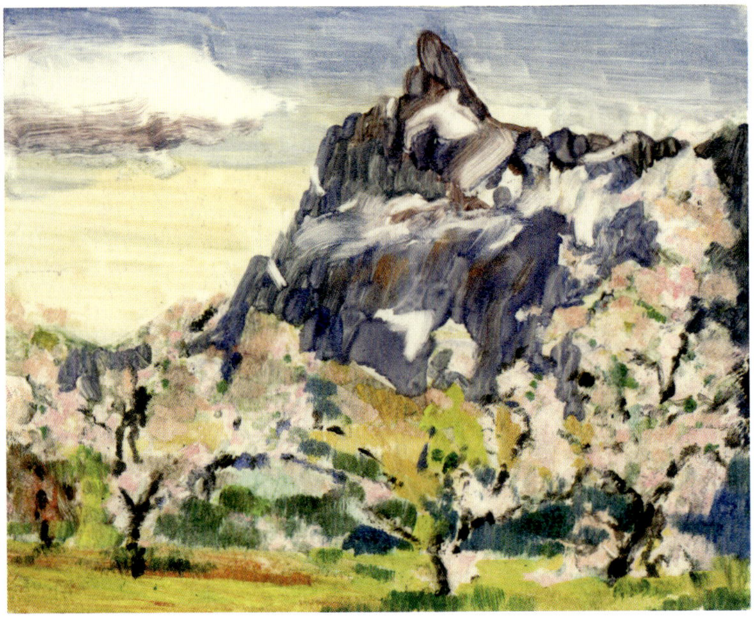

(top) Untitled, ca. 1935, drypoint with watercolor and gouache, 7 3/8 x 8 7/8 in. Private collection

(bottom) Untitled, ca. 1932, monoprint, 5 x 6 in. Private collection

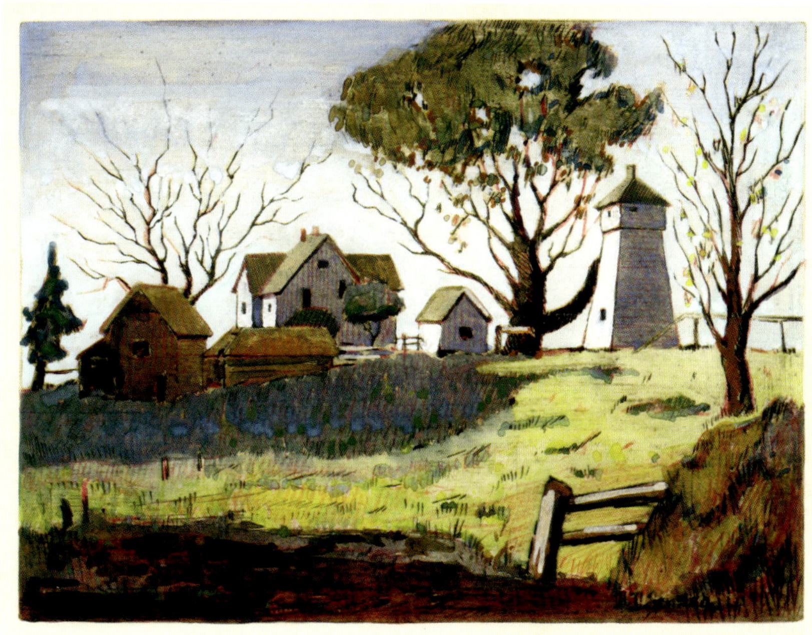

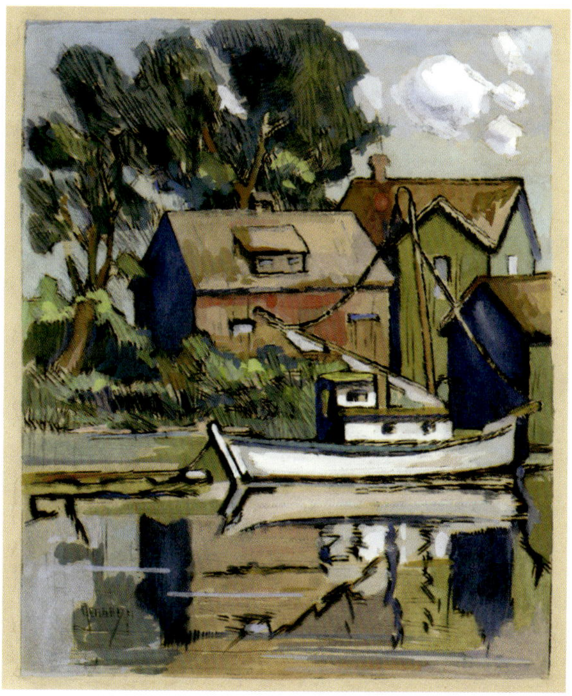

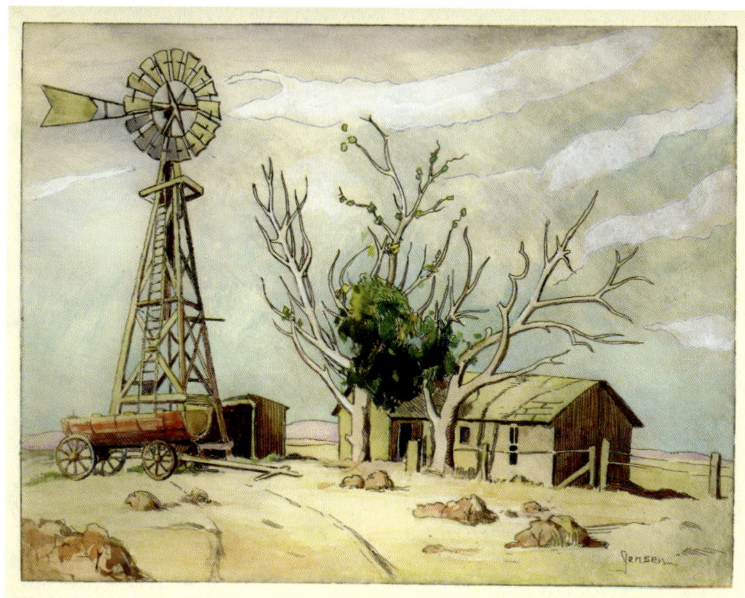

(top) Untitled, ca. 1932, etching with watercolor and gouache, 7 ¼ x 9 14 in. Private collection

(bottom left) *Ross Homestead*, ca. 1930, etching printed *à la poupee* with hand coloring, 6 ¾ x 5 ¼ in. Private collection

(bottom right) *Deserted Farm Near Quincy*, ca. 1935, etching with watercolor, 7 ½ x 9 ¼ in. Private collection

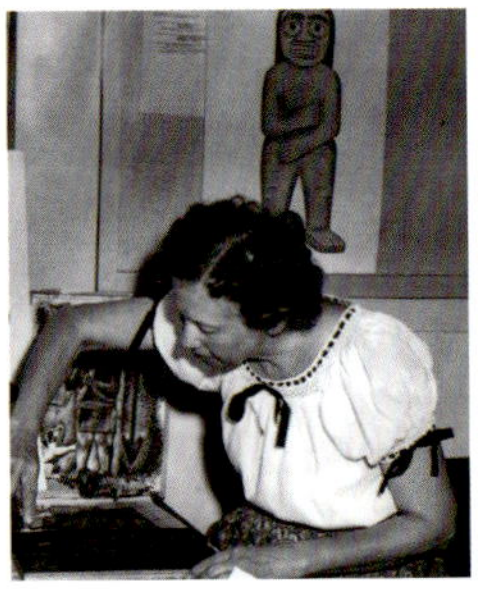

HELMI JUVONEN 1903–1985

Helmi Dagmar Juvonen was born in Butte, Montana, in 1903, the younger of two daughters of Finnish immigrants. She moved to Seattle with her mother and sister in 1918 and attended Queen Anne High School. During these years she developed a strong interest in arts and crafts. She met University of Washington art instructor Ambrose Patterson (1877–1966), who became a positive influence on her. After graduation, Helmi worked at various jobs and continued her art education by taking evening classes at the Seattle Art Club School with Fokko Tadama (1871–1937). She then set off on a career in commercial illustration. In 1929, Helmi began taking courses at the Cornish School to further her interest in illustration. The following year, she started showing symptoms of mental illness. After two suicide attempts, she was diagnosed with manic depression. Her mother committed her to the Northern State Hospital at Sedro-Wooley, Washington, where she remained for the next three years. After leaving the hospital, she concentrated on making dolls and producing portraits for local prominent families. Around this time, she began making artwork inspired by Northwest Native American culture. For the remainder of her career, Helmi would study the indigenous culture and attended numerous potlatches and dance rituals. During the war years, Helmi was employed at the Boeing Aircraft Company as a technical illustrator. For the next decade, she suffered from the effects of her illness but persevered in her art production and self-education.

Helmi had been making blockprints since the 1920s, usually for Christmas or greeting cards. In the mid-1940s, she became interested in printmaking as a fine-art expression, especially relief prints from linoleum blocks. During this time she also studied color lithography at Cornish with Emilio Amero (1901–1976).

She exhibited her first print, *Spegpegud—Winter Dance Time*, at the prestigious Northwest Printmakers Society exhibition in 1947. The lithograph won the Evergreen State Award. She would also exhibit linocuts with the society in 1948, 1953, and 1954.

With her mental health declining, she was confined again to the Northern State Hospital in 1959, and the following year entered the Oakhurst Convalescent Center in Elma, Washington, where she remained for the rest of her life. During her later years she continued to make innovative paintings, drawings, and dolls that she gave away to visiting friends and fellow artists.

Since her death, Helmi has been the subject of numerous articles, exhibitions, and publications, and her work is in many prominent institutions in the Northwest.

Photo: Helmi Juvonen inking a linoleum block, 1952. Courtesy of Dr. Ulrich Fritzsche. *Seattle Times* photo

SOURCES

Fritzsche , Dr. Ulrich. *Helmi Dagmar Juvonen, Her Life and Work: A Chronicle* (self-published), 2001.

Fritzsche, Dr. Ulrich, Helmi Dagmar Juvonen, Her Lino Prints in Public and Private Collections (unpublished).

Special Collections of The Seattle Public Library, Artists Scrapbooks.

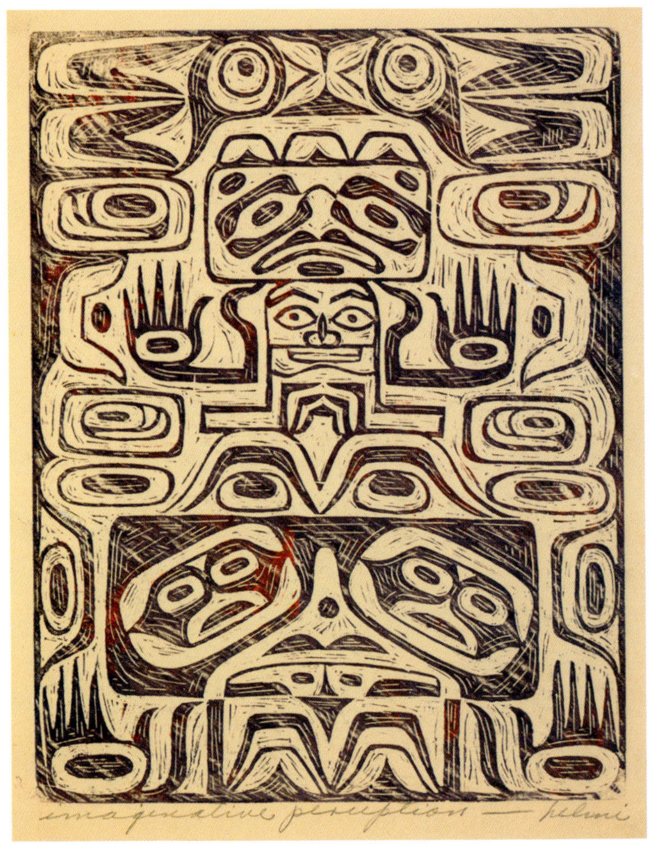

Imaginative Perceptions, 1949, also titled Symbolic Stylistic Form, linocut with monoprint inking, 12 x 9 in. Collection of the Washington State Historical Society, 88-35-23

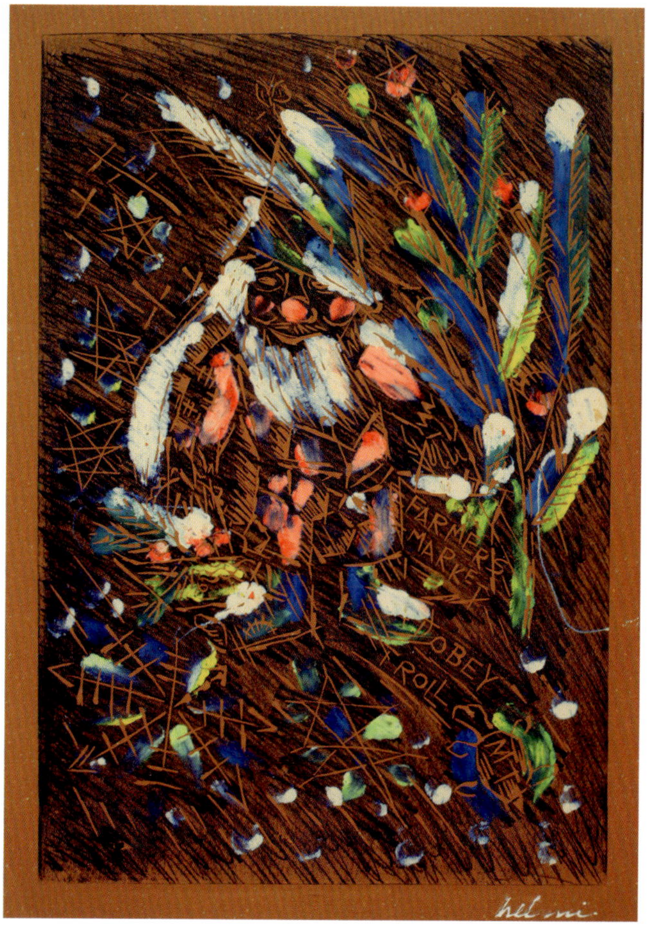

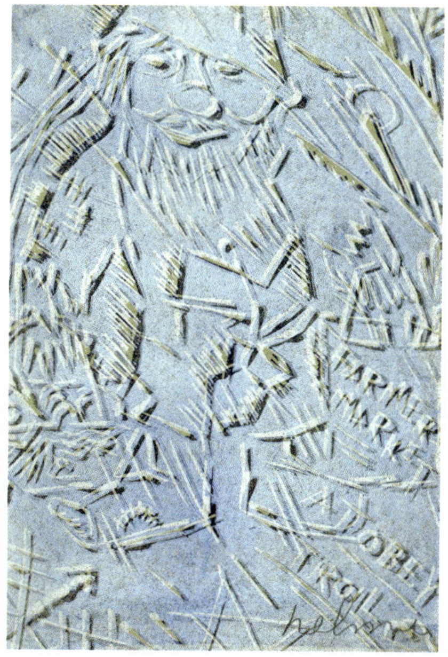

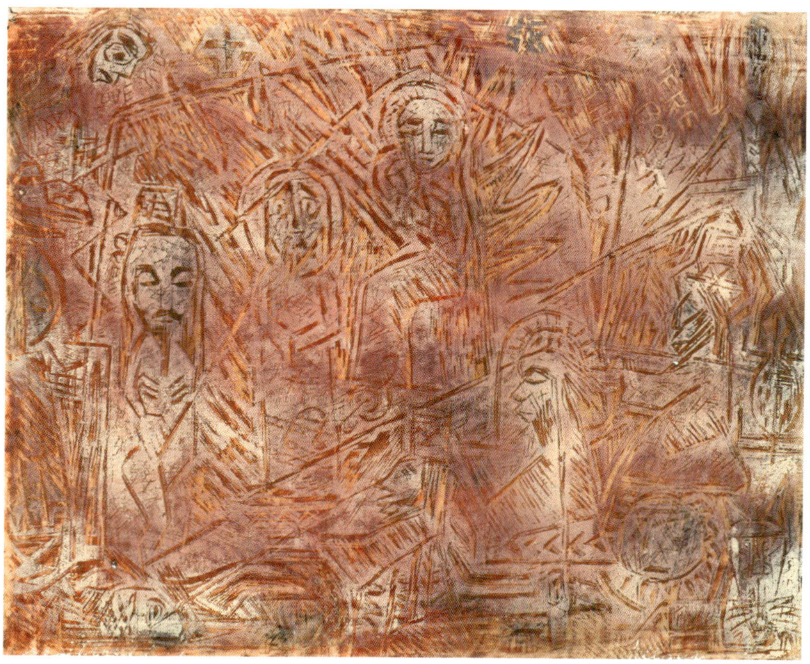

(top) *Farmers Market—A Tobey Troll*, 1954, linocut with monoprint inking, 15 x 10 in. Private collection

(bottom) *Nativity*, ca. 1955, linocut with monoprint inking, 13 ¾ x 16 ¾ in. Collection of The Seattle Public Library

(top right) *Farmers Market—A Tobey Troll*, 1954, linocut with monoprint inking, 9 x 6 in. Collection of the Washington State Historical Society, 2001.68.10

For this proof, Helmi printed it as a detail from the larger block. She used two separate pulls with one off-register by a quarter inch to give the effect of bas relief.

Helmi's color printing technique

Helmi's unorthodox color printing process was based on the carved linoleum blocks that she printed her black and white prints from. For the color proofs, she applied the inks or paint directly onto the block in a way similar to what you would do when making a monoprint. She then laid the registered paper onto the block and rubbed the back of the paper with a blunt implement, causing the appearance of a web of scribbles on the recto that integrated into the relief image lines. She would also sometimes randomly apply paint to the block and blot it with the proof, obliterating the printed lines in certain areas. Another unusual process that she employed was using the same block to make two or three pulls, offsetting the registration enough to cause a three-dimensional or bas relief effect.

None of Helmi's color prints were duplicated; her process allowed for each proof to be completely unique.

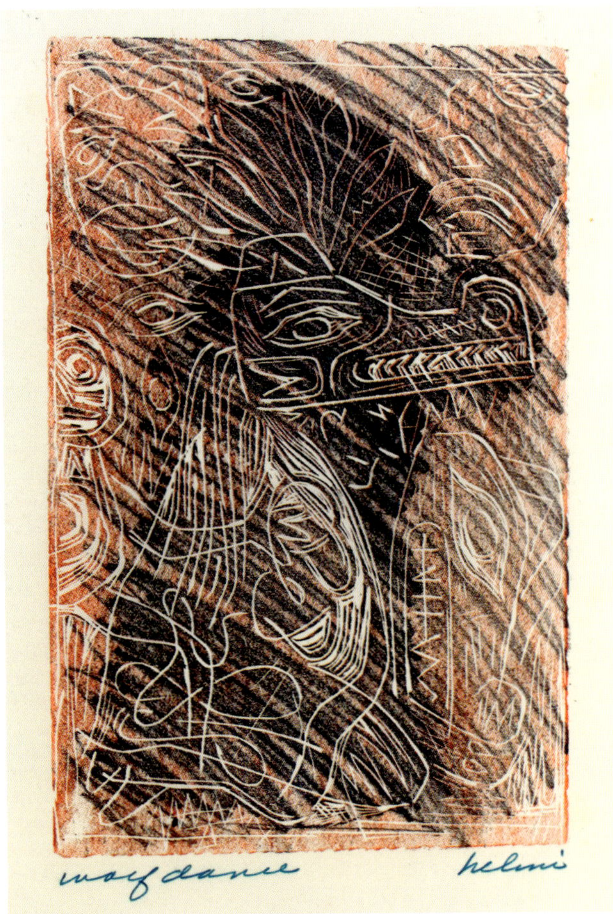

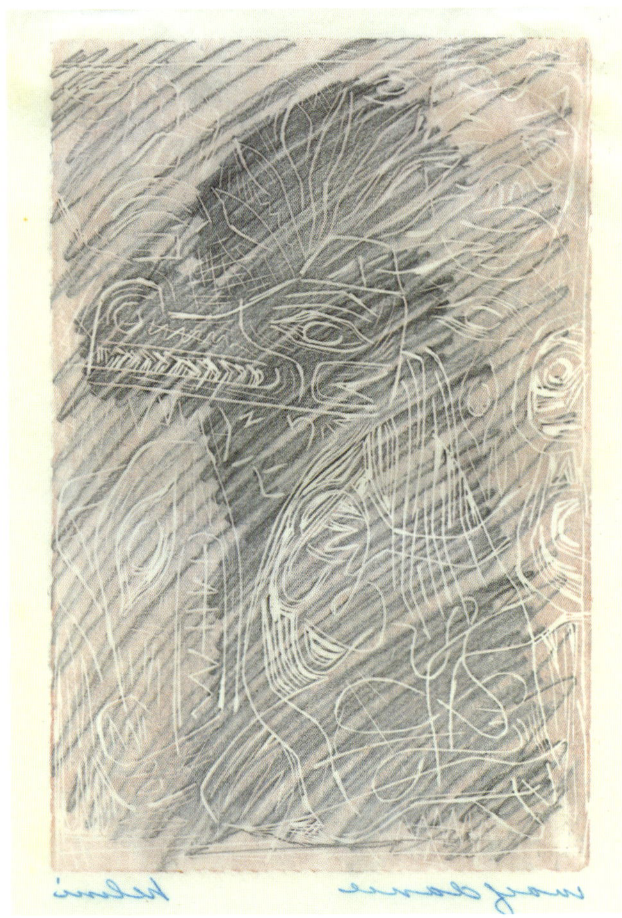

(left) *Wolf Dance*, ca. 1953, linocut with monoprint inking, 10 ¼ x 6 ½ in. Collection of the Washington State Historical Society, C1988.35.16

(right) verso of *Wolf Dance*, illustrating Helmi's printing technique. Collection of the Washington State Historical Society, C1988.35.16

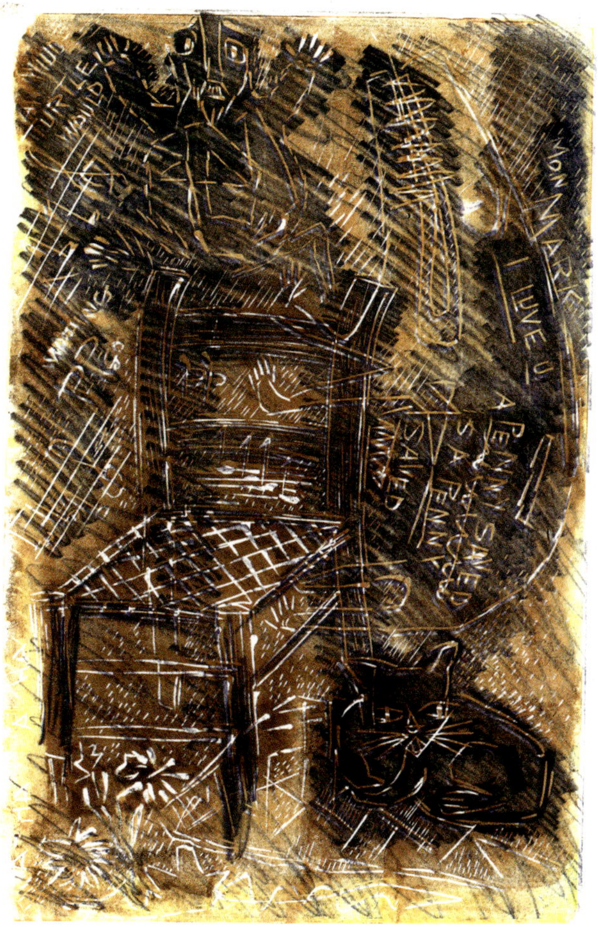

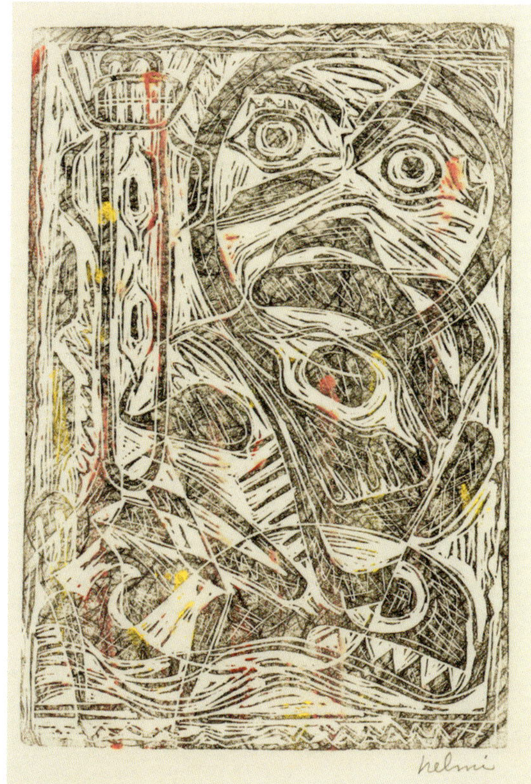

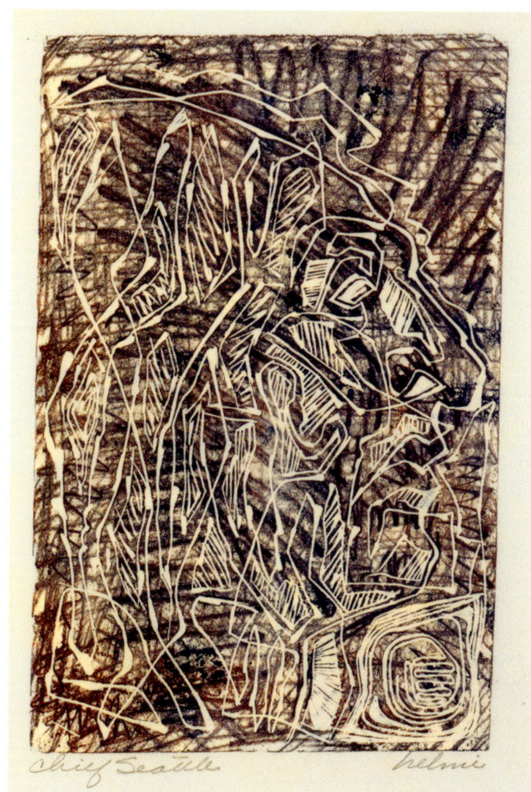

(top left) *Mark Tobey's Studio*, ca. 1955, linocut with monoprint inking, 16 ¾ x 10 ½ in. Collection of The Seattle Public Library

(top right) *Whale*, ca. 1953, linocut with monoprint inking, 10 ⅝ x 7 in. Collection of the Washington State Historical Society, C1988.35.21

(bottom right) *Chief Seattle*, ca. 1953, linocut with monoprint inking, 10 ⅞ x 7 in. Collection of the Washington State Historical Society, 88-35-15

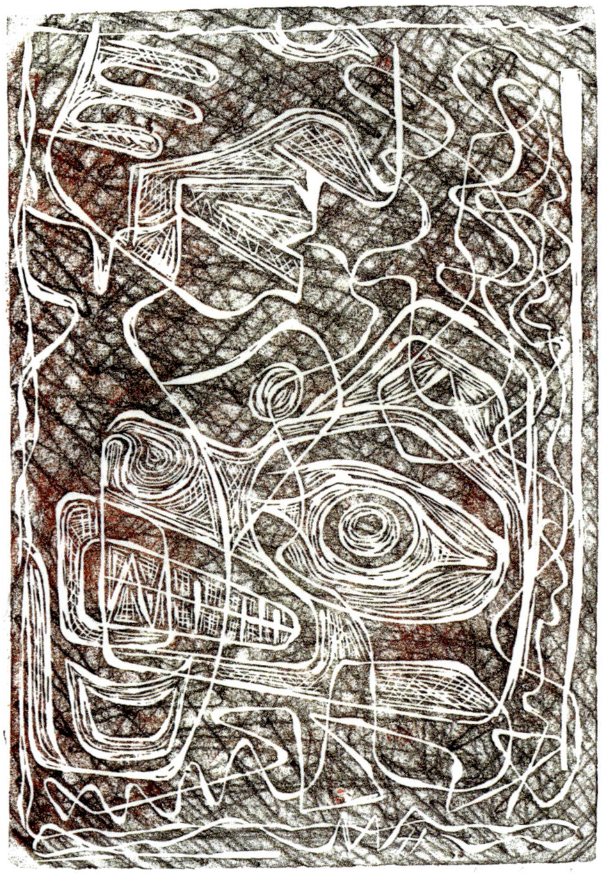

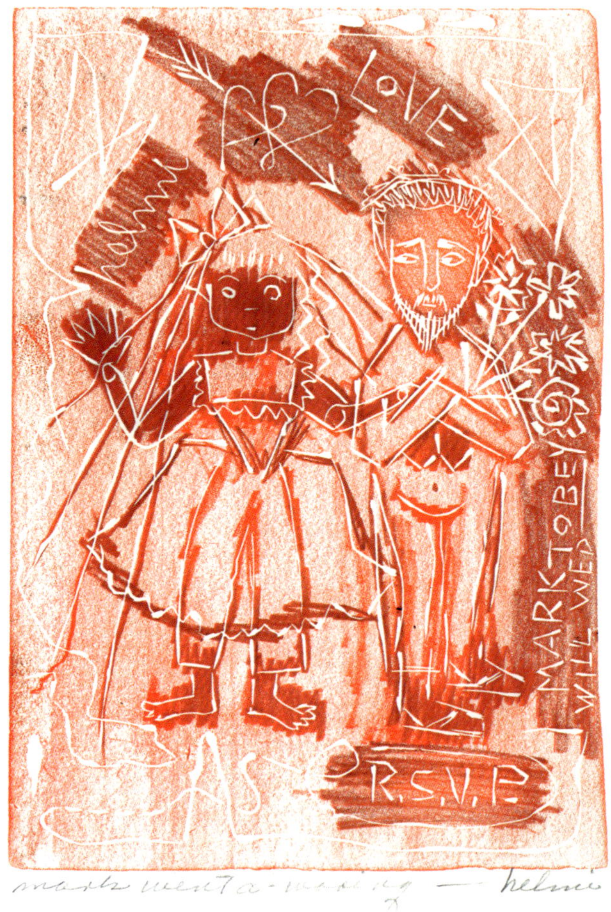

(left) *Wolf*, ca. 1953, linocut with monoprint inking, 10 ¼ x 7 in. Collection of the Washington State Historical Society, 2001.68.12

(right) *Mark Went A-Wooing*, ca. 1955–1956, linocut with monoprint inking, 12 ¼ x 7 ½ in. Frye Art Museum, Gift of Wesley Wehr, 1982.008.01

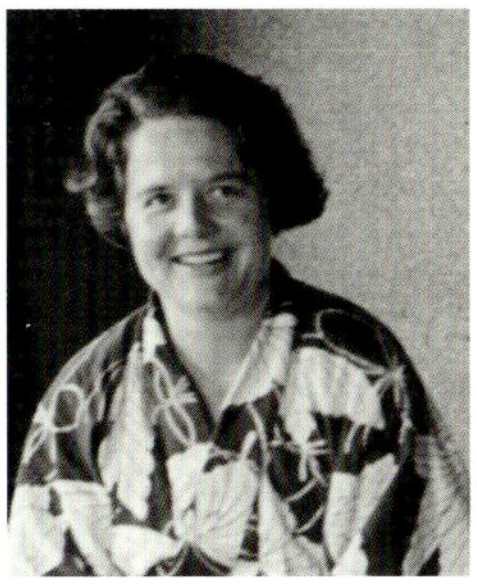

RUTH PENINGTON 1905–1998

Ruth Esther Penington was born in Colorado Springs, Colorado, and moved to Seattle with her parents in 1907. Her father was a carriage maker and worked in the budding aircraft industry when she was a child. Her mother was a creative and talented homemaker who nurtured her daughter's interest in art.

When Ruth entered Seattle's Lincoln High School, she was encouraged by her teacher Lulu Hotchkiss, one of the original faculty, who provided continuous serious art training.

Upon graduation, she enrolled at the University of Washington in 1926, earning a BFA the following year and an MFA in 1929. Her main instruction at UW had its basis in the design theories of Arthur Wesley Dow (1857–1922) and Ernest Fenollosa (1853–1908), with an emphasis on Asian art and culture. She continued her education at the University of Oregon (1931–32) and the California College of Arts & Crafts (1935).

In 1928, Penington became one of the co-founders of the Northwest Printmakers Society. She was included in almost all of their exhibitions from 1929 through 1942. She won two purchase prizes in 1937 and 1939 and the Evergreen State Award in 1942.

In 1929, she attended Columbia University's Teachers College in New York where she had her initial instruction in metalsmithing, the medium in which she was developing a serious interest at the time.

In 1942, Penington met the important industrial designer Gilbert Rohde (1894–1944) when he was a visiting lecturer at the University of Washington. Through his influence she established the Industrial Design department at the University of Washington in 1945. For the next two years, she accepted a temporary position as visiting professor at the University of California, Berkeley. During the 1940s, Penington's artistic output centered on jewelry design, silversmithing, and other craft-related areas in which she also taught at the university. In 1947, she attended a conference at the Rhode Island School of Design. The six-week session included participating in a workshop with the noted silversmith William E. Bennett (d. 1969) from Sheffield, England. In 1952, Penington spent nine months in Europe that started with six weeks working with the Michelsen silver company in Copenhagen, Denmark.

In 1954, Penington co-founded the Northwest Designer Craftsmen to support the production and exhibition of high-quality crafts in the Northwest.

Penington never married and lived with her parents for most of her life. After her mother's death in 1963, she cared for her father, who lived with her until his death at the age of one hundred and three in 1979.

Ruth Penington was a singular force in the development of design and crafts in the Northwest and received numerous awards and exhibitions.

Photo: Ruth Penington (detail), 1937. Courtesy of the Blakemore Foundation. Photographer unknown

SOURCES

Architectural Craftsmen of the Northwest: Illustrated Directory. Seattle: American Craftsmen's Council, 1960.

Vera Zimmerman

The Martin-Zambito Archive

Special Collections of The Seattle Public Library, Artists Scrapbooks.

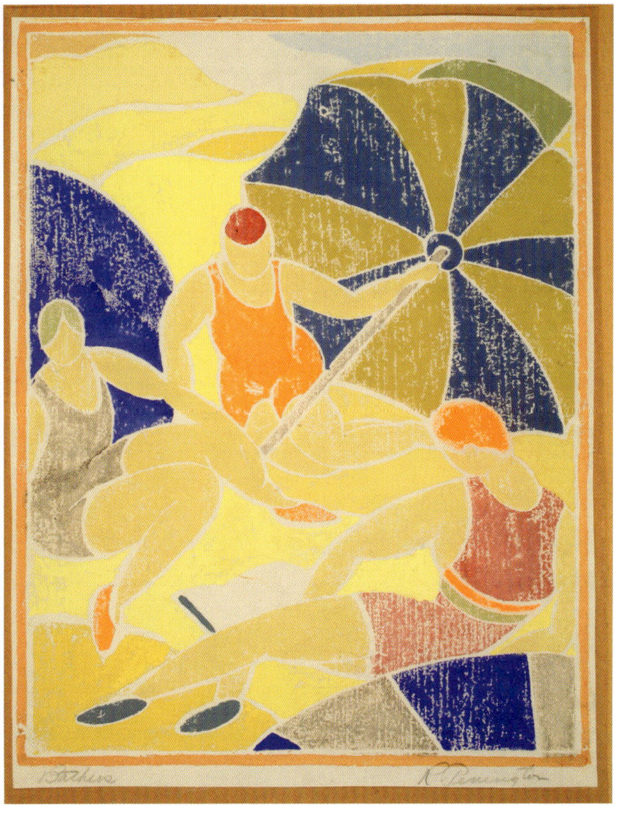

Bathers, ca. 1928, white line color woodblock print, 12 x 9 in. Collection of Vera Zimmerman

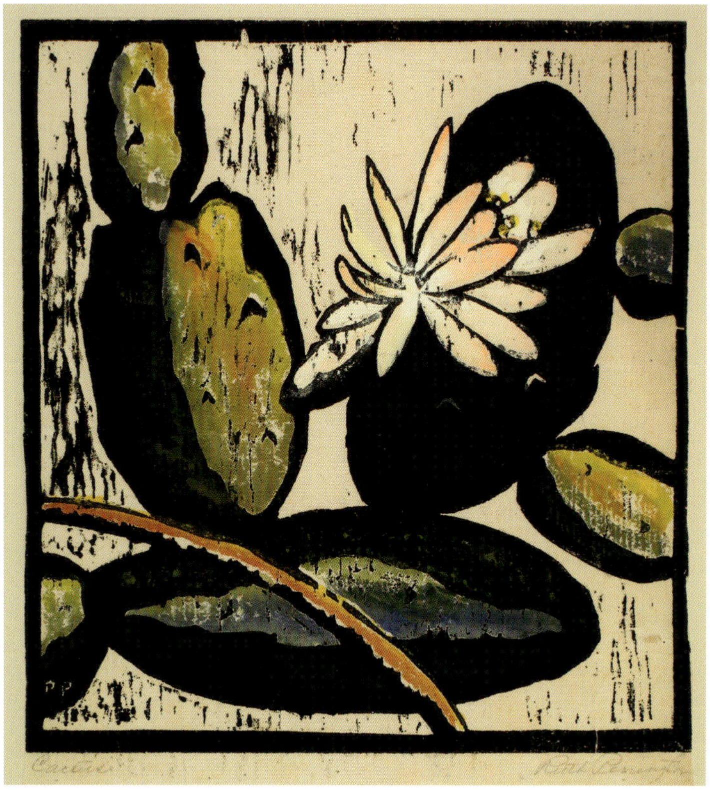

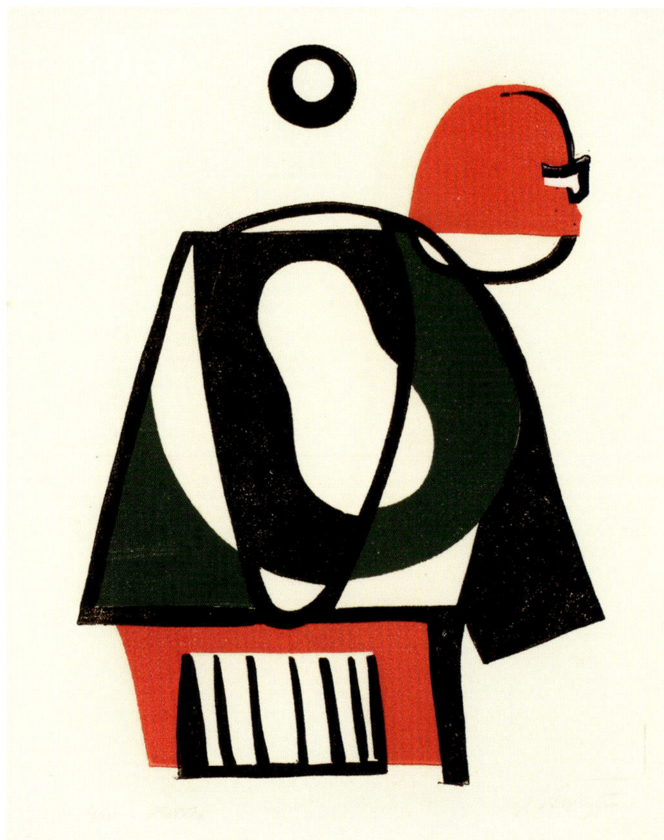

(top) *Cactus*, ca. 1930, color woodblock print, 10 x 9 in. Collection of Vera Zimmerman

(right) *Bottle*, 1934, color woodblock print, 11 x 8:½ in. Private collection

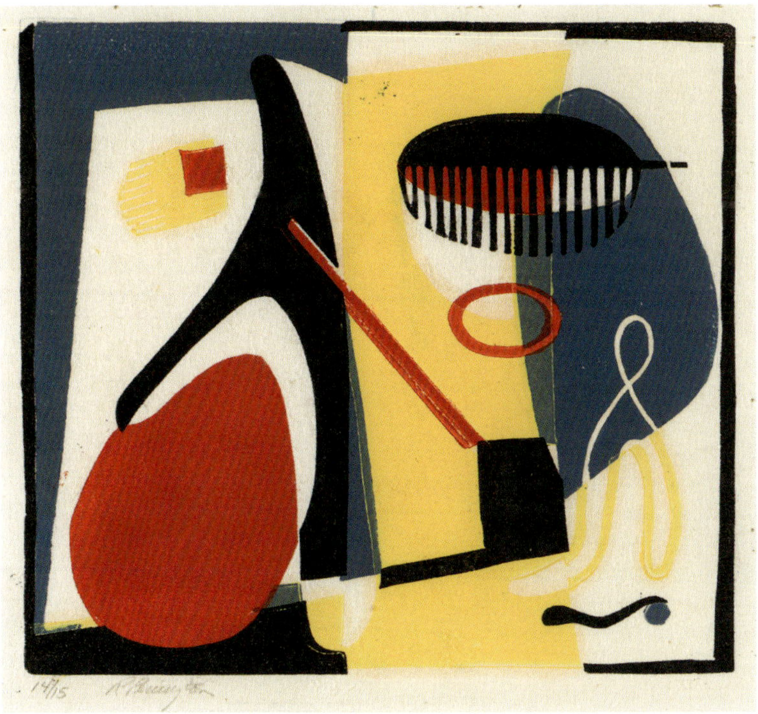

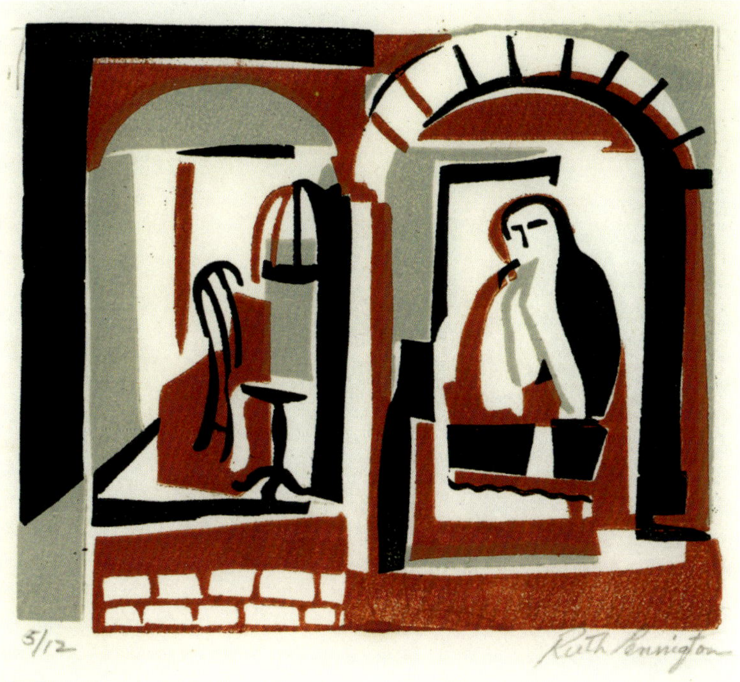

(top) *Abstract Forms*, ca. 1937, color woodblock print, 6 13/16 x 7 1/4 in.
Seattle Art Museum, Gift of the Northwest Printmakers 69.335

(bottom) *Two Windows*, 1935, color woodblock print, 5 5/8 x 6 1/4 in.
Collection of John Impert

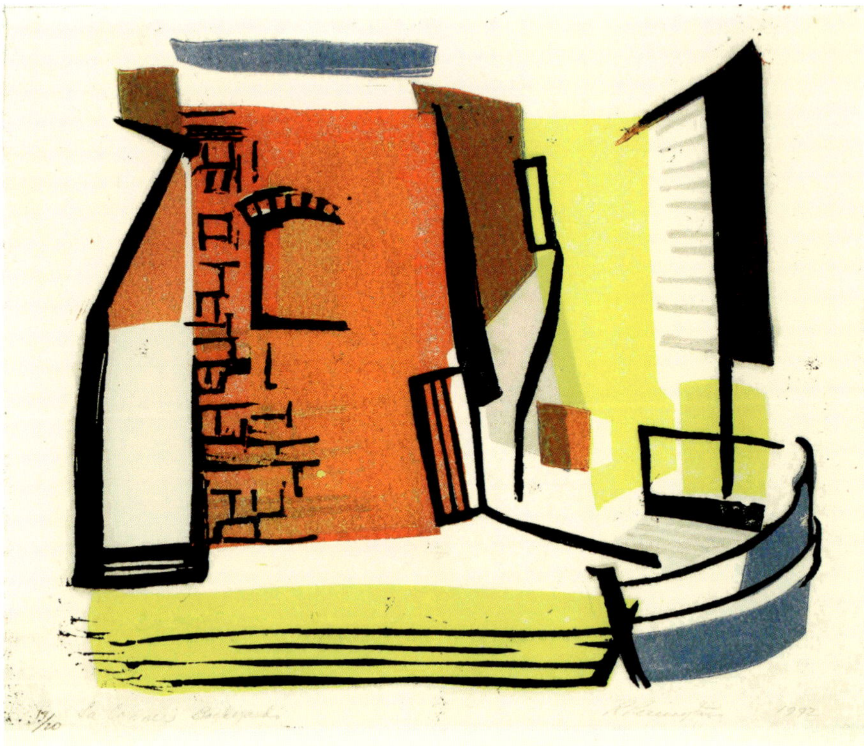

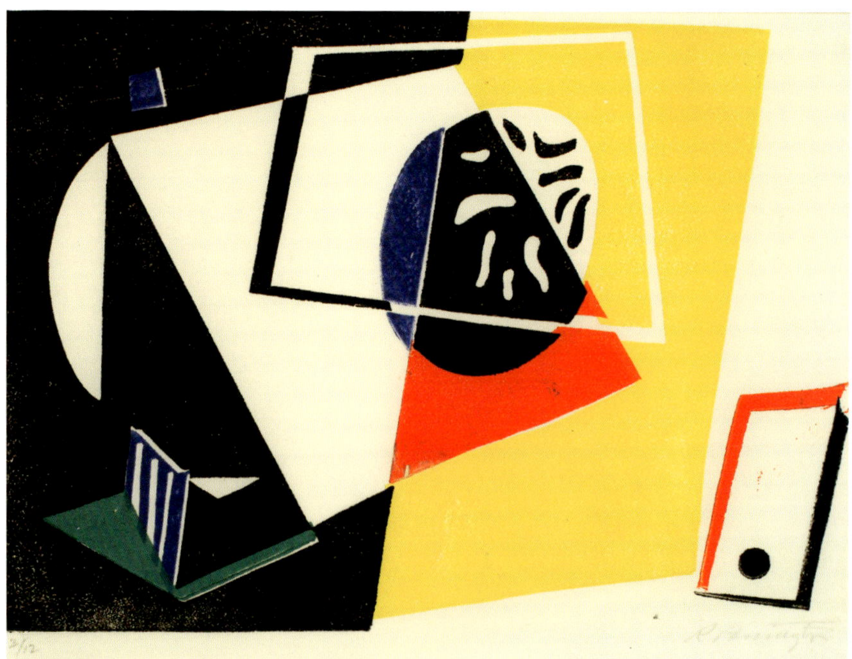

(top) *LaConner Backyards*, 1942, color woodblock print, 8 ½ x 9 ½ in.
Hagen Waer Collection

(bottom) Untitled, ca. 1936, color woodblock print, 7 ¾ x 10 ¼ in.
Collection of Vera Zimmerman

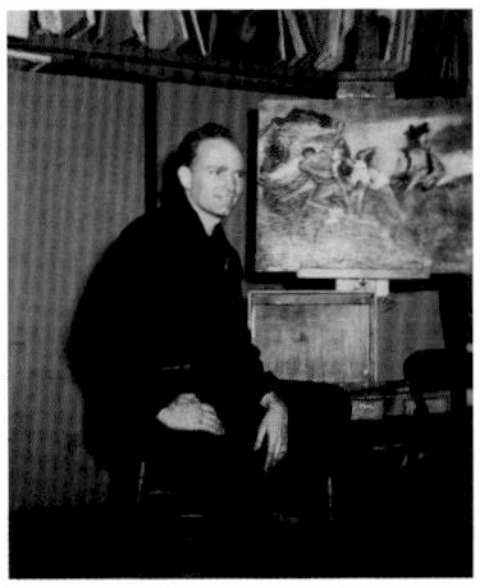

DANNY PIERCE 1920–2014

In 1958, the *Washington Post* praised Danny Pierce as "one of America's most outstanding graphic artists."

Daniel P. Pierce was born on a ranch in Woodlake, California, where he lived the life of a cowboy and developed a love of nature. His lifelong interest in art began when he was a child, sketching the horses and animals on his family's ranch. In 1939, he moved to Los Angeles to attend the Art Center School. To pay for his art education, he spent the day as a stable hand with Victor McLaglen's Light Horse Troop, which enabled him to take classes at night.

Because of the economic depression, Pierce was unable to continue working and returned to the family ranch. He was able to save some money by riding saddle broncs in regional rodeos and worked as a wrangler and packer at Lake Tahoe. He was able to save enough money to return to Los Angeles and attended the Chouinard Art Institute in 1941. Military service during WWII interrupted his art studies. He fought in two major battles and was awarded several Medals of Honor. He met Julia Rasmussen, an army nurse who attended to his combat injuries, and the two married in 1943. In May of 1945, Pierce's squadron liberated the Nazi death camp at Maulthausen in upper Austria. Following the war, he used the G.I. Bill to further his art education, initially returning to the Chouinard Art Institute and then moving to New York to attend the American Art School. In 1950, he attended the Brooklyn Museum Art School, studying with Max Beckman (1884–1950), Ben Shahn (1898–1969), and Gabor Peterdi (1915–2001), who exerted a strong influence on Pierce's printmaking technique and remained a lifelong friend.

After serving as an instructor at Hunter College in New York, Pierce and his young family moved to his wife's hometown of Kent, Washington, in 1953. He became a highly respected teacher in the region and one of the area's most prominent artists.

In 1959, Pierce created the first of nearly thirty limited-edition books that he wrote, illustrated, and—in the first few—even hand-carved the type. That year he and his budding family moved to Alaska where, under a Carnegie Grant, he became the first artist-in-residence at the University of Alaska. The following year he founded the university's art department, the first in the state. In Alaska, Pierce had a profound effect on the region's printmakers, especially such Native Alaskan artists as Bernard Katexac (1922–1997) and Joseph Senugetuk (b. 1940). In 1963, Pierce returned to Kent, Washington, and in the next few years wrote two additional limited-edition books with Alaskan themes and resumed his involvement with the Northwest Printmakers Society, which he began exhibiting with in 1952.

In 1965, Pierce and his family moved to Milwaukee, Wisconsin, where he taught printmaking until his retirement in 1984. The following year, Pierce returned to Kent and continued a distinguished career that included painting, printmaking, limited-edition books, and public murals.

In 2012, Pierce received an honorary doctorate of arts from the University of Alaska–Fairbanks. During his professional career, Pierce signed his work only with his first name—"Danny"—and included the circular conjoined letters *J A* with his signature to pay tribute to his wife Julia Ann, whom he felt was an integral part of his art.

After seventy-one years of marriage, Julia Pierce died on February 22, 2014, followed by Danny twelve days later on March 6, 2014.

Danny Pierce's work is included in numerous national and international museum collections.

Photo: Danny Pierce, circa 1947. Courtesy of the Danny Pierce estate. Photographer unknown

SOURCES

Scrapbooks and personal papers, Danny Pierce estate.

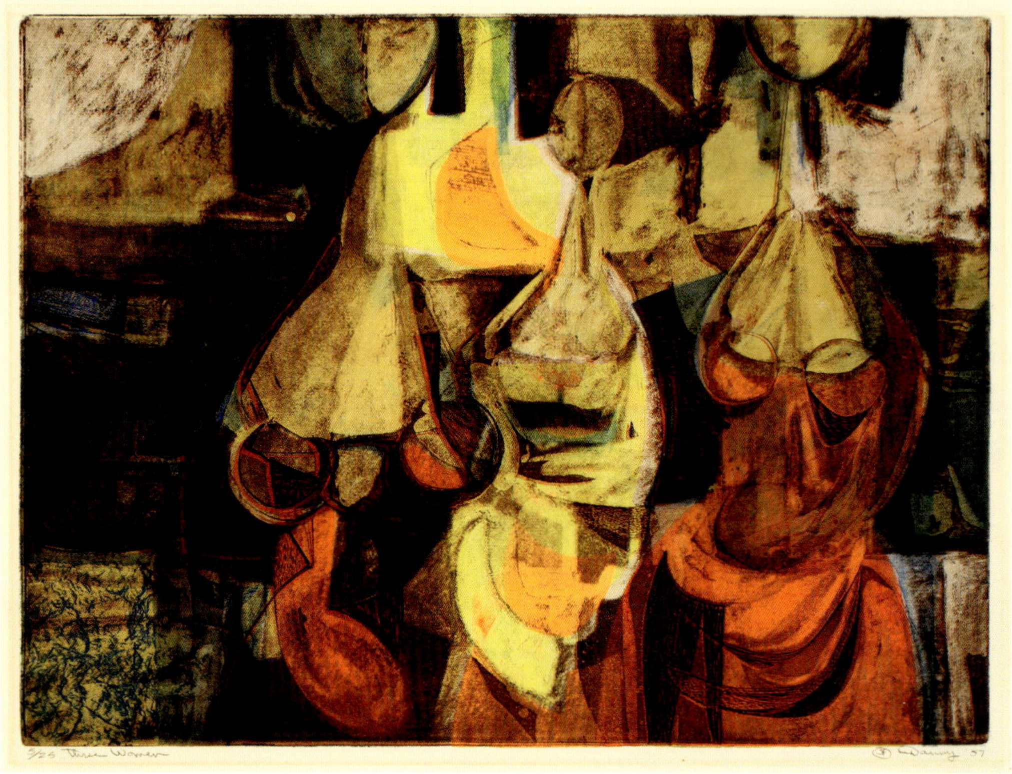

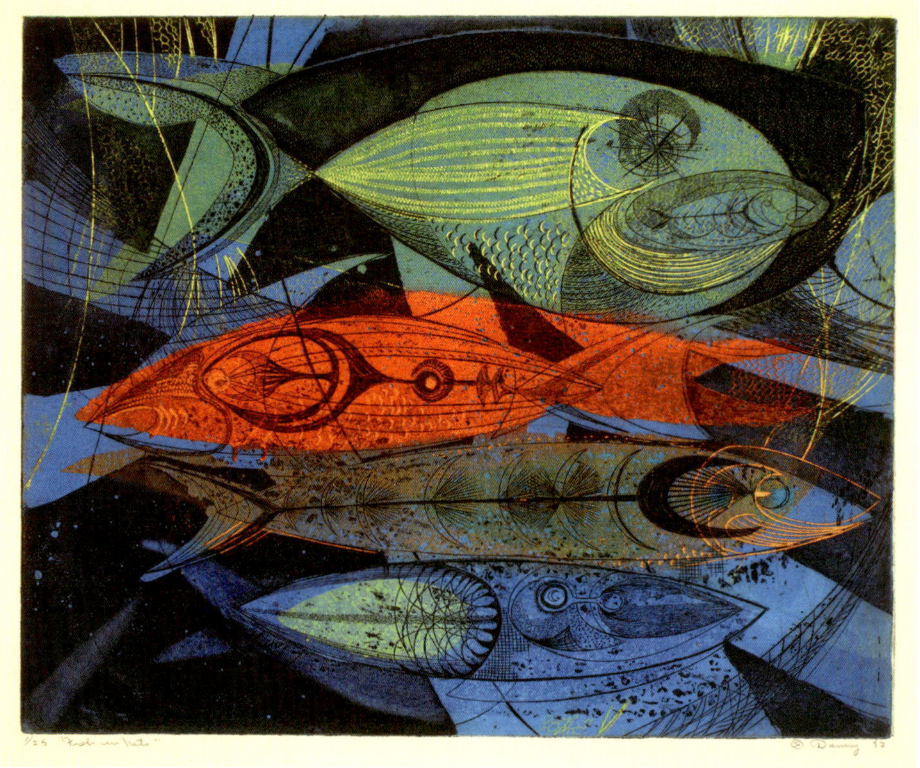

(top) *Three Women*, 1957, mixed intaglio print, 15 x 19 5/8 in. Estate of Danny Pierce

(right) *Fish in Nets*, 1952, mixed intaglio print, 15 x 17 7/8 in. Estate of Danny Pierce

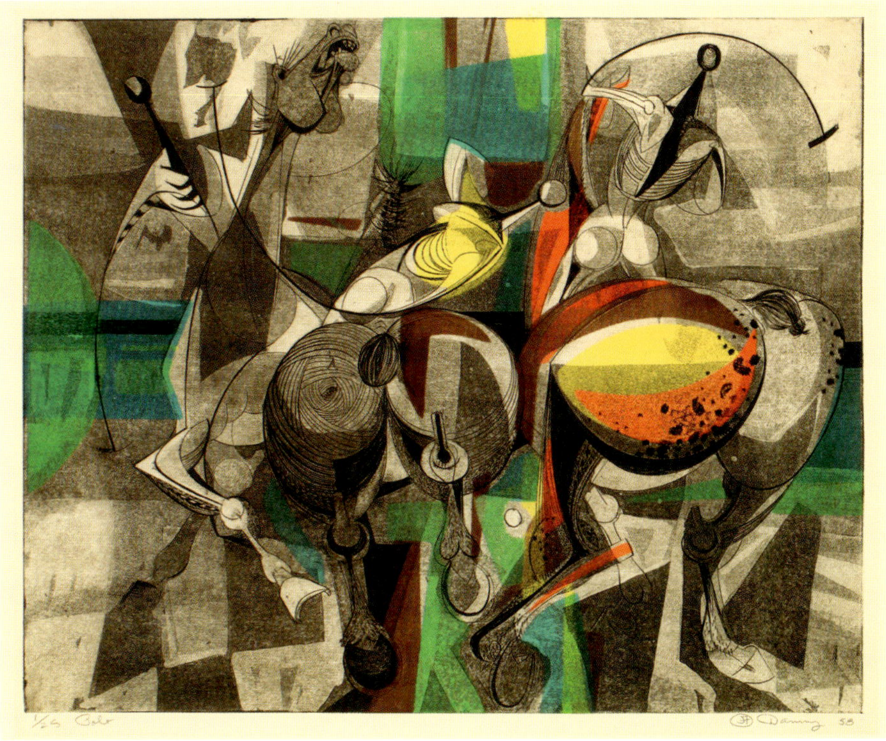

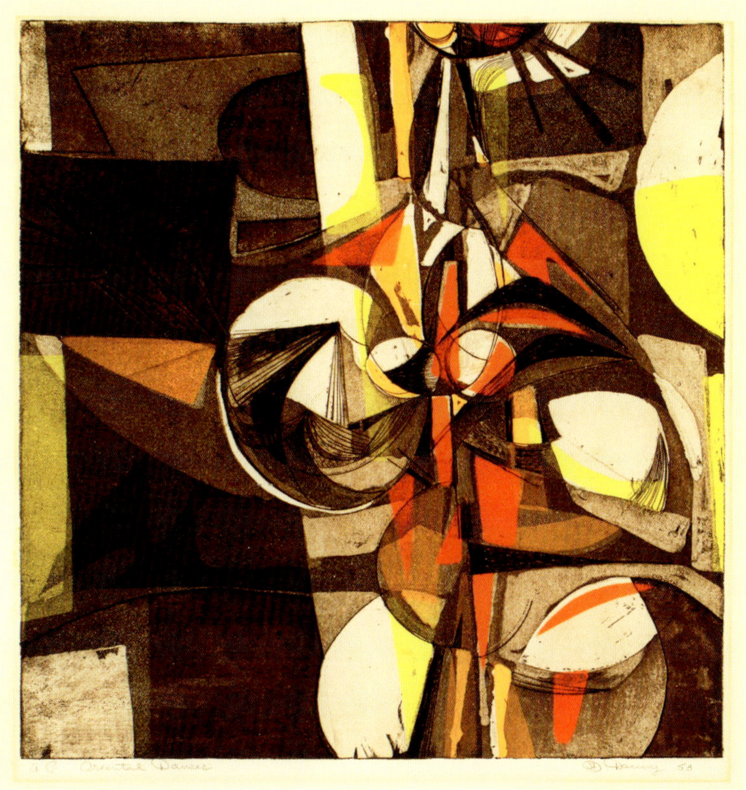

(top) *Polo*, 1958, mixed intaglio print, 14 ⅞ x 17 ⅝ in. Estate of Danny Pierce

(right) *Oriental Dancer*, 1958, mixed intaglio print, 15 ¾ x 15 in. Estate of Danny Pierce

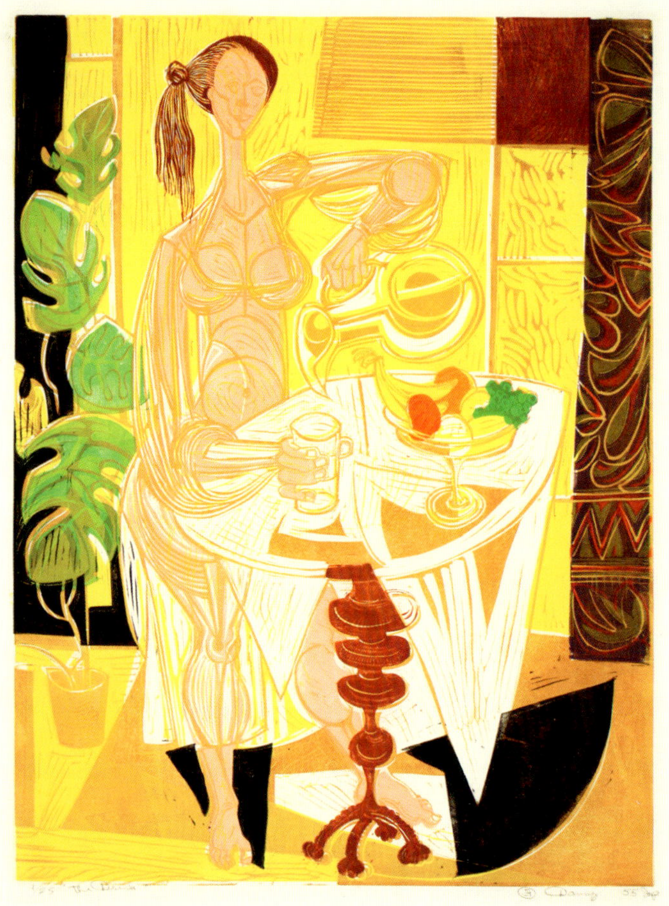

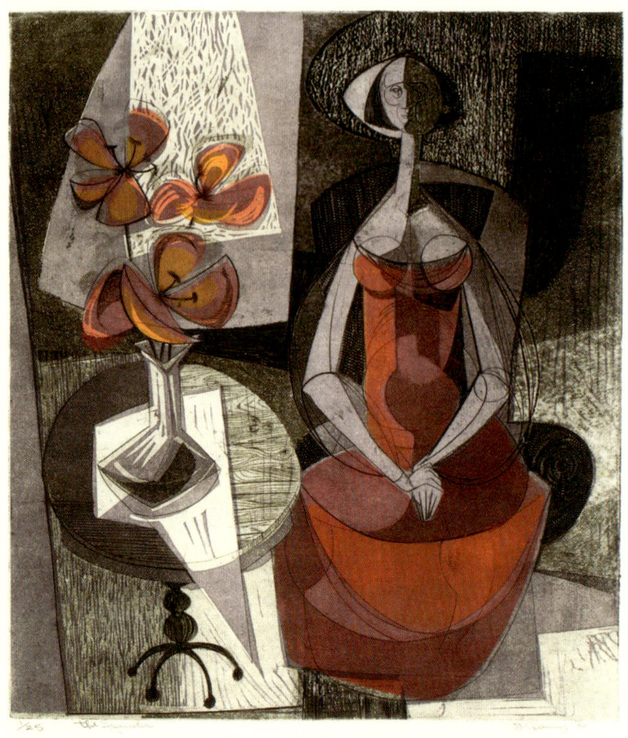

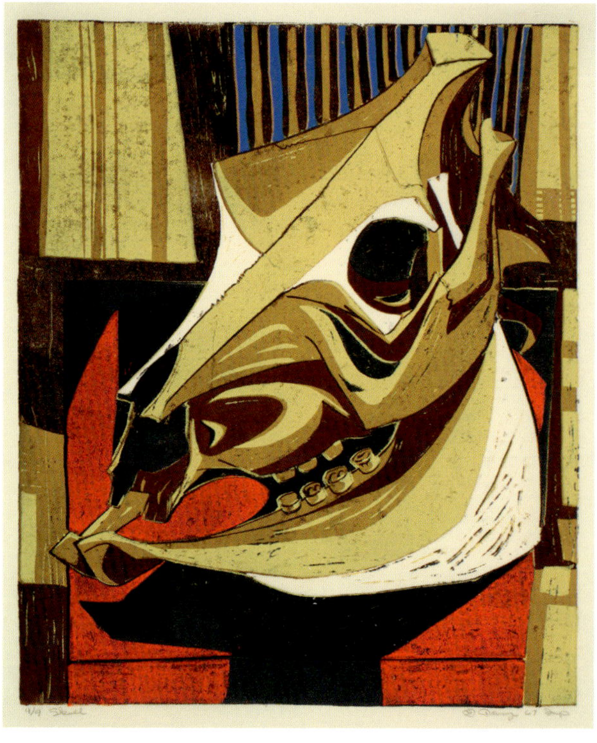

(top left) *The Drink*, 1955, color linocut, 28 x 20 3/8 in. Estate of Danny Pierce

(top right) *The Spinster*, 1958, mixed intaglio print, 17 5/8 x 15 in. Estate of Danny Pierce

(bottom right) *Skull*, 1967, color reduction print, 20 x 16 1/8 in. Estate of Danny Pierce

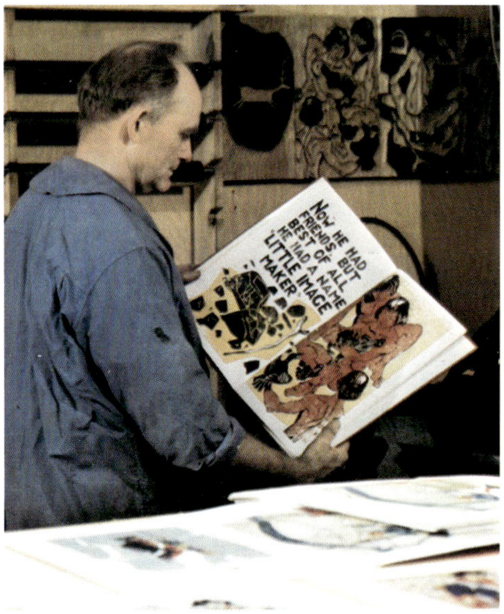

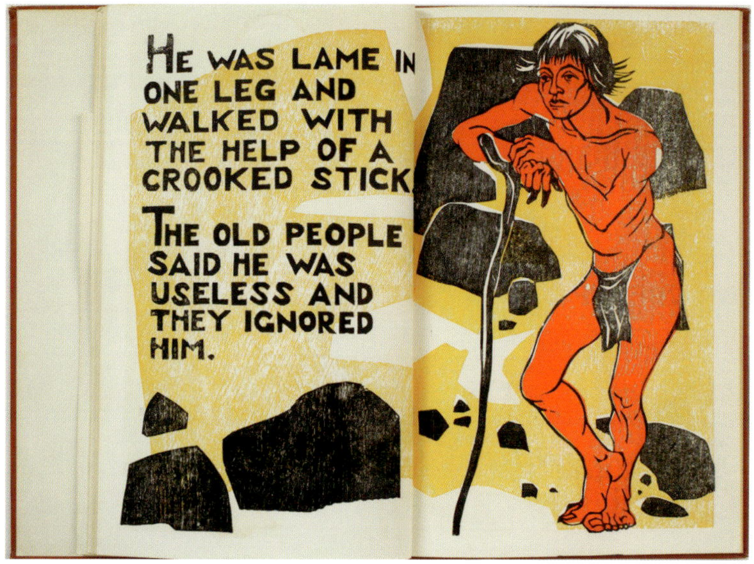

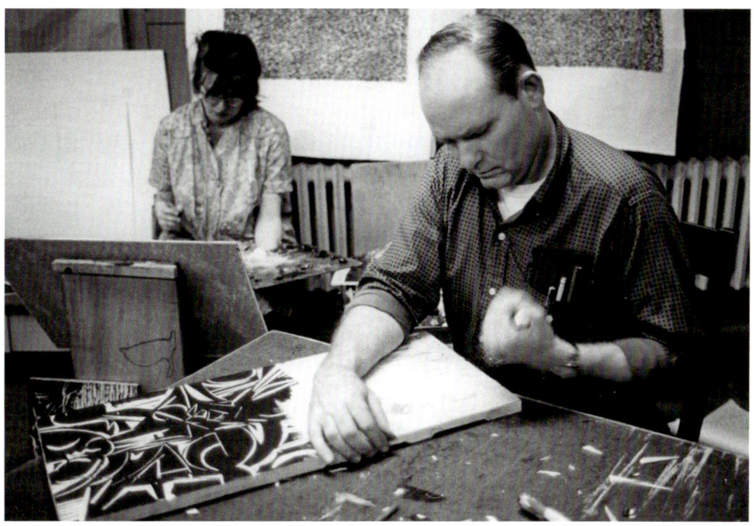

(top left) Danny Pierce inspecting his first book, *Little No Name*. Red Door Studio, Kent, Washington, 1959. Estate of Danny Pierce

(top right) Pages from *Little No Name* (1959) showing the hand-carved woodblock illustration and type. Estate of Danny Pierce

(bottom right) Danny Pierce carving a block in his studio, ca. 1958. Estate of Danny Pierce

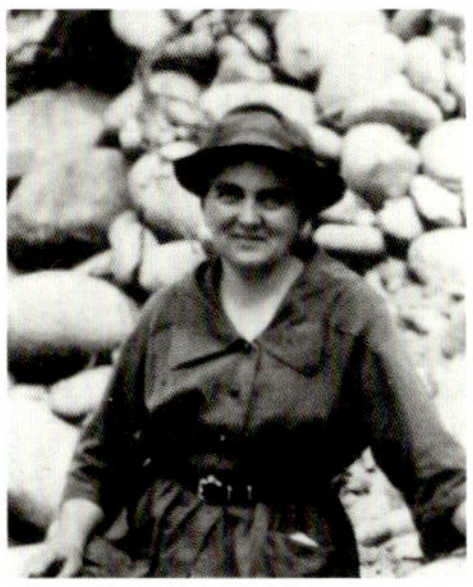

ELIZABETH WARHANIK 1880–1968

From Germantown, Pennsylvania, Elizabeth Campbell Warhanik was one of six children born to J. Addison and Anna L. Campbell, who had met while attending the Pennsylvania Academy of the Fine Arts.

Elizabeth attended Wellesley College, where she studied painting with Charles Woodbury (1864–1940) and earned a degree in Classical Literature. She served as a Wellesley student-volunteer missionary for five years, teaching in Japan before moving to Seattle with her parents in 1907. Her parents were involved in missionary work and her father was one of the founders of Seattle's University Presbyterian Church in 1908. In 1910, she married Charles Warhanik; they had three children.

As her children matured, she attended the University of Washington in 1935 and 1936, studying with Walter Isaacs (1886–1964) and Helen Rhodes (1875–1938), and privately with Paul Morgan Gustin (1886–1974) and Edgar Forkner (1867–1945). Her sister, Eleanor Brown Campbell (1894–1986), also attended the University of Washington and became an accomplished artist known for her illustrations for the popular "Dick and Jane" reading primers.

Elizabeth exhibited locally with the Seattle Fine Arts Society (later the Seattle Art Museum), where she won a prize in 1917. She exhibited in most of the region's leading venues from 1916 through the late 1950s.

In 1930, Elizabeth Warhanik became one of the founders of the Women Painters of Washington and the first president of the organization. With WPW, she exhibited locally and nationally, winning several awards. She was also an active member of the Northwest Watercolor Society and the Northwest Printmakers Society. She died in Des Moines, Washington, at the age of eighty-eight.

Photo: Elizabeth Warhanik, 1920 (detail). Courtesy of the estate of Elizabeth Warhanik. Photographer unknown

SOURCES

The Martin-Zambito Archive

Special Collections of The Seattle Public Library, Artists Scrapbooks.

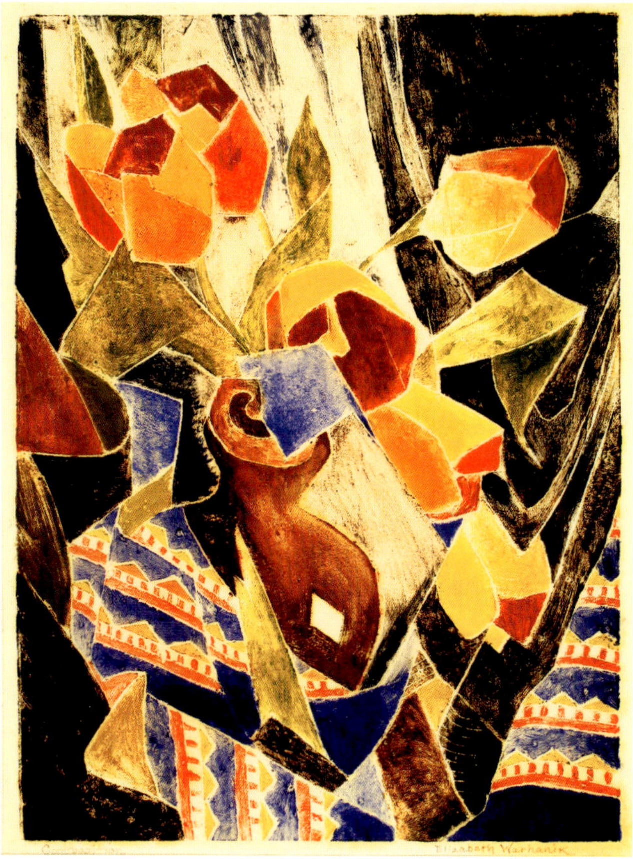

Untitled, ca. 1928, white line color woodblock print, 13 7/8 x 10 in. Private collection

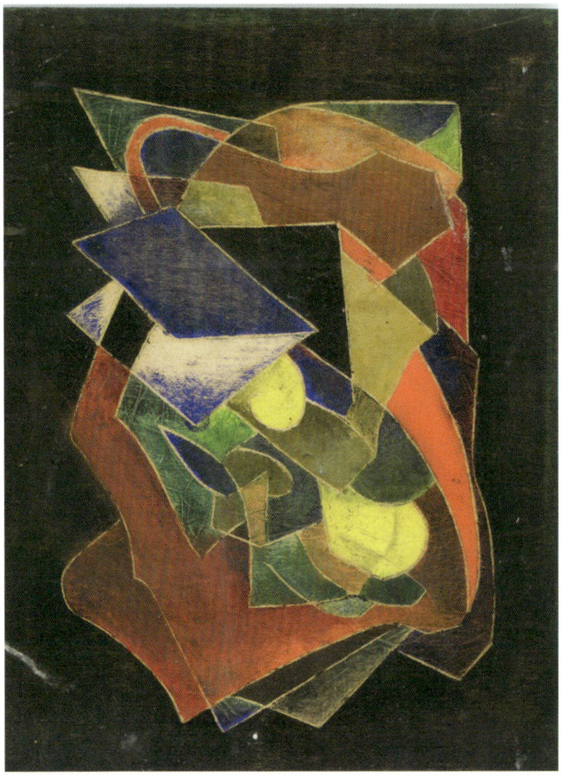

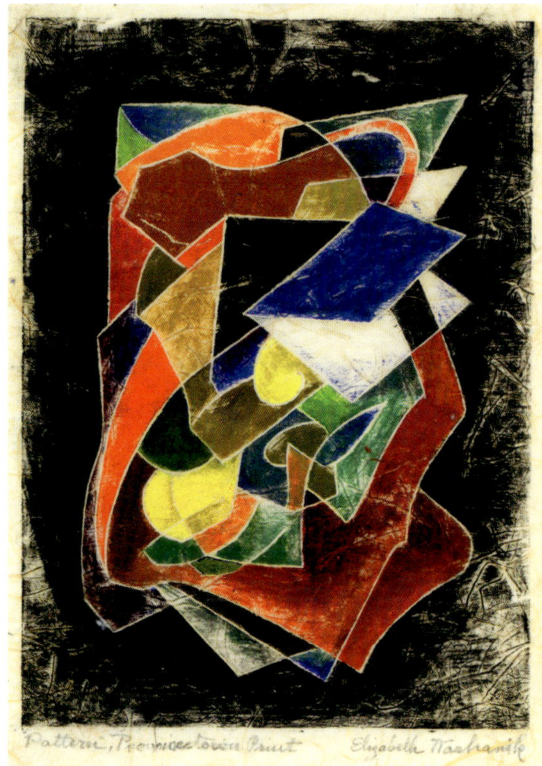

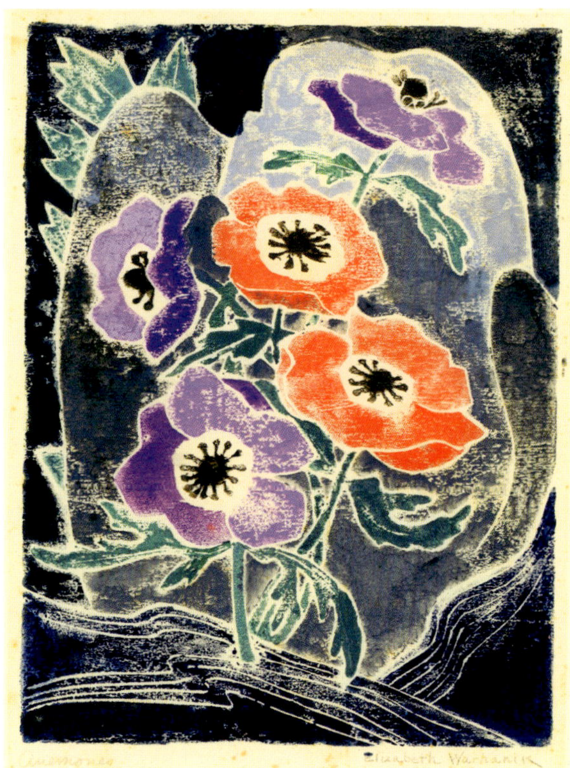

(top left) Printing block for *Pattern–Provincetown Print*, ca. 1928, Estate of Elizabeth Warhanik

(top right) *Pattern – Provincetown Print*, ca. 1928, white line color woodblock print, 9 ½ x 6 ¼ in. Private collection

(bottom) *Anemones*, ca. 1928, white line color woodblock print, 9 x 6 ½ in. Private collection

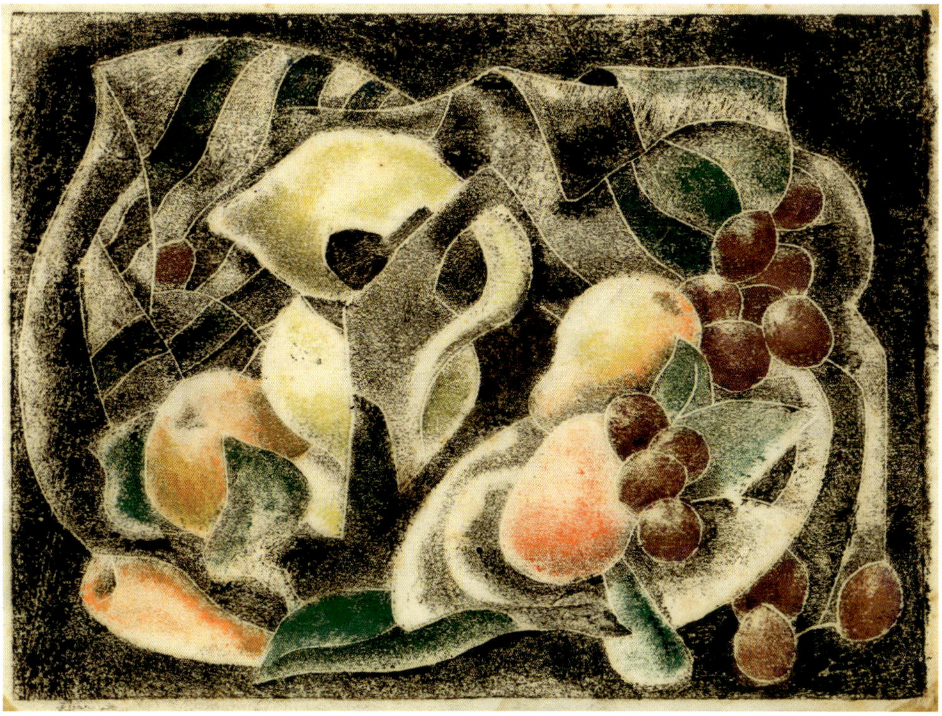

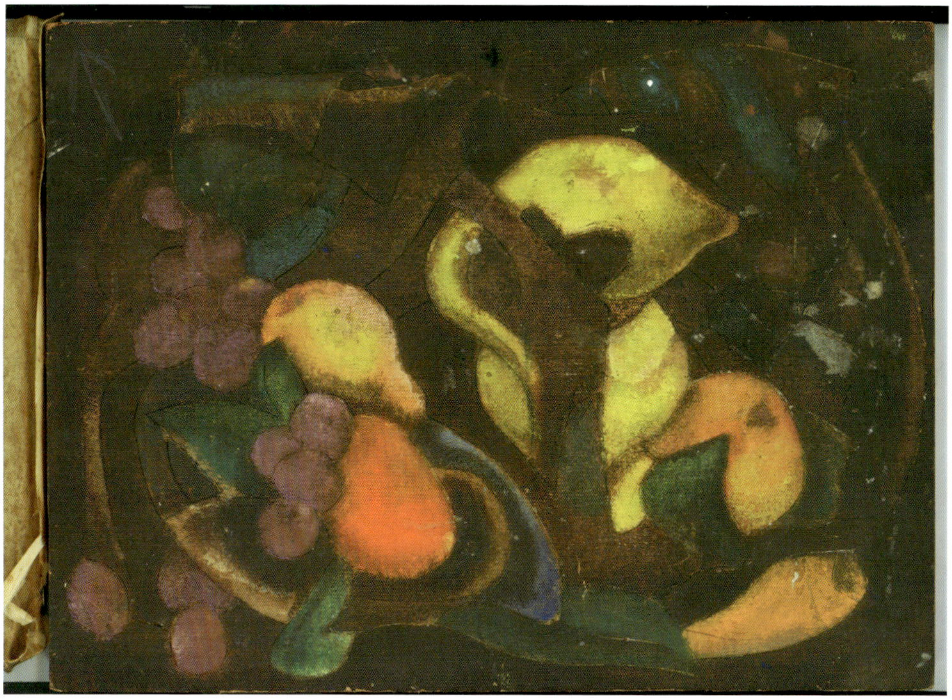

(top) Untitled, ca. 1928, white line color woodblock print, 8 x 10 ½ in. Private collection

(bottom) Printing block for Untitled, ca. 1928. Estate of Elizabeth Warhanik

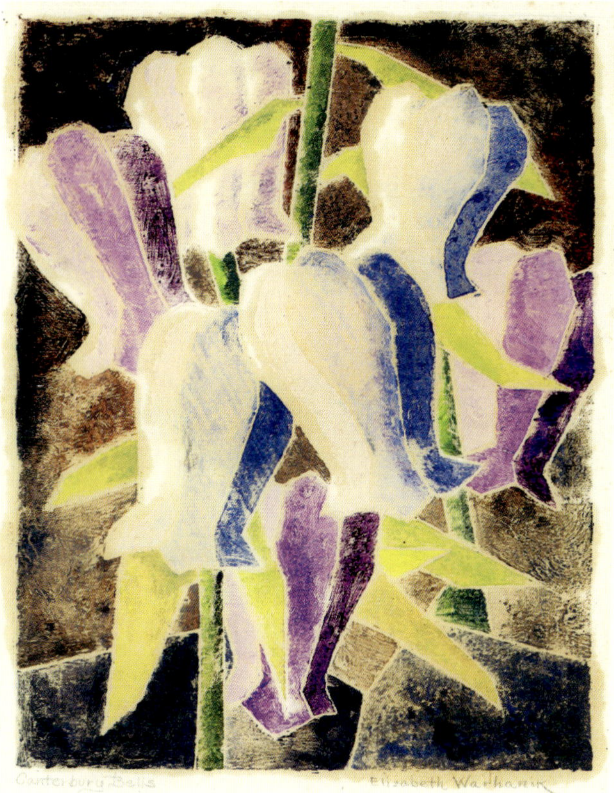

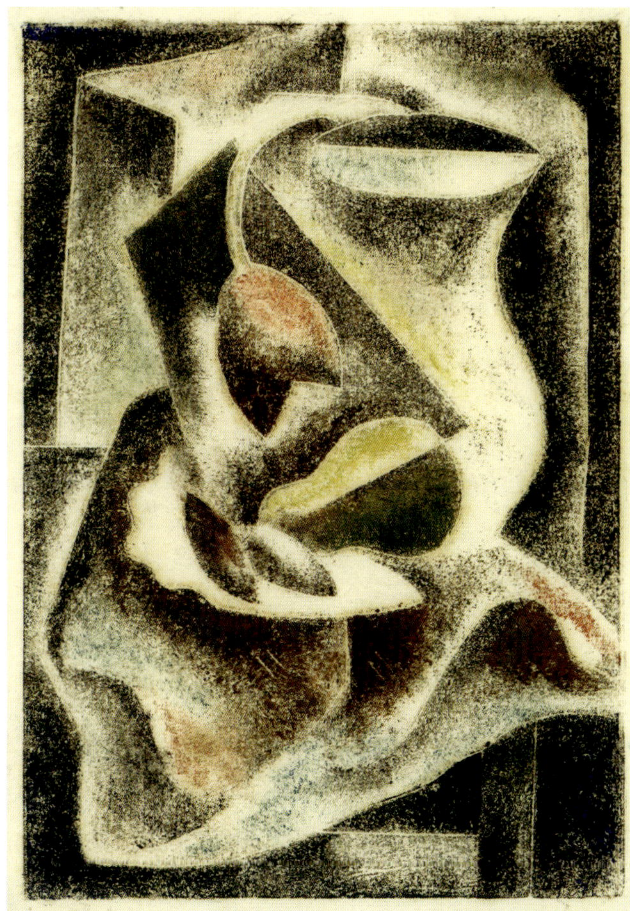

(left) *Canterbury Bells*, ca. 1928, white line color woodblock print, 8 ¾ x 6 ½ in. Private collection

(right) Untitled, ca. 1930, white line color woodblock print, 11 x 7 ½ in. Private collection

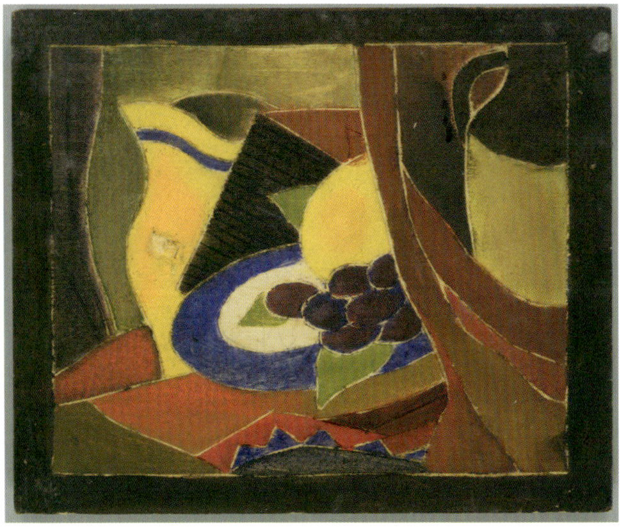

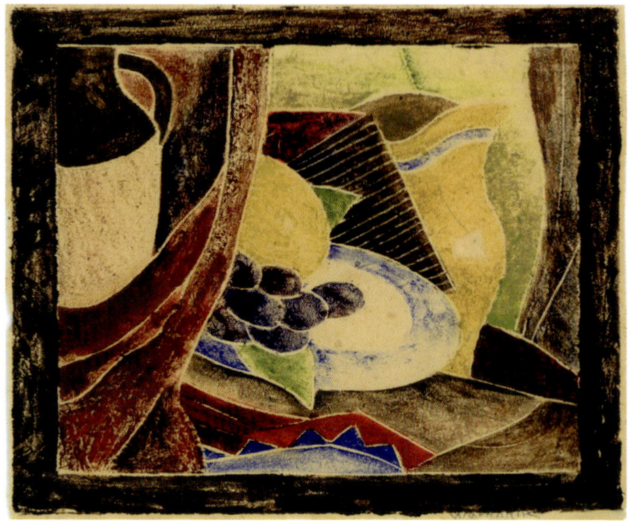

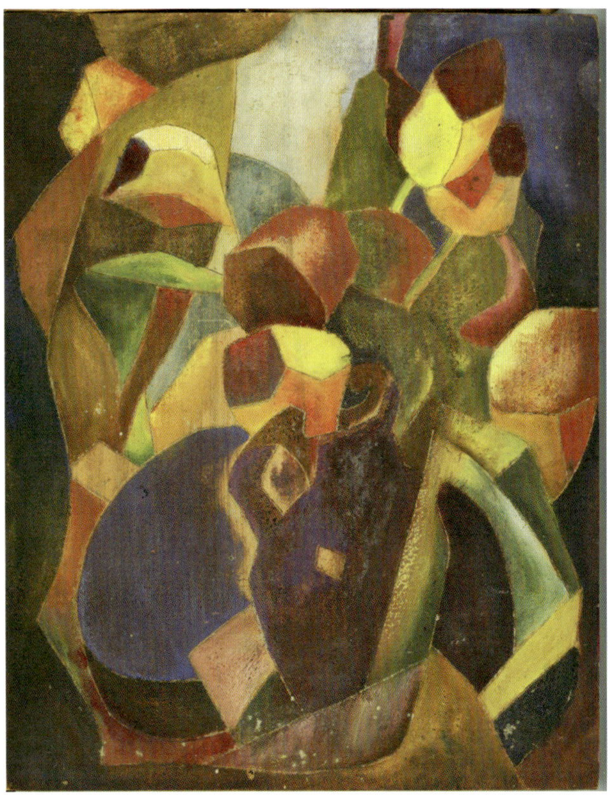

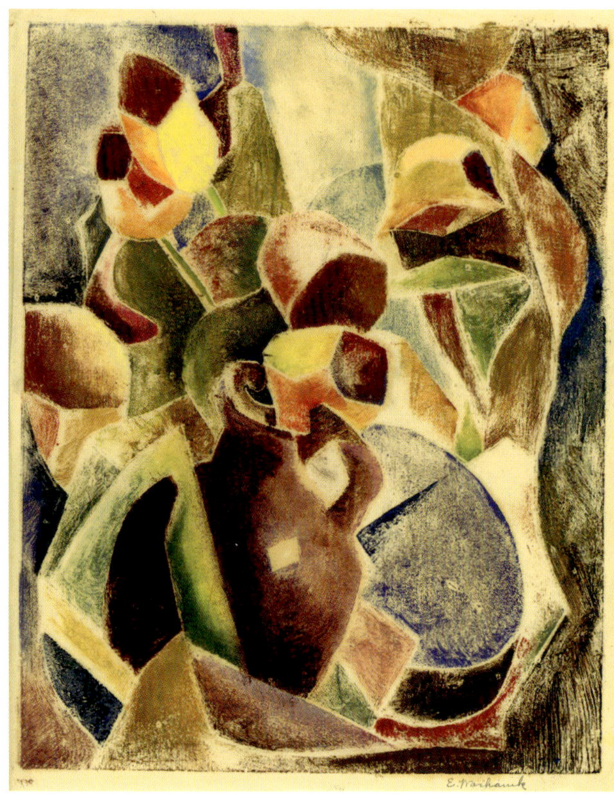

(top left) Printing block for Untitled, ca. 1928. Estate of Elizabeth Warhanik

(bottom left) Printing block for Untitled, ca. 1928. Estate of Elizabeth Warhanik

(top right) Untitled, ca. 1928, white line color woodblock print, 7 x 8 ¼ in. Private collection

(bottom right) Untitled, ca. 1928, white line color woodblock print, 10 ½ x 8 ⅛ in. Private collection

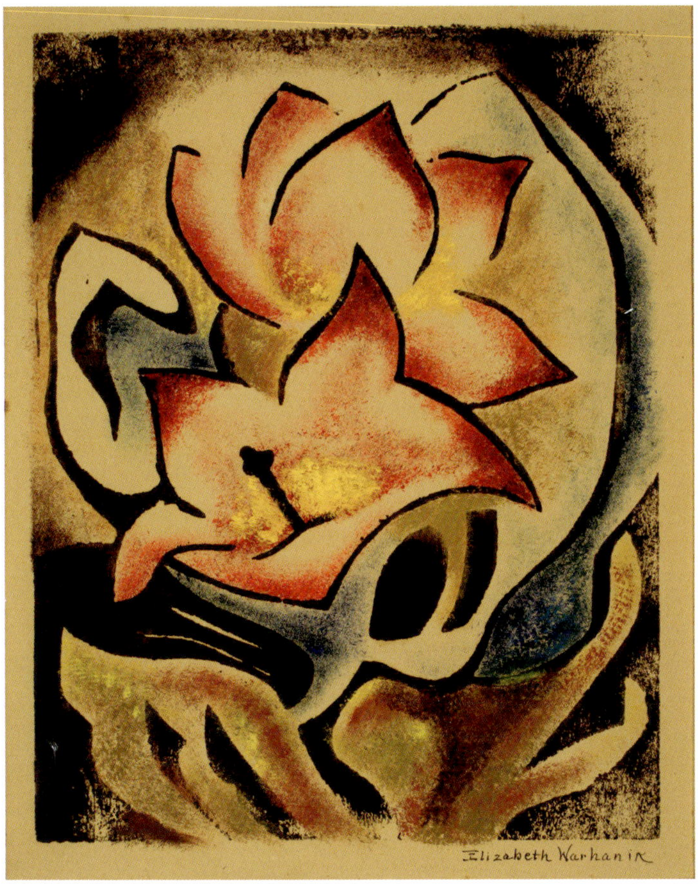

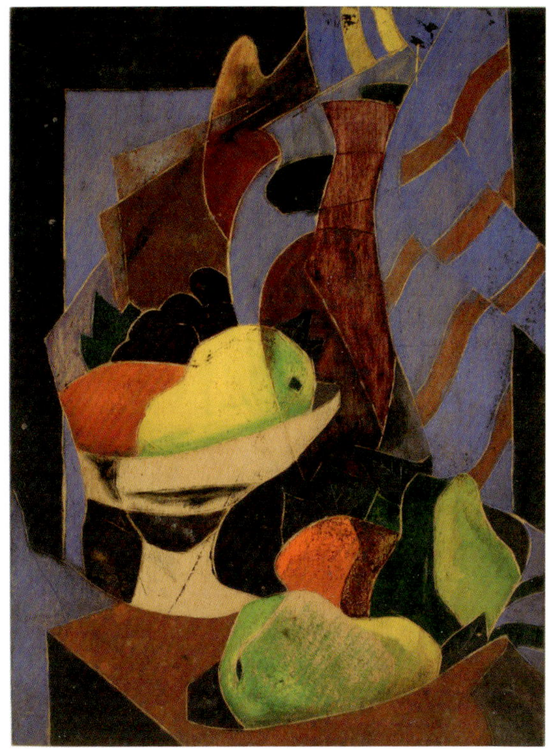

(left) Untitled, ca. 1928, color woodblock print, 10 ½ x 8 ⅛ in. Estate of Elizabeth Warhanik

(right) Printing block for an unlocated print. Estate of Elizabeth Warhanik

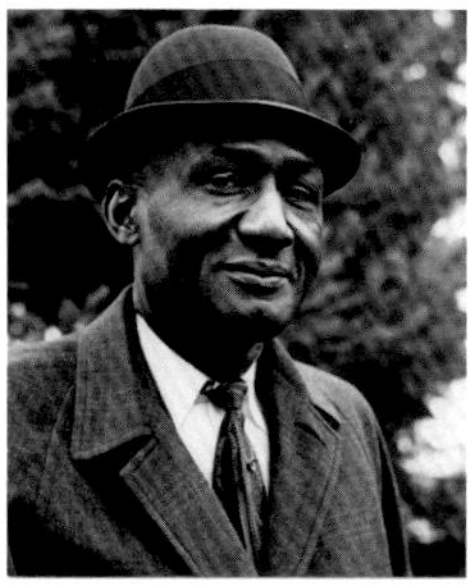

JAMES WASHINGTON, JR. 1911–2000

Born in Gloster, Mississippi, James Winston Washington, Jr. had an early interest in art and began teaching himself to draw and paint as a teenager. By 1938, he was instructing in New Deal WPA art and recreation programs at the Baptist Academy in Vicksburg, Mississippi. That same year, the Vicksburg YMCA sponsored his first exhibition of paintings.

In 1941, Washington moved to Little Rock, Arkansas, working with the U.S. Army's orthopedic division at Camp Robinson. There he befriended artist Harry Freund (1905–1999), a conscientious objector who was assigned to the camp as an artist to create posters and other military-related illustrations, murals, and portraits of some of the officers.

In 1943, he married Janie Rogella and the following year moved to Washington State where he worked as a civilian electrician at the Bremerton Navy Yard, across Puget Sound from Seattle. Some of the first artists that he encountered were members of Women Painters of Washington, several of whom became friends and supporters. Theodora Lawrenson Harrison (1890–1969) was then director of the Frederick & Nelson department store's Little Gallery. The gallery was one of the major venues for exhibiting local artists, and Harrison gave Washington his first solo exhibition of paintings in 1944. Through Harrison, he met Mark Tobey (1890–1976), who purchased several of his paintings and became an influential force in his work. In 1946, Washington studied with WPW member Yvonne Twining Humber (1907–2004) through the University of Washington's extension program. He acknowledged Humber as an important teacher, and the two remained friends throughout their lives. Another WPW member, Dorothy Dolph Jensen (1895–1977), encouraged Washington to try his hand at printmaking. She gave him his first set of tools and linoleum blocks, along with basic instruction in the medium. By 1946 he had begun his initial work in sculpture, and in 1948 studied printmaking with Glen Alps (1914–1996).

The color linocut, *Rhythm in Colors*, became his first exhibited print with the Northwest Printmakers Society in 1950. He later exhibited two additional relief prints in 1951 and 1955.

In 1950, Washington participated in the first of three yearly art events titled the *International Art Exhibition*, sponsored by the International Improvement Association in Seattle's International District. The exhibition featured the works of prominent local minority artists of black, Japanese, and Chinese descent. The event was part of the organization's yearly celebration of arts and culture by Seattle's regional minorities.

In this active period, Washington also served as Master of Ceremonies for the Mt. Zion Baptist Church Fine Arts Department Exhibit, which included art by regional artists as well as lectures and classical music performances. Washington designed and produced original blockprints as covers for the programs.

In 1951, Washington traveled to Mexico and met Diego Rivera (1886–1957) and David Alfaro Siqueiros (1896–1974), who invited him to their studios.

The following year he began the sculpting of granite, for which he would gain his widest renown. Washington's sculpture concentrates primarily on animal subject matter along with figurative works. His art philosophy was informed by his spiritual beliefs: "The creative ability of man is man's only likeness to God. True art is born of intuition and reliance on same for interpretation. That which seems impossible is brought into existence with visualization, mind control, rhythm and color."

Over the next few decades, his work was purchased by museums and high-profile collectors throughout the country. He was active in local social and political organizations such as the NAACP and became a third degree Mason.

In 1975, Washington received an honorary doctorate from the Center for Urban-Black Studies in Berkeley, California.

The house that he occupied with his wife has been made a historic landmark, and is home to the Dr. James W. Washington, Jr. & Janie Rogella Washington Foundation.

Photo: James Washington, Jr. ca. 1955. Courtesy of the Martin-Zambito Archive. Photograph by John D. McLauchlan

SOURCES

Miller, Joe. "He Paints By Night." *Seattle Daily Times*, May 18, 1952.

Ament, Deloris Tarzan. "James Washington Jr. (1911–2000): Art As Holy Land." HistoryLink.org Essay 5328, posted 3/1/2003 (accessed on 6-22-2017).

Karlstrom, Paul J. *The Spirit in the Stone: The Visionary Art of James W. Washington, Jr.* Seattle: University of Washington Press; Bellevue, WA: Bellevue Art Museum, 1989.

Special Collections of The Seattle Public Library, Artists Scrapbooks.

The Martin-Zambito Archive

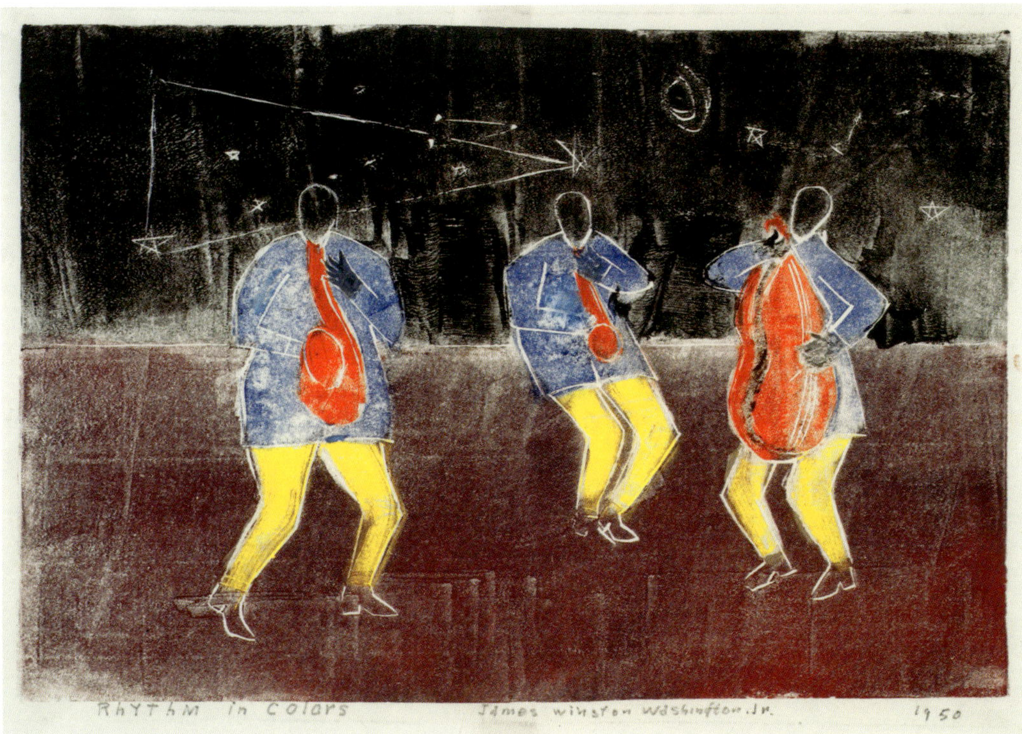

Rhythm in Colors, 1950, color woodblock print, 7 ½ x 5 3/16 in. Collection of The Seattle Public Library

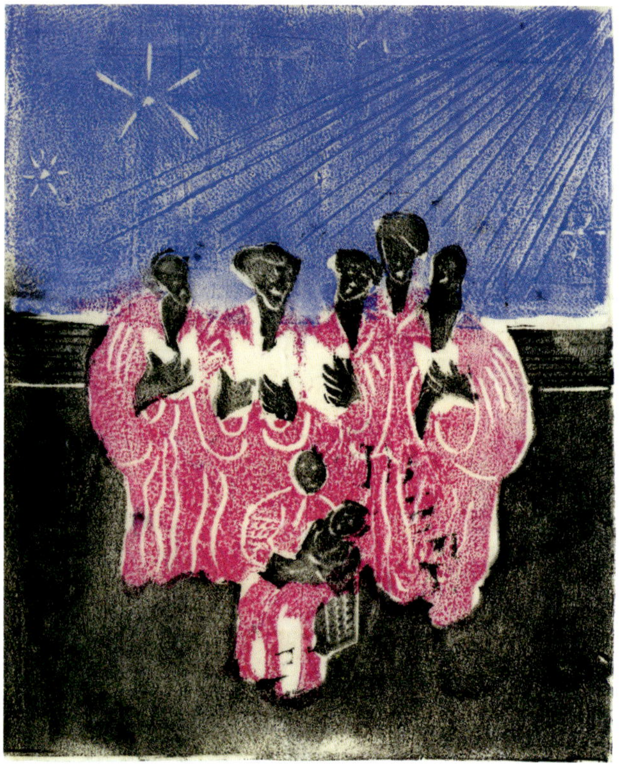

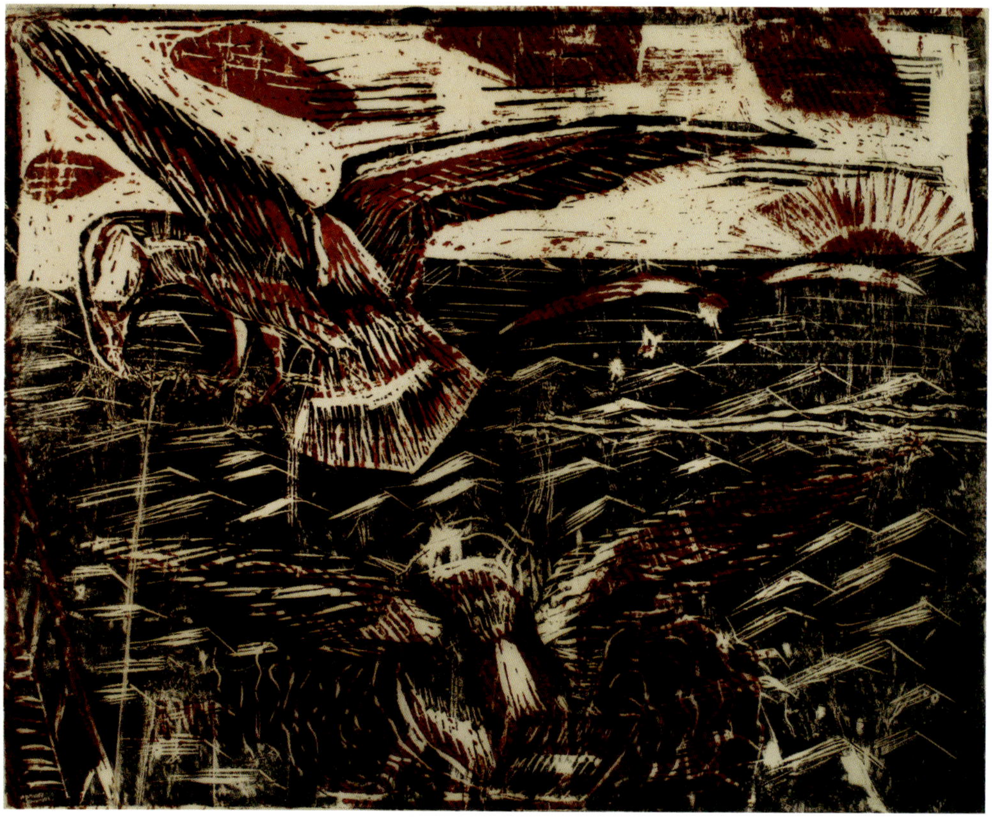

(top) Untitled, ca. 1950, color woodblock print, 6 7/8 x 5 1/2 in. Collection of the Dr. James W. Washington, Jr. & Janie Rogella Washington Foundation

(bottom) Untitled, 1947, color woodblock print, 11 x 13 1/2 in. Collection of the Dr. James W. Washington, Jr. & Janie Rogella Washington Foundation

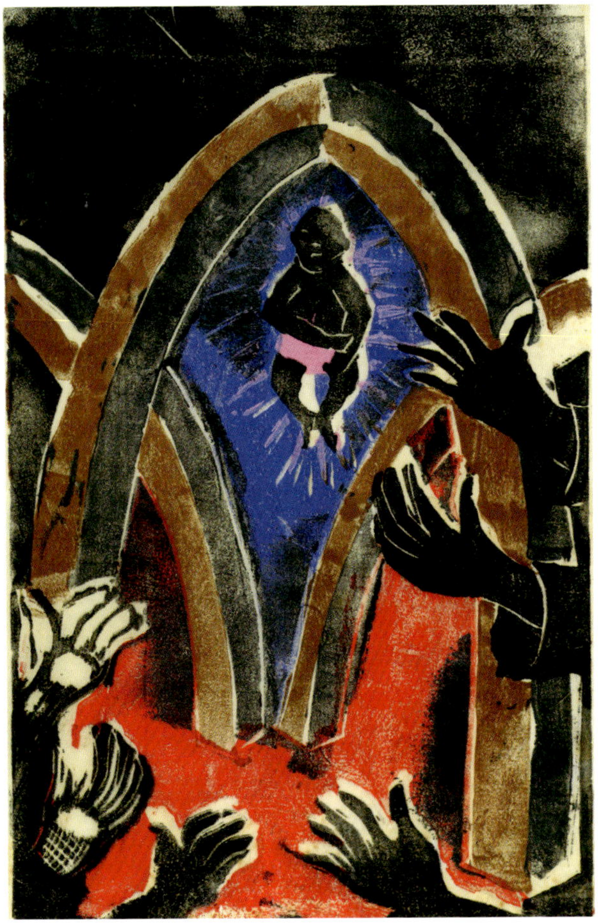

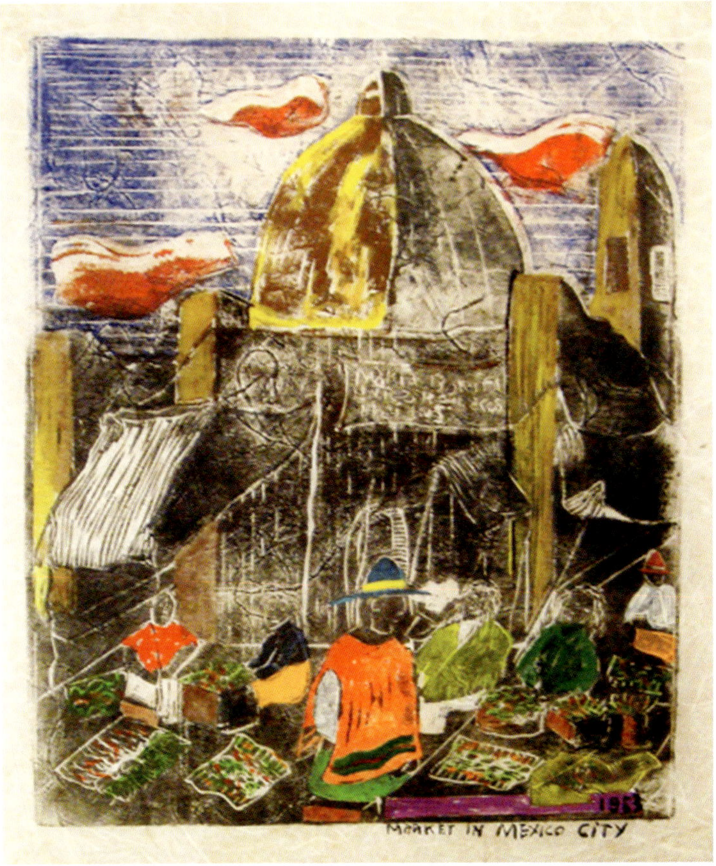

(top) Untitled, ca. 1950, color woodblock print, 8 x 5 in. Collection of the Dr. James W. Washington, Jr. and Janie Rogella Washington Foundation

(bottom) *Market in Mexico City*, 1953, color woodblock print, 17 x 12 ½ in. (sheet size). Private collection

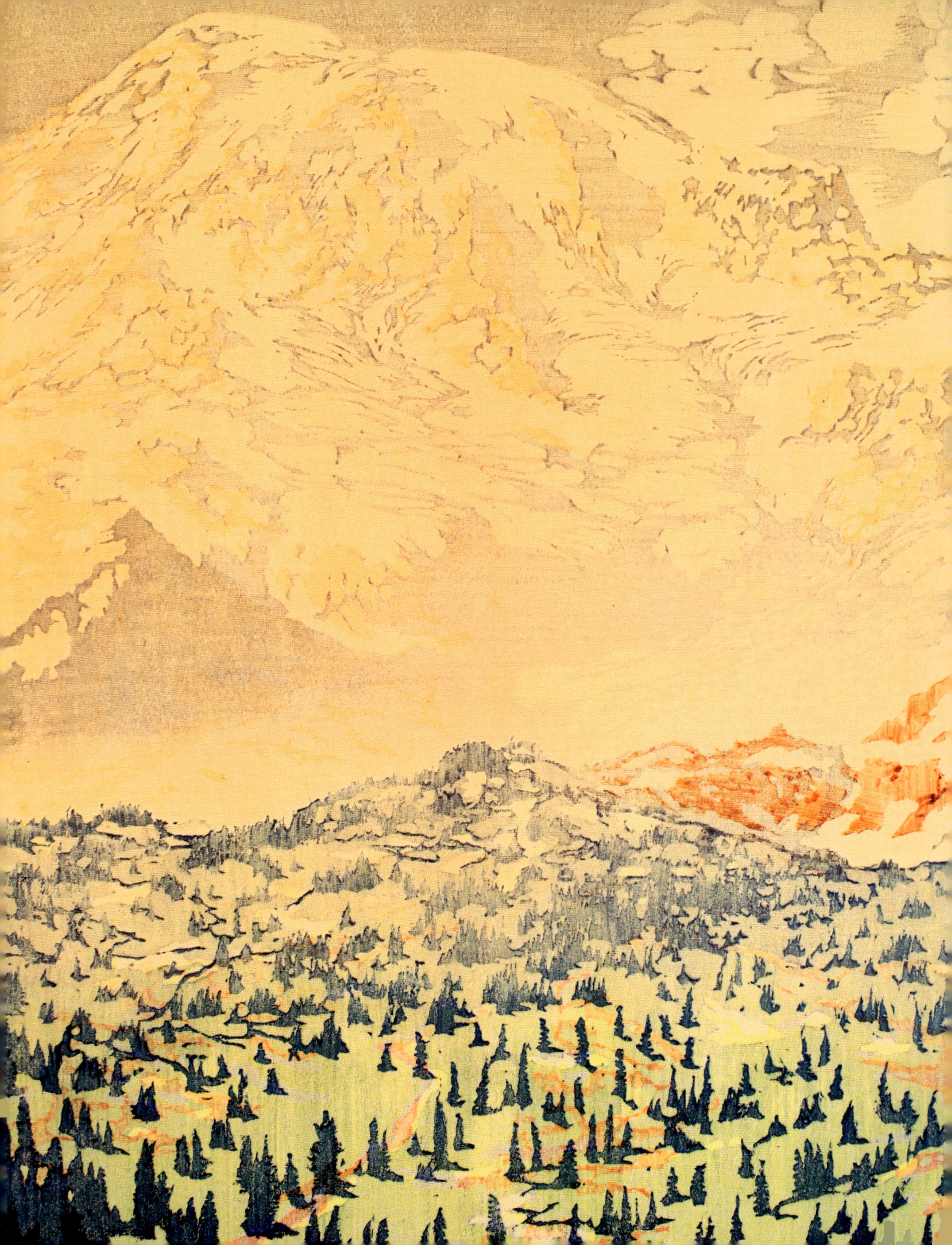

DONORS TO THE PUBLICATION

Sharon Archer & Don Eklund
Brenda & Jeffrey Atkin
Blakemore Foundation
Bibbits Brown
Wayne T. Dodge & Lawrence Kreisman
Lindsey & Carolyn Echelbarger
Beverly Criley Graham
Jane Hastings
Robert Hori
William & Ruth Ingham
Rick Johnson
Helen Johnston Foundation
Elaine Jorgensen
Kathi Knowles & Ron Outous
Christina Koons & Jim McIntire
The Kurt Lang Trust
Ann Lawler
Flora Ling & Paul Sturm
Ann Matsudaira Otani & Steve Otani
Nudelman Rare Books
David F. Plummer
Julie Pierce
Jerry W. Schroder & Y. Tokita-Schroder
Tom & Dorothy Sheehan
Milton & Sherry Smrstik
David & Janet Starr
Goro & Hatsune Tokita
Shokichi Tokita
Ned & Joyce Turner
Two Red Roses Foundation
In honor of John L. Voorhees
Jean Walkinshaw
Women Painters of Washington
Vera Zimmerman

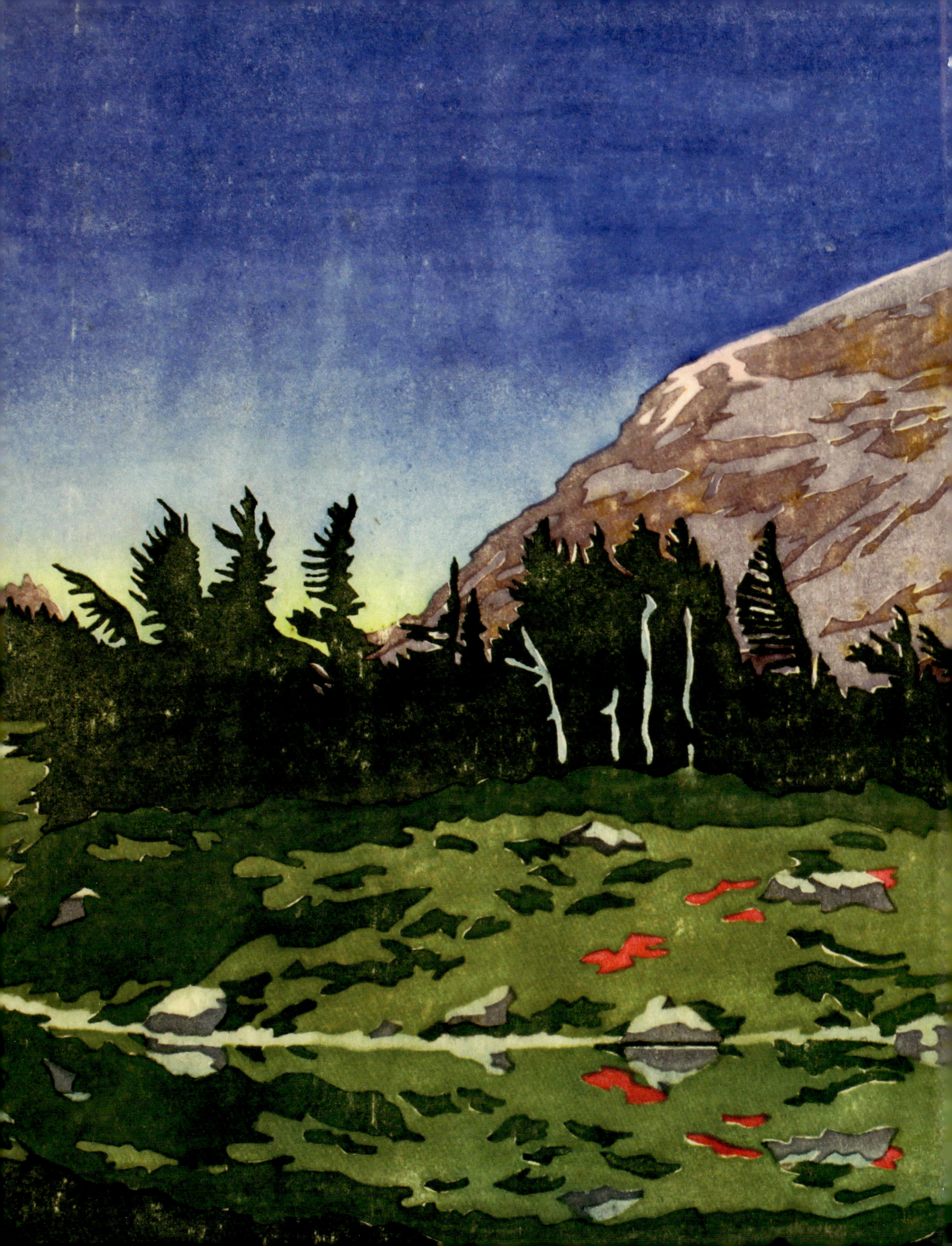

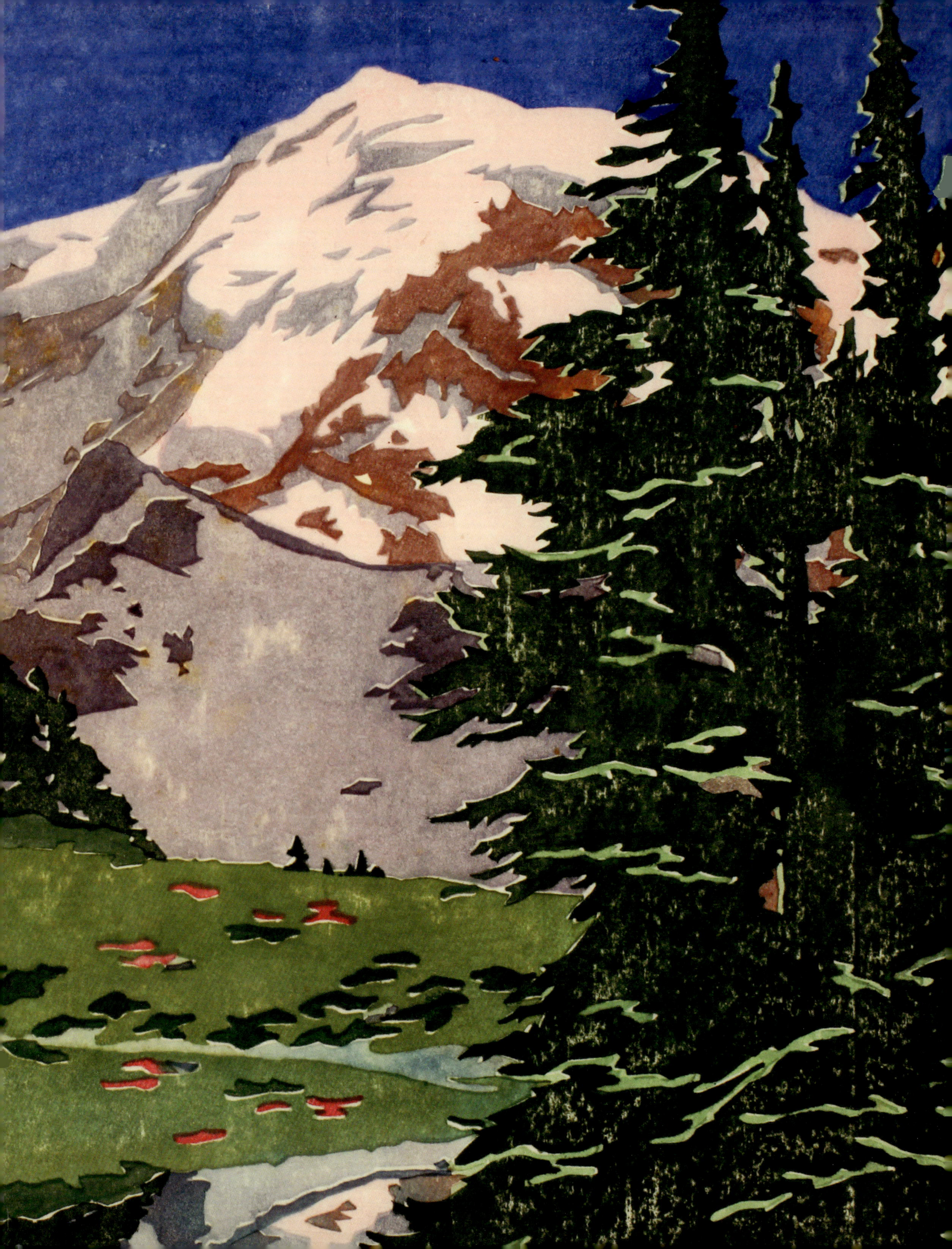

This book was published in connection with an exhibition arranged by the Cascadia Art Musuem entitled *Territorial Hues: The Color Print and Washington State, 1920–1960*. The dates for the exhibition were October 5, 2017–January 7, 2018.

Designed by Phil Kovacevich

Editorial review by Sigrid Asmus

Printed and bound in Canada by Friesen's Book Division

Front cover: ELIZABETH WARHANIK (1880–1968), *On Puget Sound* (detail), ca. 1928, white line color woodblock print, 7 x 9 1/8 in. Private collection

Back cover: GLEN ALPS (1914–1996), *Collagraph #1* (detail), 1956, collagraph, 20 3/8 x 25 7/8 in. Private collection

ISBN 978-0-9989112-0-5

Cascadia Art Museum
190 Sunset Ave #E
Edmonds, WA 98020
425.336.4809
CascadiaArtMuseum.org

Distributed by
University of Washington Press
P.O. Box 50096
Seattle, WA 98145-5096